VIOLENCE IN CANADA: SOCIOPOLITICAL PERSPECTIVES

edited by

JEFFREY IAN ROSS

Foreword by
TED ROBERT GURR

Oxford University Press
70 Wynford Drive, Don Mills, Ontario M3C 1J9

Oxford   New York
Athens   Auckland   Bangkok   Bombay
Calcutta   Cape Town   Dar es Salaam   Delhi
Florence   Hong Kong   Istanbul   Karachi
Kuala Lumpur   Madras   Madrid   Melbourne
Mexico City   Nairobi   Paris   Singapore
Taipei   Tokyo   Toronto

and associated companies in
Berlin   Ibadan

Oxford is a trademark of Oxford University Press

Canadian Cataloguing in Publication Data

Main entry under title:

Violence in Canada : sociopolitical perspectives

Includes bibliographical references and index.
ISBN 0–19–541058–0

1. Violence – Canada.   I. Ross, Jeffrey Ian.

HN110.Z9V59 1995   303.6'0971   C95–931958–1

Design: Brett Miller

1 2 3 4 – 98 97 96 95

This book is printed on permanent (acid-free) paper ∞

Printed in Canada

TABLE OF CONTENTS

FOREWORD   viii
Ted Robert Gurr

ACKNOWLEDGEMENTS   xviii

VIOLENCE IN CANADA: AN INTRODUCTION TO ITS SOCIOPOLITICAL DYNAMICS   1
Jeffrey Ian Ross

1   **VIOLENCE ON THE WESTERN CANADIAN FRONTIER: A HISTORICAL PERSPECTIVE**   10
Louis A. Knafla

2   **ON VIOLENCE AND HEALING: ABORIGINAL EXPERIENCES, 1960-1993**   40
David A. Long

3   **WORKER INSURGENCY AND SOCIAL CONTROL: VIOLENCE BY AND AGAINST LABOUR IN CANADA**   78
Kenneth D. Tunnell

4   **INTIMATE MALE VIOLENCE AGAINST WOMEN IN CANADA**   97
Walter S. DeKeseredy and Desmond Ellis

5   **VIOLENCE BY AND AGAINST CHILDREN IN CANADA**   126
Natasha J. Cabrera

6   **VIOLENCE AND THE ELDERLY**   153
Vincent F. Sacco

7   **HOMICIDE IN CANADA**   186
Rosemary Gartner

8   **VIOLENCE BY MUNICIPAL POLICE IN CANADA: 1977–1992**   223
Jeffrey Ian Ross

9 A SOCIOPOLITICAL APPROACH TO THE REPRODUCTION OF VIOLENCE IN CANADIAN PRISONS 252
Michael Welch

10 TERRORISM IN CANADA, 1960–1992 286
Anthony Kellett

11 THE RESPONSES OF DEMOCRATIC GOVERNMENTS TO VIOLENCE 316
Judy Torrance

12 CONCLUSION: SUMMARY AND FUTURE DIRECTIONS 347
Jeffrey Ian Ross

INDEX 359

TABLES AND FIGURES

Table 4.1   Wife Abuse Surveys,   102

Table 6.1   General Social Survey, 1988: Frequency of Victimization by Age,   159

Table 6.2   Canadian Urban Victimization Survey, 1982: Rates of Violent Victimization by Age,   159

Table 6.3   Canadian Urban Victimization Survey, 1982: Rates of Violent Victimization by Age and by Average Number of Evening Activities Outside the Home, per Month,   162

Table 6.4   Revised Uniform Crime Report Data: Level of Injury in Violent Crime by Age,   164

Table 6.5   General Social Survey, 1988: Feelings of Safety by Age and Gender,   168

Table 6.6   General Social Survey, 1988: Perceptions of Crime,   169

Table 6.7   Violence Against Women Survey: Proportion of Women Who Felt Worried in Specific Situations, by Age Group, 169

Table 6.8   Vancouver Urban Survey, 1984: Worry About Crime, 170

Table 7.1   Trends in Canadian Homicide Rates, 1921–1990,   193

Table 7.2   Homicides of Different Victim-Offender Relationship Types, Toronto, 1920–1990,   194

Table 7.3   Provincial Homicide Rates, by Decade,   196

Table 7.4   Regional Homicide Rates by Different Victim-Offender Relationship Types, 1961–1990,   197

Table 7.5   Average Homicide Rates for Major Cities, and Corresponding Provinces, 1981–1990,   199

Table 7.6   Sex-Specific Victimization Rates for Different Victim-Offender Relationship Types, Canada, 1961–1990,   202

Table 7.7   Sex-Specific Offending Rates for Different Homicide Types, 1961–1990,   203

Table 7.8   Native Victimization and Offending Rates for Different Regions, 1984,   206

Table 7.9   Age-Specific Rates (per 100,000 population) of
               Victimization and Offending, Canada, 1961–1990,   207

Table 7.10   Distribution of Victim-Offender Relationship Types
               Within Age Groups, Canada,   208

Table 7.11   Homicide Rates (per 100,000 population) for the
               Five Largest Canadian and US Cities, 1990,   209

Table 7.12   Selected Characteristics of Homicides in Canada,
               1961–1991,   210

Table 7.13   Selected Characteristics of Homicide in Toronto,
               1920–1990,   211

Table 8.1   Year Incident Took Place,   230

Table 8.2   Month Incident Took Place,   230

Table 8.3   Day Incident Took Place,   231

Table 8.4   Province Where Incident Took Place,   231

Table 8.5   Police Force of Accused Officer,   232

Table 8.6   Type of Real or Alleged Police Violence,   233

Table 8.7   Race/Ethnicity of Real or Alleged Victim/s and Police
               Officer/s,   233

Table 8.8   Age of Real or Alleged Victim/s and Police
               Officer/s,   234

Table 8.9   Gender of Real or Alleged Victim/s and Police
               Officer/s,   234

Table 8.10   Number of Victim/s and Police Officer/s Per
               Incident,   235

Table 8.11   Outcomes of Most Severe Sanctions of Case,   236

Table 9.1   Rates Expressed per 100,000 Total Population
               (Adults and Juveniles),   254

Table 9.2   Average Actual Count of Federal Inmate Population:
               Fiscal Years 1984–85 to 1992–93,   255

Table 9.3   Profile of an On-Register Male Offender,   256

Table 9.4   On-Register Offender Population Profile by Race,   257

Table 9.5   Definitions of Major Security Incidents,   265

Table 9.6   Major Security Incidents—National Totals,   267

Table 9.7   Minor Security Incidents in Federal Institutions—
                 National Totals   268

Table 10.1   Terrorist Incidents in Canada, 1960–1989,   288

Table 10.2   Casualties, by Group Type and Target, 1960–1989,   289

Table 10.3   Perpetrators, by Motive Type, 1960–1989,   290

Table 10.4   Terrorist Tactics in Canada, 1960–1989,   294

Table 10.5   Terrorist Targets in Canada, 1960–1989,   296

Table 10.6   International Terrorism, by Group Type, Tactic,
                 and Target, 1960–1989,   297

Figure 7.1   Trends in Canadian Homicide Rates, 1921–1990,   191

Figure 7.2   Mean Homicide Rates, by Community Size, 1978–1990,
                 198

Figure 7.3   Trends in Canadian Homicide Victimization Rates: by
                 Gender, 1921–1990,   201

Figure 7.4   Trends in Canadian Homicide Offending Rates: by
                 Gender, 1961–1991,   204

Figure 9.1   Distribution of Visible Minorities Amongst Federal
                 Inmate Population, 1990–1991,   257

Figure 9.2   Comparison of Survey and Official Data on Assault
                 Rates per 1,000 Inmates,   269

FOREWORD

BY TED ROBERT GURR

This volume offers a rich and diverse array of evidence on and interpretations of social and interpersonal violence in Canada.[1] It surpasses in scope and detail the most recent two-volume edition of *Violence in America*[2] with respect to both its detailed analyses of the dynamics of individual violence and its assessments of public policy. Encompassing social as well as interpersonal violence, it is also broader, though less definitive, than the recent multi-volume study of *Understanding and Preventing Violence*, prepared under the auspices of the US National Research Council.[3] Most distinctively, the contributors bring to bear a number of critical theoretical perspectives about the causes, consequences, and public and governmental responses to violence. On the one hand, this collection is a benchmark survey of what is known about violence in Canada; on the other, it should stimulate vigorous debate and motivate much new research.

What I propose to do here is comment on five broad themes that emerge from this book. The first is what many contributors refer to as 'the peaceable kingdom' thesis; at issue is whether and why Canada has avoided the tumult and violence of its Brobdingnagian neighbour to the south. The second theme has to do with the ways in which Canada's ethnic diversity and policies of multiculturalism are reflected in patterns of violence. Here too there are instructive comparisons to be made with the United States. The third theme concerns the consequences of social and interpersonal violence for individuals and Canadian society at large, an issue that has received less scholarly and policy attention than it deserves throughout Western societies. Fourth is the question of how Canadians go about setting the agenda for public action to control violence. Here I am led to the conclusion that policy responses in Canada are driven mainly by periodic eruptions of public concern about 'law and order', and are seldom based on informed understanding of the underlying social issues. Finally, at the most general level, the contributors to this volume raise some weighty and unanswered questions about the future of violence and social control in post-industrial societies.

THE 'PEACEABLE KINGDOM' THESIS

One might well argue that poverty and social deprivation are the main correlates of individual violence and victimization in Canada, as they are in the United States. Evidence from both countries points to the high frequency of violence against women and abuse of children in poorer households, for example. If interpersonal violence in Canada arises from the same social dynamics and manifests the same patterns and trends as in the United States and West European societies, then there should be no need for future volumes with titles like *Violence in Canada* and *Violence in America*, except perhaps to describe historical episodes, as Louis A. Knafla does in Chapter 1. In fact, some contributors devote efforts to debunking the 'peaceable kingdom myth' that Canada has relatively less social or interpersonal violence than other Western societies because of its different cultural experiences. More specifically, Canadians supposedly have greater respect for authority than citizens of the United States, have less tolerance for individual and group deviance from community norms, and are more disposed to give the state primary responsibility for maintaining social order.[4]

The evidence in this volume shows that Canada does indeed have serious problems of violence: homicide rates higher than most Western societies, high levels of violence in aboriginal communities, frequent victimization of children and women, and instances of police and prison violence that violate the standards of civil society. Nonetheless, the magnitudes of the most serious kinds of social and interpersonal violence in Canada are distinctly lower than in the United States.

A comparison of the histories of frontier violence in the two societies bears out this conclusion. Personal violence was common on the Canadian frontier, as Knafla amply documents; but collective violence of the kind associated with American vigilantism, range wars, and organized banditry was relatively rare. Canadians experienced neither a full-fledged revolution nor a civil war, and as a result no national or frontier tradition of proactive armed violence took root in Canada. Frontier rebellions by the Métis in 1869–70 and 1885 were reactive, localized, and short-lived. Knafla's accounts provide few Canadian examples of the gun battles and Indian fights that figure so prominently in American folklore and popular entertainment. The Civil War's legacy died hard in the American West, along with many of its veterans. Luckily for Canada, however, most of them stayed south of the border.

Comparisons of frontier violence between the two societies are necessarily impressionistic. Contemporary data on terrorism in the two countries provide more precise support for the same principle, that social violence has been less common and less disruptive in Canada. In Chapter 10 Anthony Kellett reports that some 500 terrorist attacks occurred in Canada between 1960 and 1989, with total fatalities of 15. The annual frequency of bombings in the United States has never been less than 500 *per year* since data were first compiled in 1969–70. In one four-year span, in the early 1970s, 26 policemen died in ambush attacks by the Black Liberation Army and similar militant groups—more than the total of all terrorist fatalities in Canada over 30 years.[5] On this count too, then, Canada has been a relatively peaceable society.

Data on homicide victimization provide another, still more exact basis for comparison. The Canadian data analyzed by Rosemary Gartner in Chapter 7 show that the homicide mortality rate for all males in the 1980s was about 3.0 per 100,000, with substantially higher rates in the west and northwest and among Aboriginal peoples. In the United States in 1988 the comparable rate was 14.2, with some of the difference due to the extraordinarily high homicide death rate of African-American males (58.2 per 100,000). Among white males alone, the US homicide rate was 7.7, two and a half times greater than the aggregate Canadian rate.[6]

Life in Canada is thus somewhat more secure than in the United States, for whatever combination of reasons. Less deadly forms of interpersonal violence may be equally common, however. Walter S. DeKeseredy and Desmond Ellis report suggestive survey evidence in Chapter 4 that male violence against female intimates, within and outside marriage, is about equally common in the two societies. Natasha J. Cabrera cautions in Chapter 5 against making similar comparisons about the incidence of physical and sexual abuse against children, for lack of solid data, but her information does suggest that child abuse is a pervasive Canadian problem. One possible inference is that Canadian levels of non-lethal interpersonal violence may be closer to their US counterparts than is the case for lethal violence. Of course this is a hypothesis in search of evidence and, if true, of explanation. Oddly, none of the contributors analyzes closely the impact of firearms and their regulation on rates or lethality of violence in Canada. The connection between the availability of firearms and US rates of violent crime has stimulated a great deal of research that is mostly inconclusive on the central policy issue of whether stricter gun controls might reduce crime rates. What is the Canadian experience and evidence?

VIOLENCE IN MULTICULTURAL SOCIETIES

It is common wisdom that ethnically diverse societies tend to have higher levels of social and interpersonal violence than more homogeneous ones: the United States and Japan are often contrasted in this way. Canada is by almost any standard the most heterogeneous of all advanced industrial societies. Close to 30 per cent of its people are members of politically active minorities.[7] Approximately one-sixth of its people were born outside the country, proportionally the largest foreign-born population of any Western society. Whereas, historically, Canada's immigrants have come mainly from other European societies, in the 1980s about two-thirds came from less-developed countries. And as most new immigrants are settling in Canada's larger cities, it has been estimated that by 2001 visible minorities will constitute as much as 45 per cent of Toronto's population.[8] In light of this diversity, why does Canada have appreciably less social and interpersonal violence than the United States?

Part of the answer lies in social attitudes and patterns of public policy. Because its ethos and distribution of wealth are somewhat more egalitarian than those of the US, Canada has fewer pockets of generationally-persistent, criminogenic poverty. In addition, Canada has long been regarded by its people as an 'ethnic mosaic'; it articulated the concept of multiculturalism at a time when most blacks in the United States were still struggling for civil rights and integration; and it instituted country-wide multicultural policies in 1971. These public attitudes and policies have reduced the potential for social violence across ethnic, racial, and communal boundaries.

Differentials in violence across groups nonetheless persist, providing a kind of litmus test of the effectiveness of Canadian policies. One might suggest, as a general principle, that the more severely a minority has been victimized or stigmatized by a dominant society, the greater its levels of interpersonal violence are likely to be. This principle helps to explain the broad differences in violence among blacks and aboriginals in Canada and the United States. Canada has a relatively small black population, and although it is of historical as well as recent origin, there is no enduring legacy of slavery, segregation, and racial stratification. Blacks in Canada face a risk of being murdered that is roughly three times that of other Canadians, whereas their male counterparts in the US are approximately eight times as likely to be murdered as white males. Aboriginals, on the other hand, have been the most stigmatized people in Canada and, according to evidence cited by David A. Long in Chapter 2 and Gartner in Chapter 7, their homicide victimization rates are seven to ten times those of other Canadians. Native Americans, by contrast, are less than half as likely as blacks to be victims of homicide.[9]

Another aspect of ethnic tensions surfaces in Jeffrey Ian Ross's analysis of police violence (Chapter 8), which provides empirical evidence that visible minorities in Canada are disproportionately likely to be the victims of physical attacks, by both private citizens and police. There is, in other words, a gap between the public ethos of tolerance and the social practice of racial victimization. That this gap exists is not surprising: what is needed is more evidence on whether the increase in immigration by visible minorities leads to greater violence by and against them.

The larger question is whether and how ethnic diversity and stratification affect levels and patterns of violence across the Canadian mosaic. Suggestive evidence is scattered throughout this volume, but none of the researchers here seems to have confronted the issue head-on and in all its complexity. What should be made of the fact that Quebec has had homicide rates at or below the country average since the 1920s? Perhaps the answer lies in Quebec's greater homogeneity, or in a tendency towards greater stability in social relationships. One could test these and other propositions by asking whether francophone Canadians outside Quebec are affected by violence in different ways than Québécois. Why have the impoverished Atlantic provinces consistently had the lowest homicide rates in the country? Are first- or second-generation immigrants more likely to be charged with or victimized by violent crime than 'old stock' Canadians? Are the answers the same for immigrants of European origin and for recent Third World immigrants? There is a large research agenda here.

THE SOCIAL CONSEQUENCES OF VIOLENCE

Knafla concludes Chapter 1 with the observation that social violence in Canada has been uncommon, not an integral part of the political process. Nonetheless, many Canadians have resorted to social violence with the aim of redressing grievances or advancing some larger social cause, and one might ask whether and under what circumstances it has served their purposes.

The frequency and intensity with which violence has been used by and against organized labour is the subject of Kenneth D. Tunnell's analysis in Chapter 3 and seems to challenge Knafla's observation. Moreover, Tunnell concludes that disruptive tactics by labour, including occupation of workplaces and attacks on anti-union workers and police, have contributed substantially to workers' gains. But very few of the violent strikes he describes have had positive outcomes for labour. Rather, management, through the use of force and the complicity of the police, has usually prevailed. A similar conclusion is implied by Michael Welch's analysis in Chapter 9 of riots and disturbances in Canadian prisons. He points out that a prisoners' rights movement took hold in the late 1960s that prompted many peaceful demonstrations and some violent incidents. But the principal consequence seems to have been the strengthening of official controls within the prisons, not institutional reform.

The evidence on labour and prison violence can be interpreted in light of William Gamson's classic analysis of the outcomes of protest movements in the United States: violence is an effective instrument of change when it is used by those who already have substantial power resources at their disposal, but it is usually fatal to the cause of weak challengers.[10] The same principle applies to the outcomes of the terrorist campaigns surveyed by Kellett in Chapter 10. None of his evidence suggests that terrorism directly or indirectly served the purposes of the groups that used it. Instead, as Judy Torrance observes in Chapter 11, the Canadian government's habitual response to violent challenges has been to resort to 'temporary measures' of coercive control. One risk, she notes, is that such measures may become permanent, leading a government 'down a path of repression that undermines the basis of its legitimacy . . .'. She suggests that Canadian governments, which have faced few serious violent challenges, may be especially vulnerable to this kind of over-reaction.

Examination of recent militancy by Canada's First Nations provides the basis for some more hopeful conclusions. In Chapter 2 Long discusses recent efforts by several individuals to use proactive and often violent tactics in efforts to 'change the rules and structures of native/state relations . . .'. These have been quite successful, both in achieving specific objectives, such as blocking unwanted exploitation of tribal resources, and in countering the suffocating paternalism that has characterized most of Canadian 'native policy'. But Long does not offer a general analysis of the extent of these successes or the reasons for them.

One might also ask what the evidence suggests about the impact of individual violence on its victims, the communities in which it occurs, and Canadian public policy. Cabrera's discussion of child abuse cites evidence that abused children are likely to become abusive and often violent offenders. This pattern has been well-documented in studies in the United States and elsewhere. DeKeseredy and Ellis's analysis of violence against women includes observations on its traumatic consequences. These are among the few nuggets of findings about what is by and large a neglected subject. One would like to have more solid evidence about the effects of assault and armed robbery on the subsequent lives of victims and their families, and more macro assessments of the economic costs of violence—in lost productivity, diversion of public and private resources to security, and so forth. Similarly, what are the consequences for the community of high levels of victimization by violence? Public policy in Canada, as elsewhere, seems preoccupied with retribution and deterrence and gives little attention or resources to remedying individual or social trauma.

PUBLIC RESPONSES TO VIOLENCE

A recurring theme in the contributions to this volume is the existence of serious discrepancies between public perceptions of violence and the reality suggested by social research. Claims about high and rising victimization of the elderly are belied by the statistical evidence surveyed by Vincent F. Sacco in Chapter 6. From time to time, concern about terrorism and other violent challenges to public order has gripped the Canadian public, when the threats actually posed have been negligible.

Violence and sexual abuse against children have come to be regarded as major public issues; yet as Cabrera shows, specific instances are often ignored or explained away at the family and community levels. On the other hand, although violence against women is exceedingly common, expressions of public concern have been only fitful. Finally, the devastating effects of interpersonal violence in aboriginal communities have been largely ignored in the broader society.

Let me suggest that a common set of dynamics is responsible for these discrepancies. Sensitization to violence has been a long historical process in Western societies. Gradually, it has led to the condemnation, criminalization, and decline in incidence of overtly brutal and violent acts in almost all sectors of public and private life.[11] Within this context, claims-makers (Sacco's term) and the mass media have scrambled to focus public attention on the existence and magnitude of problems of violence that, they claim, have gone unrecognized and untreated. The claims-makers are at work in this volume too, especially in the chapters on violence against women and children, and in Canadian prisons. But one consequence of flurries of academic and public concern is that a particular social ill can be hyped out of proportion to its significance, either objective (as revealed by quantitative evidence) or subjective (as demonstrated by the attitudes of people directly concerned).

Claims-making and media hype have real, and not necessarily beneficial, consequences for public policy. They create climates of concern that pressure public officials to respond, sometimes symbolically, sometimes with programs of legislative and policy action. Mass publics, once aroused by accounts of deviance, tend to prefer punitive responses. And policy-makers often pander to that preference, appreciating that their electoral support depends on showing how responsive they are to public demands. The risk is that the policy responses engendered in such circumstances may satisfy the perceived need for action without addressing the incompletely-understood realities of the social problem. As a consequence, their impact may be nil or even negative.

Scholars writing on public policy can contribute to such inappropriate responses by the ways in which they go about calling for a redirection of public efforts. It is not uncommon for critics to condemn existing programs and policy while at the same time calling for new ones, in the touching faith that more spending and social experiments tomorrow will accomplish what yesterday's expensive and innovative programs failed to do. Research that adds to the understanding of the general process by which the social-policy agenda is shaped in Canada could be most instructive.

On the positive side, the claims-makers may also help to galvanize private groups into action that counters interpersonal violence. DeKeseredy and Ellis's account of violence against women identifies a number of private, community-based initiatives by activists that aim either to reduce the incidence of violence or to deal with its immediate consequences. Long touches on the same issue in his discussion of aboriginal violence, pointing out that in some cases it has prompted local efforts at healing. One would like to know how widespread such community responses are, how effective they are or might be, and whether they constitute a desirable alternative to bureaucratized public programs.

EMERGING PROBLEMS OF PUBLIC ORDER IN POST-INDUSTRIAL SOCIETIES

The last general theme, one that builds on many of the preceding comments, concerns Canada's emergent problems of violence and social order. The transition to post-industrial society has led to a loss in well-paying blue-collar industrial jobs and a rise in service jobs, most of which pay poorly. Among the results are growing inequalities between the status and income of skilled and professional workers, and unskilled and semi-skilled labour. What are the long-range consequences for crime and public policy of these increasing structural inequalities? Welch believes that some of them can be seen in the way that violence is reproduced in Canadian prisons.

The immigration of growing numbers of visible minorities increases the chances of inter-ethnic hostility and violence against newcomers. Disadvantaged immigrants are also more likely than previous generations of newcomers to get locked into the low-pay, low-status service occupations, or to be locked out of the job market entirely. They may thus become the sources of future crime and social violence. To what extent can Canada's policies of social justice and multiculturalism cope with these growing tensions? Or will Canada, following the lead of Germany and Britain, try to close its gates against future immigrants?

When divisions between classes and communal groups sharpen, it becomes increasingly difficult for democratic governments to respond equitably to the interests and demands of small and disadvantaged groups. The first obligation of governments in the face of imminent crisis is to maintain control; the second—often a means to the first—is to secure majority political support. These political facts of life in heterogeneous post-industrial democracies suggest that sustained crisis has the potential to set in motion a drift towards authoritarian control, or at best a tyranny of the majority. This line of argument, like Torrance's, is of course speculative, but it is not entirely implausible.

The United States already faces these problems in significant measure. Canadian specialists on violence should be sufficiently forewarned, and cognizant of US policy failures, to design more effective responses.

NOTES

1 'Social violence' is my term for collective and individual acts of violence that are intended by their perpetrators to promote some larger social, political, or economic objective. 'Interpersonal violence' denotes acts of violence directed at others that aim to benefit or satisfy only the perpetrator(s). The editor makes a similar distinction in his introduction between political and criminological violence; I prefer the term 'interpersonal' to 'criminological' because some kinds of individual acts of violence analyzed in this volume are not consistently labelled or treated as criminal offences.

2 Ted Robert Gurr, ed., *Violence in America*, Vol. 1, *The History of Crime* and Vol. 2, *Protest, Rebellion, Reform* (Newbury Park, CA: Sage Publications, 1989).

3 The summary report is Albert J. Reiss, Jr, and Jeffrey A. Roth, eds, *Understanding and Preventing Violence* (Washington, DC: National Academy Press, 1993), prepared by the National Research Council's Panel on the Understanding and Control of Violent Behavior. Three supplementary volumes consist of detailed and critical reviews of research on the biochemical, behavioural, and social correlates of individual violence.

4 Contrasts between the formative experiences of Canada and the United States and their effects on political attitudes have attracted much scholarly attention, notably by Seymour Martin Lipset, *Revolution and Counterrevolution* (New York: Basic Books, 1968) and the contributors to Richard A. Preston, ed., *Perspectives on Revolution and Evolution* (Durham, NC: Duke University Press, 1979).

5 Most bombings have no explicit social or political purpose, so do not meet the FBI's criteria for terrorism. The FBI counted as many as 130 terrorist attacks per year in the mid-1970s, declining by the late 1980s to less than 10 per year. But abortion-clinic bombings were excluded from the count; T.R. Gurr, 'Political Terrorism: Historical Antecedents and Contemporary Trends', in *Violence in America*, Vol. 2, 201–30.

6 US data from Reiss and Roth, pp. 64, 66.

7 See the comparisons in Ted Robert Gurr, *Minorities at Risk: A Global View of Ethnopolitical Conflict* (Washington, DC: United States Institute of Peace Press, 1993), chap. 6.

8 Data from Sarah V. Wayland, 'Immigrants into Citizens: Integration and political mobilization in France and Canada', PhD dissertation, Dept. of Government and Politics, University of Maryland at College Park, 1995. A recent analysis is Hugh Donald Forbes, 'Canada: From Bilingualism to Multiculturalism', pp. 86–101 in Larry Diamond and Marc F. Plattner, eds, *Nationalism, Ethnic Conflict, and Democracy* (Baltimore: Johns Hopkins University Press, 1994).

9 Reiss and Roth, pp. 4, 62–3.

[10] William A. Gamson, *The Strategy of Social Protest* (Homewood, IL: Dorsey, 1975).

[11] The term is used by Alfred Soman, 'Deviance and criminal justice in Western Europe, 1300–1800: An essay in structure', *Criminal Justice History: An International Annual* 1 (1980): 1–28. I discuss the implications for violent crime in 'Historical Trends in Violent Crime: Europe and the United States,' *Violence in America*, Vol. 1, pp. 24–5 and 44–9.

ACKNOWLEDGEMENTS

This project originated when, as an undergraduate, it became clear to me, as it still does today, that research on violence in Canada is a relatively neglected field. When I was a student of Ted Robert Gurr's, we had a series of conversations about the possibility of editing a book of this nature. This idea was temporarily abandoned while I completed my graduate education, but was later resuscitated when my dissertation was coming to a close. The actual soliciting of chapters, however, began in earnest during the fall of 1990, when I organized a number of panels at the annual meetings of the American Society of Criminology, Academy of Criminal Justice Sciences, and Canadian Association for Security and Intelligence Studies. This book depends on the contributions of a team of respected historians, political scientists, sociologists, criminologists, and educators, many of whom are activists, to improve our ability to understand violence in Canada.

Attempts were made to invite well respected scholars, experts, and activists in the field; to have contributors who represented different genders, ethnic, and racial groups in Canada; and to have almost every conceivable subtopic covered. This latter objective was not possible. Approximately eleven subjects could not be covered, mainly because I could not locate individuals to write the chapter, persons who promised me manuscripts never produced them, and due to resource constraints I could not write them myself. Had I waited longer to fill the gaps, this book might never have been published.

During the course of the organization of this book, however, I have incurred a series of debts. First, I would like to thank my contributors for their scholarship, diligence, and patience.

Second, I would like to thank Paul Bond for his capable research assistance.

Third, many thanks to anonymous volunteer internal reviewers (i.e., other contributors to the book) who took the time from their busy schedules to provide thoughtful and helpful criticisms on the chapters.

Fourth, the work of the external reviewers, especially Mary Lorenz Dietz, was greatly appreciated.

Fifth, special thanks goes out to Brian Henderson, formerly of Oxford University Press, and Phyllis Wilson and Ric Kitowski, also of Oxford, who inherited the project, for patience and encouragement and giving me the opportunity to let this project move forward.

Sixth, the wise council, encouragement, love and support of my wife, Natasha J. Cabrera, was indispensable at several critical stages of this project.

This book is dedicated to Natasha, who taught me that good work takes time, to maintain a healthy balance in life, and whose life and mine was filled with too much violence before we met.

VIOLENCE IN CANADA

An Introduction to its Sociopolitical Dynamics

JEFFREY IAN ROSS

Increasingly, violence commands government, public, media, and academic attention. Violence is both a social and a policy problem endemic to many countries' cultural, economic, social, and political systems. Canada, one of the largest countries in the world, is not immune to various manifestations of violence. Violence has become a frequent occurrence in this Anglo-American country, particularly since the 1960s. In fact, according to a recent study, Canada has the second-highest violent crime rate in the Western world, surpassed only by the United States (Canadian Press, 1992).[1]

LITERATURE REVIEW

Although a growing body of academic and government research has been conducted on the subject of violence in Canada, this work is not easily accessible. Since the early 1970s, only three edited collections on the general topic of violence were published. Although these works provide us with a necessary beginning and have sensitized students, academics, and policy-makers to the problem of violence in Canada, they have a number of shortcomings. Richard P. Boles et al.'s *Protest, Violence and Social Change* (Prentice-Hall, 1972) is primarily an edited collection of articles and letters to the editor that appeared in main-stream and student newspapers, and speeches on the general subject of violence and protest in Canada. Besides being dated, the selections are very superficial, rendering it an inadequate introduction to this topic. Another book, Mary A.B. Gammon's *Violence in Canada* (Methuen, 1978), is also dated, mainly concentrates on criminal violence, and does not cover political violence. In fact, despite its title, only seven of the fifteen chapters of the book focus on violence in Canada per se, and six of the fifteen contributions were previously published in other forums. Finally, James M. MacLatchie's *Violence in Contemporary Canadian Society* (John Howard Society, 1985) presents the oral proceedings of a conference held on the same subject. Even though these presentations primarily focus on criminal violence, they lack both historical and theoretical depth, a conception of the prevalence of different forms of violence in Canada, as well as sophisticated explanations of the causes and effects of violence. In general, none of these collections have a theoretical or analytical framework guiding the selection of the chapters. Moreover, they are also quite limited in their range and scope.

Since these books have been published, a small cadre of scholars have investigated the dynamics of both criminally- and politically-motivated violence in Canada in an effort to gain insights into the cultural, economic, ideological, political and social cleavages that shape Canadian life and to provide policy-makers with recommendations on how to minimize the incidence of violence, as well as the pain and suffering it causes.

In order to mitigate the shortcomings of the previously reviewed edited books and organize this one, Ted Robert Gurr's (and Hugh Graham's) *Violence in America*, which is already in its third revised edition, is taken as a point of departure for this volume.[2] I reviewed the three editions, performed a content analysis of the subject matter of the chapters, and attempted to replicate the same types of topics for a book on the subject of violence for Canada. A number of themes and chapters emerged. In many cases, the approach taken by Gurr and Graham was perhaps narrow in coverage and ethnocentric in focus as well as limited in topics. I have tried to rectify these problems by organizing a more comprehensive treatment of violence in Canada. Hence, the present book becomes the counterpart to the American one, but it goes beyond *Violence in America* by providing a comparative perspective. Additionally, the contributors to this book, unlike Gurr's and Graham's, focus more on policy and its impact in the control of violence.

Violence in Canada: Sociopolitical Perspectives includes chapters dealing with important subtopics of violence written by a number of well-known and respected scholars, many of whom have done extensive field research in Canada and live or have lived there. The collection consolidates research on particular types of political and criminal violence. Why, however, is it subtitled *Sociopolitical*? To begin with, most of the contributors are political scientists or sociologists or their research deals with these broad areas of research. Additionally, because contributors come from a limited number of social science disciplines, the book's perspective cannot be said to be entirely interdisciplinary.

OBJECTIVES

This book provides an overview of the prevalence of violence both committed and experienced by individuals, groups, and organizations. This approach is helpful in identifying and comparing this social and policy problem between Canada and other similar countries such as other Anglo-American democracies.

Second, *Violence in Canada* primarily focuses on violence since the 1960s. It is heavily laced with research, statistics, and examples drawn primarily from Canada's contemporary history. Although the past is extremely important, the issue of violence did not really become a policy concern until the 1960s.

Third, it challenges the perception that Canada is a 'peaceable kingdom'. Although there are a variety of versions of the so-called myth of the peaceable kingdom (Torrance, 1986), it generally refers to the misconception that Canadians have been, and remain, a thoroughly non-violent people (Kelly and Mitchell, 1981). As this book demonstrates, Canadians both commit and experience a considerable amount of violence.

Fourth, several approaches to the study of violence in Canada were considered including interdisciplinary, criminological, political, and sociological. Whether to produce the volume as a one- or two-volume set (i.e., criminological and political) was also debated. The decision to publish a one-volume set of manuscripts was motivated by the reality that it was not easy to classify contributors and their papers into one discipline or another and that sociopolitical seemed to better capture the contributors' work rather than interdisciplinary. Regardless, the book is built around a social sciences theoretical core and chapters specifically address the sociological and political dimensions.

Fifth, the effects that some of this violence has had on Canadian legal, social, and political structures due to interventions by various levels of government is analyzed. Conterminously, in place of treating the data as static events, the contributors emphasize the dynamic bases of conflict which lead to violence.

Sixth, *Violence in Canada* presents an overview and analysis of different subtypes of political and criminological violence in Canadian society. The forms of violence which have dominated the last three-and-a-half decades are analyzed. Many theorists suggest that both the intensity and frequency of violence experienced in advanced industrialized democracies have increased and that it is technically and physically different from that of the pre-Silent Revolution (e.g., Inglehart, 1977). This predicament is true of Canada. Canada's experience of violence covers the whole gamut of styles of individual, group, and institutional action ranging from individual to collective violence, from vigilantism to violent strikes to open rebellion (Torrance, 1986).

Seventh, the contributions to the book are original (i.e., have never been published elsewhere), use empirical methodology and in some cases quantitative and/or qualitative methods of analysis. The emphasis is on physical rather than psychological or structural violence (e.g., Galtung, 1964). This is not to devalue the importance of psychological or structural violence, it simply makes the task more manageable. Each chapter includes a brief theoretical, historical, policy, and comparative treatment of the subject; the literature reviewed covers the past thirty-four years (i.e., since 1960).

Before reviewing the forthcoming chapters, however, it is wise to have some idea concerning the rate of violence in Canada. Unfortunately, the most comprehensive statistics are official statistics on criminal violence.[3] According to Statistics Canada, the annual national murder rate of two per 100,000 population is the same as it was for 1988, except for 1991 when it was three. Statistics Canada attributes the fact that the rate for all crimes of violence in '1992 was nearly 25 percent higher than in 1988 . . . due to the greater willingness of Canadians, particularly sexually assaulted women, to report personal crimes to the police'. Nevertheless, in general, Canadian statistics are very distant from American ones. For example, 'the Canadian assault rate is 850 per 100,000; the American 2,550 per 100,000' (Corelli, 1994).[4]

Data on political violence in Canada is idiosyncratic (Ross, 1988a). Although there are attempts to ameliorate this situation (Ross, 1988b; 1992), a comprehensive data base on political violence in Canada does not exist. Finally, there is a perception that the average Canadian does not want statistics on violence. As Wallace (1993: 12) has written, 'Canadians do not need statistics to tell them that their lives are less safe now than they were a generation ago. They receive a steady dose of frightening news. . . . Canadians are seething with anger at what they view as a justice system gone awry. . .' (Wallace, 1993: 12).

Violence can be classified into a number of categories and studied from a variety of perspectives including its causes, effects, perpetrators, and victims. Another dimension to investigating this phenomenon is whether or not the analysis is comparative, collective, criminal, cultural, historical, individual, institutional, political, psychological, and sociological. The thorough understanding of what violence entails and how it can be explained and predicted is best achieved by using a combination of analyses and perspectives.

The first chapter, Knafla's 'Violence on the Western Canadian Frontier' presents a historical perspective on various forms of violence, including murder, suicide, and 'accidental' death (i.e., caused by personal and corporate negligence) in the region we now refer to as Western Canada. Drawing largely on court records and archival newspaper accounts, he finds that the incidence of violence on the Canadian frontier had both similarities as well as important differences from that in the United States. He concludes that the dramatic contrast in images—the wild, lawless American west, versus the peaceful Canadian one—are the result of two radically different legal traditions.

Violence results from an interaction among perpetrators, victims, and environments or institutions. This logic is used to organize the next eight contributions.

In 'On Violence and Healing: Aboriginal Experiences, 1960–1993' Long analyses the legacy of individual and collective violence by and against Native Canadians in the context of internal colonialism. The remainder of the chapter marshals evidence regarding the extent of criminal and political violence by and against Natives in Canada over the past three decades. The chapter takes a structural perspective, and addresses such issues as the principles of adaptation-level, and relative deprivation. These factors lead us to look at mediating influences, such as de-individuating conditions, relative payoffs, and the level and type of communication and power of the actors involved in conflict situations. Long focuses on three types of violence: homicide, family violence, and suicide. The chapter concludes with an examination of 'healing initiatives' that native communities have turned to in recent years.

Tunnell's 'Worker Insurgency and Social Control: Violence By and Against Labour in Canada' argues that violence in labour disputes has been a fairly consistent tendency from before Confederation to contemporary times, though it has been much more pronounced during particular periods in our history. It has also been more evident in certain regions during specific time periods. A number of factors must be taken into account in analyzing the level of labour-related violence in Canada compared to other countries: 1) the close connections between capital and the state in Canada at both the federal and provincial levels through the nineteenth and much of the twentieth century; 2) the relatively weak position of organized labour as an influence on the body politic in Canada; 3) the relative strengths of social democratic, socialist and labour parties and their influence on the state in the United Kingdom and Europe as compared to Canada; 4) a higher than usual (among advanced industrialized countries) reliance upon resource extraction and agriculture in Canada with resulting economic instability and major disruptions in the labour market; 5) the overlapping of nationalism and ethnicity with class conflict which has often characterized labour relations in Canada; and 6) the nature and ideology of Canadian police forces and our judicial institutions. He concludes with a discussion of state-corporate crime.

DeKeseredy and Ellis, in 'Intimate Male Violence Against Women in Canada', point out that this is by no means a new phenomenon. It appears, however, that media and statistics are now strongly revealing its prevalence. Their chapter addresses violence against women by tracing its roots and by suggesting that physical violence may be conceived as an extension of patriarchal and capitalist dominance. They examine the incidence of the various forms this violence can take; the causes of violence against women; and community and state responses to violence against women. The chapter concludes with a brief examination of how violence in Canada compares to that experienced in the United States.

Cabrera, in 'Violence By and Against Children in Canada', examines the last type of family violence. She reviews the incidence of, relationships between, and literature on violence by and against children in Canada. She places this social and policy problem in an inter- and intranational context. Some notion of who the victims, perpetrators, and families are is also conveyed. Her chapter reorients policy and guides future research.

Sacco addresses the problem of 'Violence and the Elderly'. He argues that the problems of violence in later life did not begin to attract significant research until the late 1960s. Since that time, an impressive empirical literature which describes the involvement of older people as victims and offenders in violent crime has developed. The data consistently show that the risks associated with violent offending and violent victimization decline substantially with advancing age. Moreover, in several ways elderly people's experiences with violent crime differ from those of the non-elderly. Generally, these patterns of elderly offending and victimization are best explained in the context of theoretical models which stress the importance of lifestyle or routine activity factors. Most recently, research has focused on violence by and against the elderly in domestic settings. Parallels are drawn between such violence and other forms of family violence both in Canada and the United States.

Gartner, in 'Homicide in Canada', reviews the most severe type of criminal violence in Canada by focusing on murder patterns in Canada during this century. More specifically, her piece examines definitions and data sources; presents patterns in Canadian homicides since 1961 using Statistics Canada data and Canadian homicide rates using other data sources; and addresses particular concerns about homicides. Part of the analysis includes gender-specific data on homicide victimization in Canada since the 1920s, and an explanation for the increase in homicide rates in the late 1960s and early 1970s. She concludes with an examination of the Americanization of Canadian homicide.

In 'Violence by Municipal Police in Canada' Ross analyses the frequency of real or alleged violence by police against citizens in urban environments in Canada. The author argues that the majority of research on police violence in Canada is anecdoctal and the available statistics are primarily situational. He develops an original data base, based on newspaper sources, to introduce the problem of police violence in Canada and argues that a complete understanding of the dynamics of police violence requires an understanding of the multicausal nature of causes and controls.

Welch's analysis of 'The Reproduction of Violence in Canadian Prisons' looks at several important aspects of prison violence, including motives (expressive and instrumental), levels (collective and individual), forms (among inmates, by inmates against guards, and by guards against prisoners), and causes (including underlying political and economic forces). He concludes with a critical examination of policies commonly used to control prisoners and violence.

'Terrorism in Canada, 1960–1992' draws on a detailed database of terrorist incidents recently developed by Kellett and his colleagues for the Solicitor General of Canada in order to examine patterns of international versus domestic events, incidence, geographical and temporal occurrence, perpetrator group-type, tactics employed, targets attacked, etc. Using the database and other sources, Kellett examines the groups involved, their resort to various criminal acts (robbery, etc.) to understand their threat capability. For comparative purposes the study also examines global trends in terrorism.

Torrance, in 'The Responses of Democratic Governments to Violence', provides examples of violent incidents in which the Canadian government has been involved to highlight the difficulties confronting a government and the decisions it must make. Included in the analysis are the government's perceptions of an incident, the choices open to it, the diverse interests that must be accommodated, and the policy decisions that emerge. Finally, some analysis is directed towards defining what constitutes an appropriate governmental response to violence.

In the final chapter, 'Conclusion: Summary and Future Directions', Ross answers what have we learned from the contributors to this volume? He reviews the various typologies, patterns uncovered in violent victimization, and the adequacy of data on the subtypes of violence and processes reviewed in this book, briefly reviews the causes and effects of violence in Canada, and makes an number of suggestions for future research.

Violence has had and continues to play an important role in Canadian society. The time is ripe to acknowledge this reality, and consolidate research on this topic in order to understand it better, and work towards the goal of lessening its occurrence and better controlling and preventing it. *Violence in Canada: Sociopolitical Perspectives* is the beginning of this much needed process.

NOTES

An earlier version of this chapter was presented at the Annual Meetings of the Canadian Association for Security and Intelligence Studies, Ottawa, June 1992. Special thanks to Natasha J. Cabrera and anonymous reviewers, for comments.

[1] Not all Canadian criminologists agree with these findings and some question the report's methodology (e.g., Canadian Press, 'Criminologists question study on Canadian Crime', *Toronto Star*, Sunday 2 August 1992: 14).

[2] Clearly, others such as Weiner, Zahn, and Sagi (1992) could have been used, but *Violence in America* is often considered the original model. Additionally, the first two editions were co-edited, while the last was edited by only Gurr.

[3] It is unfortunate because not all individuals report crimes to the police. Thus victimization rates are often a better indicator of crime rates in a community.

[4] For discussions on crime statistics in Canada see, for example, Evans and Himelfarb (1992); Gomme (1993: Chapter 8); and Sacco and Johnson (1990).

REFERENCES

Boles, Richard P., et al. (1972). *Protest, Violence and Social Change*, Toronto: Prentice-Hall.

Canadian Press (1992). 'A not-so peaceful nation', *Calgary Herald*, 31 July: A3.

Corelli, Rae (1994). 'Murder Next Door', *Maclean's*, 18 April: 14–15.

Evans, John and Alexander Himelfarb (1992). 'Counting Crime'. Pp. 57–90 in Rick Linden, ed., *Criminology: A Canadian Perspective*, 2nd ed. Toronto: Harcourt Brace Jovanovich.

Galtung, Johan (1964). 'A Structural Theory of Aggression', *Journal of Peace Research* 1, 2: 95–119.

Gammon, Mary A.B. (1978). *Violence in Canada*, Toronto: Methuen.

Gomme, Ian McDermaid (1993). *The Shadow Line: Deviance and Crime in Canada*. Toronto: Harcourt Brace Jovanovich.

Gurr, Ted Robert and Hugh David Graham (1969). *Violence in America*, 2 vols. Newbury Park, CA: Sage.

Inglehart, Ronald (1977). *Silent Revolution: Changing Values and Political Styles among Western Publics*. Princeton: Princeton University Press.

Kelly, Michael J. and Thomas H. Mitchell (1981). 'The Study of Internal Conflict in Canada: Problems and Prospects', *Conflict Quarterly* 2, 1 (Summer): 10–17.

Kennedy, Leslie and Robert A. Silverman (1993). *Deadly Deeds: Murder in Canada*. Scarborough, ON: Nelson.

MacLatchie, James M. (1985). *Violence in Contemporary Canadian Society*. Toronto: John Howard Society.

Ross, Jeffrey Ian (1988a). 'An events data base on political terrorism in Canada: Some conceptual and methodological problems', *Conflict Quarterly* 8, 2 (Spring): 47–65.

———— (1988b). 'Attributes of domestic political terrorism in Canada, 1960–1985', *Terrorism: An International Journal* 11, 3 (Fall): 213–33.

———— (1992). 'Contemporary radical right-wing violence in Canada: A quantitative analysis', *Terrorism and Political Violence* 4, 3 (Autumn): 72–101.

Sacco, Vincent F. and Holly Johnson (1990). *Patterns of Criminal Victimization in Canada*. Ottawa: Ministry of Supply and Services.

Torrance, Judy (1986). *Public Violence in Canada*. Montreal: McGill-Queen's University Press.

Wallace, Bruce (1993). 'Fighting back: Canadians are fed up with crime-and the coddling of criminals', *Maclean's*, 20 September: 12–14.

Weiner, Neil Alan, Margaret A. Zahn, and Rita J. Sagi, eds (1992). *Violence: Patterns, Causes, Public Policy*. Toronto: Harcourt Brace Jovanovich.

Chapter One

VIOLENCE ON THE WESTERN CANADIAN FRONTIER

A Historical Perspective

LOUIS A. KNAFLA

Historically, violence has been viewed in two different ways: as the violent acts of humans against one another, and as behaviour that has been defined as unlawful by the customs and laws of either the local community or the state. The same paradigm has infused the historical study of crime. Historical research has concentrated traditionally on subjects that can be clearly defined with regard both to topic and to a specific research agenda. Thus historians have seldom felt capable of writing about violence apart from criminal law, or about crime apart from those acts that have been prosecuted in the courts.[1] The purpose of this chapter is to examine the history of violence on the western Canadian frontier within the parameters of British and Canadian law. But since the subject of violence cannot possibly be seen within a legal context alone, an attempt will also be made to place the history of violent crime within the larger social, geographic, and demographic contexts.

Perhaps the most pervasive organizing factor of Canadian history is regionality. A confederation of disparate colonies of varied social, political, and linguistic origins, Canada is made up of regions that have always been inward-looking, tied more by family, kin, community, language, ethnicity, religion, and the cultural and economic forces of Britain and the United States, than by the ties that were created between the regions to form a confederation along the vast frontiers of the American border below and the Arctic hinterland above. This factor has also been the driving force of its historiography. Too much Canadian history, however, has been written from an urban perspective.[2] A traditional approach to the history of violence in Canada has been to use the urban centres of provinces as the organizing principle. The more difficult, and interesting, task is to take a larger geographical perspective and examine the hinterlands in their totality as a moving borderland.[3] Thus this study will explore the history of violence—specifically, murder/suicide, accidental death, and collective force—in western Canada from Manitoba to British Columbia, focusing primarily on the larger landscape and looking at the legal history of the frontier as a moving borderland—an approach that is becoming an established research method in southern North American history.[4]

The thesis of this chapter is that violence was part of the human landscape of the western Canadian frontier. The traditional interpretation is that the people arriving in what was to become Canada shared with the British peoples of the late-eighteenth and nineteenth centuries a deep belief in the superiority of British institutions over the lawlessness that reigned south of the forty-ninth parallel, in the land of guns, vigilantism, wars, and revolution.[5] This interpretation was promoted in part by anglophones who wished to see themselves as independent of that aggressive society driven by change and dynamic growth instead of stability and tradition, and in part by community leaders who wished to attract immigrants and homesteaders away from the competition: that is, the states to the south. It continues to the present not only in North America but in Europe: television viewers in the United Kingdom today are exposed to 'Malcolm the Mountie', a lager-swigging mountie who 'always gets his can' along with his man. This contemporary commercial image reflects the traditional views of the people who settled the Canadian western frontier as distinct from those who settled to the south, contrasting a land based on peaceful coexistence with one permeated by endemic violence.[6]

One difficulty in using the term 'frontier' to define a particular society in a specific stage of its development is that the word implies an 'advance' from one stage (undeveloped) to another (industrial society). This is the fundamental thesis of 'Whig history': that history comprises an inexorable march of progress from a less-developed to a more-developed era.[7] In actual fact, however, the people of the Canadian 'western frontier' in the nineteenth century had no such progressive motivation: they were simply living on the 'far outer periphery of the British-Atlantic world'.[8] Hence the term 'frontier' as used in this study denotes a particular space and time, not a historical stage of development. Indeed, the evidence presented here reveals that violence was not an aberration of the 'frontier', but a part of everyday life in the regions that comprised the landscape of the Canadian west.

Indeed, violence was an integral part of European as well as North American society in the great era of imperialism from the late eighteenth century to the early twentieth.[9] Moreover, evidence from the United States reveals a nation that, from its origins in the 1760s to the 1960s, experienced a kaleidoscope of uninterrupted criminal activities and collective acts of violence. The nation was able to withstand them only because of the institutional stability of the central government and the abundant natural resources that underpinned a long-term secular trend towards growing prosperity.[10] The author of the first history of crime in Canada presents a similar picture of almost uninterrupted criminal activities by both citizens and the state. This work provides an equally unflattering survey from very selective examples, without much original research and with considerable exaggeration.[11] One of the purposes of this chapter will be to identify the causes and extent of the history of violence in the Canadian west, and place it in the continental as well as the national context.

The three early Canadian western frontiers developed in the first half of the nineteenth century in Rupert's Land in the District of Assiniboia, in the northern Rocky Mountain and Mackenzie River region, and in the northern Pacific Coast area. Containing sparse populations, and serving commercial and British imperial interests, these three frontiers will be surveyed briefly in this era from historical writings and printed primary sources. Since the thesis of this chapter is that violence was part of the landscape of the western frontier, it is important to demonstrate that violence did not come with the later settlement process and the development of the frontier from a commercial trading society to an agrarian and industrial one, but was already part of the vernacular culture.

Violent Crime in the Early Commercial Frontiers

The Assiniboia Frontier

The Hudson's Bay Company's charter of 1670 gave the Company (HBC) ownership of and jurisdiction over all the lands drained by rivers flowing into Hudson Bay.[12] While the purpose of the charter was commercial, the fact that it was issued by royal proclamation rather than act of Parliament, and that there was no firm indication of the land subject to the charter or of the nations of aboriginal peoples already resident, gave the charter questionable legal authority that would come to haunt the Company when problems such as the rebellions of 1869–70 and 1885 arose in later years. The Company's first century was profitable, but by the early 1800s the rise of competing fur-trading companies in the United States and Lower Canada, and a decline in both the market for and prices of fur products caused by embargo in the Napoleonic Wars of 1797–1814, created a crisis for the HBC from which it would never fully recover.[13]

In Assiniboia, the evidence for the history of violence begins with the celebrated conflict between the Hudson's Bay Company and the North West Company in the second decade of the nineteenth century. This conflict, which was initially commercial, grew out of the Company's grant of 116,000 square miles to Thomas Douglas, Earl of Selkirk, in 1811 for establishing the colony of Assiniboia.[14] Epitomized by the Seven Oaks killings of June 1816, which involved Lord Selkirk's settlers and the traders/voyageurs, violent death became part of the life cycle of the region. (One should note that this event became deeply engrained in the mentality of later generations as the myth of a 'massacre' by Métis 'savages' was created to justify dispossessing them of their lands in 1870.[15]) The ensuing trade wars, battles, killings, kidnappings, assaults, and thefts occupied the officials not only of Upper and Lower Canada, but also of Westminster and Whitehall, until the amalgamation of the two companies in 1821.[16] In 1817–18 alone, more than 200 arrests for criminal offences allegedly committed by both sides were sent for trial to Toronto, Montreal, and Quebec City.[17] The trials have never been fully studied, even though editions of the transcripts were published by both companies.[18] Technical problems with the Canada Jurisdiction Act of 1803[19] caused many cases to be dropped or end in acquittals. But the mounds of evidence that were collected provide a rich source for information about the violence that took place and the disputes between governments and companies.

Law enforcement to keep the peace would have to wait until the district of Assiniboia developed in population and was given legal institutions. The district was reconstituted in 1822, but its administrative structure was weak; the General Quarterly Court created by the HBC in 1835 never sat, and the Company's penal codes were perfunctory.[20] Not until a Recorder's Court was appointed in 1839 were criminal prosecutions undertaken in the district under English law. The records of the Company bear testimony to the continuation of the violent forces that had been at work from the foundation of the settlement.[21] A factor contributing to violence was the influence of Adam Thom, the first recorder.[22] Thom was an anglophone from Scotland whose reputation stemmed from his fiery prose for the prosecution, conviction, and execution of the francophones who had participated in the Rebellions of Lower Canada in 1836–38. His racist attitudes encouraged settlers and traders to ignore the rights of aboriginals and Métis, increasing the occasions for violence and ensuring that racist attitudes spread to the northern prairies. In his judgement against James Calder for a homicide on 17 August 1848, in what is today the Peace River country of northwest Alberta, Thom—lacking both jurisdiction and authority—declared that all the HBC's discoveries north to the Arctic Ocean and west to the Pacific were an extension of the Charter of 1670 (a questionable position in law), and that any attempted jurisdiction of Lower or Upper Canada, 'even if valid in point of law is utterly repugnant to justice and humanity'.[23] His position was quite consistent with the Company's documented recourse to economic pressure, physical intimidation, and 'recreational' violence in its efforts to control its society.[24]

This not to say that the HBC had any general power to control events. More often than not, the Company would attempt to manage a situation but then be placed in a position of crisis management. In the Guillaume Sayer trial before Judge Thom in 1848, for example, the Court attempted to use pressure and intimidation on the jurors to bring a conviction, but it failed. The verdict was guilty, but with mercy. Thus when Sayer walked outside and raised his hands, the assembled armed mob cheered him as a victor.[25] Perception is often as important as reality. Company control was fleeting and unsteady, lacking in both personnel and institutional structures to force adherence to its decrees. The HBC acknowledged that both its employees and the First Nations people were subject to native customary law where relevant. But Thom's lack of knowledge and appreciation of English law, in addition to his personal and overbearing lectures in court, precluded social harmony and allowed company employees to disregard some of the most basic common law doctrines which included the primacy of local custom.[26] Thus the Company provided the environment not only for itself but also for others to assert their place in society through violence. Likewise, when the HBC surrendered its charter to the British Crown in 1869 and Rupert's Land was transferred to the Dominion of Canada, it was the absence of real control that permitted the Métis to create a provisional government, with the result that the Canadian government had to send in troops to exercise its authority.

The problems that in the 1830s and 1840s the HBC had exhibited with aboriginals and mixed bloods were re-engaged with the transfer of its charter to the Dominion of Canada in 1869.[27] The story of the 1869–70 'Rebellion' is well known.[28] But it is important to note that the source of the problem was an inability of the Canadian government to act promptly in assisting the access and rights to land of the non-white settlers, in recognizing their linguistic, religious, and cultural identities, and in curbing the move of land-hungry Protestant settlers from Ontario. The conflicting signals of the Dominion government's prosecution of the 'rebels' in the spring of 1870, together with the Métis provisional government's conviction and execution by court martial of the Ontario labourer Thomas Scott, revealed the inability of legal measures to resolve festering economic, religious, and political problems.[29] The response of Prime Minister John A. Macdonald was a punitive military campaign against the non-whites that summer. The government would not address the problem of what would constitute the criminal law of the North-West Territories until the Judicature Act of 1886.[30] In the meantime, the Company continued to exercise its own informal criminal law jurisdiction with a heavy hand that lacked clear authority and demonstrated confusion and uncertainty.[31]

Discontent among the Métis in the Fort Carlton-Prince Albert-Batoche area over economic crisis and the security of land tenure along the South Saskatchewan River prompted them to recall the exiled Louis Riel to serve as leader. The peaceful protest against government inefficiency that began in the summer and autumn of 1884 turned violent when the government delayed an investigation of Métis claims and Riel responded by seizing arms and ammunition at Batoche on 18 March 1885. The Métis declaration of a provisional government sealed the armed conflict that followed, which ended with the final defeat of the Métis at Batoche on 12 May.[32] The controversy over Riel's trial for treason will never be resolved.[33] The proceedings against the other 71 'rebels' did mark an attempt, however feeble, to do justice, but the proceedings were marked with errors and inconsistencies. For the aboriginals and mixed-bloods who precipitated the conflict, the choice was largely between starvation or violence.[34]

In the 1870s the Canadian government attempted to resolve the difficulties posed by conflicts between native peoples and settlers by initiating treaties to set aside land reserves. It is worth noting that the First Nations entered the treaty process in good faith.[35] Only when their petitions were ignored did they turn to rebellion. The government quashed the rebels harshly and with bloodshed. The trials of those who survived can be interpreted as efforts on the part of the Canadian state to demonstrate its monopoly on the 'legal' use of violence in a manner that parallels the earlier history of the region under the aegis of the HBC.

In summary, the history of violence in western Canada had its origins in the conflicts that arose out of the competing interests of the Hudson's Bay and North West companies in the district of Assiniboia in the second decade of the nineteenth century. The inability of the HBC to exercise effective control allowed it to continue, and the situation was exacerbated by the controversial jurisdiction of Adam Thom as recorder of Rupert's Land in the 1840s. Thus the racist attitudes both towards and among francophones, aboriginal people, and Métis that marked the early history of the Canadian west and were to persist for many decades contributed to outbreaks of violence.

THE MACKENZIE FRONTIER

The HBC's policies towards First Nations peoples were little different in the northerly regions. The scant documentation available suggests that for a company whose daily authority was often characterized as weak, the HBC could be extremely harsh on occasion. One notable example occurred in January 1832, when 14 people at the Company post of Hannah Bay, near Moose Factory, were visited by 24 starving native people. Two days later, 9 residents at the post including women and children were found dead, their corpses mutilated, and goods taken. A search for the perpetrators a month later found two, of whom one confessed to his people's depredations and begged for a pardon, which was refused. Over several days in late March the search party found 6 natives who were alleged to have been at Hannah Bay. John McTavish, Chief Factor in charge of the post, had ordered all the adult males found to be shot on the spot, without inquiries. His orders were carried out.[35]

An equally chilling event occurred in the northern Mackenzie and Athabaska region several years later. In a major examination of the 'Mackenzie River Murders', Hamar Foster has shown more precisely how the HBC investigated and prosecuted violent crime in the Mackenzie fur-trade district in the 1830s.[37] Baptiste Cadien, Creole La Graisse, and Baptiste Jourdain were prosecuted, at Trois Rivières, Quebec, in March 1838, for the murder of 11 members of the Hare band at Lake Puant in the Mackenzie region in the last weeks of December 1835. The accused, who were 'scamps' of the HBC, had been sent north from Fort Norman to retrieve the fish they had caught that summer near Fort Good Hope. Stopping by the camp of the small Hare band, where Cadien had been pursuing a local woman for some time against postmaster William Mowat's orders, the accused fired on and killed the Hare including several children and a pregnant woman in 'defence' of Cadien's taking 'an Indian man of his woman'. The Company prosecuted Cadien and La Graisse on the testimony of Jourdain. The accused were sent south to Fort Simpson, then east to Norway House on Hudson Bay by the autumn of 1836, and finally to Trois Rivières for trial in the spring of 1838.

The incident was prominent in the newspapers of Lower Canada between the two rebellions. The *Montreal Herald*, whose editor was now Adam Thom, was given HBC documents supporting in lucid details its view of the murders. His accounts, describing the accused as cut-throat cannibals who ate their victims, reflected his racist view of native and French-speaking Métis peoples. Chief Justice Reid, who supported the obliteration of French culture, demanded the death penalty. However, a petition by the Lower Canadian francophone community induced Governor General Lord Grey to reduce the sentence to transportation to Australia.

A pioneering attempt in 1989 to write an ethno-legal history of the imposition of Canadian law by the Royal Canadian Mounted Police (RCMP) upon the Inuit at Coronation Gulf at the mouth of the Coppermine River uncovered a tragic story of murders, staged trials, and hangings which had occurred over previous decades. This, the study estimated, had destroyed the culture and law of the aboriginal people.[38] The violence exhibited in the fur-trade era, however, should not be seen as imposing entirely new codes of conduct on native communities. The pioneering ethnologist Diamond Jenness was told by Inuit males in approximately 1916 that each of them had killed at least once.

THE PACIFIC FRONTIER

The settlement of the Pacific coast region dates from the English incursions into Vancouver Island in the early 1840s. The earliest indication of violent crime in the region, however, dates from 1817, when, in what was perhaps Canada's first case of cannibalism, seven men of the North West Company had lost their boats and provisions on the Columbia River north of Revelstoke; eventually all but one died, to be eaten by their survivors. The one man who lived to be tried had slit the throat of the second to last survivor.[39] The case was tried at Montreal.

Equally controversial, but with larger ramifications, was the murder of John McLoughlin, an HBC clerk at Fort Stikine, Vancouver Island, in April 1842.[40] His father, Dr John McLoughlin, was the HBC's Chief Factor at Fort Vancouver. The son, considered adventurous, was killed when he tried to discipline some Company men and prevent them from stealing Company goods to buy the favours of native women. The evidence suggests that a group of men drew up a contract to kill him that night, and that Urbain Heroux committed the act. The men, however, first gave a concocted story to George Simpson, Governor of the HBC, alleging that McLoughlin had got roaring drunk and terrorized them, and that the killing was a matter of self-defence. Simpson accepted the story and initially made no attempt to conduct a full investigation. Normally, there would have been no prosecution. But Dr McLoughlin was not easily swayed. He devoted several years of his life to obtaining a full investigation and trial. Heroux, the interpreter, was sent east to Norway House with 11 witnesses, but after numerous investigations over several years no trial took place. The matter was shelved in 1846 when McLoughlin's father finally gave up the quest for a prosecution.

Simpson's preferred policy of not invoking the criminal law won the day. It was not, however, his policy alone. The HBC had used it for decades. For instance, when Peter Skene Ogden, a Company official, investigated a homicide during an expedition into the Snake country, he buried the body, asked the culprit a few questions and, concluding that he was 'miserable and unhappy, and will let it remain quiet', let the man go.[41] This was consistent with other acts of Company officials west of the Rockies.[42] A trial in England would have cost the HBC some £10,000.

Partly in response to problems such as these, in 1843 the HBC established a post at Fort Camosack (later Victoria) at the southern tip of Vancouver Island to serve settlers and First Nations from the Oregon to the Alaska territories.[43] A common-law regime was established in 1849 after the 49th parallel was settled as the border between British colonial lands and the United States in the west. The HBC received an exclusive trading charter, and Vancouver Island was made a Crown colony with Governor, Assembly, Justices of the Peace, and English law.[44] But the Company never surrendered real legal authority until the gold rush of 1857–58, which brought an influx of miners from California and New Zealand with their own popular assemblies, criminal codes, and 'camp justice'.

These developments hastened the end of the HBC's legal authority in the Pacific region. Its charter was revoked in 1859, when a new colony of British Columbia was established for the mainland. In order to circumvent the problems that had plagued Assiniboia, the modern English law of 1858 was introduced and a chief justice appointed who had stellar academic and legal credentials. Matthew Baillie Begbie brought modern English criminal law to the two colonies that were united as British Columbia in 1866 and admitted into Confederation in 1871.[45] While the violence between immigrant settlers and First Nations would expand to other ethnic groups and employer-employee relations in the following decades, much of it would at least be adjudicated at English common law.

Murder and Violence in the Emerging Agrarian and Industrial Communities

British Columbia

Famous murder cases have become part of British Columbia's historical heritage. Two of them deserve particular mention: the McLean gang case of 1879, and the Sproule case of 1885. The trial of Alexander Hare and Allan, Charlie, and Archie McLean for the murder of constable John Ussher in December 1879 was a *cause célèbre*.[46] The 'Kamloops outlaws' were a gang of mixed-blood teenagers whose horse thefts, assaults, and jail-breaks were depicted by the local population as acts of 'terror'. Ussher had been shot through the head by Archie from 18 inches while trying to arrest the young men. Eventually hunted down by a posse, they were sent to the jail at New Westminster because the Kamloops townsfolk threatened to lynch them and the jail there was not secure. Tried before a special commission of assize at New Westminster in March 1880, they were found guilty, but the verdict was quashed after a heated controversy between the government and the Supreme Court justices over the legality of the special commission and the choice of venue. Following a second trial with an additional murder charge, however, the young men were convicted again and hanged in January 1881.

The 'Kamloops outlaws' can be considered a Canadian version of the Jesse James story: wild young men outside the mainstream of white society who took to violence in order to give themselves a profession and a public identity. People of mixed blood had no position in white society beyond their work as unskilled labourers. Governments sought to keep them in their marginalized position by arresting them for any infractions to appease local élites, while the courts tried to maintain their independence by adhering to the strict letter of the law in insisting upon hard evidence for convictions. By the 1880s in the BC interior, more than half the people jailed in some districts were aboriginals or mixed-bloods.[47]

Similar problems faced the Oriental labourers who had been welcomed during the gold rush and the building of the CPR, but who by the mid-1880s were seen as threats to the social and economic order. Although they may have constituted the largest single ethnic minority group in the region following the collapse of the gold boom, they soon formed a large proportion of all people who were arrested for trial in the local courts.[48] Thus local and municipal governments persistently excluded, ghettoized, and harassed them.[49] This culminated in the Vancouver riots of 1887 and 1907.[50]

With development of a settled anglophone society in BC in the late nineteenth century, it was the people who had become marginalized that bore the brunt of the criminal law. Policing the interior north of Kamloops can be seen in the work of the officers of the Yukon, who often served the masters who paid them instead of the inhabitants they were sworn to protect.[51] Thus aboriginals, mixed bloods, and Orientals became both the objects and perpetrators of violence. As victims, they had no recourse against the illegal, extralegal, or discriminatory measures used against them. They lacked the knowledge or resources to defend themselves, and faced swift repression when they took actions to publicize their plight.[52]

The Queen vs Robert Evan Sproule for the murder of Thomas Hammill, a miner at the Bluebell mine, Kootenay Lake, in the BC interior on 1 June 1885, reflected the violence that occurred in mining communities which were in early stages of development. The trial was heard before the Supreme Court at Victoria in December 1885.[53] No motive was clearly established, and the evidence was circumstantial. The jurors had great difficulty. Retiring at 4:30 p.m., they returned at 9:45 p.m. to announce that they could not agree; sent back to reconsider, the jurors finally brought in a verdict of guilty at 11:00 p.m., recommending mercy for Sproule.

Sproule's appeal was based on the problems noted above. Claiming innocence of the murder, he said there was a conspiracy against him, and that he was not allowed to defend himself from this in his last words to the court because it would have been 'new evidence'. Justice Gray, in defending his decision not to poll the jury, said it was too late in the night. Defending the jury verdict of guilty, which necessitated his statutory sentence of hanging, he wrote that while the evidence was circumstantial, it 'formed in my opinion an unbroken chain that left no possible doubt of the prisoner's guilt.'[54] The case dragged on for almost another year, involving the Supreme Court of Canada. Eventually Sproule was hanged despite a petition of more than 600 persons for his release. Miners traditionally objected to the interference of 'foreign' courts in their communities.

The problem in assessing the extent of violence in this period of BC's history is that there are discrepancies between the official and unofficial records. Officially, the provincial and municipal governments were able to portray through advertisements and the press an image of law and order conducive to settlement.[55] By contrast, contemporary literary evidence paints a dramatic picture of violence. According to major provincial newspapers such as the *Daily British Colonist*, the lower western mainland, the upper Fraser River, and the Cariboo area were plagued with 'outrageous and foul murders', 'cold-blooded atrocities', 'heavy robberies', and 'rife Rowdyism'.[56]

The court records for the province as a whole suggest a more moderate view. The criminal trial calendars of the assizes are generally short, and they do not contain many capital felonies.[57] They do, however, reveal a very broad mixture of criminal indictments. Apart from violent crimes such as murder, assault, break and enter, indecent assault, and poisoning, they also include non-violent crimes such as bribery, conspiracy, forgery, gambling, perjury, and theft which frequently embodied an element of violence.[58] Data on 'reported' crime, however, do not include what criminologists would call the 'dark figure'—those crimes that were not reported or investigated. Published case studies suggest that while crime on the BC frontier may not have been frequent, when it was committed it was frequently violent.

Another perspective can be attained by examining a particular region of the frontier in more depth. The Kootenay region of BC numbered some 55 small communities that were heavily engaged in mining. These settlements had their origins in the 1860s with the construction of the Dewdney Trail, and developed rapidly in the 1890s with the creation of an internal network of rail and steam lines. The incidence of crime in the area cannot be studied from judicial records because there were few local police or magistrates courts and the circuit court of assize met only occasionally at the southern towns of Kootenay Bay, Nelson, and Rossland.[59]

Thus few legal officials were seen in the communities of the east and west Kootenays. In the early, frontier years of the 1860s-90s, those judges who did visit held their court sessions in tents or log huts,[60] and their trial calendars were not large. As in the rest of the province, there was a broad mixture of indictments without any particular crime or offence predominant. The trial calendars, moreover, do not enable one to see inside the cases to ascertain the amount of violence they may have contained.

The 'literary' as opposed to the 'records' evidence, however, reveals a different picture. There were 54 newspapers published in the region in this era, representing some 55 communities and their surrounding areas. While some of these papers were short-lived, others lasted for decades. Their contents reveal a mining culture with distinct political, economic, social, and cultural values. The law, moreover, was at the top of their agenda. In a town where an assize or local court was sitting, the full trial calendar would be published. When 'foreigners' were involved, the court house would be packed to see justice done, and juries and judges would be praised for exacting the full measure of the law.

The major problem was that there were few officials empowered to investigate or arrest. In their absence, the people of the Kootenay supported the idea of frontier justice. For example, in 1867 men crossed the border to shoot down an American thief who had killed a local constable.[61] They also lynched a suspected murderer in 1884. Thirteen years later, when a Frenchman named Pierre was accused of stealing a sack of flour and 100 pounds of bacon, 60 vigilantes searched him out, then shot and hanged him.[62] Miners were well-armed, knew how to use their weapons, and were not cowed by the threat of death. A lieutenant-colonel reported that they were ideally suited as potential militiamen to defend the country from an American invasion.[63] Given the past history of capital criminal prosecutions on the western Canadian frontier, perhaps the reliance on 'self-help' contributes to an understanding of the divergence between the official records and the 'dark' figure of violent crime.

THE NORTH-WEST TERRITORIES AND ALBERTA

The Canadian prairies were opened to settlement following the creation of the North-West Territories in 1870, which bridged the gap between Manitoba (the former Assiniboia) and British Columbia. The first settlements were established by the Métis along the North Saskatchewan River following the Rebellion of 1869–70, and by immigrants from Ontario, Britain, and the United States who followed the construction of the Canadian Pacific Railway across the southern prairies. But the status of 'Canadian' law in the North-West Territories remained in limbo until the Administration of Justice Act (1886), enacted in the wake of the 1885 Rebellion, introduced the law of England as of 1870.

Initial studies from official records suggest that violence, including assault, armed robbery, and arson, was prevalent on the prairies following the construction of the CPR from Winnipeg to Banff in the early 1880s. Loss of life, however, was surprisingly low.[64] One of the landmarks of the early period on the prairies west of Manitoba was the Cypress Hills 'massacre' of 1873. An extensive study of the event suggests that violent personal relationships and occasionally anarchy had accompanied direct contact between the Plains tribes and Canadian and American commercial ventures in this region as it had elsewhere.[65]

Although recorded evidence is unfortunately minimal for Saskatchewan, it is substantial for Alberta.[66] The large number of homesteads and rural communities scattered over a vast landscape makes the use of literary sources questionable.[67] Therefore records evidence will be used here, specifically from the judicial district of Red Deer which extended from the Saskatchewan border to the Rocky Mountains.[68] The wide variety of communities, economies and social structures in this district—which included the mining and forestry area of the Rockies, the dry arable region of the prairies, and the mixed agricultural and agrarian-based industries of the central parkland—provides a credible cross-section of frontier prairie society.[69]

The history of the Holt-Dubois gang of cattle rustlers is one of the great unwritten stories of prairie Canada. A series of indictments laid in 1909 by Serjeant Robert W. Ensor of Stettler, Alberta, against James and Irven Holt, John F. Dubois, and other individual members of the gang reveal a cattle-rustling operation that stretched from Alberta to Idaho and Montana.[70] Dubois and his sidekicks not only stole liberally from the ranches of the region, but they also terrorized the local population with threats of physical violence to the point that witnesses reneged on giving testimony in court, and it was openly stated that no jury would convict them, no matter how solid the evidence. Ensor wrote that many people were also 'in terror' of Dubois because he would run their cattle off their land.[71] In the end, only one member of the gang was convicted (his sentence was only nine months in prison). Since James Holt himself had previously been sentenced to 12 years for horse theft in Idaho, the Crown prosecutor expressed the view that the only way to get rid of the problem was to deport the whole gang to the United States.[72]

In fact, cattle and horse rustlers, often toting firearms, dominate the criminal court records of the region. Although some of the culprits were from the United States and played the border and jurisdictional question with great success, others were members of the marginalized native and Métis communities who were often the targets of law enforcement in the earlier period. Moreover, a survey of the court records of the judicial district of Fort Macleod in the late 1880s and early 1890s reveals that approximately 60 per cent of arrests and indictments were of aboriginals for the crimes of horse and cattle theft, assault, arson, carnal knowledge, and rape.[73] Records for the judicial district of Northern Alberta reveal that Métis and non-anglophone European immigrants were prominent in prosecutions there.

The prevalence of violence made law enforcement hazardous indeed. Constables and policemen were frequently assaulted in Alberta, as in the rest of the country.[74] In Red Deer, for instance, in 1913, Police Chief George Bell was called to the Crown Café to deal with some abusive patrons who were urinating on the sidewalk. When he entered the café, J.D. Kelly, a brakeman, told him to get out; Bell refused to move, and Kelly slugged him in the face.[75] Two years earlier Kelly had shot Bell through the stomach in the course of resisting arrest, and the town had almost lynched him.[76]

Violent sexual offences were also endemic in prairie frontier society. Considerable work has been done on this subject, but much more remains to be researched in the original judicial records.[77] The large number of prosecutions for incest, carnal knowledge, gross indecency, attempted rape, and rape suggests that such crimes were much more common than the literary evidence would suggest.[78] The victims were often young girls; the perpetrators fathers, relatives, and family friends; the locations frequently small immigrant communities and towns. The names of victims and suspects represent most ethnic groups, and no particular one is predominant. The high standards of evidence used by the judiciary, together perhaps with a male bias against female testimony, resulted in a very low conviction rate and thus an inability to enforce the Criminal Code.

The problems in prosecuting sexual offences can be seen in Rex v. Weir in Knee Hill Valley in 1910. The Crown filed three charges against Henry Weir for illicit connection, seduction, and carnal knowledge with Sarah Anne Hibbert, aged 14–16.[79] The charges included threats of bodily harm, and were laid only after Hibbert bore a child as a result of one incident. Weir escaped to North Dakota, but even after he was returned to Canada, the Attorney-General tried to persuade Hibbert's father to drop the charges. After three consecutive trials stretching over 19 months, no further attempts were made to indict Weir. In numerous other cases throughout the region, families would lodge complaints, demand indictments, and face not-guilty verdicts or, at best, convictions with light sentences.[80]

CORPORATE VIOLENCE AND ACCIDENTIAL DEATHS

'Accidental death' is one of the great black holes in legal-historical scholarship both in North America and Europe. This makes the recovery of coroners' inquests absolutely essential for historical study. Deaths ruled accidental did not go to criminal trial. Coroners' inquest juries heard, and often recorded, the evidence, and would present the matter for trial only if they found the death not accidental and presented evidence implicating a suspect. Many kinds of violent death ranging from homicide and infanticide to suicide and mercy-killing went no further than the coroner's inquest.[81] This process demonstrates how local communities could have a decisive impact upon how the criminal law *worked* by deciding which violent deaths would be prosecuted and tried, and which ones would not.

Taken at face value, accidental death may not seem to constitute violent crime; however, I would suggest that in some instances it does. On one level, when the prosecutorial energy moved from the private individual to the state in the early nineteenth century, a murder was reported once an official deemed a death to stem from unnatural causes. The decision as to how a death would be defined was solely that of the investigating official. Thus when the landscape is a frontier— where there were few officials—and where a single industry was often the major employer and sole economic base of the region, one can expect that such decisions between murder and non-murder may often have been questionable. Such was the case in the Kootenay region of southeastern BC in the late nineteenth century.

A series of exposés in *The Brooklyn News* of Brooklyn, BC, in the autumn of 1898, reveals the extent of the problem. A Swede working on a rock face was ordered to fire several kegs of dynamite; the improperly fixed location resulted in an explosion that knocked down 600 pounds of rock, killing him. At Smith Falls, three men were ordered to climb up and loosen the contents of 20 kegs of charged dynamite that had failed to explode; they were blown to 'smithereens'. John Oleson of Trail was ordered to do a similar job with just a few kegs of dynamite; the explosion sent the tool he was using through his heart and out his back.[82] These events were never formally investigated. The district had no coroner, and often the bodies of persons who may have died of suspicious causes had to wait several weeks before the next of kin were allowed to bury them.[83] Companies whose success depended on not meddling in the day to day life of the workplace were not keen to embrace an investigatory institution.

The historian might classify the cause of such deaths as the conscious negligence on the part of the mining companies, but the incidents did not enter the registers even as 'accidental' until long after they had occurred. Human tragedy became a common feature of this hard-rock mining region. Often bodies were found floating down the rivers of the Kootenays, and often the cause of death was never examined.[84] Local residents complained in 'letters to the editor', but little seems to have been done. Thus the idea of the law's inability to provide adequate regulations for companies, protection for workers, inquiries for accidents, and possible prosecutions for negligence became deeply ingrained in the region's culture, forming a foundation not only for vigilantism, but for the violent strikes and industrial actions that would mark the future.

The situation with miners was replicated in the early frontier history of the North-West Territories: in particular, the vast coal reserves of the Rocky Mountains and the adjacent foothills region, the 'badlands', and the southern grasslands of the Territories. Some of the exploitative conditions of these regions were later well documented in the Alberta Royal Commission of 1919,[85] the conditions of which contributed in part to the strikes and workers' 'rebellion' of that year across western Canada. The seeds, however, were sown in the pre-war years as mining companies refused to acknowledge liability for 'industrial accidents' that might oblige them to compensate the victims' next of kin.[86] In this they may well have followed the example of the CPR, which set the pattern for corporations that wished to avoid the legal and financial obligations arising from the violent deaths of employees in the workplace. The use and extent of common-law limitations on the liability of corporate employers for industrial accidents was significant.[87]

The railway arrived at Fort Calgary in 1882. As the city grew, the CPR did little to safeguard the lives of those crossing its tracks. Signals and barriers were lacking, and by the early years of the twentieth century people and animals were being injured, often mortally, every week. The legal position of the CPR was that the city should teach people *and* animals how to avoid injury, or erect crossings and barriers to protect them.[88] In 1898, a government mail clerk travelling on the Calgary and Edmonton Railway (which leased the track from the CPR) sustained multiple injuries when the train derailed on a bridge and fell into the ravine below. The Company defended the resulting lawsuit (which it lost) despite overwhelming evidence that the railbed was poorly maintained.[89] Similarly, when two CPR trains collided head-on near Pincher Creek in 1910, the Corporation denied liability for the deaths because the day was a Sunday, and under the Lord's Day Act there could be no liability because commercial transactions to haul passengers could not lawfully take place on such days.[90] Justice Nicholas Beck supported the claim against the CPR, stating that the Corporation was as responsible for the deaths as if it had placed 'a large body of dynamite upon the tracks.'[91]

In 1908 the CPR was sued for compensation in the death of John Toll, a locomotive engineer who was killed when he stuck his head out the window and had it crushed when struck by a mile post marker standing 22.5 inches from the cab; by regulation, such markers were to reach no closer than four feet from the cab. Richard Bennett, lawyer for the CPR, argued that the death was an accident because no one had seen Toll's head hit the post. Losing to the trial jury, the CPR appealed the judgment of Justice Stuart and was denied by the full court.[92] The purpose of the CPR's defence was to make it prohibitively expensive for any employee's next of kin to sue for deaths caused by the Corporation's negligence.

SUICIDE

Another manifestation of violence on the human landscape of the prairies was the incidence of crimes of suicide. In the late twentieth century, Alberta has the highest rate of suicides per capita in the country with BC a close second. The evidence from coroners' reports suggests that the rate was equal, if not higher, in the late nineteenth and early twentieth centuries.[93] Suicides involved virtually all members of the diverse prairie community and social structure. In the judicial district of Red Deer, for example, Frank August Swan, a farmer of Red Willow, cut his throat and drowned himself in his water tank in 1909.[94] Harry A. Wilson, the NWMP constable for Innisfail, shot himself through the mouth with his revolver on Christmas Eve 1909; there were two whiskey bottles on the table, one empty and one full.[95] Two days earlier he had unhitched the runaway horses that ran down an old man, and watched a drunk doctor perform a grisly amputation of the man's damaged leg. In 1910 Charles Kyme Wright of Red Deer shot himself in the forehead with his rifle just before Christmas; apparently he had been worried about gossip concerning himself and the lady whose boarding-house he resided in.[96] And homesteader Egbert Hagin of Donalta was charged with attempting to kill his wife and himself in November 1913; though he had stabbed her, and then himself, both survived. The judges ruled that, Swedish-born and illiterate, he was unfit to stand trial and he was released.[97]

CANADIAN CONTEXTS: VIOLENCE IN FRONTIER SOCIETIES

Selected cases and regional studies should be viewed in the larger context of frontier society. The statistical analysis of historical crime, however, is fraught with difficulties. And the problems that beset the study of crime statistics in Great Britain and the United States pale in comparison with those of Canada's western hinterland.[98] Nonetheless, I will attempt to construct from my own research a larger landscape in which to view the historical incidence of violence on the western Canadian frontier.

The most accurate statistical figures available are those concerning convictions for capital offences. Analyzing the years 1870–1919, including a geographical breakdown for the Saskatchewan and Alberta districts of the North-West Territories before 1905, the following conclusions can be drawn. First, on a per capita basis convictions in the west are nearly twice as numerous as for all the other provinces combined;[99] within the western provinces, the figures for capital convictions are significantly higher for BC (125) and Saskatchewan (54) than for either Manitoba (47) or Alberta (39). Second, the percentages of persons convicted who were also executed show a similar discrepancy: 58 per cent for BC, 57 per cent for Saskatchewan, 45 per cent for Manitoba, and 49 per cent for Alberta.[100]

A broader comparison can be made by correlating statistics on all indictable offences (1891–1911), which I have compiled for western and central Canada, with the census figures.[101] On the prairies, indictable offences per capita rose from .07 per thousand in 1891 to 2.1 in 1911, and for BC, from 1.25 to 2.6; for Ontario and Quebec, by contrast, they actually declined from 2.5 to 1.7. It is interesting to compare these per capita figures with rough historical estimates for England over the centuries: approximately 10.0 in 1260, 3.0 in 1600, 2.5 in 1750, 1.2 in 1900, and 1.0 in 1950. In the late nineteenth century, therefore, recorded criminality in general was rising to historic highs in the Canadian west, while it was declining in both England and central Canada.[102]

A detailed study of the years 1888–97, however, for all criminal prosecutions, both violent and non-violent, and including victimless and regulatory offences, would seem to contradict the above comparison of Prairie Canada with Ontario. In this decade, all prosecutions amounted to .96 per thousand for the North-West Territories and 1.14 for Ontario. However, the figures for crimes against the person were .72 in the North-West Territories and 2.21 for Canada as a whole.[103] This latter figure suggests that personal crimes were far more frequent for the country as a whole than for the Prairies. It appears, however, that the Prairie West, if not also BC, had a tendency not to report crimes against the person, thereby confirming one of the themes of this chapter.

The reports of the superintendants of the NWMP describe a Canadian west relatively free of crime, with the police firmly in control—the very picture of a law-abiding society.[104] That picture was supported by crime statistics that under-reported criminal offences by omitting the large number of indictable offences heard at summary jurisdiction. Local police also neglected to report violence between native peoples and between foreign immigrants.[105] Since there was approximately one Mountie for every 70 square miles in the west, the physical difficulty of reporting together with the policy of not including prosecutions before summary courts could explain such discrepancies.

Finally, an examination of recorded crime in the prairies by demographic region is also revealing. Using my own study of selected judicial districts in the region of Alberta, 1889–1909, the following conclusions can be offered based on a geographical division of the region into parkland, grassland, foothills, and urban centres.[106] For total indictments, the parkland comprised 12 per cent, grassland 44 per cent, foothills 10 per cent, and cities 33 per cent. But for crimes against the person, the indictment figures were 38 per cent for parkland, 47 per cent for grassland, 5 per cent for foothills, and 11 per cent for cities.[107]

Placed within the context of the conclusions that have been developed above, these percentages suggest that the great majority of public prosecutions were conducted in the southern grasslands and urban centres, but that the prosecution of violent crime was conducted largely in the less densely populated rural parkland and grassland communities. The percentages also support the suggestion that violent crime and deaths in the mining (mountainous) districts of BC and Alberta were beyond the pale of the law. Contrary to the view that originated with public officials and chambers of commerce, violence in the Canadian frontier west appear to have been at least equal to that in the rest of North American society.

North American Contexts: Violence in Frontier Societies

The radically different images of the 'lawless' American frontier and the 'peaceful' Canadian one stem from two conflicting traditions in English legal culture. One tradition, emanating from the juridical writings of Sir Edward Coke and the radical authors of the English Civil War of the seventeenth century, can be seen in the conception of parliamentary sovereignty that culminated in the American Revolution: where the right to dissent incorporates the right to revolt, and where the right to revolt conveys the right to own and carry arms in order to defend one's 'rights' when they are threatened. Known in recent years as the 'No Duty to Retreat Rule', the law of the American west was based on the principle that any person who was attacked had the legal right to stand his/her ground and blast away the aggressor.[108] This principle explains both the role and the prevalence of vigilantes in all American frontier societies from the eighteenth to the twentieth centuries. It assumes that since 'English' common law treated any killing as homicide, a social custom that legitimized acts of violence was 'American'.[109] The resulting 'rule' was made legal precedent by Supreme Court Justice Oliver Wendell Holmes when he reversed the conviction of a Texan who had shot his knife-wielding assailant.[110] The rule provided a legal rationale for what was known as the 'Code of the West', and was sufficiently prominent to be noted by the English writer Rudyard Kipling in his travels through the American west.[111]

The significance of the Code of the West is that it has enabled historians to depict the history of the American west in the 1850–1920 period as the 'western civil war of incorporation'.[112] The Code provided the legal authority for the 'commanders of industry' to hire gunslingers to drive off anyone who impeded the capitalistic exploitation of the land by ranchers and the owners of railways, mining, forestry, and financial companies, and contributed to the use of weapons for offensive as well as defensive purposes. The corporation gunman, romanticized in the 1902 novel *The Virginian*, represented the rise of violence in the service of the law in the western 'wars' of the 1890s.[113] Recently the Code of the West has also been applied by historians of Mexico to the gunslingers of American companies who operated in the Mexican states of Chihuahua and Sonora in the late nineteenth century, and to the origins of the Mexican Revolution of 1910.[114] Moreover, it has also been proposed for the history of the North American west stretching from Mexico to Canada.[115]

The second legal tradition stems from the development of the mixed constitutional monarchy of the seventeenth century. Here the emphasis was not on 'parliamentary' sovereignty but on the dual legal tradition of law and custom.[116] According to this more mystical conception, law was embodied not only in the written statutes of Parliament and judgements of the common-law courts, but in the unwritten customs of the people. While Parliament became supreme in the course of the nineteenth century, law was still infused by the 'ancient constitution' and had become a living culture.[117] Judges could no longer 'make' law, but their wide powers of judicial discretion enabled them to interpret law in such a way as to make it relevant to the society or community in which a dispute arose. This dual tradition of law *plus* custom, sometimes known as 'the municipal law', became the dominant legal culture of the anglicized western Canadian territories and provinces, especially Rupert's Land and BC, in the nineteenth century.[118]

Several historians of the Canadian west have seen the American 'Code' at work here, although in less dramatic circumstances. Brown and Brown wrote of the Mounted Police as embodying the British imperial and martial law traditions with their use of physical force, exploitation of native women, alcoholism, corruption, and repression of political dissent.[119] And Macleod has written of the police as an instrument of the 'National Policy' of Sir John A. Macdonald to 'Canadianize' the west as the hinterland of eastern Canadian interests.[120] More recently, Reid has put the case for the role and influence of aboriginal law in contributing to violence on the western Canadian frontier. In a broad survey of killings involving First Nations and Métis, he argues that native law permitted 'avengers of blood' to kill any member of a slayer's kin group, or nation, in compensation. He also argues that British, Canadian, and American fur trappers adopted these values for property as well as personal crimes.[121]

Foster has observed that the opening of the Canadian west was more peaceful than that of the American.[122] This general conclusion can be supported by the absence of gunslinging 'heroes' and 'wars of incorporation' that stigmatized the early American west. But the proposition that the deep convictions of Canadians in the superiority of British law and institutions precluded them from engaging in the kinds of violent activities and vigilantism that occurred in the United States is not supported by the evidence presented in this study.[123] Nor is the more recent view that, even if the BC frontier was not peaceful, the prairie frontier was.[124] The most recent assessment of law and order on the western Canadian frontier suggests that much of the violence that occurred there was no different from the violence that is always present in all societies, and had nothing to do with economic, social, or class conflict.[125] The evidence presented here does not support this view either.

What the evidence does support is that the carriers of English law to the Canadian west in the early nineteenth century had a mindset in the dual tradition of English municipal law that accorded equal weight to local custom, and that contact with aboriginal people through the fur trade led the HBC to incorporate the more violent dispute-resolution systems of the First Nations and the Métis into its own legal culture. In addition, the evidence suggests that this more violently oriented legal culture developed in intensity in the three regions from the 1840s to the 1880s, and had a perceptible influence on the new public and corporate entities that emerged as 'civilizing', 'nationalizing', and 'industrializing' elements from the 1870s to the early 1900s.[126] The creation of the NWMP, the CPR, and the National Policy added institutional layers to the landscape which mirrored on the one hand the regime of the HBC, together with English municipal law and aboriginal custom, and on the other the instrumentalist intervention of the rules of industrial capitalism.

Part of the difficulty is that Canadian historians have tried too hard to follow the paradigms that have been established on the basis of European and American experiences.[127] The current model for the study of violence in North America is Gurr and Graham's *Violence in America*.[128] Some of the themes of that work are relevant here: the role of the competitive hierarchy of immigrant groups, economic exploitation, reservations for aboriginal societies, restrictions on immigrant groups, large-scale socioeconomic change, and the violence generated by governments and corporations. Other aspects of the American experience have at least partial parallels in the Canadian west: these include racial and ethnic strife, vigilante activities, and conflicts between large corporations, employees, and communities. But some themes are not so relevant in the Canadian context: for example, the use of violence to nurture a law-abiding mentality, and the link between the rise of violence and the growth of the nation state. Nor did the Canadian west experience a considerable amount of military activity, federal intervention in local affairs, direct extermination of First Nations, organized crime, or political violence. Thus the thesis of Charles Tilly, that violence is integral to the political process, and that there is an indissoluble link between collective violence and political life,[129] receives little support from the evidence presented here. Yet even this old myth is still applied to the Canadian west.[130]

In the end, we must recognize that definitions of violence change over time. We must perceive the subtle interchange of humanity and environment, and how the product of that interchange leads to behavioural values which inform our notions of law and custom, of right and wrong, and of legitimate and illegitimate forms of violence. We must also recognize the importance of balanced interpretations that do not see a society through a lens which is focused exclusively on violent or non-violent activities. Only then can one assemble a more relevant typology of violence that is rooted in human actions which gave rise to its physical manifestation and mental images, and make the essential connections between the world we have lost and the world in which we live.

NOTES

I wish to thank Sarah Carter, Warren Elofson, Hamar Foster, Walter Hildebrandt, Greg Marquis, Jeffrey Ian Ross, and Jonathan Swainger for their very useful comments and criticisms on various drafts of this chapter, and Janice Erion, Hamar Foster, Robert Omura, and Russell Smandych for their assistance on sources and certain technical points. All errors and omissions remain my own.

[1] This has been the case for those countries that have a rich tradition of historical literature on the subject: particularly England, Germany, the Low Countries, and the United States, in addition to Canada. The exception has been France, where the *Annales* School has used a broader range of sources such as notarial act books, ecclesiastical and communal records, and folk customs to encompass a larger vision of criminality.

[2] For example, the recent collected essays edited by R.C. Macleod, *Lawful Authority: Readings on the History of Criminal Justice in Canada* (Toronto: Copp Clark, 1988); and by Susan Lewthwaite, Tina Loo, and Jim Phillips, eds, *Crime and Criminal Justice in Canadian History* (Toronto: Osgoode Society, *Essays In Canadian Legal History* V, 1994).

[3] Lawrence M. Friedman, 'The law between the states: Some thoughts on southern legal history' in *Ambivalent Legacy: A Legal History of the South*, eds David J. Bodenhamer and James W. Ely, Jr (Jackson, MS: 1984); and David J. Langum, *Law and Community on the Mexican-California Frontier: Anglo-American Expatriates and the Clash of Legal Traditions, 1821–1846* (Norman, OK: 1987). For an engaging survey of legal-historical writing on western Canada, see Russell Smandych and Rick Linden, 'The transformation of legal ordering and social control in the Canadian West before 1850: A study of co-existing forms of aboriginal and private justice', *Justice and Reform* (1993): 1–42. I wish to thank Dr Smandych for sharing this with me prior to its publication.

[4] For treatments of other areas, see Jim Phillips' guide to the literature: 'The history of Canadian criminal justice, 1750–1920' in *Criminology: A Reader's Guide*, eds R. Ericson, C. Shearing, and J. Gladstone (Toronto: University of Toronto Press, 1991), 65–97, and the bibliography at 97–124. A historiographical analysis of this literature is in his chapter on Canada in *Crime Histories and Histories of Crime*, eds Clive Emsley and Louis Knafla (Westport: Greenwood Publishing, 1995).

[5] Paul F. Sharp, 'Three frontiers: Some comparative studies of Canadian, American and Australian settlement', *Pacific Historical Review* 24 (1955): 369–77; Robin W. Winks, *The Myth of the American Frontier: Its Relevance to*

America, Canada and Australia (Leiceser and New York: University of Leicester Press, 1971); and James G. Snell, 'The frontier sweeps northwest: American perceptions of the British American prairie west at the point of Canadian expansion (circa 1870)', *Western Historical Quarterly* 11 (1980): 381–400.

6 In particular, Richard Maxwell Brown, 'The American vigilante tradition' in *The History of Violence in America*, eds Hugh David Graham and Ted Robert Gurr (New York: Oxford University Press, 1969). For the problem of lawlessness on the frontier, see Hamar Foster, 'Shooting the elephant: Historians and the problem of frontier lawlessness' in *The Political Context of Law*, eds Richard Eales and David Sullivan (London: Hambledon Press, 1987), 135–44.

7 For example, Herbert Butterfield, *The Whig Interpretation of History* (London and New York: G. Bell & Sons, 1931; repr. 1969 ed.).

8 Gordon Wood, 'The creative imagination of Bernard Bailyn' in *The Transformation of Early American History*, eds James Henretta, Michael Kammen, and Stanley Katz (New York: Knopf, 1991), 40–1.

9 See Charles Tilly, 'Collective violence in European perspective', in *Violence in America. Historical and Comparative Perspectives*, eds Hugh David Graham and Ted Robert Gurr (Beverly Hills and London: Sage, rev. ed. 1979), 83–118; and his revised essay in the 1989 edition, *Violence in America*, Vol. ii: *Protest, Rebellion, Reform*, ed. Gurr.

10 Ted Robert Gurr, 'The history of protest, rebellion, and reform in America: An overview' in *Violence in America* (1989 ed.), 11–22; and Richard Maxwell Brown, 'Historical patterns of violence', ibid. 23–61.

11 D. Owen Carrigan, *Crime and Punishment in Canada: A History* (Toronto: McClelland and Stewart, 1991), which suffers from research and interpretive problems in addition to the lack of secondary studies.

12 *The Canadian North-West: Its Early Development and Legal Records*, ed. E.H. Oliver (Ottawa: King's Printer, 1915), Vol. i, 135–53, for a copy of the text of the charter.

13 In general, E.E. Rich, *The Fur Trade and the Northwest to 1857* (Toronto: McClelland & Stewart, 1967); Arthur S. Morton, *A History of the Canadian West to 1870–71* 2nd ed. (London and Toronto: Nelson & Sons, 1939; repr. 1973), 508–617; and Glyndwr Williams, 'The Hudson's Bay Company and the fur trade', *Beaver* 314 (1983): 4–86.

14 W.L. Morton, *Manitoba: A History* 2nd ed. (Toronto: University of Toronto Press, 1957), 37–93.

15 Lyle Dick, 'The Seven Oaks incident and the construction of a historical tradition, 1816 to 1970', *Journal of the Canadian Historical Association* (1991): 91–113.

16 The most convenient summary is that of Rich, *The Fur Trade*, 208–35.

17 Gene M. Gressley, 'Lord Selkirk and the Canadian Courts' in *Canadian History Before Confederation: Essays and Interpretations*, ed. J.M. Bumsted (Toronto: Oxford University Press, 1972): 287–304. See the recent assessment of Hamar Foster, 'Forgotten Arguments: Aboriginal title and

sovereignty in *Canada Jurisdiction Act* Cases', *Manitoba Law Journal* 21 (1992): 344–89 at 370–7.

[18] Transcripts of the trials were published by both the HBC and the Northwest Company; see *Report of Trials in the Courts of Canada, Relative to the Destruction of the Earl of Selkirk's Settlement on the Red River; with Observations*, ed. A. Amos (London, 1820) and *Report of the Proceedings Connected with the Disputes between the Earl of Selkirk and the North-West Company at the Assizes, Held at York, in Upper Canada, October 1818* (London, 1819), respectively.

[19] An Act for extending the Jurisdiction of the Courts of Justice in the Provinces of Lower and Upper Canada, 1803 (43 George III, c. 138).

[20] Oliver, *Canadian North-West*, 283–305 and 485–502 for the early codes. The later ones were published in the *Consolidated Statutes of Manitoba* (Winnipeg: Queen's Printer, 1880), pp. liv-lxxx.

[21] Roy St George Stubbs, *Four Recorders of Prince Rupert's Land. A Brief Survey of the Hudson's Bay Company Courts of Rupert's Land* (Winnipeg: Peguis Publishers, 1967), 1–47.

[22] See, in general, Kathryn M. Bindon, 'Hudson's Bay Company law: Adam Thom and the institution of order in Rupert's Land 1839–54' in *Essays in the History of Canadian Law*, ed. David H. Flaherty (Toronto: University of Toronto Press, 1981), i 43–87.

[23] *Western Law Times* 2 (1891), 1–11, the quote at p. 10.

[24] John Foster, 'Paulet Paul: Métis or "house Indian" folk hero?', *Manitoba History*, 9 (Spring 1985): 2–8.

[25] W.L. Morton, *Manitoba*, 77.

[26] For example, the laws of marriage, divorce and inheritance later confirmed by the Quebec court of Queen's Bench: *Connolly v. Woolrich* (1867), *Lower Canada Jurist* 11 (1866): 197–265, and the appeal in *La Revue légale* (1869): 253–400.

[27] For the historiography of the era, see Frits Pannekoek, 'The historiography of the Red River settlement, 1830–1868', *Prairie Forum* (1981): 75–86.

[28] A.S. Morton, *Canadian West*, 870–909. Native and Métis writers today refer to it as the 'Resistance'.

[29] See *Alexander Begg's Red River Journal and Other Papers Relative to the Red River Resistance of 1869–70*, ed. W.L. Morton (Toronto: Champlain Society, 1956), for the details.

[30] The legislation and the law that emerged from it are discussed in Louis A. Knafla, *Law & Justice in a New Land* (Toronto: Carswell, 1986), 51ff.

[31] Desmond H. Brown, 'Unpredictable and uncertain: Criminal law in the Canadian North West before 1886', *Alberta Law Review* 17, 3 (1979): 497–572.

[32] The most sensitive survey of the 1885 Rebellion is in Gerald Friesen, *The Canadian Prairies* (Toronto: University of Toronto Press, 1984), 220–36. For details, see the major study of Bob Beale and Rod Macleod, *Prairie Fire: The 1885 North West Rebellion* (Edmonton: Hurtig, 1984).

[33] Thomas Flanagan and Neil Watson, 'The Riel trial revisited: Criminal procedure and the law in 1885', *Saskatchewan History* 34, 2 (Spring 1981):

57–73; the trial documents in *The Queen v Louis Riel*, ed. Desmond Morton (Toronto: University of Toronto Press, 1974); and the account of Beale and Macleod in *Prairie Fire*.

[34] Beale and Macleod, *Prairie Fire*.

[35] The misunderstandings have been set out, for example, in *The Spirit of Alberta Indian Treaties*, ed. Richard Price (Montreal: Institute for Public Policy, 1979). See *Indian Treaties and Surrenders* (Ottawa: Queen's Printer, 1891).

[36] Province of Alberta Archives [hereafter PAA], the Anderson Papers, 74.1, box 5, which contains all the details of the expedition and relevant correspondence. There is a brief published account in *John McLean's Notes of a Twenty-Five Year's Service in the Hudson's Bay Territory*, Vol. 19 (Toronto: Champlain Society, 1932), 99–101.

[37] Hamar Foster, 'Sins against the great spirit: The law, the Hudson's Bay Company, and the Mackenzie's River murders, 1835–1839', *Criminal Justice History: An International Annual* 10 (1989): 23–76. The material below is taken from Foster's article, the complexity of which has scarcely been touched upon here.

[38] Sidney L. Harring, 'Rich men of the country: Canadian law in the land of the Copper Inuit', *Ottawa Law Review* 21, 1 (1989): 1–64. For background on aboriginal law, see *Aboriginal Peoples and The Law: Indians, Métis and Inuit Rights in Canada*, ed. B. W. Morse (Ottawa: University of Carleton Press, 1989).

[39] The case has been discussed by Hamar Foster in 'Long-distance justice: The criminal jurisdiction of the Canadian courts west of the Canadas', *American Journal of Legal History* 34 (1990): 31–2. While a trader claimed that the accused, named La Pierre, was acquitted, Foster has not found the original court record of the case.

[40] Details can be found in E.E. Rich, *History of the Hudson's Bay Company 1763–1870*, 711–16, and various volumes of the Hudson's Bay Record Society—especially *The Letters of John McLoughlin from Fort Vancouver to the Governor and Committee: Second Series, 1839–44*, ed. E.E. Rich, introduction by W. Kaye Lamb, pp. xi–xlix. A recent, full analysis of the case is by Hamar Foster, 'Killing Mr John: Law and jurisdiction at Fort Stikine, 1842–1846', in *Law for the Elephant, Law for the Beaver: Essays in the Legal History of the North American West*, eds John McLaren, Hamar Foster, and Chet Orloff (Regina and Pasadena: Great Plains Research Centre, 1992), 147–93.

[41] 'The Peter Skene Ogden Journals', ed. T.C. Elliott, *Quarterly of the Oregon Historical Society* 10 (1909): 342.

[42] See Kenneth Coates and William R. Morrison, *Land of the Midnight Sun: A History of the Yukon* (Edmonton: Hurtig, 1988), for examples.

[43] Rich, *Hudson's Bay Company*, ii 563–734 for the history.

[44] John C. Bouck, 'Introducing English law into the Province: Time for a change?', *Canadian Bar Review* (1979): 74–87.

[45] David R. Williams, *The Man for a New Country: Sir Matthew Baillie Begbie* (Sidney, BC: Gray's Publishing, 1977).

[46] Hamar Foster, 'The Kamloops outlaws and commissions of assize in nine-teenth-century British Columbia' in *Essays in the History of Canadian Law*, ed. David H. Flaherty (Toronto: University of Toronto Press, 1983), ii 308–64. The following discussion is taken from Foster's major study.

[47] For example, British Columbia Archives and Record Center (hereafter BCARC), GR 574, the registers of Fort Hope.

[48] For example, BCARC, GR 713, the Richfield Assize Book.

[49] Roy, *White Man's Province*. For the American northwest, see John R. Wun-der, 'The Chinese and the courts in the Pacific Northwest: Justice denied?' *Pacific Historical Review* 52 (1983): 191–211.

[50] Patricia Roy, *A White Man's Province: British Columbia Politicians and Chi-nese and Japanese Immigrants, 1858–1914* (Vancouver: University of British Columbia Press, 1989).

[51] See Thomas Stone, 'The Mounties as vigilantes: Perceptions of commu-nity and the transformation of law in the Yukon 1885–1897', *Law and Society Review* 14 (1979–80): 83–114.

[52] Roy, *White Man's Province*.

[53] W.F. Bowker, 'The *Sproule* case: Bloodshed at Kootenay Lake, 1885', in Knafla, ed., *Law & Justice in a New Land*, 233–66, which is fully explored in all its details. The discussion below is taken from Bowker's study.

[54] Quoted from the Public Archives of Canada [hereafter PAC] by Bowker, 'Bloodshed at Kootenay Lake' 251.

[55] For example, Patricia E. Roy, 'The preservation of the peace in Vancou-ver: The aftermath of the anti-Chinese riot of 1887', *BC Studies* 31 (1976): 44–59.

[56] *Daily British Colonist*, 17 Aug. 1865, p. 3. This paper merged with the *Vic-toria Chronicle* in 1872, and became the *Daily Colonist* in 1887.

[57] For example, the Assize calendars in the BCARC, GR 996 (1883–1888); and the coroners inquests in GR 1327–8 (1859–1876).

[58] For example, the transcripts of preliminary hearings made by the Attor-ney-General's office, located at BCARC GR 419, B-395 (1857–1891).

[59] BCARC, GR B-1989(1), and GR 715, 577, 581, 657–8, 996, for the surviving court records for the period.

[60] Gray to Edward Blake, 12 July 1877, in PABC Add. MSS 54, folder 12/66.

[61] *The Cariboo Sentinel*, 25 July 1867, p. 1. David Williams has questioned whether the men were Canadians or Americans.

[62] *The Ledge*, 23 Sept. 1897, p. 2.

[63] Reginald H. Roy, ed., 'The First Military Intelligence Report of the Inte-rior of British Columbia', *BC Studies* 1 (Winter 1978–69): 20–6, dated 27 Oct. 1897.

[64] W.A. Waiser, 'The North-West Mounted Police, in 1874–1889: A statistical study', *Research Bulletin* (Ottawa: Parks Canada, 1980). I wish to thank Dr Waiser for bringing this to my attention.

[65] Philip Goldring, 'Whisky, horses and death: The Cypress Hills massacre and its sequel', *Occasional Papers in Archaeology and History* 21 (Ottawa: Canadian Historic Sites, 1979): 41–70.

66 Virtually every Alberta judicial district, from 1886 to the present, has a complete set of Supreme Court reports from the judicial circuits to the full court, Justice of the Peace and Coroner returns, crime reports and correspondence in the Attorney-General's office. In Saskatchewan, fire and floods have accounted for major losses in their court records, together with some early disposition schedules.

67 In contrast to rural Ontario and British Columbia, for example, there were few local newspapers, and no tradition of writing to the government until Alberta gained provincial status in the early 20th century.

68 The records base from which the account and examples in this section have been taken is all the files for the judicial district 1907–1914 from PAA 79.220, 66.166, and 72.26. I wish to thank Dr Jonathan Swainger who has been working on these files with me as part of a project provisionally entitled 'The prosecution of crime in the judicial district of Red Deer, 1907–1914'.

69 The region ranged from parkland in the north to dryland in the south, and arable farming in the east to mixed farming in the centre, and mining and forestry in the west.

70 PAA RDC 170, 216a-b, 217, 235-6; and PAA 219 66.166, file #979.

71 PAA 66.166, file #797 (14 April 1909).

72 PAA 66.166, file #979 (23 Jan. 1910).

73 PAA 78.235, boxes 1–5.

74 Greg Marquis, *A History of Policing in Canada* (Toronto: University of Toronto Press, 1993). I wish to thank Dr Marquis for sharing some of his observations with me prior to my obtaining his book.

75 PAA RDC 826 (30 April 1913). Kelly is also spelled Kelley.

76 PAA 66.166, file #1158 (3–5 June 1911).

77 For example, Terry L. Chapman, 'Sex crimes in Western Canada, 1890–1920' (PhD dissertation, University of Alberta, 1984). Dr Chapman has also written a number of articles concerning these crimes for *Alberta History*. See most recently her article on '"Inquiring minds want to know": The handling of children in sex assault cases in the Canadian West, 1890–1920' in *Dimensions of Childhood: Essays on the History of Children and Youth in Canada*, ed. Russell Smandych et al. (Winnipeg: University of Manitoba, 1991), 183–204.

78 Historians use the term 'records evidence' to refer to official public records, and 'literary evidence' for unofficial, private records such as correspondence, memoirs, newspapers, etc.

79 PAA RDC S55, S72; and PAA 66.166 file #797.

80 Knafla and Swainger, *supra*, note 68.

81 For example, see the various coroners' records in England which have been edited by Dr Roy Hunnisett, who is currently writing a history of the coroner.

82 *Brooklyn News*, 20 Aug., 3 and 10 Sept. 1898.

83 *Brooklyn News*, 29 Oct. and 5 Nov. 1898, respectively.

84 *Brooklyn News*, 8 Oct. 1898, where the phenomenon is reported and the problem discussed.

[85] *Alberta's Coal Industry 1919*, ed. David Jay Bercuson (Calgary: Historical Society of Alberta, 1978).

[86] For example, 'Report of the Royal Commission on the Coal Mining Industry in the Province of Alberta 1907', PAA.

[87] The literature on industrial accidents has been discussed generally by R.C.B. Risk, '"This nuisance of litigation": The origins of workers' compensation in Ontario' in *Essays in the History of Canadian Law*, ed. David H. Flaherty (Toronto: University of Toronto Press, 1983), i 418–91.

[88] Louis A. Knafla, 'Richard "Bonfire" Bennett: The Legal Practice of a Prairie Corporate Lawyer, 1898 to 1913' in *Beyond the Law: Lawyers and Business in Canada, 1830 to 1930*, ed. Carol Wilton (Toronto: University of Toronto Press, 1990), 344–9 for the corporate policies.

[89] *Kenny v Canadian Pacific Railway Co.* (1901–1902), 5 *Territorial Law Reports* 420–38; and PAA 69.305, File (1902).

[90] *Rise v Canadian Pacific Railway Company* (1910), 3 *Alberta Law Reports* 154–66.

[91] Ibid., p. 166.

[92] *Toll v Canadian Pacific Railway Company* (1909), 1 *Alberta Law Reports* 244–7 and 318–23. The case is discussed in Knafla, ' "Bonfire" Bennett', 340.

[93] I am currently engaged in the collection of coroners' reports for a study of suicide on the prairies, 1870–1914.

[94] PAA 68.261, file #1141.

[95] PAA 67.172, file #1.

[96] PAA 67.172, file #120.

[97] PAA RDC 942, and PAA 68.29, file #11.

[98] See, for example, the critique of 19th c. criminal statistics by V.A.C. Gatrell and T.B. Hadden, 'Criminal statistics and their interpretation' in *Nineteenth-Century Society: Essays in the Use of Quantitative Methods for the Study of Social Data*, ed. E.A. Wrigley (Cambridge: Cambridge University Press, 1972); and the comparative study of Ted Robert Gurr, 'Historical trends in violent crime: A critical review of the evidence', *Crime and Justice* 3 (1981): 295–393.

[99] PAC, RG 13 C.1. The files are organized in chronological order for the whole country, and thus the numbers have been compiled from the capital files by apportioning the file numbers to separate lists for each province. The results here and below are from my rough calculations from the statistics tabled in Parliament. The subject is deserving of a full study.

[100] Ibid. Until recently the capital case files were restricted in their use; they are now open without restrictions.

[101] Government of Canada, *Sessional Papers*, Crime Statistics, for the annual volumes of Sessional Reports 1891–1911; and Statistics Canada, census figures, for the censuses of 1881, 1891, and 1911. A more accurate account would come from an examination of the trial calendars of selected jurisdictions.

[102] See the discussion of the current literature in the 'Historiographical Introduction' to Knafla, *Crime, Police and the Courts in British History* (Westport: Meckler Publishing, 1990), pp. ix-xiv.

[103] An unpublished paper by Gwen Taylor, 'A crime study of the West 1888–1897' (University of Calgary, Dec. 1992). The cumulative calculations are my own, obtained from Ms Taylor's tables.

[104] The annually printed *Report of the North West Mounted Police* for the years 1888–1901.

[105] In order to maintain a positive public profile for continued immigration, and to quell any apprehension over 'wild Indians', violence within these communities was not a priority of policing.

[106] These figures have been obtained from the files in the PAA, Supreme Court of North-West Territories, and Supreme Court of Alberta, for several judicial circuits, each one of which has been divided into the demographic regions listed above. Again, the lists are rough ones, and the subject is deserving of a complete study.

[107] See, for example, T. Thorner and H. Watson, 'Patterns of Prairie Crime: Calgary, 1875–1939' in *Crime and Criminal Justice in Europe and Canada*, ed. Louis A. Knafla (Waterloo: Wilfrid Laurier University Press, rev. ed. 1985), 219–55. It should be noted that assault was the most common violent offence, and could be tried either summarily before a local police court or magistrate, or before a Supreme Court justice on circuit.

[108] Richard Maxwell Brown, *No Duty to Retreat: Violence and Values in American History and Society* (New York: Oxford University Press, 1991).

[109] Garrett Epps, 'Any which way but loose: Interpretive strategies and attitudes towards violence in the evolution of the Anglo-American "retreat rule"', *Law and Contemporary Problems* 55 (Winter, 1992): 303–31.

[110] *Brown v. United States*, 256 U.S. 335 (1921).

[111] *American Notes: Rudyard Kipling's West*, ed. Arrell Morgan Gibson (Norman: University of Oaklahoma Press, 1981), 53.

[112] See the stimulating article of Richard Maxwell Brown, 'Western violence: Structure, values, myth', *The Western Historical Quarterly* 24, 1 (Feb. 1993): 5–20.

[113] For example, those close to the Canadian border in the Johnson County, Wyoming, War of 1892 in Helena Huntington Smith's *The War on Powder River* (New York: McGraw-Hill, 1966); and Robert Wayne Smith's *The Coeur d'Alene Mining War of 1892: A Case Study of an Industrial Dispute* (Corvallis: Oregon State University Press, 1961).

[114] Paul J. Vanderwood, *Disorder and Progress: Bandits, Police, and Mexican Development* (Lincoln, 1981).

[115] Richard W. Slatta, *Cowboys of the Americas* (New Haven, 1990).

[116] Louis A. Knafla, 'Common law and custom in Tudor England: or, "The best state of a commonwealth"' in *Law, Literature, and the Settlement of Regimes*, ed. Gordon J. Schochet (Washington, DC: Folger Shakespeare Library, 1990), 171–86.

[117] J.G.A. Pocock, 'Historiography and the Common Law', in his *The Ancient Constitution and the Feudal Law: A Study of English Historical Thought in the Seventeenth Century: A Reissue with a Retrospect* (Cambridge: Cambridge University Press, 1987), 335–88.

[118] Louis A. Knafla, 'From oral to written memory: The common law tradition in Western Canada', in Knafla, ed., *Law & Justice*, 31–77, and especially 60–4.

[119] Lorne and Carolyn Brown, *An Unauthorized History of the RCMP* (Toronto: James Lewis and Samuel, 1973).

[120] R.C. Macleod, 'Canadianizing the West: The North-West Mounted Police as Agents of the National Policy, 1873–1905' in *Essays on Western History*, ed. Lewis H. Thomas (Edmonton: University of Alberta Press, 1976) 101–10.

[121] John Phillip Reid, 'Principles of vengeance: Fur trappers, Indians, and retaliation for homicide in the transboundary North American West', *Western Historical Quarterly* 24, 1 (Feb. 1993): 21–43.

[122] Hamar Foster, 'Law enforcement in nineteenth century British Columbia: A research agenda' (unpublished paper, Oct. 1983). I thank Professor Foster for sharing this with me.

[123] Sharp, 'Three Frontiers'; and Winks, *The Myth of the American Frontier*.

[124] Robin Fisher, 'Indian warfare and two frontiers: A comparison of British Columbia and Washington Territory during the early years of settlement', *Pacific Historical Review* 50, 1 (1981): 31–51.

[125] R.C. Macleod's 1992 article on 'Law and order on the Western Canadian frontier' in *Law for the Elephant, Law for the Beaver*, 90–105.

[126] For the role of violence in the building of corporate entities in western Canada, some of which can be seen as unintentional, see some of the cases discussed in Knafla, 'Richard "Bonfire" Bennett.

[127] For example, Jim Phillips has argued persuasively that there still is no general thesis about crime, and the role of the criminal law, in Canadian society: 'The history of Canadian criminal justice, 1750–1920' in *Criminology: A Readers' Guide* (Toronto: University of Toronto Press, 1991), 96.

[128] Graham and Gurr, eds, *Violence in America* and Gurr's vol. ii, *Protest, Rebellion, Reform* (Newbury Park, CA: Sage). The most relevant essays here are those of Brown, Gurr, Hartz, Guillemin, and Graham.

[129] Charles Tilly, 'Collective violence in European perspective', in *Violence in America* i 4–44, and ii.

[130] *Riel to Reform. A History of Protest in Western Canada*, ed. George Melnyk (Saskatoon: Fifth House, 1992), 1–11.

Chapter Two

ON VIOLENCE AND HEALING

Aboriginal Experiences, 1960-1993

DAVID A. LONG

The chances for an Aboriginal child to grown into adulthood without a first-hand experience of abuse, alcoholism or violence are small.

Indian and Inuit Nurses
of Canada, 1991.

The following analysis provides support for the Hobbesian view that violence is a fact of human life, especially in the lives of many of Canada's aboriginal peoples.[1] However, Hobbes did not distinguish between political and criminal violence, since for him all of human life was simply 'brutish and short'. In contrast, since the 1969 White Paper[2] much of the writing on the relationship between Canada's aboriginal peoples and violence has focused on the more structural causes and expressions of political violence (Adams, 1989; Cardinal, 1969; Fleras and Leonard Elliott, 1992; Long, 1992; Manuel and Posluns, 1974; York, 1989). The picture that has emerged in the social-science literature and the popular press is one of colonially dispossessed peoples collectively fighting for their basic human rights against an oppressive, paternalistic, bureaucratic nightmare.[3] Indeed, Canada's human-rights commissioner noted in 1989 that an Indian youngster had a better chance of ending up in prison than of completing university (Yalden, 1989).

There have been significant changes both in the experiences of Canada's native people and in writing by and about them since the early 1960s. As the Canadian public has learned more about the conditions of life and expectations of aboriginal people in this country, awareness has grown that many of the 'post-contact' problems that aboriginal people have experienced are attributable to the cultural and structural impact of European colonization. And while much academic research up until the early 1960s perpetuated the image of aboriginal people as 'passive victims', since then scholarship and other writing have gradually begun to shift in focus and intent (Havemann et al., 1985: 159). One of the most important developments in social-science research in this area has been increased attention to the structural effects of colonialism.

Following a brief discussion of the data used in this study, this chapter will provide a socio-historical analysis of the relationship between colonialism and violent political activity involving Canada's native people. Yet there is another dimension of the violence that it is equally important to understand. Although various chapters in this book suggest that criminal violence in Canada is an everyday reality for many Canadians, relatively few attempts have been made to document or examine it in a systematic and comprehensive manner. The same can be said for the study of criminal and non-criminal violence involving native people. There have been national and provincial task forces, non-government organizations, and individual researchers who have examined many aspects of aboriginal life in Canada, but generalizable, quantifiable data on the broad spectrum of violence by and against native people is lacking. The analysis of criminal and non-criminal violence included in this chapter thus seeks to fill part of this gap in our understanding by discussing homicide, family violence, and suicide among First Nations and Inuit people in Canada.

For the purposes of this discussion, violence is defined as physically reckless, aggressive, or destructive behaviour (Bachmann, 1993: 2). Such acts may represent aggression directed either outwards, as in the case of political violence, homicide, and family violence, or inwards, as in the case of suicide. Violence here is also examined from a sociological perspective that draws on the work of several researchers. Touraine (1982), Cornell (1988), and Guillemin (1989) are especially helpful because they examine the relationship between social structure and human agency in political violence. I also draw on the work of Bachmann (1993), who has examined the incidence and causes of physical violence among native people in the United States.[4] The discussion that follows, therefore, considers the past thirty years of political and criminal violence involving native people in Canada as much more than a series of unfortunate incidents involving isolated victims, since these people have been both victims and perpetrators of both forms of violence for centuries. I also wish to raise a number of questions, including where the responsibility lies for the perpetuation of violence among aboriginal people in Canada, and how change should occur. In the past, state representatives contributed to violence by and against native people in this country through the politics of internal colonialism; now they must work to alleviate aboriginal violence by changing state policies and practices. At the same time aboriginal people must use all available resources in order to bring about the changes they desire. As the following analysis illustrates, aboriginal people in Canada have taken a variety of paths in response to the conditions of their lives over the past thirty years. And because native violence is an expression of their anger, frustration, and fear that change will not occur, it is proper to examine even their most violent actions in relation to their movements towards healing. After discussing the causes of aboriginal violence in Canada, therefore, the chapter will conclude with an analysis of various 'healing initiatives' that have been tried, as well as some of the obstacles that have stood in the way of healing.

THE DATA

The data included in this study come from many sources: submissions to the Royal Commission on Aboriginal Peoples (RCAP); National, Provincial and Territorial Task Forces on Criminal Justice, Family Violence, and Suicide in Canada; and Statistics Canada data from the Ministry of Health and Welfare and the Canadian Centre for Crime Statistics, as well as government and non-government studies, reports, and discussion papers relating to political as well as criminal violence. In all, the data support the view that native people in Canada have been both perpetrators and victims of violence for well over the past thirty years. It is my view that much of violence 'initiated' by native Canadians has arisen in response to the problems of colonialism. In other words, the conditions of colonialism are directly related to aboriginal acts of political violence as well as to rates of suicide, homicide, and family violence among the aboriginal peoples, which are disproportionately high in comparison to similar rates for the Canadian population as a whole.

For various reasons, there has not been a great deal of social-scientific research examining violence by and against native peoples, especially from data generalizable to national or even provincial levels. The oppressive character of relations between the Canadian state and native peoples did receive increased attention just before and after the 'fall' of the 1969 White Paper (Berger, 1977; Boldt and Long, 1985; Cardinal, 1969; Manuel and Posluns, 1974; Weaver, 1981), but relatively little systematic attention has since been given to the extent and impact of state-initiated violence. With the exception of writing on the 1990 'Oka Crisis' (Gabriel, 1992; Thompson, 1992; York and Pindera, 1992), such historical events as the Red River and North West conflicts in the late nineteenth century (Torrance, 1977) and more recent conflicts between government forces and First Nations bands and tribes (Long, 1992), comparatively little study has been focused on the politically violent aspects of native-state relations.

Moreover, during the mid-1980s many social scientists, recognizing that reliance on statistical data was blurring their understanding of the profoundly subtle and diverse character of human social life, began to focus on community-level research (Minore et al., 1991). Support for community-based understanding and initiatives has continued into the 1990s. Countless submissions to the RCAP have asserted that the uniqueness of the cultures, organized social structures, and everyday experiences in aboriginal Nations, settlements, and communities across Canada continues to challenge those who wish to generalize about them (RCAP, 1993b: 7–8). Nonetheless, community-level understanding is not without its limitations. For example, Auger et al. (1992: 318) found in their study of three Northern communities that

> people in the three communities differed, sometimes dramatically, in their estimates of how frequently various specific forms of disorder occurred in their communities. Similarly, they varied in their views of whether these problems should be dealt with by the community itself or by the police and the courts.

According to these authors, even simple reports by respondents on the everyday life of their communities were fraught with uncertainty and inconsistency. Perhaps the most significant limitation of community-level research, however, is that it does not provide a means of moving beyond an understanding of particular communities. This is not to imply that community-based research is less valuable or desirable than research that is broader in scope. Yet having an overall sense of the extent of political violence, as well as the pervasiveness and relative proportions of criminal violence at the regional, provincial, and national levels, is vital if useful ways of understanding and responding to violent conditions are to be found.

The most conspicuous reason for the paucity of quantified data is that it was not until the RCAP began its hearings in 1991 that a comprehensive, national-level examination of the many different facets of native life in Canada was initiated. Moreover, it has only been in the past thirty years that some of the problems relating to violence and aboriginal people in this country have begun to be examined. Nowhere is this more evident than in the area of family violence, which only started to receive sustained attention in the past ten years (Frank, 1992: 2–3). Even when research has been carried out in native communities, a critical, positivistic attitude has undoubtedly led some social scientists to regard community-level data as unreliable and invalid. Along with a paucity of scientifically-legitimate research, there have been and continue to be many cultural, legal, political, academic, and other obstacles that have hindered the collection of useful, reliable data on violence as it relates to Canada's native peoples (Dyck, 1993). Whether we are examining data from regional, provincial, or national inquiries, uniform crime report statistics, or community-level studies, it is important to recognize the limited reliability and generalizability of all statistics. Even when data appear to be reliable, it is often the case that regions, cities, reserves and settlements with vastly different economies, cultures and structures are lumped into the same data pool for the simple reason that they exist side by side. Though the following analysis draws on a wide range of data involving native peoples in Canada, generalizing from this study to all First Nations and Inuit people in Canada should therefore be done only with considerable caution.

THE SOCIO-HISTORICAL CONTEXT OF NATIVE-STATE RELATIONS

Most of the pre-contact societies of aboriginal peoples were well organized, culturally distinct, and economically viable. Indeed, it was the 'intelligent manipulation of nature backed by supportive social structure that made survival possible under extremely difficult conditions' (Dickason, 1993: 30). The picture of life in the Americas painted by the early explorers was quite different from that experienced by those already settled there. While the former wrote of a 'New World', the latter had over thousands of years built great civilizations, developing agriculture into a science, producing artists, mathematicians, and deeply spiritual philosophical thinkers. The organization of native societies in pre-contact Canada varied with the conditions they faced, from the bounty of the Pacific coast, through the marginal subsistence of the north-central region, to the relative stability of life in the eastern woodlands (Dickason, 1993: chap. 4). And though native people have never been culturally or organizationally homogeneous, their long history reflects certain shared, fundamental ways of being and doing. In general, their approach to life was holistic: that is, all details of life were viewed in relation to one another. Of course, native systems of social control did not always work perfectly within or between bands and tribes: taboos against killing did not prevent inter-tribal raids and fighting for purposes of revenge or to take slaves (Dickason, 1993: 67–9, 79–92). Although most pre-contract societies were not overly violent, they were willing and able to take violent action when the situation warranted it.

Since the turn of this century, scholarly estimates regarding the size of the indigenous population of pre-Columbian North America have varied between 1 million and 10 million; today the general consensus is that by the end of the 1400s between 2 million and 5 million people were living north of the Rio Grande. By 1650, 85 to 90 per cent of them had been wiped out through disease, massacre, and suicide (Cornell, 1988: 51–3). For those who survived this 'holocaust' life changed profoundly. At first, the fur trade provided a substantial increase in goods and income in eastern and northern Canada, and many natives benefited from their relations with the European traders who depended on their expertise in trapping, hunting, and knowledge of the territories (Rich, 1991: 158–68). But rising competition in trade also increased the divisions between tribes that were already divided (Adams, 1989:

chap. 3), and when the fur trade went into decline, difficulties arose among natives who had become dependent on European goods. The most profound changes in native life, however, followed the signing of treaties.

The first treaty agreement in pre-Confederation Canada was signed on 29 May 1680 between the Mohawk, Nipissing, and Algonquin Indians and the government of France. As European settlers pushed farther west and north, agreements and treaties were made with various tribes. Although pre- and post-1867 treaties involved different concessions, most arranged for First Nations peoples to cede their interest in large tracts of land in return for reserves along with small annuities, the right to hunt and fish on the reserves or on unoccupied Crown land, the right to limited educational services, and, in treaties negotiated after treaty six, (1876) the provision of a medicine chest (Taylor, 1991: 208). By the time of Confederation, Canada had a fully developed Indian policy inherited from the British imperial and colonial governments and already administered by the Crown Lands Department (eventually to become the Department of Indian Affairs and Northern Development, or DIAND). The last of the eleven numbered treaties was not signed until 1921, but native people had begun to mobilize in response to problems associated with the policies and practices of the colonizers long before then.

POLITICAL VIOLENCE

Indeed, organized, sometimes violent political action by native people started well before the turn of the century, as evidenced by the Red River conflict of 1869–70 and the North-West conflict of 1885. Torrance's (1977: 494–5) contention that Canadian governments have historically responded promptly and decisively to violent political actions with little if any sympathetic interest in what may have precipitated them was illustrated early on by the highly restrictive legislation passed at the end of the 1860s and, later, by the deployment of hundreds of North-West Mounted Police to Saskatchewan during the North-West conflict. Effecting change became difficult for First Nations, since it was illegal to use band funds for political organization or to leave the reserve without a pass from the Indian agent (Cardinal, 1969: 103). Moreover, any legal actions that First Nations people might have wanted to initiate that were undoubtedly stifled by the fact that until 1961 it was illegal for lawyers to represent Indians in actions against the Crown. Nonetheless, the numerous violent and non-violent political activities during the early part of this century prepared important ground on which later activists would build. Through the 1930s and 1940s native tribes, bands, and communities worked to organize and develop lines of communication

within and across provincial boundaries. Finally, in 1951, increased lobbying, demonstrations, and violent confrontations on behalf of native
people served to pressure the federal government into 'amending' the
Indian Act, which had remained virtually intact since its enactment in
1876 (Cardinal, 1969: 108–9). These amendments in the 1951 Act,
which conferred special benefits, subsidies, and exemptions, especially
for natives on reserves, set some First Nations' concerns to rest for a
time. In general, the 1950s and early 1960s saw a subsiding of violent
political activity and a slowing of organized interest and pressure to
effect change.

Nevertheless, two developments in the late 1960s were important
catalysts for the resurgence of both violent and non-violent efforts at
change on the part of native people and their supporters. One was the
establishment of the National Indian Brotherhood (NIB), the first
national organization run by and for Canada's First Nations. Though
the organization was to have a turbulent history, largely as a result of disagreements within and without over funding and agendas (Ponting,
1986: 40–1), NIB board member Harold Cardinal (who was also president of the Indian Association of Alberta) noted in his controversial
book (1969: 107) that the creation of the NIB was a turning-point. The
second occurrence that served as a focal point for organized native
interests at this time was the introduction by the Minister of Indian
Affairs of the 1969 White Paper. For aboriginal people in Canada, the
White Paper served as a symbol that helped to crystallize the 'problem'
they faced. Native leaders from across Canada immediately and categor-
ically rejected what they termed the 'genocidal' implications of the
White Paper, and in 1970 adopted the Indian Chiefs of Alberta's position paper *Citizens Plus* as their national response. As an outspoken representative of two of the most recognized native organizations in the
country, Harold Cardinal was both hopeful and wary. He warned that
failure of the NIB and other similar organizations, especially if Canadian
governments were at fault, could result in aboriginal peoples' 'taking
the dangerous and explosive path travelled by the black militants of the
United States' (Cardinal, 1979: 107).

Numerous violent political incidents during the 1970s and 1980s
seemed to fulfil Cardinal's prophecy. It is important to note, however,
that most of these incidents have been strategically planned: they have
not been the spontaneous, unexpected occurrences that media and
state representatives often make them out to be (York and Pindera,
1992). Moreover, Native people have often 'initiated' such action only
after they have exhausted other, more legitimate means of attempting
to bring about change. One example of the tireless legitimate efforts by
native people involves the Lubicon Lake Indian band of northern
Alberta, who have been fighting for their rights with the federal and

provincial governments for over fifty years. In addition to lobbying government officials, speaking to the media, and joining in coalition with other native and non-native supporters, the Lubicon have compiled a library that includes letters to and from other native leaders and supporters, lawyers, Canadian and international politicians, and corporate executives, as well as newspaper articles, press releases, interviews and leaked government documents. Though the Lubicon people and their supporters have yet to engage in violent confrontation with state representatives, they have at times expressed frustration and anger at the repeated lack of good faith and effort on the part of Canadian governments to bring the dispute to resolution. The Mohawk people had followed a similar path prior to the crisis at Oka in the summer of 1990.

From the perspective of state representatives, a change in native organizations during the 1970s from issue-oriented to more bureaucratic, institutionally-based organizational structures increased the credibility of those organizations (Frideres, 1988: 282). However, the ideological compromises that often accompany bureaucratization also led to growing frustration among those aboriginal people and their supporters who had been trying to bring about radical political and social change. Increased frustration and aggression towards the state were especially apparent during the 1980s, when a large number of native students began graduating from Canadian and American universities. Armed with a rediscovered respect for their cultural traditions and histories, a number of these educated young leaders joined with others in blending and alternating legitimate and illegitimate organizational goals and techniques (Frideres, 1988: 269). Supporters of native rights could now be expected to intersperse their peaceful lobbying, negotiating, and demonstrating activities with violent political action. And although the targets of their actions have varied—including logging and other private companies, the military, non-aboriginal communities, and at times factions within their own communities—the primary concern of most politically active native people over the past thirty years has been to challenge the policies and practices used by state representatives at one level or another to gain native consent to state rule.

Challenging the state has been both difficult and costly, however, largely because of the internal colonialism that has so long affected every area of native life. Among the policies and practices that have been (and continue to be) used by the state are the following: publicly supporting native sovereignty by negotiating treaties with First Nations peoples, while at the same time assuming the fundamental principle of Crown sovereignty (Boldt, 1993: 5); manipulating sentiment through 'guilt management' by painting a particular picture of state-native relations (Boldt, 1993: 18–21); the social and geographical isolation of native people on reserves (Dickason, 1993: 257); political co-optation of key native leaders (Hammersmith, 1992: 55); manipulation of the discourse used in native-white relations (Jensen, 1993: 350–2); and widening the divisions between tribes and bands by sponsoring competitive specialized funding programs for community development projects and research into specific tribal histories for land-claims arguments (Frideres, 1988: 286). For well óver a century aboriginal people in Canada have not had meaningful control of their lands, funds, business interactions, or educational, social, community, and local-government activities. Although the federal government's stated goal for its native wards was and continues to be full and equal participation in Canadian society, the route of separate development enshrined in the Indian Acts of 1876 and 1951 has continued in many ways to lock many native communities and individuals into a structure that has done little more than perpetuate their political, legal, cultural, and social marginality (Erasmus, 1989: 295).

Despite their colonially-enforced marginality, during the 1970s and 1980s many natives began lobbying government representatives and using various legal channels in order to challenge the policies, legislation, and practices of European colonization. For example, in the early 1960s Mary Two Axe-Early was joined by other native women in openly condemning the Indian Act for its discrimination against native women and lobbying for changes to it. Continuing throughout the 1970s, these efforts resulted in the Canadian government's promise, in 1979, to remove section 12(1)(b) of the Indian Act, a promise that was finally honoured in 1985 when the Act was amended and Indian women were offered 'official' reinstatement (Silman, 1987: 235).[5] Aboriginal people also recognized that mass-media coverage of their activities could bring added attention to their concerns and possibly help them cultivate a broader social support base. For example, in 1993 members of the Peigan Indian nation in central Alberta focused national attention on their grievances against the provincial government and members of the local community by organizing a violent protest against the building of the Old Man River Dam. The mayor of the town cancelled a ceremony scheduled to celebrate the opening of the dam because he and others 'feared for their lives' (*Edmonton Journal*, 25 June 1993, p. A5). Although accounts vary as to what happened and why, native leader Milton Born with a Tooth was eventually convicted on five counts of dangerous use of a firearm. No doubt such militant, sometimes violent political actions have often angered those whose interests they threaten, but they have also enabled native people and their supporters to draw local, national and international attention to their ongoing experience of colonialism and their desire for change.

The most widely publicized recent occurrence of political violence involving native people was the 1990 'Oka Crisis'. During the summer of that year, the Mohawks of Kanasetake engaged in an armed standoff with the Canadian military on the grounds that the extension of a local golf course onto their land would have broken an agreement between the government of Quebec and the Mohawk people. This confrontation received unprecedented national and international attention (York and Pindera, 1992). But it was by no means the only occasion in Canada on which police and army personnel have been dispatched to quell potential 'native uprisings'. Among the more newsworthy examples have been the Montagnais Indians' 1969 demonstration during which they threatened to burn down a fishing club near Montreal in protest against the provincial government's violation of their fishing rights; the native People's Caravan of 1974, in which hundreds of natives and their supporters travelled from Vancouver to Ottawa to protest their treatment in front of the Parliament buildings at the opening of Parliament; the 1974 occupation of the DIAND office in Morley, Alberta, by members of the Stoney band in order to bring attention to their concern and to secure discussions with the federal Minister of Indian Affairs; and the four-month occupation, in 1983, of their band office by native women of the Tobique reserve in New Brunswick in order to attract attention to the problems facing them. More recently, the Lubicon of Northern Alberta lobbied, set up road blockades, and protested in various other ways throughout the 1980s to bring attention to their fifty-year-old land-rights dispute and to prevent large-scale deforestation of their territory; the Dene and Métis of Northern Alberta have protested and lobbied against proposed pulp-mill projects on the Peace and Athabasca Rivers; the Haida of British Columbia have stood in the path of logging machines ready to clear-cut their forests; the Lonefighters of the Peigan Indian Nation in Alberta forced an armed standoff, in 1990, with local and provincial authorities because of their land-rights and environmental concerns around the proposed building of the Old Man River Dam; and the Tin Wis coalition of British Columbia, a group of natives, labour groups and environmentalists, have continued to use violent protest as well as international boycotts against MacMillan Bloedel for destroying the rainforest in the Clayoquot Sound region.

These and many other examples illustrate the preparedness of aboriginal people to engage in violence when they have felt it was necessary. Various expressions of political activism, ranging from passive resistance to the use of violent, armed confrontation, also highlight the tension that has characterized native-state relations since the arrival of the European explorers. As early as 1974 the Royal Canadian Mounted Police (RCMP) described the native movement as the single greatest threat to national security. Although this may now be viewed as a rather gross overstatement, what the RCMP does appear to have understood is that those with relatively little power can and do resort to violence in order to effect change (Gurr, 1970: 210–12). By contrast, others including Prime Minister Pierre Trudeau dismissed the early militant outbursts as insignificant actions by a small and desperate group of extremists (York, 1989: 251). While the Trudeau assessment may have contained a grain of truth—certainly many such incidents did reflect a degree of desperation—a more credible interpretation would have viewed native political violence as a response to the experience of oppression resulting from social, economic, legal and political inequality.

Most aboriginal people in Canada would undoubtedly have preferred that their social, economic, political, and legal problems be resolved in peaceful ways. However, the development, during the 1970s and 1980s, of an ideological agenda that expressed itself in an often violent manner was for many native people a matter of survival (York, 1989: 260–1). To continue to turn the other cheek would have meant accepting the prospect of cultural and physical genocide. Strategic use of violent political action also served to shock other Canadians into realizing that the vision of their country as a 'peaceable kingdom' was little more than a state-perpetuated myth (Boldt, 1993: 21), and that aboriginal people's part in constructing a new and truly democratic Canada could no longer be ignored or co-opted (Boldt, 1981: 215). As the following discussion of criminal violence will illustrate, political activism is by no means the only vehicle through which native peoples have expressed their pain and frustration. Nonetheless, it has taken over thirty years of political activity, non-violent and violent, for other Canadians to begin to ask why the conditions in which many native people live continue to fall short of the general standard of living in this country, why certain rates of criminal violence are comparatively higher for native people than for the Canadian population as a whole, and what the response to such problems should be. Given the size and increasing relative growth of the aboriginal population of Canada, as well as the awareness most Canadians now have regarding the average socio-economic conditions of life among aboriginal people, these questions are becoming ever more pressing.

CRIMINAL VIOLENCE

A recent DIAND report (1993: 29) estimates that the aboriginal population in Canada of approximately 958,000 in 1991 represented 3.5% of the total Canadian population. Between 1961 and 1988 the annual population growth for the aboriginal population averaged roughly 3% (Frideres, 1988: 140–1). DIAND also estimates that most aboriginal groups will increase their proportion of the total population into the year 2001, growing to roughly 1,145,000 at an annual rate of 1.8% and with a mean age 10 years younger than that of the rest of the Canadian population (DIAND 1993: 30). These and other demographic trends reflect a number of factors, including a lowering of mortality rates and an increase in life expectancy among the native population as a whole. For example, the infant mortality rate decreased from 82/1,000 in 1960 to 16.5 in 1985, while in 1986, the overall mortality rate was only 5.3—half of what it had been in 1950 (Frideres, 1991: 116). Further, though the life expectancies for aboriginal males and females in 1976 of 61.1 and 67.6 years respectively were both almost 10 years less than for their non-native counterparts (Statistics Canada, 1990), this gap decreased significantly between 1960 and the late 1980s (Frideres, 1991: 117). But even though the discrepancies between native and non-native birth, death, and life-expectancy rates have been closing over the past three decades, the rates continue to differ significantly. The same is true of causes of death: unlike the rest of the Canadian population, the majority of native people in Canada continue to die as a result of violence/accidents (Comeau and Santin, 1990: 79). Along with problems linked to increases in population, aboriginal people have long experienced the worst socio-economic and living conditions of any group in the country. Hawthorne (1966) reported that the average yearly income of native Indians in Canada at the time was $1,361, compared to $4,000 for non-natives. By 1981, the average First Nations income was $8,326, compared to $14,044 for others in Canada. Moreover, these averages may mask the real poverty experienced by many native people, for there is a high degree of socio-economic diversity among Canada's aboriginal people. For example, in 1978 the per capita annual income in various First Nation bands across the country ranged from over $10,000 for those living on oil-rich reserves to as low as $550 (Frideres, 1988: 162), a relative distribution that has continued into the 1990s. According to DIAND (1991) data, throughout the 1980s approximately 40% of native Indians of working age living on reserves were unemployed; the unemployment rate in all the rest of Canada was 7 to 10%. Frideres (1991: 123) places the unemployment figures even higher—near 55%—and argues that even these figures are lower than they should be since underemployed, seasonal, and part-time workers are included in the calculations. As for living conditions, comparisons require some caution, since people's priorities differ. Nevertheless, whereas the proportion of on-reserve homes with furnaces in the late 1980s was only about 3 in 10 (Comeau and Santin, 1990: 26–7). Some conditions have shown substantial improvement—88% of homes on reserves had adequate water supplies in 1991, and 80% had adequate sewage disposal, compared to 53 and 47% respectively in 1978—the proportion of on-reserve homes with furances in the late 1980s was only about 3 in 10. Conditions for native people living in urban centres are often no better, and sometimes worse, than those on some reserves (Frideres, 1988).

While living standards and experiences vary widely, there is much evidence that many aboriginal people in Canada have experienced relatively impoverished living conditions. A number of analysts suggest that it is important to take such conditions into account, since they appear related to crime and violence. According to Avio and Clark (1976) and Land and Felson (1976), for example, there is a relationship between living conditions and crime. Hartnagel and Lee's (1990) assertion that crime is associated with relative deprivation supports the research of Bachmann (1993: 57), who goes even farther in asserting that long-term economic deprivation, coupled with hopelessness, frustration, and anger, contributes to the potential for violence that may be turned either inward or outward. As we will see in the sections that follow, native death rates from homicide and suicide average between 2 and 4 times the national rates, with some communities reporting rates as much as 20 times the national rates (Westcott et al., 1987).

HOMICIDE

Two incidents illustrate a number of major problems concerning the relationship between aboriginal peoples and justice in Canada. Both events occurred in 1971, the first when a young Cree woman, Helen Betty Osborne, was brutally assaulted and murdered just outside The Pas, Manitoba (York, 1989: 158–9). Though the young white man who had used his father's car for the abduction told dozens of people about the murder (including the local police chief), charges were not laid until 1986. Two white suspects subsequently went to trial, though only one of the four who were in the car was eventually convicted. The second incident involved the Micmac teenager Donald Marshall, who had been convicted and sentenced to prison for the May 1972 murder of Sandy Seale in Sydney, Nova Scotia. The Royal Commission that ordered the case reopened in 1982 found Marshall not guilty when it was discovered that police investigators had ignored certain evidence and not reported everything they knew about the case, and he was released after almost eleven years of incarceration (Harris, 1986). Although these are only two isolated cases, the argument that native people experience structurally-induced discrimination at the hands of the Canadian criminal justice system is supported by the research of Havemann et al. (1985), LaPrairie (1990), and Trevethan (1993), among others. Trevethan, for example, found that aboriginal people are significantly over-represented both as victims of violent crime and as offenders in the three western Canadian cities that she studied. Although natives represented only 2% and 5% of the total populations of Calgary and Regina in 1990, they comprised 6% and 30%, respectively, of the victims of violent crimes in these cities (Trevethan, 1993: 27).[6] Violent-crime offence rates were found to be similarly disproportionate: conviction rates for aboriginal offenders in Calgary (1,800/100,000), Regina (344/100,000), and Saskatoon (2,020/100,000) were 6, 15, and 14 times the rates for non-aboriginal offenders in those cities (Trevethan, 1993).

Research shows similar trends in homicide victimization and offence rates. National and provincial government data on homicide victims suggest that native people are proportionately much more likely to become victims of homicide than other Canadians, with aboriginal males being the most victimized of all. Comprising roughly 2.5% of the Canadian population between 1962 and 1984, aboriginal people represented just over 17% of all homicide victims in Canada during that period (Moyer, 1992: 390). During the 1980s, their overall victimization rate was 15%, ranging from a low of 12% to a high of 19% (Kennedy et al., 1989). The percentage of aboriginal homicide victims in 1988 was 17.6, 2.5% higher than the previous ten-year average (Statistics Canada, 1991c: 68). Males generally were more likely to be victims of homicide than females, with aboriginal males comprising the highest percentage of victims. From 1962 to 1984, non-aboriginal males represented 82% of all homicide victims killed by aboriginal people, while aboriginal males killed by aboriginal suspects accounted for almost 68% of all homicides against aboriginal people. Moreover, in 58% of homicides committed against aboriginal people by non-aboriginals, the victims were male. Among homicides by non-aboriginal suspects, there was a more equal 'gender split' of victims, with just under 52% involving non-aboriginal male victims. Of these, 90% were committed by male suspects (Moyer, 1992: 398). Further, 58% of homicides by non-aboriginal suspects involved male aboriginal victims, and approximately 80% of these were committed by males.

Moyer (1992: 390) also notes that, between 1962 and 1984, native homicide victims were more likely to have been related to the person suspected of killing them (52.2%) than were non-aboriginal victims (39%). Although fewer women than men were victims of homicide among both native (563 females and 1,097 males) and non-native populations (2,773 females and 4,470 males) during this time, females were more likely to have known the person who killed them (Moyer, 1992: 376). Rates for aboriginal and non-aboriginal female victims from 1962 to the early 1980s appear relatively close: just over 60% of female native victims were killed by their conjugal partners, compared to 57% of female non-native victims.[7] Data from 1981 to 1990 suggest that these trends have continued for aboriginal women. During this period, 48% of all female native homicide victims were killed by a spouse/ex-spouse, while 27% were killed by an acquaintance (Department of Justice, 1988).

Disproportionately high rates are also recorded for homicides involving native suspects. From the early 1960s until the end of the 1980s the percentage of aboriginal people charged with homicide, relative to all homicides committed in Canada, fluctuated between 18% and

22%. By contrast, similar rates for non-aboriginal people fluctuated between 74% and 82%. According to Moyer (1992), from 1962 to 1984 native people represented over 19% of all suspects charged with homicide, a figure that increased to 22% by 1988. Over the same period, the percentage of non-native suspects decreased from just over 80% of all suspects between 1962 and 1984, to 74.5% in 1988. These statistics are significant when we consider how small a percentage of the Canadian population natives comprised during this time—but exactly how they should be interpreted is debatable. Numerous studies have pointed to the problem of racial bias in the ways in which police officers and others administer justice in relation to native people (Department of Justice, 1988; Havemann et al., 1985; Law Reform Commission of Canada, 1991; McKaskill, 1985).

Similar patterns of violence are evident when the sex of homicide victims and suspects is taken into account. Overall, from 1962 to 1984, males in Canada took the lives of a greater number and proportion of victims than did females. Native males were charged with almost 81% of homicides against native victims and 78% of those with non-native victims. Non-native males were also more likely to kill than their female counterparts: males were responsible for 88% of homicides involving native victims and 93% of homicides involving non-native victims.

That there is more to the homicide picture than killing and being killed is suggested by Moyer's (1992: 399) report that aboriginal offenders are less likely than their non-aboriginal counterparts to have been convicted of first- or second-degree murder. Between 1976 and 1980, 75% of native offenders charged with homicide were found guilty of manslaughter, compared to 46 per cent of non-native men and 56 per cent of non-native women. Overall, only 3 per cent of convictions for first-degree murder during this period involved aboriginal offenders. This suggests that homicides committed by aboriginal people are more likely to be spontaneous than those committed by non-aboriginals. It is also important to recognize the problems that aboriginal people experience at the hands of the justice system in Canada, since, as was noted in the report of the Law Reform Commission of Canada (1991), many native people plead guilty to crimes even when they are innocent. Misunderstanding on the part of native suspects, as well as racial bias and discrimination on the part of enforcers and administrators of justice, thus needs to be taken into account. Other factors that must be carefully examined include the presence of alcohol (Havemann et al., 1985; Moyer, 1992; Task Force on Aboriginal People in Federal Corrections, 1989); the living conditions of both suspects and victims; the relationship between victims and suspected offenders; and the specific contexts in which homicides occur. These will be discussed in more detail in the Causes section below.

FAMILY VIOLENCE

Research on family violence among aboriginal people in Canada is relatively recent. Thus it is difficult to know exactly how new a phenomenon it is, the extent of the violence that occurs in 'family' situations, and whether the incidence has increased, remained constant, or decreased over the past thirty years. For many reasons—changing perceptions of what constitutes assault; the economic, physical, and sometimes emotional dependency of the woman on the man she lives with; cultural expectations of loyalty to one's community; fear of reprisal by family or community members; fear of having one's children taken away or one's sole source of support put in jail; lack of awareness of available services; fear of the police, threats, and loss of privacy—family violence tends to remain hidden both from public view and from potential sources of support for those involved (Frank, 1992: 15–18). As a result, it is estimated that for the Canadian population as a whole, police become aware of family violence in only approximately 50% of assaults by a spouse or former spouse (Appleford, 1989: 3). A study on family violence in the Northwest Territories estimated that 'only between 10 to 30 per cent of assaults ever come to the attention of social services. For the many more who never seek help, violence is simply a part of their everyday experience' (Report to the Government of the Northwest Territories, 1986: iii). It is therefore difficult even to estimate the extent of family violence experienced by the Canadian population as a whole and by native people in particular.

MacLeod's (1980) 'conservative estimate' that every year 10% of Canadian women are abused by their spouses or partners was based on her study of the number of women in transition homes, combined with the number of women filing for divorce on the ground of physical cruelty.[8] In a subsequent study, MacLeod (1987) estimated that almost 1 million women are abused in Canada each year. A recent inquiry in Manitoba reported that one in six women in that province had been abused, and that the figure for aboriginal women was much higher. Another report to the same inquiry stated that spousal homicides accounted for 40% of all homicides in Canada (Indian and Inuit Nurses of Canada, 1991), and for native women in Canada the story is probably worse. Not only is the incidence of family violence among these women believed to be much higher, but the pressure to be loyal to one's spouse and community is felt very strongly both by those who are in abusive situations and by others who may be aware that abuse occurring (Frank, 1992: 16). In a 1989 study on family violence involving native women in Ontario, 42% of the respondents indicated that when family violence occurs in their communities, it is not talked about. In the same study, only 48% of respondents stated that family violence is reported when it occurs; 28% said that it is not reported, and 24% said they did not know.

In addition, 54% of respondents indicated that they thought very few aboriginal women who experienced family violence actually sought social, medical, or legal help (Ontario Native Women's Association, 1989: 21). A representative of the Child Protection Centre of Winnipeg estimated that while only 10% of non-aboriginal women testify in court against their abusive partners, the numbers of aboriginal women willing to take their cases to court are even lower.[9] Frank (1992: 18) reports that 65% of respondents to a Helping Spirit Lodge survey stated that many native people are discouraged from receiving medical treatment because of the fear of reprisals from the abuser or the abuser's family. Moreover, approximately 65% of the aboriginal population in Canada live in rural and remote parts of the country where information and services are lacking because of inadequate government funding and program development, financial hardship, or language and other cultural differences (Northern Alberta Development Council, 1988: 8). In many respects, the struggle against family violence by aboriginal women and men is also a struggle against oppression and towards self-understanding and self-determination (Frank, 1993: 7).

Estimates vary widely as to the extent of victimization among native women in Canada. A 1989 study in British Columbia indicated that 86% of native respondents had experienced family violence (Frank, 1993). In a study carried out by the Ontario Native Women's Association (1989: 18–20), 84% of respondents indicated that family violence occurred in their communities, while a further 80% indicated that they had personally experienced it.[10] In the same study, 78% of respondents indicated that more than one member of the family were victims of regular abuse. A similar study carried out by the Yukon Task Force on Family Violence estimated that roughly 700 women in the Yukon are assaulted each year (1985: 13). Other research suggested that, overall, one in three aboriginal women in Canada is abused by her partner (Jamieson, 1987), and 40% of respondents to Statistics Canada's Aboriginal Peoples Survey (1993) reported that family violence is a problem in their community.[11] Based on RCMP statistics, the incidence of spousal assaults[12] in the Yukon in 1985 was 526/100,000, substantially higher than the national average of 130/100,000 though substantially lower than the 1 in 6 cited in the Manitoba study. In their report to the Yukon Task Force on Family Violence (1985: 15), representatives from the Transition Home in Whitehorse reported that their organization provided shelter to an average of 160 women and 170 children per year. They also noted that 80% of their clients had fled violent home situations. According to one study, such statistics suggest that physical abuse has become an 'acceptable way of resolving conflict and of getting one's own way' that is being passed from generation to generation in many native communities (Yukon Task Force on Family Violence, 1985: 4). Of course, however, as the findings of Macleod (1987) and DeKeseredy and Ellis (this volume) suggest, viewing physical abuse as an acceptable means of resolving conflict is not unique to native communities.

Family violence is both an intensely isolating, individual experience and a disturbingly social phenomenon, and it is as difficult to understand as it is to address. Rates of victimization and offence, while important for our understanding of the pervasiveness of family violence involving native people in Canada, barely scratch the surface of the physical, emotional, psychological, and spiritual suffering that is involved. Moreover, because the available statistics are at times contradictory, there is a need for research that is not only more collaborative, but more rigorous and comprehensive.

SUICIDE

If murder is the most extreme outward expression of aggression, suicide is the most extreme expression of violence directed inward (Bachmann, 1993: 2). As is noted below, all available data show that the suicide rates for native people in Canada are significantly higher than comparative rates for non-natives. For Canadians in general, the age-specific suicide mortality rate (ASSMR) averaged approximately 13/100,000 between 1969 and 1987 (Statistics Canada, 1990b: 332). However, standardized rates often include both males and females: when we control for sex, the ASSMR for males between 1984 and 1988—22/100,000—was over three times the rate for females during that same period. Further, the 2,794 male suicides registered in 1987 represented just over 80% of all recorded suicides (Statistics Canada, 1989: 99). Unlike the relatively stable rates for females, male ASSMRs also showed a steady increase from the 1960s into the late 1980s, rising from 15.6 in 1969 to just over 21 in 1987. In general, although there were relatively minor age variations in suicide mortality rates among males in Canada during this time, their rates consistently averaged just over three times those of females in most age groups.

For native people, both female and male, the figures are much higher. In 1979, the ASSMR of 33.8/100,000 for native people was over 2.5 times the national average for non-natives (Health and Welfare Canada, 1993). By the late 1970s, suicide accounted for 10.4% of all deaths for First Nations people (Jarvis and Boldt, 1982: 10) but a mere 2%, approximately, for the general population. Between 1983 and 1986, the suicide rate for First Nations people was 34/100,000, compared to the national average of just over 14 between 1983 and 1985 (Bobet, 1980: 12–13). The overall rate for First Nations males between 1984 and 1988 was almost 58, compared to the non-aboriginal male rate of 22. By 1989, the suicide mortality rate for aboriginal males in Canada aged 20–24 was 171/100,000, more than five times the national average for males of these ages and the highest rate for that age group in the world. The standardized rates for First Nations females during this time was considerably lower, at 14.5. However, this is still more than twice the rate of 6.2 for non-native females. The highest suicide rate by age group for First Nations females was 44/100,000, and was recorded for those between the ages of 35 and 39. This was followed by rates of 16/100,000 for those aged 15–24. Significantly lower rates of 9.3/100,000 and 5/100,000, respectively, were recorded among non-native females in Canada between 1984 and 1988 (Muir, 1991). Further, between 1975 and 1986, 72 per cent of all suicides in the Northwest Territories were committed by aboriginal people, with rates for communities averaging from a low of 15.8/100,000 for Yellowknife to a high of 97.2/100,000 for Tuktoyaktuk. From the middle of the 1970s to the mid-1980s, the major regions of Inuvik, Kitikmeot, Keewatin, and Baffin registered suicide rates of 85, 75, 33.1, and 50/100,000 respectively (Westcott et al., 1987: 6–7).

The ASSMR for all aboriginal people between 1984 and 1988 was 36.1—almost three times the rate for the Canadian population as a whole. Nonetheless, statistics from the 1980s suggest that, overall, ASSMRs among portions of the native population in Canada have slowly declined. From 1984 to 1988, suicide rates among Canada's First Nations decreased by 17% from the previous four-year period (Muir, 1990: 39–40). In 1990, the suicide rate of 27.4 for registered Indians living on reserves was just over twice the Canadian rate of 13, down from the 3-to-1 ratio recorded in 1981, when the rate for registered Indian was 42.[13] It has been suggested that slowly declining rates may reflect better prevention, intervention, and follow-up programs in some native communities and urban settings (Minister of National Health and Welfare, 1988: 74–9). Simply admitting that the problem of suicide was reaching epidemic proportions, especially among native youths, also appears to be helping communities and potential victims identify and address their suicide-related 'problems' more quickly and effectively (Minister of Health and Welfare, 1988: 74), though rates continue to be comparatively much higher than for the Canadian population as a whole. According to Health and Welfare statistics (1988), the decrease in the overall suicide rate for First Nations people was most pronounced in the Yukon, though decreases were recorded in all regions. ASSMRs for males were particularly high in certain age groups, while the distribution among females was relatively even across age cohorts. In general, between 1980 and 1988, the ASSMRs for First Nations males were lowest in parts of central Canada and highest in the northern and east-coast regions of the country (Muir, 1991: 39–40). The highest ASSMRs for First Nations males from 1980 to 1984 were found in the Yukon (178.3), followed by Saskatchewan (85), Alberta (72.8), and Quebec (70.4). From 1984 to 1988, significant increases were recorded in the Northwest

Territories (from 21.8 to 53.6), Atlantic region (48.8 to 70.6), and Alberta (72.8 to 86.8). All other provinces and regions recorded declining ASSMRs. The lowest rates for First Nations males between 1980 and 1984 were recorded in Manitoba (43.5) and Quebec (47.2). ASSMRs between 1980 and 1984 for First Nations females were highest in Alberta, Saskatchewan, and the Yukon, though these same regions recorded the most significant declines over the next four-year period. ASSMRs declined in Saskatchewan from 35.1 to 18.3, in Alberta from 28.8 to 18.4, and in the Yukon from 26.6 to 9.7/100,000. The lowest ASSMRs for First Nations females between 1980 and 1984 were recorded in the Northwest Territories (0.0), the Atlantic region (2.7), Manitoba (6.3), and the Yukon (9.7), though all of these regions except the Yukon reported increases in these rates between 1984 and 1988 (Northwest Territories, 8.8; Atlantic, 15.6; Manitoba, 14.6). The highest recorded ASSMRs in 1986 for non-native females in Canada were in the Yukon (17.9), and the lowest in the Atlantic region (3.1). Muir (1991: 39) notes that the highest rates for non-active males were also found in the Yukon (65.0) and Northwest Territories (47.5), while the lowest rates were recorded in the Atlantic region (16.3) and Ontario (19.1).

The data on First Nations suicides during this time suggest a certain regional pattern. The ASSMR declined in most provinces among both males and females, with the highest rates of decline being recorded in the Yukon, Saskatchewan, Alberta, and Quebec. There also appear to be a relationship between suicide and the sex of the victim, since rates for both First Nations and non-aboriginal females are notably lower than those for males. Suicides by First Nations females were quite evenly distributed between 1980 and 1988, though again slightly higher rates were recorded in certain prairie and northern regions. Although it is possible to speculate that declining rates reflect a concentration of resources and people in certain areas of the country, research is needed to determine whether changes in rates reflect an improvement in medical reporting practices in certain areas, implementation of more successful community-awareness and suicide-prevention programs, and/or worsening of personal and social conditions.

As high as the suicide rates for First Nations people are, even higher rates have been recorded among the Inuit in the Northwest Territories. The most Inuit suicides (65.4%) between 1984 and 1988 were found in the 15–24 age group; a similar age group (15–29) had the highest rate among First Nations people as well. However, for First Nations this age group accounted for 75% of all suicides, with a rate of almost 80/100,000 (Muir, 1990: 40). It is interesting to note that in 1971 the suicide rate among the Inuit was close to the national average of 10/100,000; it was only as the impact of colonial development spread northward that these measures of violence-turned-inward took a dramatic upturn. Prior to 1970, there had been little interest in north-ern Canada on the part of those who had 'settled' this country. When a global 'oil crisis' emerged in the early 1970s, however, the possibility of accessing the relatively untapped deposits of this resource directed the eyes of developers northward. Just as the early colonizers and settlers had 'structured' violence into the lives of native individuals, families, and communities through various policies and practices south of the 60th parallel, the belief that the economic benefits of the Mackenzie Valley pipeline outweighed the potential social and environmental costs contributed to a similar spread of violence in the north. By 1978 the Inuit suicide rate had risen to over 85/100,000 (Department of Health, 1990). Though the ASSMR for the Inuit in the Northwest Terri-tories averaged 53.4 between 1978 and 1988, yearly rates fluctuated greatly over this period, ranging from a low of 18.4 in 1982 to a high of 85.7 in 1978. The four-year period between 1984 and 1988 shows a steady increase from 51.4 to 75.9 (Department of Health, 1990). Research suggests that traditionally, among the Inuit, suicide was a cul-turally acceptable way of responding to infirmity or the death of kin, and was not a serious problem prior to the 1970s (Pauktuutit, 1990: 2). From the 1970s through into the late 1980s, however, suicide emerged as a major social problem. National Health and Welfare reported that the Inuit rate for 1981 through 1985 was 3.3 times the Canadian rate, with most of the victims being young men. This increase in suicide mor-tality rates continued throughout the 1980s, and by 1988 had reached 75.9/100,000—almost four times the national average for 1988 and an increase of 35% from the average during the previous four-year period (Department of Health, 1990). By contrast, the increase for the national average during the same time period was marginal, from 12 to 13/100,000.

As violence turned in on oneself, suicide is both a final solution for those who take their lives and another reminder of lost hope for those who continue to live. Many RCAP intervenors expressed concern that both the hopelessness experienced by many aboriginal young peo-ple and their often violent response to it may continue into future gen-erations. Indeed, the numbers of suicides and suicide attempts among Canada's native population continue to be frightening. Between 1986 and 1993, the Sioux Lookout, Ontario, hospital dealt with over 600 serious suicide attempts; in 1992, 46 of the 500 Innu people living in Davis Inlet attempted suicide. Though the latter continue to receive government help and national media attention, recent newspaper reports suggest that many youths in the community are still intent on taking their lives. The mayor of Nain, Newfoundland, reported to the RCAP approximately 30 suicide attempts in his community during a recent 18-month period. Moreover, community workers estimate that for every suicide that takes place, at least seven people are directly affected. Thus violence begets more violence; for both youths and adults it appears that there is little if any way to escape, since the alternative is to try to become a part of a society that has historically treated its non-white members in oppressive, often violent ways (Comeau and Santin, 1990: 39).

CAUSES OF POLITICAL AND PHYSICAL VIOLENCE

Along with the political, legal, and socio-economic changes experienced by native people in Canada over the past thirty years, the ways in which the conditions and problems of their lives have been explained have also changed. As researchers and others have focused attention on the sources of problems associated with aboriginal health and violence, there has been less tendency to blame aboriginal people for the conditions in which they live and the violence in their midst (Havemann et al., 1985). In the 1960s, many researchers used acculturation theory to explain the social problems of native people, arguing that major social and cultural change caused stress, which in turn led to social disorganization, culture conflict, feelings of inferiority, and an inability to adjust. This view of who or what was to blame for native violence and other social problems was challenged in the 1970s by proponents of internal colonialism theory, who asserted that these problems reflected aboriginal people's colonial status.[14] According to this perspective, many aboriginal people in Canada have been unable to construct meaningful and rewarding social environments because of the oppressive effects of colonizing political, social, and economic structures (Pauktuutit, 1990: 3).

For example, while the disproportionately high rates of physical violence among Canada's native people have been attributed to such personal, social, and environmental factors as alcohol abuse, learned helplessness, social isolation, histories of abuse, overcrowded housing conditions, and poverty (Health and Welfare, 1990: 14), a more structural approach views those factors themselves as consequences of internal colonialism (Bachmann, 1993: 26). The view that internal colonialism is the underlying problem has been welcomed by those who assert that the perpetuation of physical violence in aboriginal relationships is a 'tradition' that emerged from and has been perpetuated by the assimilationist policies and practices of European colonizers. Among these policies and practices are the establishment of reserves, the sorting of aboriginal people into different categories of rights and responsibilities, the removal of children on the pretext of concern for their welfare, the creation of elected band-council systems of 'native' government, the control and/or banning of certain religious ceremonies, and the establishment of residential schools (Frank, 1993: 7).

Moreover, Bachmann (1993: 26) asserts that homicide and other acts of physical violence by aboriginal people represent their response to the loss of their culture, hope, and feelings of responsibility towards their communities. The long-term experience of colonization and economic deprivation has also contributed to feelings of powerlessness, frustration, anger and despair among aboriginal people, with physical violence representing an attempt to exert some degree of control over their lives (Bachmann, 1993: 57). This power-seeking response to relative powerlessness is particularly evident in the lives of native men who express their aggression in violence and of native youth involved in suicide. Though native women appear to be less violent than their male counterparts, their colonized status is reflected in the data showing that they are much more likely than non-native females to experience some form of violence in their lives. These and other effects of colonization continue to be perpetuated by social, political, and justice policies and practices that often blame and/or punish native people for their pain and anger as well as their violent responses to their frustration and lack of hope.

At the same time, the process of redressing these problems is hindered by the colonial nature of state funding arrangements. First, the administration of state bureaucracy continues to consume a major share of the resources available, leaving most aboriginal communities to manage state-initiated programs with inadequate funding (RCAP, 1993a: 42). Moreover, what funding is available is distributed through a myriad of agreements with individual bands, provinces, and territories, resulting in inconsistencies in services and confusion over federal-provincial cost-sharing arrangements (Health and Welfare, 1990: 107). A significant aspect of the process of colonization thus includes disputes over the allocation of human and material resources not only between aboriginal people and government but also within and between aboriginal communities. The inadequacy of the resources available to address social problems means that it is most often the symptoms rather than the underlying causes that are treated. Given the importance of alleviating pain and suffering, most native organizations would agree with Denham (1989: 22), who argues that in response to family violence, the largest portion of financial resources should be directed at providing immediate protection and safety for victims and providing services and treatment for individuals, families, and communities needing them. Unfortunately, resources have not always gone to those in greatest need (Silman, 1987: 125–35).

This is not to say that internal colonialism is the only explanation for violence by and against aboriginal people in Canada. For example, there is a great deal of disagreement among state representatives, community members, health-care representatives, and researchers on the role of alcohol in physical violence. Some argue that alcohol is used to numb the pain of experience and prevents natives from thinking and acting responsibly. Others counter with equal vehemence that it is an easy way out to blame alcohol for family and other types of physical violence (Yukon Task Force on Family Violence, 1985: 185). Bachmann (1993: 25–6), among others, asserts that the role of alcohol and other 'mitigating factors' can be meaningfully understood only in the context of socio-historical conditions and developments.

POLICY CONCERNS AND DIRECTIONS IN HEALING

The data examined in this study strongly suggest that over the last thirty years natives have been disproportionately involved as both victims and offenders in a variety of destructive activities including homicide, suicide, and family violence. At the same time, however, two related dimensions of native life have had undeniably positive results. Together, the revitalization of native spirituality and the rediscovery of some almost forgotten cultural traditions have contributed in no small way to the strengthening of native identities, the integrity of native efforts for social and political change, and the belief that healing is possible. At the community level renewal is evident in the increasing call upon native elders and traditional speakers to conduct sweetgrass ceremonies, speak at conferences, and lead aboriginal and non-aboriginal people in sweat-lodge ceremonies and spiritual workshops (Peng, 1989: 1–2). In pursuing their goals of self-determination and self-sufficiency, aboriginal communities have also increasingly taken control of their own schools, child-welfare programs and agencies, economic development and crisis intervention programs, and justice systems (RCAP, 1993b). At the organizational level, 'friendship centres' and aboriginal organizations have incorporated traditional teachings in their programs and decision-making processes (Supernault, 1993: 24–5). Finally, towards more political ends, aboriginal organizations and communities have increasingly conducted their own research and lobbied various levels of government with their findings and policy recommendations, while continuing to engage in demonstrations, protest marches, and armed confrontation (Long, 1992: 123–5).

From the perspective of some, one of the most significant problems faced by those concerned to address violence by and against aboriginal people in Canada is the sheer diversity of the conditions and people requiring 'healing and justice' (Yukon Task Force on Family Violence, 1985: 10). It is evident to many that there is no single solution that will address the needs of all aboriginal communities, women, and men (Ontario Native Women's Association, 1989: 114). Increasingly, the shared sentiment is that 'if solutions are going to work, they have to be made by, and within, the community, however that community may be defined' (Frank, 1993: 17). From the bureaucratic perspective, however, the main difficulty with the diversity of native communities is that it confounds what would otherwise be the uncomplicated application of generic therapies, community-development strategies, and national action plans. Recognizing this, many people working in community- and health-related areas have designed programs that can be adapted to unique situations and communities (Health and Welfare, 1990: 74–9). Such initiatives also often take into account the history of the community and the fact that those most likely to intervene at the community level will be para-professional volunteers, many of them natives who are sensitive to the cultures of the people they are serving (Council for Yukon Indians, 1992: 8).

One of the main reasons offered in support of community-based health, education, justice, and economic-development programs run by and for native people is that 'the system' has historically worked against rather than for native people. As Dr Jonathan Sheehan, health practitioner at the Sagkeeng First Nation, told the RCAP, many potential native clients fall through the cracks and are denied services to which they are entitled because the provincial and federal health-care systems share responsibility for aboriginal people, and both seem more concerned about saving money than addressing peoples' needs. Specific concerns relating to the planned devolution of health and other services for aboriginal peoples have centred around three main questions: Who will control the policies, funds and other resources? What is the underlying agenda of those who control the health, justice, community-development, and other budgets for aboriginal peoples in Canada? And, perhaps most important, will those who are most in need have their needs met? The answers that have been given to the first two questions suggest the directions that policy and program initiatives, and possibly even legislative developments, could take in the future.

There are those who propose that if the immediate and long-term needs of native people are to be met, native people themselves must have absolute control over policy agendas and program implementation. In the words of Dr Chris Durocher of the Yukon Medical Association, 'self-determination for aboriginal peoples is a prerequisite for healing and the development of wellness—wellness meaning of body, mind and spirit. Control of their cultural rights, land resources, education, justice system and health care delivery must come into the hands of aboriginal people first.' Central to this self-determination position is the view that the philosophies underlying health, family, justice, social, political, economic, and other agendas need to reflect the traditional world-views and lived experiences of the aboriginal people involved. Advocates of this view note that unlike most Westernized, government-supported approaches to healing, the traditional, holistic aboriginal approach seeks to integrate the physical, spiritual, mental, and emotional aspects of health (RCAP, 1993b: 52). Socio-economic problems such as poverty, unemployment, welfare dependence, and poor housing are understood in terms of the direct effects they have on the well-being of individuals, communities, and whole societies (Indian and Inuit Nurses of Canada, 1991). From this perspective,

> abuse and other imbalances of life cannot be healed by attempting to heal isolated aboriginal individuals apart from their family and their community. To get to the root cause of abuse and neglect, the entire system that allowed it to occur must be restored to balance. This means that the accumulated hurt of generations, carried to our families and our communities, needs to be released through a healing process. (Nechi Institute, 1988: 4)

Similar reports and testimonies from those sensitive to the cultural and spiritual dimensions of aboriginal life acknowledge the uniqueness of aboriginal nations and communities and the need to restore communal balance and spiritual harmony (Yukon Spousal Assault Task Force 1985: 10). As Halfe (1993: 9–10) describes the healing process, 'When the Indigenous people are allowed to dance their journey by reclaiming their visions, their personhood, their families, their societies, and all which they encompass, perhaps then we shall see a decrease in self-destructive behaviour.' Advocates of self-determination also underscore the importance of grassroots developments in aboriginal communities and focus on the healing that needs to occur within every individual and community. The most strident of these recommend that resources and efforts towards change should be directed primarily towards community-based programs and initiatives (RCAP, 1993b: 59). They also assert that respect for their traditional ways in all areas where healing is needed is vital, and that tinkering with parts of a fundamentally flawed socio-political system will not alleviate the root causes of violence by and against their people (Frank, 1993: 2).

Many others who support traditional native beliefs and practices also strongly believe that aboriginal individuals and communities can benefit from the knowledge and expertise of non-aboriginal people. Especially in health- and justice-related initiatives, these 'new traditionalists' maintain that aboriginal perspectives and practices need to be combined with non-aboriginal conflict resolution, support-group therapies, and community health and development programs (Frank, 1993: 17). They maintain that combining different perspectives, strategies, and techniques will enable aboriginal people to rediscover and strengthen their identities in the community while learning to coexist with others in the modern world (RCAP, 1993b: 60). Among the ways of

responding to family violence in native communities that have been suggested are these: greater enforcement of wife-assault policy and subsequent use of the criminal justice system; assurances from police that
they will in fact respond to calls and take appropriate action; alternative
approaches to the justice system (based on traditional values); more
transition houses, second-stage housing, and safe homes, as well as easier access for native women and children to these facilities; easier access
to counselling both in aboriginal communities and within mainstream
services; enhanced or holistic support services throughout the justice
system; increased access to legal aid; cross-cultural training of justice
personnel; cultural awareness through public education; and development of wife-assault intervention models and men's prevention programs, as well as family-counselling and mental-health teams that are
sensitive to the many different experiences and perspectives of native
people (Frank, 1993: 17). Advocates of this perspective accept that
aboriginal perspectives and traditions must play a central role in the
healing process. However, they also believe that addressing the hydra-
headed problems related to physical violence requires the type of specialized knowledge and training that most aboriginal people do not yet
have. Accordingly, they call for understanding and patience during this
time of transition in which aboriginal people are learning, among
other things, to rekindle their traditional awareness and practices, to
strengthen relations with their own people, and to build co-operative,
healthy relationships with non-aboriginal people (RCAP, 1993b: 60).

Central to all discussions regarding policy development and implementation is the issue of program effectiveness, with everyone involved
in the 'healing debates' maintaining that they have the best interest of
native people in mind. While there are some who support the inclusion
of native perspectives and people in the healing process, there are many
others whose actions suggest that they believe native people are best left
out of the dialogue (Boldt, 1993: 18–21). Advocates of this position may
pay lip service to the idea that aboriginal cultures and traditions are a
valid part of the healing process, but their policies and practices suggest
that they do not support the fundamental, systemic changes advocated
by many native people and their supporters. Evidence from the last
thirty years suggests that many people, non-native and native alike, who
benefit from supporting the status quo have been able to maintain the
positions of power and influence that enable them to stifle meaningful
change in the healing process and perpetuate oppressive colonial structures, policies, and practices.

Although DIAND and other federal and provincial government
departments have often worked with native people in developing and
initiating 'healing-related' policies and programs, the majority of these
initiatives have not been preventative in nature, nor have they been

arrived at through an inclusive, consensual process (Barnaby, 1992: 40). The analysis presented above suggests that the problem has not been merely the lack of political will or resources. Rather, there have been and continue to be at least two significant factors hindering positive, meaningful changes. On the one hand, most dialogue and efforts to implement meaningful structural changes continue to be constricted by an underlying paternalistic, bureaucratized perspective that views aboriginal peoples in Canada as wards of the state who, after more than 200 years of colonial administration, still require protection and help (Boldt, 1993: 21). In response, many aboriginal people have taken the stand that nothing short of violent protest will bring awareness to those who continue to hold to such an 'Old World' view (Long, 1992). Compounding the problem of paternalism is the unwillingness and/or inability of many aboriginal and non-aboriginal people to admit that they do not like the prospect of change, and/or that they fear reprisal from colleagues or community members for honest dissent (Dyck, 1993: 194). Numerous RCAP intervenors echoed the words of the native women interviewed by Silman (1987), most of whom noted that healing on their reserves was inhibited by native political leaders who refused to grant women an equal place and voice in their communities. They point out that many aboriginal people, especially women, have often had to be satisfied with programs and services that at best have met only their most basic needs (Health and Welfare 1990: 106), and at worst have ignored the needs of some altogether (Silman, 1987: 125).

The demands for cultural and organizational changes in native life have therefore been accompanied by demands for structural changes in health care, criminal justice, politics, and economic development policies. One of the key assumptions underlying these demands is that if the diverse needs of aboriginal people are to be met, they themselves are the ones best suited to develop the necessary policies and programs. Though many state representatives have deemed such an arrangement impossible or at best unlikely to occur in the immediate future, aboriginal people have continued to assert that those who have suffered and those who have perpetuated the violence need to be an integral part of the healing process. Along with major political and legal changes, native people and their supporters have therefore also proposed, among other things, that aboriginal people take more control over policy development, funding, and program implementation in all areas of their lives (RCAP, 1993a: 35); national forums be established to address the myriad of issues involved in the areas of physical violence, criminal justice, and community development as they relate to aboriginal people; expert advisory committees be appointed by the federal government to facilitate discussions, program implementation, and policy changes in all areas where physical violence is a problem; the federal government enact a child welfare act and establish a child welfare system by the year 2000; the federal government establish a mental-health policy for aboriginal peoples by the same year (Health and Welfare, 1990: 108–9); and that prevention, intervention, and follow-up policies and programs take into account the unique experiences and perspectives of the people they are meant to serve (RCAP, 1993a: 35). Other proposals include the establishment of comprehensive education programs in family violence, suicide, and criminal justice for leaders and other members of aboriginal communities, as well as professionals and lay practitioners working with aboriginal people in these areas (Health and Welfare, 1990: 108); cross-cultural education for non-native people in education and work-related areas; support for community-based alternatives to the formalized systems of justice, health care, family and child welfare, and economic development that incorporate customary law and traditional practices, and, where needed, facilitate healing and reconciliation (RCAP, 1993a: 35–63); implementation of social, educational, health, and justice-related services for aboriginal people living in urban areas (RCAP, 1993a: 3); and the creation of more positions for native people in the court and prison systems, to provide culturally-sensitive assistance and support to aboriginal people in those settings (Health and Welfare, 1990: 109). Finally, it is suggested that the federal and provincial governments address all outstanding land claims with integrity and as expeditiously as possible, and that the governments and courts of Canada work with aboriginal people to make self-government and self-sufficiency a reality across Canada (RCAP 1993a: 41).

Indeed, many argue that the conditions of life in aboriginal communities and lives cannot change in positive ways as long as native people lack control over their own lives, families, communities, and nations. Accordingly, they believe that only the implementation of aboriginal self-government and the restoration of native traditions will stop the cycles of violence and allow meaningful change and healing to begin. Yet for many the painful truth is that self-government, community-based control over health and other services, and traditional beliefs and practices do not, in themselves, ensure healing and growth (Yukon Task Force on Family Violence, 1985: 318). This is not to deny the significant changes that have resulted from countless community-level programs (Health and Welfare, 1990: 74). As community workers and mental-health practitioners note, however, countless aboriginal individuals and communities continue to experience violence even where programs are available. For example, traditional healing becomes next to impossible when people feel they have no choice but to leave their communities because of the violence they experience in them. Even if those who experience violence are willing to wait until support groups and programs are initiated in their communities, they still face the sobering reality that such initiatives do not ensure that the violence they experience will stop. Hence many political activists assert that nothing short of fundamental changes in the cultural and structural relations between natives and non-native people in Canada will bring healing.

The purpose of this study has been to provide a picture of violence and healing among aboriginal people in Canada. The statistical data on homicide, family violence, and suicide that have been examined show that these phenomena are in many respects a disproportionate part of aboriginal life in Canada. Numerous accounts of political violence, along with countless personal accounts and testimonies of aboriginal victims, offenders, and community health practitioners, augment the statistical reality of violence by providing a sense of the depth of human concern, suffering, and hope that are all part of aboriginal life in Canada. They remind us that behind the numbers are the emotional-filled experiences of real people. It is this understanding, of how and why others respond as they do to hopelessness, poverty, and constraint in their lives, that social scientists have the privilege to seek. If we fail to address these fundamental dimensions of social life we will invite the perpetuation of violence for people whose lives have for centuries been determined by the choices of other human beings.

NOTES

[1] This paper uses the term 'aboriginal' since it is consistent with section 35 of the Constitution Act, which stipulates that the 'Indian, Inuit and Métis' peoples comprise the aboriginal peoples of Canada. However, generalizations from the data included in this study should be made with caution, since most research focuses solely on either First Nations or Inuit populations. The reader should note when the discussion refers to these specific populations and when it refers to 'aboriginal or native people', which include Métis.

[2] In its 1969 *White Paper on Indian Policy* the federal government proposed 'an equality which preserves and enriches Indian identity and distinction; an equality which stresses Indian participation in its creation and which manifests itself in all aspects of Indian life.' The proposal was denounced by native people across Canada as aimed at divesting them of their aboriginal, residual, and statutory rights. In short, natives refused to accept this policy by which they would have become partners in cultural genocide.

[3] The nightmarish character of aboriginal experiences has been well captured in Kelly's (1987) *A Dream Like Mine*.

[4] As the work of Cornell (1988), Guillemin (1989), and Bachmann (1993) shows, the conditions of life in 'native America' parallel those of native people in Canada despite the slightly different historical path that native-state relations have taken in the US.

[5] In abolishing the discriminatory sections of the Indian Act, which had stripped any Indian woman of status upon marriage to a non-Indian, Bill C-31 reinstated all those who had lost their Indian status for financial, educational, or career reasons. It also made it impossible to gain or lose status through marriage.

[6] Statistics for Saskatoon are not available because of the different reporting practices used by police in that city. Indeed, Canada's Uniform Crime Report (UCR) data say relatively little about the relationship between race/ethnicity and violent crimes, largely because of the inconsistency of police recording practices.

[7] The statistics here are deceiving, however, for while excluding lovers, friends, and acquaintances from the 'kin relationship network' may be appropriate in the case of non-native suspect/victim relations, it is questionable whether the same is true of the extended relation networks of many aboriginal peoples.

[8] See DeKeseredy and Ellis's critique of MacLeod's research methodologies and findings in their chapter in this book.

[9] Presentation to the RCAP in Winnipeg on 10 March 1993.

[10] The response rate for the 680 questionnaires was approximately 15 per cent. In addition, 127 telephone and 40 personal interviews were conducted. Though the low response rate and lack of randomized sampling may lead some to question the findings of this study, the researchers expressed confidence in the reliability of the data.

[11] Given the findings of a number of provincial task forces on the incidence of family violence in aboriginal families and communities, the data from this national survey raise a number of important questions. Three of the more important are: (1) why is the incidence of family violence (at least 80%) reported in provincial task force and community-level surveys so high in comparison to the 40 per cent of respondents in the RCAP survey who believe that family violence is a problem?; (2) given the differences between the community-level, provincial, and national survey findings, how valid and generalizable are their data?; and (3) to what extent should the reality of family violence in aboriginal families be left open for question merely because survey data appear to differ?

[12] Assaults were coded as 'spousal assaults' only if the victim and the accused were living together at the time of the assault. This coding criterion, developed by Statistics Canada, ignores the fact that women often report being assaulted well after the relationship has formally ended.

[13] These figures can be deceiving, since the health services for which registered (status) Indians living on reserves are eligible are not as accessible to registered Indians living off reserves and not available at all to non-registered Indians or Métis people. This is significant when we consider that the combined Métis and non-status Indian populations comprised 42 per cent of Canada's native population in 1991.

[14] Neither of these theoretical perspectives, of course, attempts to explain the existence of similar problems among the non-native population.

REFERENCES

Abbott, Pamela and Claire Wallace (1990). *An Introduction to Sociology: Feminist Perspectives.* London: Routledge.

Adams, Howard (1989). *Prison of Grass: Canada from a Native Point of View,* rev. ed. Saskatoon: Fifth House Publishers.

Anawak, Caroline and Meryl Cook (1986). *Keewatin Suicide Prevention and Intervention Study.* Keewatin: Northwest Territories.

Appleford, Barbara (1989). *Family Violence Review: Prevention and Treatment of Abusive Behaviour.* Ottawa: Correctional Service Canada.

Auger, Donald J., Anthony Doob, Raymond P. Auger, and Paul Dribben (1992). 'Crime and control in three NishnawbeAski Nation communities: An exploratory investigation'. *Canadian Journal of Criminology* 3: 317–38.

Avio, K.L. and C.S. Clark (1976). *Property Crime in Canada: An Econometric Study.* Toronto: Economic Council.

Bachmann, Ronet (1993). *Death and Violence on the Reservation: Homicide, Family Violence, and Suicide in American Indian Populations.* New York: Auburn House.

Baffin Custodial Suicide Committee (1989). *Report of the Baffin Custodial Suicide Committee.*

Barnaby, Joanne (1992). 'Culture and sovereignty'. Pp. 39–44 in Diane Englestad and John Bird, eds. *Nation to Nation: Aboriginal Sovereignty and the Future of Canada.* Toronto: Anansi Press.

Berger, Justice Thomas R. (1977). *Northern Frontier: Northern Homeland, The Report of the Mackenzie Valley Pipeline Inquiry* Vol. 1. Ottawa: Supply and Services Canada.

Bobet, Ellen (1989). 'Indian mortality'. *Canadian Social Trends.* Ottawa: Statistics Canada: 11–14.

Boldt, Menno (1976). *Report of the Task Force on Suicides.* Edmonton: Minister of Social Services and Community Health.

——— (1981). 'Philosophy, politics and extralegal action: Native Indian leaders in Canada'. *Ethnic and Racial Studies* 4, 2: 205–22.

——— (1993). *Surviving as Indians: The Challenge of Self-Government.* Toronto: University of Toronto Press.

Boldt, Menno, and J. Anthony Long, eds (1985). *The Quest for Justice.* Toronto: University of Toronto, Press.

Brant, C.C., and J. Ann Brant, eds (1987). *Transcribed and Edited Proceedings of the Canadian Psychiatric Association Section on Native Mental Health.* London, Ontario.

Caputo, Tullio C. (1993). 'Crime, law, and social control'. Pp. 373–93 in Peter Li and B. Singh Bolaria, eds. *Contemporary Sociology: Critical Perspectives.* Toronto: Copp Clark Pitman Ltd.

Cardinal, Harold (1969). *The Unjust Society.* Edmonton: Hurtig.

Comeau, Pauline, and Aldo Santin (1990). *The First Canadians: A Profile of Native People Today.* Toronto: James Lorimer.

Cornell, Stephen (1988). *The Return of the Native: American Indian Political Resurgence.* New York: Oxford University Press.

Correctional Services Canada (Management Information Services) (1990). *Population Profile Report and Native Population Profile Report, Population on Register 30/06/89.* Ottawa: Supply and Services Canada.

Council for Yukon Indians (1992). 'Council for Yukon Indians family violence project'. *Transition* 4, 4.

Denham, Donna (1989). *Federal Government Consultation on Family Violence with National Non-Governmental Organizations.* Ottawa: Minister of Supply and Services.

Department of Health (Greater Northwest Territories) (1990). 'Report on Suicide in the Northwest Territories: 1978–1988'.

Department of Indian Affairs and Northern Development (DIAND) (1991). *Basic Departmental Data.* Ottawa: Minister of Supply and Services.

—— (1993). *Growth in Expenditures.* Ottawa: Minister of Supply and Services.

Department of Justice (1988). *Native Offenders' Perceptions of the Criminal Justice System.* Ottawa: Minister of Supply and Services.

Dickason, Olive Patricia (1993). *Canada's First Nations: A History of Founding Peoples from Earliest Times.* Toronto: McClelland and Stewart.

Dyck, Noel (1993). 'Telling it like it is: Some dilemmas of Fourth World ethnography and advocacy'. Pp. 192–212 in Noel Dyck and James B. Waldram, eds. *Anthropology, Public Policy and Native Peoples in Canada.* Montreal: McGill-Queen's University Press.

Englestad, Diane, and John Bird, eds (1992). *Nation to Nation: Aboriginal Sovereignty and the Future of Canada.* Toronto: Anansi Press.

Erasmus, George (1989). 'Concluding remarks'. In Boyce Richardson, ed. *Drum Beat: Anger and Renewal in Indian Country.* Toronto: Summerhill Press.

Fleras, Augie, and Jean Leonard Elliot (1992). *The Nations Within.* Toronto: Oxford University Press.

Frank, Sharlene (1993). *Family Violence in Aboriginal Communities: A First Nations Report.* Report to the Government of British Columbia.

Frideres, James S. (1988). *Native Peoples in Canada: Contemporary Conflicts.* 3rd ed. Scarborough: Prentice Hall Canada.

——— (1991). 'From the bottom up: Institutional structures and the Indian people'. Pp. 108–32 in B. Singh Bolaria, ed. *Social Issues and Contradictions in Canadian Society.* Toronto: Harcourt, Brace Jovanovich, Canada.

Gabriel, Ellen (1992). 'Kanesatake: The summer of 1990'. Pp. 165–72 in Englestad and Bird, eds (1992).

Government of Alberta (1991). *Alberta Task Force on Aboriginal People in the Criminal Justice System.* Edmonton: Queen's Printer.

Government of Canada (1969). *Statement on Indian Policy* (the White Paper). Ottawa: Supply and Services Canada.

Guillemin, Jeanne (1989). 'American Indian resistance and protest'. Pp. 153–72 in Ted Robert Gurr, ed. *Violence in America.* Vol. 2. New York: Sage.

Gurr, Ted Robert (1970). *Why Men Rebel.* Princeton, NJ: Princeton University Press.

Halfe, Louise (1993). 'Healing from a native perspective'. *Cognica* 26, 1: 7–10.

Hammersmith, Bernice (1992). 'Aboriginal women and self-government'. In Englestad and Bird, eds (1992).

Harper, Vern (1979). *Following the Red Path: The Native Peoples Caravan, 1974.* Toronto: NC Press.

Harris, M. (1986). *Justice Denied: The Law versus Donald Marshall.* Toronto: Macmillan.

Hartnagel, T., and G.W. Lee (1990). 'Urban crime in Canada'. *Canadian Journal of Criminology* 32 (October): 590–606.

Havemann, P., K. Couse, L. Foster, and R. Matonovich (1985). *Law and Order for Canada's Indigenous People.* Regina: Prairie Justice Research, School of Human Justice, University of Regina.

Hawthorne, Harry (1966). *A Survey of the Contemporary Indians of Canada: Economic, Political, Educational Needs and Policies.* 2 vols. Ottawa: Department of Indian Affairs.

Health and Welfare Canada (1987). *Suicide in Canada: Report of the National Task Force on Suicide in Canada.* Ottawa: Supply and Services Canada.

——— (1990). *Reaching for Solutions: Report of the Special Advisor to the Minister of National Health and Welfare on Child Sexual Abuse in Canada.* Ottawa: Supply and Services.

——— (Medical Services Branch) (1993). *Report on Intentional Deaths (Suicides) for Registered Indians in Canada: 1979–1991.* Edmonton.

Hughes, Ken (1991). *The Summer of 1991: Fifth Report of the Standing Committee on Aboriginal Affairs.* Ottawa: House of Commons Report.

Hunter, Robert, and Robert Callihoo (1991). *Occupied Canada.* Toronto: McClelland and Stewart.

Hutchinson, Bonnie (1988). *Breaking the Cycle of Violence: A Resource Handbook.* Ottawa: Correctional Service Canada.

Hylton, J.H. (1982). 'The native offender in Saskatchewan'. *Canadian Journal of Criminology* 24, 2: 121–31.

Indian Chiefs of Alberta (1970). *Citizens Plus.* Edmonton.

Indian and Inuit Nurses of Canada (1991). *National Family Violence Abuse Study/Evaluation.*

Jamieson, Wanda (1987). 'Aboriginal male violence against aboriginal women in Canada'. MA thesis, Department of Criminology, University of Ottawa.

Jarvis, George K., and Menno Boldt (1981). *Native Indian Mortality: A Prospective Study.* Edmonton: Department of Indian Affairs and Northern Development.

Jensen, Jane (1993). 'Naming nations: Making nationalist claims in Canadian public discourse'. *Canadian Review of Sociology and Anthropology* 30, 3: 337–58.

Kelly, M.T. (1987). *A Dream Like Mine.* Toronto: Stoddart.

Kennedy, Leslie W., David R. Forde, and Robert Silverman (1989). 'Understanding homicide trends: Issues in disaggregation for national and cross national comparisons'. *Canadian Journal of Sociology* 14: 479–86.

Laclau, Ernesto, and Chantal Mouffe (1985). *Hegemony and Socialist Strategy: Towards a Radical Democratic Politics.* London: Verso.

Land, K.D., and M. Felson (1976). 'A general framework for building dynamic macro social indicator models: Including an analysis of changes in crime rates and police expenditures'. *American Journal of Sociology* 82: 565–604.

LaPrairie, Carol P. (1990). 'The role of sentencing in Over-representation of aboriginal people in correctional institutions'. *Canadian Journal of Criminology* 32: 429–40.

Law Reform Commission of Canada (1991). *Aboriginal Peoples and Criminal Justice.* Ottawa: Supply and Services Canada.

Long, David (1992). 'Culture, ideology and militancy: The movements of native Indians in Canada, 1969–1992'. Pp. 118–34 in William B. Carroll, ed. *Organizing Dissent: Contemporary Social Movements in Theory and Practice.* Toronto: Garamond.

—— (1993). 'Oldness and newness in the movements of Canada's native peoples'. Unpublished manuscript, Department of Sociology, King's University College, Edmonton.

MacLeod, Linda (1980). *Wife Battering in Canada: The Vicious Circle.* Ottawa: Canadian Advisory Council for the Status of Women.

—— (1987). *Battered But Not Broken: Preventing Wife Battering in Canada.* Ottawa: National Health and Welfare.

Manuel, George, and Michael Posluns (1974). *The Fourth World: An Indian Reality.* Don Mills: Macmillan.

Marenin, Otwin (1992). 'Patterns of crime in Alaskan native villages'. *Canadian Journal of Criminology* 3: 339–68.

McKaskill, D. (1985). *Patterns of Criminality and Correction among Native Offenders in Manitoba: A Longitudinal Analysis.* Correctional Planning Branch, Solicitor General of Canada.

Minister of National Health and Welfare (1988). *National Task Force of Suicide.* Ottawa: Supply and Services Canada.

—— (1989). *Family Violence: A Review of Theoretical and Clinical Literature.* Ottawa: Supply and Services Canada.

Minore, B., M. Boone, M. Katt, and P. Kinch (1991). 'Looking in, looking out: Coping with adolescent suicide in the Cree and Ojibway communities of Northern Ontario'. *Canadian Journal of Native Studies* XI, 1: 1–24.

Moyer, Sharon (1992). 'Race, gender and homicide: Comparisons between aboriginals and other Canadians'. *Canadian Journal of Criminology* (July/October): 387–402.

Muir, Bernice (1991). *Health Status of Canadian Indians and Inuit, 1990.* Ottawa: National Health and Welfare.

Nechi Institute, Four Worlds Development Project, Native Training Institute & New Direction Training (1988). *Healing is Possible: A Joint Statement on the Healing of Sexual Abuse in Native Communities.* Alkalai Lake, British Columbia.

Northern Alberta Development Council (1988). *Family Violence in Northern Alberta.* Edmonton.

Ontario Native Women's Association (1989). *Breaking Free: A Proposal for Change to Family Violence.* Thunder Bay, Ontario.

Pauktuutit, Inuit Women's Association of Canada (1990). Newsletter *Suvaguuq* V, 1.

—— (1991). *Arnait: The Views of Inuit Women on Contemporary Issues.* Yellowknife.

x76   DAVID A. LONG

Peng, Ito (1989). 'Minobimadiziwin: An examination of aboriginal paradigm and its policy implications'. Unpublished manuscript, Department of Social Work, McMaster University.

Ponting, J. Rick, ed. (1986a). *Arduous Journey: Canadian Indians and Decolonization.* Toronto: Butterworths.

————— (1986b). 'Assessing a generation change'. Pp. 394–409 in Ponting, ed. (1986a).

Purich, Donald (1986). *Our Land: Native Rights in Canada.* Toronto: James Lorimer.

Report to the Government of the Northwest Territories (1986). *Choices: A Three Year Program to Address Family Violence in the Northwest Territories.* Yellowknife.

Rich, E.E. (1991). 'Trade habits and economic motivation among the Indians of North America'. Pp. 158–79 in J.R. Miller, ed. *Sweet Promises: A Reader in Indian-White Relations in Canada.* Toronto: University of Toronto Press.

Royal Commission on Aboriginal Peoples (RCAP) (1993a). *Public Hearings: Overview of the Second Round.* Ottawa: Minister of Supply and Services.

————— (1993b). *Public Hearings: Focussing the Dialogue.* Ottawa: Minister of Supply and Services.

Silman, Janet (1987). *Enough is Enough: Aboriginal Women Speak Out.* Toronto: Women's Press.

Statistics Canada (1989). *Vital Statistics Volume IV: Causes of Death.* Catalogue 84–203.

————— (1990). *Health Reports.* Catalogue 82–003, 2, 4, 332.

————— (1991a). *Aboriginal Peoples Survey: Language, Tradition, Health, Lifestyle and Social Issues.* Catalogue No. 89–533. Ottawa: Minister of Industry, Science and Technology.

————— (1991b). *Uniform Crime Reporting Survey, 1990.* Ottawa: Canadian Centre for Justice Statistics.

————— (1991c). *Homicide in Canada.* Catalogue 85–204. Ottawa: Minister of Supply and Services.

Strachan, Jill, Helen Johansen, Cyril Nair, and Mubund Nargundkar (1992). 'Canadian suicide mortality rates: First generation immigrants versus Canadian born'. *Health Reports.* Catalogue 82–003S11, Supp. 12: 327–41.

Supernault, Esther (1993). *A Family Affair.* Edmonton: Native Counselling Services of Alberta.

Task Force on Aboriginal Peoples in Federal Corrections (1989). *Final Report*. Ottawa: Minister of Supply and Services.

Taylor, John Leonard (1991). 'Canada's northwest Indian policy in the 1870s: Traditional promises and necessary innovations'. Pp. 207–11 in J.R. Miller, ed. *Sweet Promises: A Reader in Indian-White Relations in Canada*. Toronto: University of Toronto Press.

Thompson, Loran (1992). 'Fighting back'. Pp. 173–8 in Englestad and Bird, eds (1992).

Torrance, Judy (1977). 'The response of Canadian governments to violence'. *Canadian Journal of Political Science* 10: 473–96.

Touraine, Alain (1981). *The Voice and the Eye: An Analysis of Social Movements*. Translated by Alan Duff. Cambridge: Cambridge University Press.

Trevethan, Shelley (1993). 'Police reported aboriginal crime in Calgary, Regina and Saskatoon'. Ottawa: Canadian Centre for Justice Statistics.

Weaver, Sally (1981). *Making Canadian Indian Policy*, Toronto: University of Toronto Press.

Westcott, David, Sharon Freitag, and Luis Barreto (1987). *Review of Mortality Due to Suicide in the Northwest Territories, 1975–1986*. Yellowknife: Government of the Northwest Territories.

Yalden, Maxwell (1989). *Annual Report of the Canadian Human Rights Commission*. Ottawa: Supply and Services Canada.

York, Geoffrey (1989). *The Dispossessed: Life and Death in Native Canada*. London: Vintage Press.

York, Geoffrey, and Loreen Pindera (1992). *The People of the Pines*. Toronto: Little, Brown.

Yukon Task Force on Family Violence (1985). *Report of the Task Force on Family Violence*. Whitehorse.

Chapter Three

WORKER INSURGENCY AND SOCIAL CONTROL

Violence By and Against Labour in Canada

KENNETH D. TUNNELL

Men make their own history, but not of their own free will; not under circumstances they themselves have chosen but under given and inherited circumstances with which they are directly confronted.

Marx (1852: 146)

This chapter describes violence both by and against labour in Canada, particularly since 1960. Although violence takes various forms, the primary focus here is on 'public violence' (Torrance, 1986). Public violence is conducted for a greater purpose than private violence—violence typically used to settle interpersonal conflicts. Violence that occurs when individuals act on behalf of a group—for example, when individual workers act on behalf of a union, an entire labour movement, or the working class as a whole—is a form of public violence. Likewise, public violence occurs when corporate or state agents act on behalf of a corporation, an industry, or capitalism as a socio-economic way of life. Furthermore, the etiology of public violence is located in dominant social arrangements characterized by motivated behaviour aimed at rectifying perceived injustices, altering social conditions, or maintaining social order (Torrance, 1986: 15). Individuals who engage in public violence typically consider themselves victims and are often perceived by others as rebels with a cause. Victims typically are members of a recognized group (e.g., unions, police, industrialists).

Torrance's concept of public violence illustrates politics-in-action: less-powerful individuals act to alter existing social relations while those with power act to maintain and preserve such relations. Violence, Torrance (1986: 11) argues, 'both by and against governments can play a part in normal political relations'. Thus labour collectives, engaging in political protests, work stoppages, and picketing have sometimes engaged in political violence, although most commonly (in the latter part of the twentieth century) for instrumental rather than expressive objectives. Nonetheless, because of differential power relations, labour collectives often have little choice but to participate in activities beyond widely accepted political arenas and to engage in demonstrations, strikes, etc., that may result in violence initiated by workers seeking change, industry seeking to subjugate workers, or the state seeking to maintain order and the differential power relations from which such violence emanates.

Such politics-in-action, union organizing, strike activity, and public violence by and against labour in Canada have received little attention from academics. Both Jamieson (1968) and Abella (1974) refer to the near-absence of attention to these issues as the 'conspiracy of silence'. By ignoring such issues, the subtle implication is that Canada's labour history is a peaceful, non-violent one, markedly different from that of the United States—one characterized by violence, bloodshed, and near-anarchy (Taft and Ross, 1979). In fact, however, the Canadian experience has been little different from the American. The first fifty years of the twentieth century were especially important, for they marked the real 'take-off' period for organized labour in Canada. The politico-legal system favoured employers, and clashes with both state and privately hired police forces were common. The process was costly for business, which lost profits as well as property, but above all it was working-class men and women who suffered as, time and again, the state sided with capital and did whatever it deemed necessary to contain the 'threat' that labour posed to law, order, and continued capital accumulation. Having fought (both violently and non-violently) for the right to unionize and bargain collectively for wages, working hours and conditions, and job security, Canadian workers eventually won the right to form trade unions in 1948 (later than US workers). During these early unionization efforts, labour-initiated violence often occurred as workers struggled to gain legitimacy in the political arena (Grant and Wallace, 1991). Such legitimacy, however, has assured them full-fledged membership: they remained a 'weak-insider' group. As a result, primarily as a reaction to the sociopolitical context of their struggles and their interactions with the state, labour has at various times engaged in violence (Grant and Wallace, 1991: 1126).

During the key strikes of the first half of the twentieth century, the state relied on the Royal Canadian Mounted Police (RCMP) (e.g., in Winnipeg and Estevan) as well as municipal and provincial police forces in Windsor and Regina (Abella, 1974). Furthermore, government policies and legislation sided with employers, leaving workers who attempted to organize to not only engage in conflict with the employer but with a politico-legal system that was far from neutral.

Research on labour struggles from 1958 to 1967, after workers won the right to unionize, indicates that labour violence most often was a defensive measure as workers, now legitimate players in politico-economic conflict, came under attack from industry, its privately-hired police, and public police forces. Violence often resulted from labour's disadvantaged position in relation to its employers' power (e.g., economic might, political clout, legal protections) (Grant and Wallace, 1991).

The remainder of this chapter describes various confrontations between labour, capital, and the state. To this end, a sample of post-1960 cases will serve to illustrate typical examples of violent behaviour by labour, capital's representatives, and state managers. These cases of work-related violence are by no means exhaustive but are used here for their typicality. Other cases perhaps could have been selected, but the central lesson would have remained the same. By using these specific vignettes, I show the public nature of the violence, while describing the relative power of labour, capital, and the state, and show that such differential power relations contribute to violence both by and against labour. First, however, a brief history of Canadian labour unrest is essential to situate more recent occurrences within their historical context.

EARLY CANADIAN LABOUR UNREST

The Lachine strikes of 1843 are classic examples of labour violence originating in conflict between employer and employee. At the same time they illustrate how such actions can self-destruct when workers themselves are divided. The Lachine canal originally was a public-works project. The labourers, most of them Irish, were paid in cash. Soon, however, the state retained a private contractor to build the canal, who then paid the workers less than the state had guaranteed. Meanwhile, word spread to the US that the Canadian employer planned to work during the winter, and Irish workers there, whose livelihoods were in jeopardy because of an economic depression, flocked to Lachine, flooding the market with an excessive number of labourers clamouring for the few jobs available. When the workers received their first pay, which was not only less than they had expected but in the form of credit which was valid only at company-owned businesses, they struck and seemed, for a time, unified. However, old antagonisms among Irish workers (Corkmen and Connaughtmen) re-emerged and came to a head as they took up arms against each other. The military was called in to confiscate weapons and maintain peace. The workers returned to work with the guarantee that wages would soon increase to the old state-rate. As the date of the promised increases approached, however, the private employer began systematically laying off labourers. The workers, in turn, struck a second time and on this occasion with wide support among the local citizens. The employer, further dividing workers, replaced the striking Irish workers with French Canadians. The Irish workers took up arms, clubs, and whatever could be used as weapons and forcibly drove the Québécois from the area (Pentland, 1948). Although little resistance was offered, this is an example of an early working-class movement that relied on violence as a means of settling public disputes. Not only did the workers suffer economic 'violence' as their private employer cut pay and paid in credit, but the state used the threat of force, which is in itself a form of violence. Workers engaged in public violence as the Irish used force to rid themselves of the threat that the French-Canadian workers posed to their jobs, economic security, and livelihoods. Each of these actions, both by and against labour, is an example of public violence—violence committed for a public objective.

Canadian labour history is rife with cases where working-class interests were thwarted due to ethnic, racial, religious, and gender differences. Often ideological differences contributed to strikes as well as working-class divisions (Jamieson, 1973). The Lachine strike is but one in a long series of events that ultimately gave rise to unionization efforts beginning in the 1850s and was encouraged by rapid unionization progress in Britain and the US (Jamieson, 1973). By the 1860s the workers' movement had taken on a national and international character, and the 1870s witnessed the first Canadian labour movement that coalesced around the nine-hour work day and garnered much public and political sympathy (Pentland, 1948).

In the early part of this century, strikes occurred most often in the construction industry; however, most were brief with few workers participating. Strikes were, however, violent including such actions as riots and mob violence, property damage, injuries and deaths, the imposition of marital law, and military intervention. Strikes involving coal miners typically were the most violent.

Although Canada has witnessed its fair share of labour unrest and violence (Jamieson, 1973), most instances have been regionally contained; national labour unrest has been rare. But there have been exceptions: the Winnipeg general strike of May and June 1919 was one (Bercuson, 1974a; 1974b); another was the national strike by the Public Service Alliance of Canada in 1991 (discussed below) (Wilson-Smith, 1991). At Winnipeg, with public-sector workers violating strike laws and joining in the general strike, and with increasing loyalty to the One Big Union,[1] industry and state managers organized special makeshift police forces (Bercuson, 1974b). Public-sector police were ordered back to work; when they refused, they immediately were fired and replaced by untrained, trigger-happy special forces (Bercuson, 1974a). Soon Mounties, the militia, and civilian special forces—a total of 800 troops— began policing Winnipeg. On 21 June troops attacked protesting strikers, injuring several of them. Immediately afterwards the strike was ended, with the workers gaining none of their demands (Bercuson, 1974a; 1974b). Repeatedly across Canada, as workers sought collective bargaining rights, increased wages, improved working conditions—for example, in Estevan, Stratford, Oshawa, Windsor, Quebec—they were met with the force of the state as it overtly sided with capital (Abella, 1974). Winnipeg, as did other strikes, illustrated the public violence of such actions; workers refused to work—no doubt action that can be interpreted as a violent affront to business, further capital accumulation, and state revenue. Likewisè, the state engaged in public violence by hiring strike-breakers as police officers who ultimately attacked the workers. The issues at hand were public and the violence resulting from their disagreements also was public.[2]

Perhaps the greatest show of worker solidarity was the now-famous On-to-Ottawa trek in 1935. After months of struggle in British Columbia between workers, capitalists, and state managers over the miserable conditions of the relief camps, the workers struck and occupied the Hudson's Bay Company store in Vancouver. Nearly everyone, regardless of political ideology, sympathized with the occupants of relief camps, recognizing the camps' deplorable and inhuman conditions. Nevertheless, the Department of National Defence forbade any organization of collective representation whatsoever (Liversedge, 1973). Vancouver's mayor and business leaders attempted to isolate the workers by denouncing their organization as communist and revolutionary. The RCMP was called out on more than one occasion when large public rallies were held, but no violence occurred. The striking workers, unable to break the stalemate, decided to take their cause to the people of the country by riding the railroad to Ottawa. On 1 June about one thousand unemployed workers jumped a freight train with the railroad's blessing and to the relief of Vancouver's Mayor. Officials and business leaders assumed the On-to-Ottawa trek would soon fizzle out but were proven wrong (Brown, 1987).

News quickly spread across the country as the striking trekkers held rallies at various stop-over points. Encouraged by the public support, the strikers continued on eastward across the country. Authorities reported no misdeeds, violence, or law-breaking by the strike participants. However, seeking help from city officials along the way, they occupied Calgary's Relief Office and held a few authorities hostage for three hours until assistance was granted. These tactics alarmed city and criminal justice officials east of Calgary. Hundreds more joined the trek as it left Calgary on 10 June and the prevailing belief was the numbers would reach into the thousands by the time it reached Ottawa. The next day, fearing that hundreds more would join in solidarity when it reached Winnipeg, the federal government initiated plans to stop the trek at Regina. Thus the groundwork was laid for a violent confrontation (Howard, 1985).

Orders were given to arrest the Trek's leaders and speculation spread across the country that perhaps hundreds ultimately would be arrested. The police and the RCMP, wielding small baseball bats previously issued by corporate and state managers, descended on a mass meeting of strikers and sympathizers. Witnesses reported afterwards that the police, using their bats, had indiscriminately clubbed and beat whomever crossed their paths. To prevent further attacks, the strikers overturned cars to block the path of the police and took up rocks and debris to throw at them. The police fired, wounding several. The fighting, which lasted for two hours, marked the end of the conflict; the protestors took refuge in a stadium and were provided transport home on 5 July, thus halting a national campaign to raise consciousness about the conditions of relief camps and to further solidify working-class men and women across the country (Brown, 1987). During the riot, over 100 strikers were arrested and eight ultimately were convicted and sentenced to prison for up to 15 months.

This struggle is particularly relevant for understanding contemporary labour issues because of its national character and its ability to garner enormous public support, sympathy, and political and material changes for working-class men and women. Furthermore, this strike illustrates the near powerlessness of workers even in circumstances of unusual solidarity among themselves and public support for them. The strike easily was quashed by the force of the state; strikers were physically attacked and subjected to the wrath of the criminal justice system. Again, public violence was used to settle an ongoing public debate.

In 1937, in Sarnia, Ontario, employees at the Holmes Factory, toiling under miserable, sweat-shop-like conditions, attempted to form a union for collective bargaining with management over wages and working conditions. When a union was formed, management refused to recognize it or negotiate with the employees as a collectivity. The workers used a tactic that had worked well in the United States: a sit-down strike in which they occupied the plant with the objective of stopping production. As was typical for that time, the workers were immediately met with physical aggression and violence.

> The small group of sit-downers was beaten and driven from the Holmes plant by an enraged armed mob of local Anglo-Saxon citizens, encouraged by the plant management and assisted by the law enforcement bodies. The strike was an ugly incident that was conditioned not solely by anti-unionism but also by the exploitation of racial tensions. (Snow, 1977: 3)

A riot ensued and resulted in the hospitalization of twenty strikers for serious injuries. All the strikers were fired and some convicted of trespassing. Pertinent to this case, as was the situation during the Lachine strikes, the working class was once again at odds with itself, divided over easily recognizable differences among them—race, ethnicity, religion, and gender—which disallowed cohesive working-class solidarity regarding issues that have as their common denominator social class. Furthermore, we learn that the industrialists again relied on law enforcement using their legitimate power and authority to crush the workers' resistance and defiance.

The struggle for union representation took place outside legitimate political arenas: these battles were waged and won in factories, relief camps, shanty towns, soup kitchens, the streets, mines, and police stations and courts across the country. The individuals who initiated such social change (e.g., worker representation, unemployment compensation, and decent housing) had little access to legitimate political circles and were left to their own devices. Thus they struck out at their common enemies: their employers and the agents of social control, including the state and the criminal justice system (Brown, 1987).[3]

RECENT CANADIAN LABOUR VIOLENCE

Since the mid-twentieth century, labour unrest has perhaps occurred less frequently in Canada, but it has remained tumultuous, violent, disruptive, and consequential for workers, social institutions, and the dominant social order. Violence by and against labour remains a fundamental ingredient of strikes, collective bargaining, challenges to immanent socio-economic changes, and changes in the very nature of work. Both private and public employees have challenged industry and government over such diverse issues as wages, benefits, job security, contracting services and manufacturing out to non-union, lower-paid workers, free-trade agreements, and structural changes pertinent to work including lay-offs through attrition, task consolidation, and work environment changes. Although governmental response to such challenges has oscillated, since the mid-1980s increasingly conservative policies and agendas have been imposed on workers, further limiting their collective power and material gains—arguably a subtle yet gravely consequential form of economic violence against labour. But, during the 1960s, labour unrest was particularly violent and usually was accompanied by military or police intervention, repression, arrests and criminal convictions (a state strategy to apply criminal sanctions to individuals engaged in political misdeeds, e.g., Turk, 1982).

In the early 1960s, bitter and violent strikes occurred most often in low-wage occupations. For example, in 1960 a violent strike erupted at the Hormel meat-packing plant in Brandon, Manitoba. The striking workers engaged in a variety of tactics, some violent, some merely strategic; mass picketing, threatening non-union workers, obstructing roads, and damaging property were common. However, as the Royal Commission of Inquiry found, the company had precipitated an already violent situation by illegally presenting 'false and misleading information' to the union during collective bargaining which no doubt contributed to the long and protracted violent strike (Jamieson, 1968: 407).

In Toronto, the residential construction industry was the setting for much labour unrest, strikes, and violent confrontations. Strikes that included thousands of workers primarily, at that time, were measures for organizing the unorganized. Work stoppages were common. During such activities, pickets were established around non-union work sites, and violent confrontations, including fist fights, violent destruction of property, and violent threats between union and non-union workers, were commonplace. Typically, union members were arrested and prosecuted for their activities (Jamieson, 1968), yet another indication of the relative powerlessness that organized labour had and the power, in the form of state force and administration, available to capital.

Perhaps the most violent and widely publicized strike of the early 1960s involved the Seafarers' International Union (SIU). The SIU battled with the newly created Canadian Maritime Union (CMU). There were numerous physical confrontations that often were violent between the two competing organizations. For example, some ships that docked in the United States were shot at and bombed and the crew members beaten by sympathetic US union members. Thus, a violent Canadian labour dispute, involving power struggles over organizations, became a transnational violent confrontation, as workers in the US participated in violent support for the union.

The 1963 pulpwood cutters' strike in Ontario marked the first time in three decades that a labour dispute resulted in deaths by gunfire (Jamieson, 1968). The action reached its climax in February when striking workers planned a raid on the Val Rita Cooperative, a non-union organization that had encouraged stockpiling logs for further shipment. When about 400 strikers arrived at the camp they were met by police. As they rushed past and attempted to disrupt the stockpiling, the non-union Val Rita workers emerged and fired guns randomly into the crowd. Two strikers were killed instantly, a third died later, and several others were wounded. The police disarmed the non-union assailants and charged 20 with non-capital murder. In a blatant example of state support for the non-union side, the murder charges were later dropped but 223 strikers were convicted of 'unlawful assembly'. The strike was settled soon afterwards (Jamieson, 1968: 414).

The Teamsters' Union consistently has been active in union organizing and strike activities. The Ontario strike of 1966 included 8,500 workers, lasted 14 weeks, and witnessed sporadic acts of violence including gun shots fired at non-union truckers, physical clashes with the police, damage to trucks and trailers, and various assaults (Jamieson, 1968). Such violence was often initiated by strikers, non-union workers, agents of capital, and state forces, most commonly the police. As the Teamsters began organizing the unorganized and working toward improvements in wages and working conditions, they were met with typical forms of repression, both covert and overt forms of violence. Union workers, likewise, often precipitated violent actions against employers, their property, and non-union workers and their property.

Other strikes in the mid- to late 1960s involving violence by and against labour included those by the International Nickel Company employees of Ontario, the Steel Company of Canada employees in Ontario, and the Longshoremen's Union of the St Lawrence. Each had similar precipitating events, quality and quantity of violent confrontations, and outcomes (e.g., Jamieson, 1968).

During the late 1960s in Quebec, several prolonged strikes resulted in shutdowns, violence, damage to property, police intervention, arrests, injuries, and a few deaths. Labour historians report this period's unrest:

> Among such disputes were a strike against Domtar in 1969, in which two kraft paper plants were seized and occupied by armed strikers; a series of construction workers' strikes in several areas in the province that, according to one official account, featured bombings, goon squads and inter-union quarrelling; a prolonged strike of postal truck drivers in Montreal in the course of which it was reported that numerous trucks were sabotaged and strike breakers attacked and threatened with knives, axes, and crowbars. (Jamieson, 1973: 98)

Thus, history shows that violent confrontations involving labour represent ongoing conflicts that labour at times initiated while at other times reacted to when government and private police forces were allowed to use repressive control tactics.

In 1971, a strike involving Canada's most widely read French-language newspaper, La Presse, led to violent clashes with police that culminated in hundreds of injuries and one death. The next year, in Quebec, over 200,000 public employees struck. The strike leaders were arrested and sentenced to a year in jail for ignoring court orders to return to work. In response, workers across the province joined in a general solidarity strike that resulted in mass violence, property damage, plant seizures, and, ultimately, the use of the state force in the form of police repression to end the strike and return some order to society (Jamieson, 1973).

The postal workers' and mail carriers' strike of 1965 was perceived as especially threatening to legitimate order, for a disruption of mail delivery, some argued, could cripple the country. The strike certainly had far-reaching implications for Canada and industrial relations. As a result, and indicative of the strike's impact, the government responded with threats, misinformation, and false promises—clearly not overt violence, but nonetheless state misdeeds. The striking workers returned to their jobs (Jamieson, 1968). However, postal workers' resolve has not diminished and they continue engaging in working-class solidarity movements.

Public postal employees have struck twelve times since 1965. Although postal labour problems date back decades, they were compounded in the late 1960s when the post office proceeded with plans to mechanize its operations—not an undesirable move in itself, but one that had negative consequences for workers. As changes in work settings were implemented, workers found themselves spending the better part of their waking hours in environments that, according to critics, were

> designed by engineers who had a malicious outlook on human nature. They are horrible places to work. The big plants were the worst thing they could have done. Everybody admits that now, but the plants are still there, the machines are still there, and the bad feelings are still there. (*Maclean's*, 1987: 12)

Workers became increasingly militant. There seemingly was little government continuity and decisions about postal operations and workers' issues were scattered across a variety of government departments including 13 different ministers since 1968. As labour situations worsened, major strikes erupted seven times between 1965 and 1981. In 1978 then Prime Minister Trudeau ordered that the post office (at that time a fully public-sector enterprise) be converted into a Crown corporation and emulate the practices of the private sector, with the objective of increasing efficiency (*Maclean's*, 1987). Canada Post, born three years later, began an intensive recruiting campaign for hard-hitting managers who would streamline the postal service and treat its employees as workers are treated in the private sector.

In June 1987, the 20,000-member Letter Carriers' Union of Canada (LCUC) ordered a series of rotating strikes across the country in response to Canada Post's demands for major concessions on issues such as job security and working conditions. Although reluctant to actually strike, workers believed that they were forced to take such drastic action by management's confrontational demands. Canada Post quickly hired replacement workers to take the jobs. Violence resulted as strikers fought replacement workers and as riot police battled strikers, making dozens of arrests. In Montreal, 1,000 letter carriers circled the post office, disrupting traffic and mail flow, while others invaded and then vandalized the post office. Shortly afterwards, letter carriers in Toronto, where half of Canada's mail is sorted, joined the strike. Although workers returned to work after 19 days without a renewed contract, each side clearly had different agendas—the workers to gain a new contract with wage increases and Canada Post to wrest concessions, such as job security and working conditions, from workers. In this dispute, the letter carriers were unable to garner public support and the business community vehemently criticized them for their unwillingness to accede to Canada Post's demands. The President of the Canadian Federation of Independent Business publicly commented, 'Why should they be mollycoddled when everybody else has had to take cuts?' (Gee, 1987: 11)—except corporate heads and state managers. The letter carriers claimed that at the heart of the dispute was Canada Post's five-year plan to eradicate its deficit by eliminating more than 10 per cent of the jobs, close hundreds of rural post offices, gain concessions from the larger Canadian Union of Postal Workers (CUPW), eliminate the no-layoff guarantee, contract some services to non-union labour, and increasingly rely on temporary workers (Gee, 1987). In the end, the letter carriers accepted a 31-month contract with wage increases of three per cent annually.

Just four months later, in October 1987, the CUPW went on strike. This time, however, Canada Post had initiated some preemptive strategies designed to allow business to operate as usual. For example, it hired hundreds of replacement workers and put in place elaborate security systems for their safety. Security guards were hired, chain-link fences were erected around mail-sorting plants, helicopter pads were constructed for flying mail in and out, and fleets of buses were rented for transporting the replacement workers across picket lines. Although mail service was disrupted in several centres (St John's, Halifax, Montreal, Ottawa, Hamilton, Edmonton, and Victoria), the strike was fairly calm and uneventful. As in the June strike, workers found themselves with little public support and were forced to negotiate with a new breed of conservative business-minded managers who were determined to force concessions from them (*Maclean's*, 1987).

In the private sector, employees have engaged in various strikes across Canada. Canadian members of the United Steelworkers of America in Ontario and Alberta voted by an unprecedented margin of 95 per cent to walk off their jobs after negotiations broke down. They, much like public-sector employees, struck over wages and over corporate practices of contracting work out to non-union lower-paid workers. Thus, they not only struck for their own immediate material conditions, but for long-term job security and continued work. Strike-related violence typically took the form of skirmishes between strikers and replacement workers attempting to cross picket lines and police officers monitoring the situation. In addition, both corporate and strikers' property was damaged.

Employees at Pacific Western Airlines (PWA) struck in early 1986 for similar reasons. Although PWA had seen a profit of $18.7 million in

1984 (a 14.3 per cent return on investment over five years), in order to cut costs it demanded increased productivity from its workers. Furthermore, among the 200 concessions PWA asked of its employees, it wanted to hire increasing numbers of part-time workers and demanded longer working days and lower salaries for new employees. As strikers walked the picket line, PWA hired 600 replacement workers who were paid less than the unionized workers had earned. Violence erupted as individuals tried crossing the line and as strikers distributed literature to the public warning them of the inexperienced workers in whose hands they were placing their lives (Nikiforuk, 1986). Again, this is an example of workers violently confronting other workers over scarce resources—jobs.

In recent years miners' strikes have centred on similar issues, but they have involved much more violence than either other Canadian labour strikes or miners' strikes in the United States. In January 1992, contract negotiations between Royal Oak Mines, Inc. and the Canadian Association of Smelter and Allied Workers (CASAW) quickly disintegrated. CASAW had demanded better pension benefits, improved working conditions and wage increases, but the company, claiming declining gold prices, refused and demanded that workers accept their offers. On 23 May 1992, the 240 union workers at the Yellowknife mine struck and violence erupted immediately. The mine's general manager and family were evacuated from their home after receiving a bomb threat; miners allegedly confronted and threatened a manager's son; power lines were mysteriously severed; a bomb blast damaged a satellite dish at the mine; and another bomb exploded inside one of the mine's buildings. Royal Oak immediately brought in 150 replacement workers who were attacked by striking miners on the picket line. Strikers, replacement workers, and management engaged in rock fights; union members attacked a busload of replacement workers; and an RCMP officer was attacked with a baseball bat while other officers fired warning shots into the air. Finally, on 18 September a bomb blast inside the mine killed nine replacement workers, six of whom were local men. The violence spread into the community as residents supporting the strikebreakers assumed the union miners were responsible for the deaths. Fights broke out between union members and locals; a beer bottle was thrown through the union hall's window, injuring two women; some union members received death threats; the union strike headquarters was vandalized; and a week later the RCMP announced that they were treating the miners' deaths as homicides (Kopvillem, 1992). One man, a member of the union, was charged.

A recent Canadian strike that perhaps had the least public support was the Ontario medical doctors' strike of 1986[4]—the first since 1962, when doctors in Saskatchewan refused to render medical services to protest the enactment of medicare. The primary issue in the 1986 strike was legislative limits placed on what doctors can charge their patients ('extra billing'). The Ontario Medical Association (OMA) called on its members to shut down their offices. They initially agreed to continue providing emergency services. However, a few days into the strike, emergency rooms were without doctors (Gee, 1986). Doctors saw the fundamental strike issue as not money itself but governmental control of their private freedom to charge what they wanted.

As the strike wore on, the potential for social harm—non-criminal yet socially injurious behaviour—became obvious. Doctors' offices were closed, emergency rooms did not function, and services were denied to patients in need. Soon, however, violence took a more traditional form. In Toronto, 700 militant doctors stormed the legislature, clashed with security guards, and fought their way through barricades to gain entry. The public was clearly behind the government, although the doctors had the support of the Conservative members of Parliament evidenced by Tory Richard Treleaven maintaining a filibuster for five early morning hours to a near-empty chamber (Aikenhead, 1986).

In 1991, a strike by the widely recognized and self-proclaimed pacifist Public Service Alliance of Canada (PSAC), representing 155,000 employees—the majority of federal civil servants—shut down governmental services and caused general chaos across the country. The central concerns in this, Canada's first national pubic-sector strike, were threats of wage freezes and threats to job security. For two days, service at Toronto's airport was disrupted by skirmishes between PSAC and non-striking workers who tried to cross picket lines. Traffic was delayed at harbours as well, waterways were closed, and border crossings were jammed. Industrial production reeled. As a result, the business community (e.g., the Canadian Manufacturers' Association) condemned the strike and demanded that authorities immediately legislate back-to-work orders. The government swiftly announced that it would request that Parliament order workers back to work and extend contracts with no wage increases. Although many were irritated and inconvenienced, Canadians generally supported the strikers' demands for a wage increase (Wilson-Smith, 1991; Allen, 1991). The union, believing the government planned to eliminate many jobs, pointed out that increasing numbers of part-time temporary workers were being used, that 13,000 workers had been displaced since Prime Minister Mulroney had taken office, and that 2,000 had lost their jobs permanently. Just one day before the government was to table its back-to-work order, workers entered a new contract with wage increases and improved job security, and the strike ended (Allen, 1991).

These cases of strikes and the roles of labour, industry and its police, the state and its police, especially since 1960, indicate that violence by and against labour is central to Canadian labour conflicts just as it was at the turn of the century. Indeed, violence in resolving labour struggles is apparently a fundamental component. For labour, though, violence usually is not a central ingredient by design, but is often the by-product of ongoing struggles, especially when union workers' jobs are threatened, when they are locked out of their places of work, and when non-union workers are hired to replace them. For industry, while perhaps undesirable, violence has often been initiated to maintain production schedules, minimize production costs, and minimize company losses. The state has also been the initiator of violence as the police—guardians of order—often are those individuals who contribute to violence by simply their presence, posture, resolve to maintain order by force, and their socialization into and dependency on tactical force to contain insurrection (Marx, 1972; Ross, 1992).

Workers undoubtedly have participated in violent acts during their struggles for pecuniary and non-violent objectives. Capital has resisted workers' advances, for labour victories are considered losses for capital. When costs to capital are defined as extreme, the state, its managers, and repressive forces are used to contain threats toward a system that is dependent on further capital accumulation and is, by design, unequal. As a result of such obvious taking of sides, questions arise about the state's neutrality and legitimacy. Recent attention to injurious behaviour resulting from the inter-dependent relationship between corporate and state powers has re-directed our inquiries and given rise to a new concept, state-corporate crime, that is pertinent to this discussion of violence by and against workers in Canada. This concept and its application to the Canadian experience are described below.

STATE-CORPORATE VIOLENCE AGAINST LABOUR

In recent years a growing body of literature has examined state-corporate crime, a broadly constructed concept referring to (1) criminal actions of the state in tandem with corporate institutions, (2) regulatory violations of the state and corporations, and (3) moral transgressions by the state in conjunction with corporate institutions (e.g., Kramer, 1990; Kramer, 1992; Aulette and Michalowski, 1993). Some of these state-corporate actions are criminal and others are not; the fundamental component is the social harm produced by such powerful institutions as they seek increased capital accumulation without due regard for human life, safety, and health. State-corporate crime has been defined as

> illegal or socially injurious actions that result from a mutually
> reinforcing interaction between (1) policies and/or practices in
> pursuit of the goals of one or more institutions of political

governance and (2) policies and/or practices in pursuit of the goals of one or more institutions of economic production and distribution. (Aulette and Michalowski, 1993: 175)

State-corporate transgressions, on the other hand, occur when the state and its agencies working in conjunction with capitalist producers either commit actions that result in social harm or fail to act in ways to prevent socially injurious actions. The state's complicitous role in such transgressions is especially pertinent as we consider acts of public violence against workers—acts that while not criminal, nonetheless are harmful and avoidable.

First applied to the explosion of the US space shuttle *Challenger*, the concept is used here to refer to state actions that are both violent and socially harmful, yet not necessarily criminal. Technically, the space shuttle's explosion resulted from faulty seals; however, the broader causes include the 'hurry up' agenda of NASA and the management of Morton Thiokol, the seal's private producer. The fatal consequences were the result of both private producers and state managers whose concern for production, schedules, and a financially self-sufficient space-shuttle program overshadowed their concerns for human life (Kramer, 1992). The direct victims in this case of violence were workers, no doubt highly-paid professional individuals, but nonetheless, labourers who died on the job as result of state-corporate transgressions.

In September 1991, another act of state-corporate violence that directly victimized workers occurred in the United States—the Imperial chicken processing plant fire in Hamlet, North Carolina. From both corporate acts and state omission, 25 workers died at their place of work (Aulette and Michalowski, 1993). From these and other cases of state-corporate transgressions, we learn that capital and states engage in mutually beneficial actions that often bring death, disease, and various horrors to workers—individual citizens and employees who suffer the consequences of these oft dysfunctional organizations.

Canadian workers are confronted with such state-corporate transgression in the form of subtle, institutionalized, public violence that typically escapes debate—their work. Work-related deaths, injuries, and occupationally-related diseases have been on the rise in Canada in recent years. For example, between 1969 and 1978 there was a 35 per cent increase in work-related injuries and 69 per cent increase in disabling injuries. In 1975, the third leading cause of death in Canada was work-related (these figures did not include occupationally-related diseases and thus were conservative). Just a decade ago a Canadian worker died on the job every six hours (Reasons, Ross, and Patterson, 1982). Commentators have observed that:

Canada has a history of violence enacted through legitimate institutions, in contrast to a pattern of individual and group violence in the United States. Much of the violence we experience in Canada may be through legitimate institutions such as work. (Reasons et al., 1982: 56)

Union leaders such as Henri Lorraine, former president of the Canadian Paperworkers' Union, have accused corporations of refusing to invest in safer working conditions for their workers and the state of refusing to force them to do such (Reasons et al., 1982). A prime example of such occupationally-related harm that has gone unchecked is the asbestos exposure that, by most accounts, has resulted in the deaths of thousands of workers.

Canadian authorities (like their US counterparts) view these transgressions as unfortunate but for the most part unavoidable costs of doing business. They do not blame capital for such misdeeds, and state complicity is a non-issue for state managers, police authorities, and government officials.

Given this particular form of social harm, the state can be described as both a crime-regulating and a crime-generating institution (Barak, 1993). On one hand the state is the moderator of socio-legal conflicts, but on the other, the state is complicitous in ongoing disreputable behaviour towards workers and their efforts at promoting labour unions and work settings that are safe from immediate and long-term life-threatening situations (Tunnell, 1995).

CONCLUSION

This chapter has described several cases of public violence oft initiated by labour as a means of affecting social change for both instrumental and expressive benefits. Often, however, public violence is initiated by business aided by the state and its agents to prevent social change and to maintain the status quo. Such public violence, unlike private, occurs in the pursuit of a common rather than an individualistic objective. Violence by and against labour clearly is a form of public violence.

Descriptions of violence by and against labour in Canada dispel widely held beliefs that Canada is the 'peaceable kingdom' for workers' gains have only been achieved through conflict—persistent, steadfast protest that has relied on occupying places of work, taking hostages, violating laws, and engaging in violent confrontation including attacks on anti-union workers, police, and management. Such actions are not anomalies but rather ongoing initiatives in labour's struggles for union representation, collective bargaining, job security, and wage increases.

Furthermore, industry and the state (that is widely believed to be neutral) have played various roles in contributing to labour unrest and violence against working-class men and women. The state, that body that its citizens assume objectively applies the law while protecting its subjects, has engaged in violent acts against labour that have been just as consequential as any that labour has initiated against industry or the state. Thus, each party in Canada's ongoing labour disputes has been equally guilty of violent actions resulting in varying degrees of social harm. Labour no doubt has caused injury, loss of property, and loss of revenue to industry and the state. Industry and the state, however, have caused their fair share of harm, violence, injury, and even death to working men and women. In the final analysis, it is working men and women who have had the most to lose due to power differentials and it is they who indeed have suffered inordinately.

NOTES

An earlier version of this paper was presented to the American Society of Criminology, Phoenix, November 1993. Special thanks to Jeffrey Ian Ross for his comments on an earlier draft and to Todd Flynn for his research assistance. This chapter has also benefited from the comments of the anonymous reviewers.

[1] The One Big Union (OBU) of Canada was formed in 1919 in opposition to the Trades and Labour Congress (TLC). Proclaiming a much more radical agenda than the TLC, including revolutionary socialism, the OBU attempted to organize workers by industry rather than trade (Jamieson, 1973) and also became a rallying point for workers involved in the Winnipeg general strike (Bercuson, 1974b). By about 1920, however, the OBU had lost most of its power as the more conservative TLC gained wide acceptance with both workers and state managers. Years later, with the merger of the AFL and CIO in the US, the OBU and TLC merged into the Canadian Labour Congress.

[2] For further details about early twentieth century labour struggles, see Abella and Millar, 1978.

[3] For further details about the labour movement during the first half of the twentieth century, see Abella, 1978.

[4] This strike had little public support because the striking medical doctors were seen as opposing a social program that provided necessary services to Canadian citizens—services that Canadians had fought long and hard to win. The strike contributed to social harm, a subtle form of 'violence', but its physical and psychological effects on the Canadian people. During such a widespread strike, both in its numbers and in its execution, there is little doubt that individuals physically and psychologically suffered due to the lack of accessible medical resources.

References

Abella, Irving (1974). *On Strike*. Toronto: James Lewis and Samuel.

—— (1978). *The Canadian Labour Movement*. Ottawa: Canadian Historical Association.

Abella, Irving, and David Millar (1978). *The Canadian Worker in the Twentieth Century*. Toronto: Oxford University Press.

Aikenhead, Sherri (1986). 'Reaching the boiling point'. *Maclean's* 99 (26): 8–9.

Allen, Glen (1991). 'Saying no to zero: Civil servants show a tough new face', *Maclean's* 104 (September 23): 32–4.

Aulette, Judy R. and Raymond Michalowski (1993). 'Fire in Hamlet: A Case Study of State-Corporate Crime.' Pp. 171–206 in Kenneth D. Tunnell, ed., *Political Crime in Contemporary America: A Critical Approach*. New York: Garland.

Barak, Gregg (1993). 'Crime, criminology and human rights: Toward an understanding of state criminality'. Pp. 207–30 in Kenneth D. Tunnell, ed., *Political Crime in Contemporary America: A Critical Approach*. New York: Garland.

Bercuson, David J. (1974a). 'The Winnipeg general strike'. Pp. 1–32 in Irving Abella, ed., *On Strike*. Toronto: James Lewis and Samuel.

—— (1974b). *Confrontation at Winnipeg*. Montreal: McGill-Queen's University Press.

Brown, Lorne (1987). *When Freedom was Lost: The Unemployed, the Agitator, and the State*. Montreal: Black Rose.

Gee, Marcus (1986). 'A bitter doctors' strike', *Maclean's* 99 (June 23): 19.

—— (1987). 'A bitter confrontation', *Maclean's* 100 (26): 10–11.

Grant, Don Sherman and Michael Wallace (1991). 'Why do strikes turn violent?' *American Journal of Sociology* 96, 5: 1117–50.

Howard, Victor (1985). *We Were the Salt of the Earth: The On-to-Ottawa Trek and the Regina Riot*. Regina: University of Regina.

Jamieson, Stuart M. (1968). *Times of Trouble: Labour Unrest and Industrial Conflict in Canada, 1900–1966*. Ottawa: Task Force on Labour Relations.

—— (1973). *Industrial Relations in Canada*, 2nd ed. Toronto: Macmillan.

Kopvillem, Peeter (1992). 'Death in the deeps' and 'The hunt for a killer', *Maclean's* 105 (October 5): 18, 31.

Kramer, Ronald C. (1990). 'From white collar to state-corporate crime'. Paper presented to the North Central Sociological Association, Louisville, Kentucky, March.

——— (1992). 'The space shuttle Challenger explosion'. Pp. 214–43 in Kip Schlegel and David Weisburd, eds, *White Collar Crime Reconsidered*. Boston: Northeastern University Press.

Liversedge, Ronald (1973). *Recollections of the On to Ottawa Trek*. Toronto: McClelland and Stewart.

Maclean's (1987). 'Drawing the battle lines', *Maclean's* 100 (41): 10–12.

Marx, Gary T. (1972). 'Civil disorder and the agents of social control'. Pp. 75–97 in Gary T. Marx, ed., *Muckraking Sociology: Research as Social Criticism*. New Brunswick, NJ: Transaction.

Marx, Karl (1852 [1974]). *The Eighteenth Brumaire of Louis Bonaparte*. In D. Fernbach, ed., *Surveys from Exile: Political Writings*. New York: Vintage.

Nikiforuk, Andrew (1986). 'Deadlocked in bitterness', *Maclean's* 99 (February 3): 50.

Pentland, H.C. (1948). 'The Lachine strike of 1843', *Canadian Historical Review* 29: 255–77.

Reasons, Charles, Lois Ross, and Craig Patterson (1982). 'Your money and your life: Workers' health in Canada', *Crime and Social Justice* 17: 55–60.

Ross, Jeffrey Ian (1992). 'The outcomes of public police violence: A neglected research agenda', *Police Studies* 15: 1–12.

Snow, Duart (1977). 'The Holmes Foundry strike of March 1937: We'll give their jobs to white men', *Ontario Historical Society* 69 (March): 3–31.

Taft, Philip, and Philip Ross (1979). 'American labour violence: Its causes, character, and outcome'. Pp. 187–241 in Hugh Davis Graham and Ted Robert Gurr, eds, *Violence in America*. Beverly Hills, CA: Sage.

Torrance, Judy M. (1986). *Public Violence in Canada, 1867–1982*. Montreal: McGill-Queen's University Press.

Tunnell, Kenneth D. (1995). 'Crimes of the capitalist state against labor'. Pp. 207–33 in Jeffrey Ian Ross, ed., *Controlling State Crime*. New York: Garland.

Turk, Austin T. (1982). *Political Criminality: The Defiance and Defense of Authority*. Beverly Hills, CA: Sage.

Wilson-Smith, Anthony (1991). 'Mulroney vs. the unions', *Maclean's* 104 (September 23): 30–1.

Chapter Four

INTIMATE MALE VIOLENCE AGAINST WOMEN IN CANADA

WALTER S. DEKESEREDY AND DESMOND ELLIS

Various forms of male violence against female intimates—whether wives, ex-wives, cohabitors, or dating partners—have become highly politicized topics for the general public, researchers, policy-makers, and the mass media. The growing concern for the plight of battered women is evident in a growing number of state-sponsored reports, the federal government's 15 August 1991 establishment of the Canadian Panel on Violence Against Women, two federally funded national surveys (DeKeseredy and Kelly, 1993a; Statistics Canada, forthcoming),[1] the creation of special community organizations (e.g., the Ottawa Regional Coordinating Committee to End Violence Against Women), and the many academic journal articles and books on male-female assaults that are published every year. In fact, advances in the sociological study of this problem have outpaced some of the major developments in the physical sciences (Schwartz and DeKeseredy, 1988).

'Atrocity tales' (Goffman, 1961) of men's brutal attacks against female partners are also commonplace in television shows, newspaper reports, and feature films (Messerschmidt, 1986).[2] According to the Sub-Committee on the Status of Women, created by the Standing Committee on Health and Welfare, Social Affairs, Seniors and the Status of Women (1991: 5):

> Rarely a day goes by in this country in which Canadian media do not carry reports of sexual and physical assaults, perpetrated by trusted persons and strangers against girls and women. The frequency with which incidents of this nature are reported in the media would lead most Canadians to conclude that violence against women is, indeed, a serious problem in Canada.

Of course violence is not restricted to conjugal, dating, and estranged marital relationships. Many children are victimized by their fathers, uncles, siblings, etc., and a large number of senior women are assaulted by their male offspring (DeKeseredy and Hinch, 1991; Podnieks, 1990). Whereas a great deal of sociological work has been done on these issues in the US, however, very few Canadian studies and theories are available. Clearly, much more attention should be devoted to violence against elderly people and children; however, it is beyond the scope of this chapter to address these problems.[3] Given that the vast majority of relevant Canadian research focuses on female victimization in adult heterosexual relationships, we have chosen to narrow our focus here to empirical and policy issues related to this problem.

In the sections that follow, we define violence against women in heterosexual relationships; discuss the incidence, prevalence, and distribution of this problem within Canada; and critique five different policy responses. Finally, we compare Canadian data with those gathered in the US and make some brief suggestions for further policy development.

WHAT IS VIOLENCE AGAINST WOMEN?

The social-scientific study of violence against women is characterized by a wide range of definitions. Indeed, there is considerable disagreement over what acts should be included in definitions of this variant of female victimization. Some definitions are so broad as to suggest that almost all women who are or have been intimately involved with men are victims of violence. One of the best Canadian examples of a broad formulation is provided by Stark-Adamec and Adamec (1982),[4] who argue that the term 'spousal violence' refers to anything a male spouse has done or not done to his partner that is perceived as psychologically, socially, economically, or physically harmful. Measures of violence derived from this definition include 'fractures, stitches, bruises, semen in the vagina and/or anus, browbeating, restriction of educational and employment opportunities, economic threats . . . adultery.' According to this definition, violence against female intimates in Canada is 'frighteningly pervasive' (1982: 8).

Influenced, perhaps, by critics who assert that grouping many types of abuse together makes it impossible to determine the causes of violence (Gelles and Cornell, 1985), most Canadian researchers offer definitions that are much narrower in scope. They limit their attention to sub-lethal acts of physical violence, such as punches, kicks, and slaps (Brinkerhoff and Lupri, 1988; Kennedy and Dutton, 1989; Lupri, 1990; Smith, 1987; 1989a; 1989b; 1990a; 1990b; 1991). This position is rejected mainly by feminists who contend that in focusing only on physical assaults, researchers appear to assume that these behaviours are more painful than psychological abuse and 'economic brutality' (Breines and Gordon, 1983; DeKeseredy and MacLean, 1990; 1991; MacLeod, 1987). In many cases, however this notion does not reflect the reality experienced by victims. Walker (1979), for example, found that most of her respondents considered incidents of psychological humiliation and verbal abuse to be their worst experiences, regardless of whether they had been physically attacked.

We agree with the feminist argument that physical assaults, economic abuse, and psychological abuse should all be considered forms of violence. However, since the primary objective of this chapter is to review the current state of sociological knowledge on only the first of these three problems, violence is defined here as any intentional sub-lethal physical assault on a woman by a husband, estranged husband, cohabitor, or dating partner. Consistent with Gelles and Straus (1988), our formulation covers a wide range of behaviours, from pushing and shoving to attempted murder.

VIOLENCE AGAINST WOMEN: ITS EXTENT AND DISTRIBUTION

Some, perhaps many, abused women 'suffer in silence' (Pizzey, 1974). In addition, a large number of men do not publicly reveal their mistreatment of female intimates. Others relate their experiences as victims or perpetrators to researchers in response to questions asked of them in victimization and self-report surveys. In these studies, a relatively small number of men, women, or couples are selected in such a way (e.g., a probability sample) as to enable the researchers to generalize their results to the entire population (city, province, or country) from which the sample was selected.[5]

In other cases the police are informed. However, fewer cases of woman abuse are reported to police than to survey researchers (DeKeseredy and Hinch, 1991). One major exception, of course is the very serious crime of homicide. Most murders, including the murders of women in intimate relationships, are known to the police. Femicide statistics are among the most accurate data produced by the police. Because these statistics are presented in this book by Gartner, only victimization and self-report data on various forms of sub-lethal violence will be reported here.

VIOLENCE AGAINST WIVES

Based on definitions formulated by DeKeseredy and Hinch (1991) and Ellis (1989), for the purposes of this chapter a wife is any woman who is legally married or is sexually and emotionally linked to a male cohabitor.[6] So far, most of the Canadian sociological data on husband-to-wife violence are derived mainly from three sources: women's shelters, three state-sponsored victimization surveys, and national, provincial, and city-wide surveys that used the Conflict Tactics Scale (CTS) (Straus, 1979). The shelter data were collected in two studies by MacLeod (1980; 1987). In the first, based on methodologically problematic transition-house and divorce-petition data, she argues that 'every year, 1 in 10 Canadian

women who are married or in a relationship with a live-in lover are battered' (1980: 1). In her second report, which also has methodological
limitations, MacLeod (1987) contends that at least one million women,
or one in eight, were assaulted by their male partners in 1985.

MacLeod's estimates, especially her first, are stated so often in
Canada that they are considered by many to be truisms. However, her
research is not methodologically sound and thus does not provide reliable incidence rates of wife abuse. In fact, as Smith (1989a) correctly
points out, MacLeod's conclusions are only slightly better than guesses
because of two major shortcomings. First, shelter residents are not representative of the entire Canadian female population who are married
or in cohabiting relationships. Second, some of the women included in
the divorce data collected in MacLeod's first study probably also stayed
in transition houses. In sum, both shelter and divorce data can only provide information on women who are officially designated as victims
(DeKeseredy and Hinch, 1991). Only representative sample surveys can
enhance our knowledge of the extent of wife assault in the Canadian
population at large (Smith, 1987). Three widely cited surveys of this
kind were conducted by state agencies: the Canadian Urban Victimization Survey (CUVS), the third cycle of the General Social Survey (GSS),
and the Women's Safety Project (Government of Canada, 1993).

In 1982, with the assistance of Statistics Canada, researchers working for the Statistics Division of the Ministry of the Solicitor General of
Canada conducted the CUVS. In this seven-city victimization survey,[7] a
random probability sample of more than 61,000 household residents 16
years of age or older were interviewed by telephone. One of the main
objectives of this study was to collect data on the frequency and distribution of reported and unreported crimes that occurred between
1 January and 31 December 1981 (Solicitor General of Canada, 1983).
Although the CUVS was not specifically designed to produce information
that could be used as a basis for estimating the incidence of wife abuse
in the seven large cities surveyed, some relevant information was provided because 'respondents were asked to state what their relationship
to the offender(s) was' (Solicitor General of Canada, 1983).

Even so, because it was a general victimization survey that focused
on a variety of personal and property offences rather than wife abuse
specifically, and because of several methodological limitations (see
DeKeseredy and Hinch, 1991; DeKeseredy and MacLean, 1991), in
comparison with other studies to be reviewed further on, the CUVS yields
an incidence rate that greatly underestimates the amount of wife assault
in Canada. Excluding threats with no physical attacks, the incidence
rate is very low—less than one per cent. Despite several methodological
improvements upon the Seven Cities study, the wife-assault data generated by the GSS are not much better.

Conducted in January and February 1988 by Statistics Canada, the GSS (Sacco and Johnson, 1990) was a telephone survey that gathered accident and criminal victimization data from a representative sample of 9,870 persons 15 years of age and older in ten provinces. Like the CUVS, this larger study was not designed specifically to examine the extent and nature of wife abuse. Sacco and Johnson's report on the findings, *Patterns of Criminal Victimization in Canada*, does not present a detailed analysis of the relationship between perpetrators and victims. Nevertheless, Canadian Centre for Justice Statistics researcher Johnson (1990) offers some relevant GSS data. She studied wife assault which she referred to as 'assaults or sexual assaults against a female victim by her spouse or ex-spouse' (1990: 169). These assaults ranged from face-to-face verbal threats to physical attacks with minor injuries, and 'sexual assault' referred to rape, attempted rape, and molesting (Statistics Canada 1990). The incidence rate reported by Johnson (1990) is not much higher than the CUVS statistic—1.5% or approximately 1,500 victims per 100,000 women. She states that this finding should be used with caution because it has high sampling variability.

If the wife-abuse data gleaned by the CUVS and GSS are problematic, the same can be said of the Women's Safety Project. Conducted in Toronto by Haskell and Randall and sponsored by the Canadian Panel on Violence Against Women, this study found that 27% of the women interviewed (N = 420) stated that they were physically abused by a husband, cohabiting partner, boyfriend, or date (Government of Canada, 1993). Unfortunately, data on variations across these marital-status categories are not reported. Thus we do not know whether married men are more or less dangerous than other male intimates. Perhaps subsequent reports on this study will offer more complete information on the extent of male-to-female violence in marriage and other intimate heterosexual relationships.

Representative sample self-report and victimization surveys that use the Conflict Tactics Scale (CTS) (Straus, 1979) offer much more reliable estimates of wife assault than the above three surveys because they were formulated specifically to do so.[8] Even though it has been highly criticized,[9] several variations of the CTS are clearly the most common measures of intimate violence in both Canada and the US.[10]

Table 4.1[11] presents the CTS incidence and prevalence rates of violence reported by either victims or perpetrators (or both) in national, provincial, and city-wide Canadian studies conducted to date. Based on these findings, we can conclude that at least 11% of the women who live with men are abused by them in any given year.

Wife abuse is not evenly distributed across the Canadian population. The small amount of survey research done to date shows that the most 'consistent risk markers'[12] (Hotaling and Sugarman, 1986) are

Table 4.1: Wife Abuse Surveys

	Description of Surveys				Abuse Rates			
Survey	*Survey location & date*	*Sample description*	*Interview mode*	*Measure of abuse*	*Abuse past year* %	*Severe abuse past year* %	*Abuse ever* %	*Severe abuse ever* %
Brinkerhoff & Lupri (1988)	Calgary 1981	526 men and women	Face-to-face & self-administered questionnaire	CTS (men only)[a]	24.5	10.8	—	—
Kennedy & Dutton (1989)	Alberta 1987	1,045 men and women	Face-to-face & phone	CTS (aggregate)	11.2	2.3	—	—
Lupri (1990)	Canada National 1986	1,530 married or cohabiting men and women	Face-to-face & mail questionnaire	CTS (men only)	17.8	10.1	—	—
Smith (1985)	Toronto 1985	315 women aged 18–25	Phone	CTS/open questions & 1 supplementary question	10.8	—	18.1	7.3
Smith (1987)	Toronto 1987	604 presently or formerly married or cohabiting women	Phone	CTS & three supplementary questions	14.4[b]	5.1	36.4[c]	11.3

[a] men as aggressors

[b] past-year rates based on CTS data alone

[c] abuse-ever rates based on CTS data (25.0, 7.8) plus supplementary questions

youth, low income, and marital estrangement (divorce or separation). Educational attainment, occupational status, and employment status are defined as 'inconsistent risk markers' (Hotaling and Sugarman, 1986) because the data on their influence are mixed (Smith 1990a). The influence of several other determinants, such as religion and ethnicity, has not received sufficient attention. Therefore Smith contends that 'conclusions about these variables would be premature at present' (1990a: 45).

More accurate information is also sorely needed on woman abuse in dating relationships. It is to this variant of female victimization that we now turn.

VIOLENCE AGAINST WOMEN IN DATING RELATIONSHIPS

There are various definitions of dating relationships. In fact, defining this concept is the subject of much debate. Much of the controversy surrounds the question of whether cohabiting is a form of dating.[13] Consistent with DeKeseredy and Hinch (1991: 44), however, we contend that cohabiting is not a particular type of dating, and their definition informs our analysis of the issues to be addressed below.[14] For the purposes of this section, dating relationships are defined as

> associations between unmarried males and females that address at least four needs. These are recreation, socialization, status achievement, and mate selection (Skipper and Nass, 1966). Some relationships are considered 'serious' because they involve a high degree of commitment and intimacy. Others are defined as casual because both partners seek a 'good time' with no future commitment or obligation. (Eshleman, 1978)

Survey research shows that violence against women in the above contexts is a major problem in the US.[15] Until relatively recently, however, there were no comparable Canadian studies as sociologists focused primarily on violence against married and cohabiting women, specifically in Toronto and Alberta. Now national representative survey data are available (DeKeseredy, 1994; DeKeseredy and Kelly, 1993a), along with statistics gathered from several non-probability samples of high-school and university students in Winnipeg and various parts of Ontario (Barnes et al., 1991; DeKeseredy, 1988; DeKeseredy et al., 1992; Mercer, 1988; Sudermann and Jaffe, 1993). These studies show that many Canadian women are at great risk of being assaulted by their male dating partners.

For example, DeKeseredy and Kelly's (1993a) national survey of undergraduate university/college students (1,307 men and 1,835 women) generated the following CTS data on violence in post-secondary school courtship:

13.7 per cent of the male respondents stated that they physically abuse their dating partners in the year before the study, while 22.3 per cent of the female participants reported being victimized.

Since they left high school, 17.8 per cent of the male respondents stated that they assaulted their dating partners, while 35 per cent of the women reported having been victimized.

DeKeseredy and Kelly's findings are similar to those produced by DeKeseredy (1988) and DeKeseredy et al. (1992). However, Barnes et al.'s (1991) male prevalence rate is higher. Approximately 42% of their male sample (N = 245) reported using some form of violence while attending university. This inconsistency probably reflects differences between the specific variants of the CTS employed by the four studies. For example, Barnes et al.'s version included a sexual-assault item and several other different measures.

Violence is also common in Canadian high-school dating relationships. Based on memories of their past experiences, 1.4% of DeKeseredy and Schwartz's (1994) national male sample stated that they 'intentionally physically hurt' their dating partners, while 9.1% of the females reported having been victimized in such a way. Higher female victimization rates were obtained in non-probability sample surveys. For example, 11% of Mercer's (1988) female participants reported being physically abused, and approximately 15% of Sudermann and Jaffe's (1993) sample experienced this problem.

Although some young people start dating while they are in elementary school, courtship activities are much less common in this context; therefore, fewer very young people are likely to be either victims or perpetrators of intimate violence. In other words, they are less likely to spend 'time-at-risk' (Ellis and DeKeseredy, 1989). Empirical support for this thesis is provided by DeKeseredy and Schwartz (1994) who report that 7.2% of the women in their sample stated having been intentionally physically hurt by their elementary-school dating partners. Fewer men (3.6%), on the other hand, reported that they engaged in this behaviour. Similar findings were obtained by DeKeseredy et al. (1992).

So far, there are no data on the risk markers associated with violence in Canadian high-school and elementary dating relationships. Surveys of university/college students, however, reveal five strong predictors of violence in post-secondary school courtship: an adherence to the ideology of familial patriarchy (DeKeseredy and Kelly, 1993b); male peer support (DeKeseredy, 1988; DeKeseredy and Kelly, 1993b); alcohol consumption; violence and parenting in the family of origin; and personality stress (Barnes et al., 1991).

In sum, the findings presented in this section challenge Straus et al.'s (1981: 32) assertion that the 'marriage license is a hitting license'. This thesis includes two arguments: first, that marriage is a unique relationship that places women at great risk for abuse, and second, that married women are more likely to be beaten than unmarried women. The abuse of women in intimate relationships is clearly not restricted to the conjugal home. Additional evidence of major variations across marital-status categories is found in the literature on post-separation violence, an equally if not more serious Canadian problem. Here, 'post-separation violence' refers to any intentional physical assault on a woman by her estranged husband or cohabiting partner. When homicide figures are considered, the extent of this crime is even more startling.

POST-SEPARATION VIOLENCE

If we accept the argument that the marriage licence is a hitting licence, then one logical solution to the problem of wife abuse is legal separation or divorce (Ellis, 1990). This goal may be difficult to achieve, but many, even most, battered wives and cohabiting partners eventually do (Schwartz, 1989). For some of them, however, separation does not solve the problem of intimate violence. According to Okun (1986: 43), 'even if she doesn't stay, he may keep showing up,' and if he does, the results can be deadly. For example, in 21% of the cases of intimate femicide recorded in Toronto between 1974 and 1990, the victims were separated from either their legal or common-law male partners (Crawford and Gartner, 1992). Moreover, over 80% of multiple murders, including murder-suicides, involved women, children, and ex-mates (or prospective ex-mates) (Ellis, 1987). Generally, in these cases, the man kills the woman, often the children too, and then commits or at least attempts suicide.

Separated and divorced women are also disproportionately represented among victims of sub-lethal assaults. For example, both the CUVS and the GSS found that members of these marital-status categories had much higher rates of physical assault than did married females. The CUVS assault rates were 1 per 1,000 married women, 8 per 1,000 divorced women, and 27 per 1,000 separated women (Statistics Canada, 1990). Using a combined category of 'separated or divorced', the GSS assault rates were significantly higher: 6 per 1,000 married women and 38 per 1,000 separated or divorced women.

Again, these state-sponsored studies were not specifically designed to measure the extent of violence against women in intimate relationships. Hence it is necessary to turn to other research for accurate data. In his national study, using the CTS, Lupri (1990) found that 18% of his married or cohabiting male respondents physically assaulted a partner. However, a much higher figure (30%) was obtained from divorced or separated respondents. Kennedy and Dutton's (1989) Alberta study also shows that separated and divorced women are much more likely to have been attacked than married respondents. The incidence rates for cohabiting and married people are 24.4% and 8.7%. In sharp contrast to these figures, the rates for divorced and separated people are 39.8% and 54.8%.

In a less sophisticated study, by Ellis and Wight (1987), an even higher rate of post-separation violence was obtained. Here 46% (N = 89) of separated or divorced female respondents reported some form of physical abuse and/or threats of physical assault by their estranged male partners. Furthermore, 26 out of these 41 victims stated that they were not victimized prior to separation. Further Canadian and US evidence demonstrating the frequent victimization of separated and divorced women is provided by MacLeod (1980), Smith (1990a), Ellis and Stuckless (1992), Bowker (1981), Giles-Sims (1983), Browne (1987), Gaquin (1978), Levinger (1966), O'Brien (1971) and Russell (1982).

Except for a handful of studies, little work has been done to identify the major correlates of post-separation violence. Based on the research done by Ellis (1987), Ellis and Stuckless (1992), Ellis and Wight (1987), and Ellis et al. (1987), it appears that the following are significant predictors: pre-separation violence, power differences between men and women, privacy norms, alcohol and drug abuse, lawyer styles, and marital conflict mediation.

POLICY RESPONSES TO VIOLENCE AGAINST WOMEN

What is to be done about male violence against Canadian women in intimate heterosexual relationships? Some of the major attempts to answer this question can be subsumed under five headings: policing, mediation, economic policies, social services, and pro-feminist programs for violent men.

POLICING

An influential group of therapists and scholars (e.g., psychiatrists, psychologists, social workers) have, since the mid-1970s, worked very hard to assist abused and battered women. The general focus of their approach has been to improve the response to different forms of woman abuse, especially wife-beating, adopted by various agents of the state, including policemen, social workers, psychologists, and counsellors employed in various community agencies.[16]

Initially, it was thought that the policing of wife assault would be improved if police officers were trained in crisis-intervention techniques specifically geared to domestic violence. Police officers trained in this way were made part of a team that included social workers from community agencies responsible for the welfare of Canadian families (Jaffe and Thompson, 1979; Levens, 1978). More recently, because of feminist lobbying and education initiatives, the state's response to a 'legitimation crisis' (Habermas, 1975), empirical research, attitudinal changes among police officers, and the 'federal government's readiness to comply with the wishes of important people' (Rock, 1988: 48), the focus seems to have shifted toward a more specifically law-enforcement response to wife assault (DeKeseredy and Hinch, 1991).[17] Thus police chiefs and attorneys general in various jurisdictions have issued directives requiring police officers to arrest perpetrators, and the law has been changed to require that victims testify in court.

While we have a rapidly growing amount of Canadian survey data on the extent and distribution of male violence against women, at present there are no national Canadian official statistics on the numbers of men arrested for engaging in these behaviours. For example, except for homicide, the Uniform Crime Reporting System (UCR) does not include any data specifically on the physical abuse of women in intimate contexts. The relationships between victims of assault and their assailants are also excluded from the US Uniform Crime Reports. Relevant Canadian government data on policing, however, are collected by the Solicitor General of Canada, the Royal Canadian Mounted Police (RCMP), and a few provincial, territorial, and municipal police departments (MacLeod, 1987).

One of the most recent Canadian studies on the response of the police to violence against wives/cohabitors was conducted in Metropolitan Toronto by Leighton (1989), a researcher for the Solicitor General of Canada. Based on an analysis of the police and court response to 2,910 incidents of 'spousal assault', he found that (1) no charges were laid in 30.2% (N = 844) of the incidents; (2) 24.1% (N = 675) of the victims were advised by police officers to turn to a justice of the peace to lay their own charges; (3) in 15 incidents, the police laid charges on their own but did not arrest the offenders; in 31.3% (N = 876) of the incidents offenders were both arrested and charged; (4) the police investigated a further 11.2% incidents (N = 314), and arrested but did not charge offenders in another six; and (5) in 40 incidents offenders were arrested for another act, while in another 28 cases other outcomes were determined.

Leighton's study does not tell us whether arresting violent husbands and/or male cohabiting partners reduces the amount of physical harm done to their female intimates. However, Jaffe et al.'s (1986) London, Ontario, study does. These researchers studied the long-term effects of laying charges in wife-assault cases. Post-charge assaults were measured by counting the number of contacts abusers had with police in the following year, and by examining wives' reports of their husbands' violence during the 12-month period after arrest. With the significant exception of violence involving weapons, all other forms of violence were considerably reduced during the year following arrest. Kicking, biting, or hitting with a fist, for example, declined from 57.2% to 22.9%.[18]

Even though there is some scientific support for the mandatory arrest of violent male spouses, some Canadian critical criminologists (e.g., Currie and MacLean, 1992; Snider, 1990) are sharply opposed to a punitive, 'law and order' approach for the following reasons. First, because arrest policies are not implemented evenly across Canada, many battered women do not receive police protection. In Ontario, for example, the Race Relations and Policing Task force (Lewis et al., 1989) found that black women were less likely to receive police support than white women.

Second, many victims do not want their violent partners arrested because the men may be fined or lose their jobs. For these women, arrest is a major threat to their (and their children's) material well-being. Other women fear that arrest will only anger their husbands and lead them to seek revenge by increasing the frequency and severity of their violent behaviour (MacLeod, 1987).

The third, and probably most important, reason why some critical criminologists oppose pro-arrest policies is that they see such policies as diverting attention from the wider cultural and structural conditions that reproduce violence in intimate relationships (Currie and MacLean, 1992; Snider, 1990). For this reason, as well as the other two described above, Currie and MacLean question whether criminalization is really a victory for women.

Peacemaking criminologists, such as Pepinsky (1991), Knopp (1991), and Quinney (1991) are also sharply opposed to punitive state responses, and they call for a program based on mediation, mutual aid, and reconciliation. It is to the effectiveness of one of these peacemaking strategies—mediation—that we now turn.

MEDIATION

Historically, mediation was the most common method of settling conflicts in many societies around the world (Gulliver, 1979; Merry, 1989; Volpe, 1991). Mediation is 'a relatively short-term participatory intervention process that enables disputing parties to resolve their differences with the assistance of a third party, known as a mediator, in an informal, face-to-face, private, and confidential setting' (Volpe, 1991: 198). Mediation is rarely used in Canada because the federal government is not interested in funding it (Horrocks, 1982; Kennedy, 1990), even though research shows that it is a successful way of resolving some criminal cases (Volpe, 1991): for example, the participants seem to be very satisfied; they are highly likely to agree with each other; they view the settlements as fair; and when agreements are reached, they gener-ally comply with their terms (Beer, 1986; Cook et al., 1980; CDRCP, 1989; Davis et al., 1980; Felstiner and Williams, 1980; Volpe, 1991). However, is mediation effective in cases of male violence against female intimates?

According to Pepinsky (1991: 310),

> through a trusted intermediary, if not face-to-face, giving a woman a safe opportunity to confront the offender with her anger and pain, and to ask the offender to account for himself, must offer more relief than praying that one's rapist doesn't hit the streets, and will probably have a more favourable impact on the rapist.

However, he and other advocates of mediation do not provide empirical support for their proposals. In fact, research shows that mediation is ineffective in wife-abuse cases, and can be extremely dangerous for the victims.

Among the reasons why, in its current form, mediation does not help battered women is the fact that the latter do not have equal bar-gaining power; that most mediators are not neutral; that mediation ignores and does not punish the man's past behaviour; and that com-munication with mediators is often not kept confidential (Knopp, 1991). Research also demonstrates a link between marital mediation and continuing violence against wives and cohabiting partners who par-ticipate in mediation. More specifically, mediation can perpetuate the abuse of female participants (Ellis, 1990; Ellis et al., 1987).

These findings are not surprising to feminist scholars such as Ler-man (1984). For some time now, she has argued that the support pro-vided to abused women by lawyers is less likely to be associated with post-separation abuse than the support provided by mediators. The main reason for this is that mediators are less likely than lawyers to focus on battering as the issue, to clearly assign responsibility to the batterer, and to take legal steps to separate the abuser from his victim. Where lawyers see a victim and a violent offender, mediators tend to see two interactants who make equal contributions to the signing of a mediation agreement focusing on the future of the man, the woman, and the chil-dren (Ellis, 1987).

In some cases, these agreements constitute a licence to hit. For example, Lerman cites agreements in which the husband is required to stop beating his wife and the wife must not do things that provoke her husband; if she does violate the agreement by provoking her husband, then 'he has been granted tacit permission to beat her again' (1984: 12). As Ellis (1987) correctly points out, the mediation agreement is a form of social support for violence against women.

Ellis points to several other serious problems with allowing wife abusers to participate in mediation. He contends that such an approach

> enhances their persuasive strength *vis-à-vis* their wives. Abused women are often timorous around their husbands. Timorous wives usually do not make good advocates for their own positions. They tend to be neither forceful nor articulate in stating their legitimate claims to custody, support, and property when they must do so facing the men who have beaten them. The end result may be that they sign agreements which are economically disadvantageous. Difficult post-separation economic circumstances . . . tend to invite new relationships with men who abuse them. (1990: 335)

In sum, mediation in its present form is, to say the least, an ineffective mode of curbing intimate violence. Moreover, it does not induce broader social change, it neutralizes both class and gender conflict, and it is easily absorbed into the punitive social-control system, widening the net of oppressive social control documented by some feminist critics of policing (Schwartz and DeKeseredy, 1991). Instead of empowering battered women, mediation appears to serve the needs of the bureaucratic state system (Selva and Bohm, 1987). If mediation does not address the wider social forces that perpetuate and legitimate woman abuse, however, the same thing cannot be said of 'left-realist' economic policy proposals.

ECONOMIC POLICIES

Although male-to-female violence occurs among all Canadian socio-economic groups, the highest rates are found among lower-class people (Smith, 1990a). Before examining polices that focus on this problem, it is necessary to explain why the advanced capitalist system affects lower-class men in particular in such a way as to perpetuate woman abuse.

According to Schwartz (1988), Rubin's (1976) analysis of working-class married life may help to answer this question. Rubin argues that compared to middle-class men—who may assert but not necessarily practise marital equality, and who have more work and lifestyle choices—working-class men are more likely to dominate and/or victimize their wives/partners because: (1) they are not able to demonstrate their personal power outside a conjugal relationship; (2) they do not have the money to pay for child care, leisure activities, and other relief from the pressures of a marital relationship; and (3) they have been socialized into a context that legitimizes both violence and familial patriarchy.

It should also be noted that many battered women cannot escape their husbands because they are financially dependent upon them and cannot survive without their economic support (Barnett and LaViolette, 1993). Moreover, even if they do find employment, the fact that approximately 73% of Canadian women work in low-paying, 'pink ghetto' jobs (Parliament, 1990) means that they are not likely to be able to live and take care of their children on their own. Thus economic desperation leads many women to remain with violent men, increasing their time-at-risk for victimization.

Policies that directly target the above problems are in short supply. DeKeseredy and Hinch (1991) contend that some initiatives proposed by US 'left realists' have the potential to reduce the numbers of Canadian battered women, especially those who are economically disenfranchised. Among these proposals are the policies advocated by Michalowski (1983), Currie (1985; 1989), and Messerschmidt (1986).

Michalowski addresses the negative effects of unemployment and low wages, suggesting strategies designed to place the financial burden on capitalists instead of the welfare state. They include:

- Tax surcharges on industries attempting to close plants or permanently reduce a community's work force.
- State laws requiring retraining and job placement for all workers displaced by new industrial technology.
- A minimum wage level that is approximately 150% of the poverty level (1983: 14–18).

Unlike Michalowski's proposed structural changes, Currie's left-realist agenda calls for increases in both public and private support. Included in his 'social-environmental' or 'human ecological' platform are the following reforms:

- Increased wages for women.
- A wage policy informed by Scandinavia's 'solidaristic' (Rhen, 1985) program.
- Publicly supported, community-oriented job creation. Improving the quality of work available to disadvantaged people.
- Intensive job training and supported work designed to help both young and disabled people obtain stable careers.
- Paid work leaves.
- Job creation in local communities.

Messerschmidt's (1986) economic agenda is similar to those of Michalowski and Currie. His strategies, and the others set forth here, move beyond the narrow boundaries of criminal-justice reform to address the wider economic forces that contribute to woman abuse.

Even though some of the policies proposed by American left realists have been successfully implemented in other countries, given the current conservative Canadian political climate (Hatt et al., 1990), DeKeseredy and Hinch argue that it is not likely that Canadian politicians, or most of the general public will embrace their progressive proposals. Their scepticism reflects Barak's (1986: 201) view that left-realist policies will not be implemented until 'politicians, policy analysts, and the public are exorcised of current crime causation myths, and . . . many people are ready to challenge some of our most inbred cultural and political assumptions.' The exorcism that Barak calls for will not be easy to achieve, because implementing major elements of the above proposals would mean eliminating the gains that powerful Canadians, especially males, have made under the patriarchal capitalist order (DeKeseredy and Schwartz, 1991).

It is not a lack of expertise that has precluded Canadians from addressing the wider economic and social forces that perpetuate and legitimate woman abuse. Rather, the hurdles are political and ideological (Currie, 1985). As was noted above, many people are reluctant to restructure Canadian society because they profit greatly from the current political and economic state of affairs. Other people recognize that economic forces are major factors in woman abuse and other types of violent crime, but have decided that the advantages of changing them are not worth the costs. They choose to maintain a society that is conducive to male physical, sexual, and psychological assaults on women (Currie, 1985).

Social Services

As we pointed out earlier, many battered women stay with their partners because they are financially dependent and cannot survive without their spouses' economic support. This problem is more severe for unemployed women and their children. With no refuge from violence, many women are forced by their material circumstances to remain in dangerous intimate relationships. Others, because they are denied access to emergency shelters, state-subsidized housing, and living quarters with either family members or friends, resist their violent partners by living on the streets (Harman, 1989). In fact, many homeless women who are labelled by both the general public and state officials as 'bag ladies', 'vagrants', and 'urban transient females', have been severely brutalized by their male partners (Bard, 1988; Barak, 1991; Mallin, 1987). These people would rather face the indignities, humiliation, neglect, social and economic isolation, and criminal dangers associated with living on the street than be beaten, raped, and psychologically assaulted by male intimates (Barak, 1991).

Needless to say, a homeless 'lifestyle' has serious health implications.[19] Short-term emergency shelter and housing assistance must be provided not only for abused women but for any woman who lacks adequate housing. The number of Canadian women's shelters has tripled since 1979 (MacLeod, 1987); this is a positive reform. But even so, emergency shelters are usually overcrowded, and many battered women are reluctantly turned away. Clearly the state should build new shelters and increase funding to those already in place. Moreover, government funding agencies should give private citizens money to look after abused women who are denied access to emergency housing (Bowker, 1983). To date, this type of state support has been offered primarily by some provincial/territorial governments to private homes or 'safe houses' in rural and isolated areas (MacLeod, 1987).

Women's shelters and safe houses, however, are not enough. In order to guarantee women safety, autonomy, and self-reliance, state-subsidized housing is essential. Again, if victims are unable to afford homes or apartments, they may have to live on the streets or stay with their abusive partners (Ellis, 1987; Harman, 1989). Or, they could end up becoming totally dependent on the shelter system, which is a reflection of the wider patriarchal forces that reproduce both gender inequality in the marital home and woman abuse. For example, based on her ethnographic study of a feminist hostel in an Ontario city, Harman concludes:

> The hostels replace traditional female roles by being modelled after homes and requiring women to do daily housekeeping chores, and by subjecting them to the rules and regulations of a larger structure that makes the decisions and has disciplinary power. In other words, they teach, foster, and reward domesticity. (1989: 106)

PROFEMINIST PROGRAMS FOR VIOLENT MEN

Obviously, the victims of the three variants of intimate violence discussed in this chapter require more social support. However, some researchers contend that therapeutic treatment programs for violent men are also desperately needed (Finkelhor and Yllo, 1985). Many shelter workers and feminist scholars alike sharply reject this argument because they maintain that the state contributes little money toward solving the problem of woman abuse, and that the meagre amount that is allotted should go only to social-support services for victims (Dobash and Dobash, 1992; MacLeod, 1987). Some critics of programs for men also point out that many women perceive these initiatives as calls for them to nurture violent males (Schechter, 1982).

Of course women should not be denied funds so that their violent partners can receive assistance; as we stated earlier, they should be given more support. Nevertheless, pro-feminist treatment programs for men can be beneficial to some degree, and, like other feminist-inspired left-realist initiatives, they can help to 'chip away' at patriarchal capitalism (Messerschmidt, 1986). Indeed, men's programs and shelters can work together to curb woman abuse (Dobash and Dobash, 1992; Schechter, 1982).

There are various types of programs for men, including the insight, ventilation, interaction, cognitive-behavioural, and pro-feminist models (Adams, 1988). These programs were first created in the US in the mid-1970s and started in Canada in the early 1980s. Currently there are at least 130 Canadian programs for abusive men; however, only a handful employ the pro-feminist approach (Storrie and Poon, 1991). The dominant perspective is the cognitive-behaviourial approach (Correctional Services of Canada, 1988; Storrie and Poon, 1991), which, among other limitations,[20] fails to address the wider social forces that reproduce violence against women. Since pro-feminist programs focus directly on the influence of societal and familial patriarchy, they are the ones we have chosen to advocate here.

Among the Canadian examples of pro-feminist treatment programs—sometimes referred to as anti-sexist male collectives—are New Directions, Vivre sans Violence, and Entre-Hommes. Agencies such as these offer telephone 'hot-lines' for men to call when they feel like assaulting their wives, girlfriends, cohabiting partners, or ex-partners (Finkelhor and Yllo, 1985). They also provide an all-male peer-group education in which woman abuse is regarded not as a product of individual or couple pathology but as learned behaviour that is a function of patriarchal social norms (Adams, 1989). These anti-sexist male collectives are influenced not only by feminism but by social learning theory, the progressive 'men's movement', radical therapy, and political experiences (Adams, 1989; Shechter, 1982).

The primary objective of group-therapy sessions is to stop participants from physically attacking women. Even if clients achieve this goal, however, Dankwort (1988: 2) argues that unless the underlying attitudes that motivate them to beat women are changed, men will resort to other forms of abuse, such as psychological and economic cruelty. Thus pro-feminist treatment groups also encourage men not to use non-violent means of patriarchal control. Group sessions are contexts of feminist education in which members encourage each other to stop all behaviours that undermine gender inequality and their partners' autonomy.

Nevertheless, anti-sexist collectives have some limitations. Seldom do they have more than one or two dozen clients at a time, for the simple reason that most men lack motivation to end their abusive behaviour or to seek help. Most of those who participate in self-help groups do so for two reasons. First, their female partners have left them and they were told to change if they want them to return. Second, they were caught by the police, and counselling was ordered by judges or probation officers (Finkelhor and Yllo, 1985). Unfortunately, research shows that coerced therapy is not as effective as voluntary participation (Hornick et al., 1988).

CONCLUSION

Canada's rate of 'street crime' is much lower than that of the US (Silverman, 1992). However, some of the figures presented in Table 4.1 show that Canadians are equally, if not more, violent in intimate heterosexual contexts. For example, the incidence rates of husband-to-wife violence reported in two national US surveys were 12.1% and 11.3% respectively (Straus et al., 1981; Straus and Gelles, 1986), while both Lupri's (1990) national Canadian estimate (18%) and Brinkerhoff and Lupri's (1988) figure (24.5%) are considerably higher. Smith's (1987) Toronto survey also produced a higher incidence rate (14.4%).

Canadian rates of dating violence also approximate those of the US. DeKeseredy et al.'s (1992) victimization incidence rate, for example, is only slightly lower than the national US figure reported by Stets and Henderson (30%). At present, unfortunately, reliable comparisons between the rates of violence reported by US and Canadian estranged male partners cannot be made because only one US survey examined post-separation violence (Shulman, 1979). This study yielded a rate lower than comparable Canadian statistics (43%). While it may be premature to draw conclusions based on the limited amount of US research, it appears that separated and divorced Canadian men are more violent than their US counterparts.

The above comparative statistics clearly challenge the assertion that Canada is a 'peaceable kingdom'. Together with the efforts of feminist activists, they have also contributed to the widely-held belief that we are now experiencing an 'epidemic' of male-to-female violence (DeKeseredy, 1992b). This assumption is incorrect. In fact, violence against women has existed in Western societies for centuries (Dobash and Dobash, 1979). Moreover, since Canadian researchers only started examining this issue in the early 1980s, we cannot conclusively state whether the rate of violence against women in this country has increased or decreased over time. However, historical data suggest that today's men are no more violent, and possibly less so, than their ancestors (DeKeseredy, 1992b; Straus et al., 1981).

Regardless of whether or not rates of violence against women have changed over time, the key question for many Canadians, especially women, is what is to be done about it. Some policy analysts argue that the present approaches are ineffective because they do not target the broader political, economic, and cultural forces that perpetuate and legitimate violence against women, such as patriarchy. According to DeKeseredy (1992b), for example, the current strategies assume that minor adjustments to the status quo, such as arresting more offenders, or increasing funding to shelters, will make a considerable difference. Yet large numbers of women are still beaten on a regular basis, despite some of the most active and sweeping feminist-inspired reforms ever undertaken (Schwartz and DeKeseredy, 1988; 1991). We are not opposed to some short-term policies; even so, we maintain that a problem rooted in structural inequality is not going to be eliminated simply by tinkering with the current social order. Perhaps it is time to direct our policy initiatives towards macro-level determinants, such as patriarchy and economic inequality.

NOTES

[1] At the time of writing, Statistics Canada had not yet released its telephone-survey findings.

[2] One outstanding US example of the media attention devoted to wife-beating was the Lisa Steinberg murder case. Lisa's mother, Hedda Nussbaum, was viciously beaten on a regular basis by her husband, Joel Steinberg, and when Nussbaum appeared on the witness stand 1988, NBC, CBS, and ABS pre-empted their soap operas to broadcast her testimony. According to Ehrlich (1989) she became New York City's 'biggest daytime star'.

[3] See DeKeseredy (1992a), Cabrera (this volume), and Sacco (this volume) for critical reviews of Canadian research on these variations of family violence.

[4] Canadian researchers Brown (1990) and MacLeod (1987) also offer very broad definitions.

[5] These results are usually stated within statistically estimated degrees of error. Thus one might say that 20 per cent of all Canadian women now living with men were beaten at least once during their relationship, and this estimate is accurate to plus or minus two percentage points. This means that would be the actual percentage could vary between 18 and 22 per cent.

[6] See DeKeseredy and Hinch (1991) for critical responses to this definition. For example, some maintain that marriage and cohabiting are two distinct relationships.

[7] The seven cities surveyed were Greater Vancouver, Edmonton, Winnipeg, Toronto, Montreal, Halifax-Dartmouth, and St John's.

[8] The most widely used version of the CTS includes 18 items that measure three different ways of resolving conflict in marital relationships: reasoning, verbal aggression, and physical violence. The items are categorized on a continuum from least to most severe, with the first 10 describing

non-violent strategies and the last eight describing violent tactics. The last five items from kicking, biting or hitting with a fist to using a knife or a gun make up the severe violence scale.

[9] See DeKeseredy and Hinch (1991), DeKeseredy and MacLean (1990), and Dobash et al. (1992) for criticisms of the CTS.

[10] Various versions of the CTS are also integral components of North American research on both physical and psychological forms of woman abuse in dating relationships.

[11] This is a modified version of a table constructed by Smith (1989b). Except for Brinkerhoff and Lupri's study (1988), all the surveys included in this table include separated and divorced respondents.

[12] A risk marker is any attribute of a couple, victim, or assailant that is associated with an increased probability of husband-to-wife abuse (Smith, 1990a). It may or may not be a causal variable (Last, 1983).

[13] See DeKeseredy (1988) and DeKeseredy and Hinch (1991).

[14] Except for the exclusion of cohabiting, their definition is exactly the same as DeKeseredy's (1988).

[15] See DeKeseredy (1988), DeKeseredy and Hinch (1991), Sugarman and Hotaling (1989), and Currie and MacLean (1993) for reviews of the literature on US incidence and prevalence rates.

[16] See Dutton and Levens (n.d.), Levens (1978), Byles (1980), Jaffee and Thompson (1979), and Jaffe and Burris (1984).

[17] See DeKeseredy and Hinch (1991) for a review of the relevant literature on the factors that caused this shift in focus.

[18] US research both supports and challenges the assertion that arrest deters men from beating their wives. See DeKeseredy and Hinch (1991) and Hirschel et al. (1992) for reviews of empirical attempts to test the deterrent effect of mandatory arrest policies.

[19] For example, homeless women experience hunger, various physical illnesses, sleep disorders, disorientation, and phobias; in addition, strangers often rob, rape, or try to rape them (Bard, 1988; Barak, 1991; Coston, 1988). The physical and psychological problems associated with homelessness are also experienced by battered women who remain in abusive homes (Bard, 1988).

[20] See Adams (1988) and Storrie and Poon (1991) for a more detailed critique of this perspective.

REFERENCES

Adams, D. (1988). 'Treatment models of men who batter: A profeminist analysis'. In K. Yllo and M. Bograd, eds, *Feminist Perspectives on Wife Abuse*. Beverly Hills: Sage.

——— (1989). 'Feminist-based interventions for battering men'. In P. Caesar and L. Hamberger, eds, *Treating Men Who Batter: Theory, Practice, and Programs*. New York: Springer.

Barak, G. (1986). 'Is America really ready for the Currie challenge?', *Crime and Social Justice* 25: 200–3.

—— (1991), *Gimme Shelter: A Social History of Homelessness in Contemporary America*. New York: Praeger.

Bard, M. (1988). 'Domestic abuse and the homeless women: Paradigms in personal narratives for organizational strategists and community planners'. Doctoral dissertation, University of Michigan, Ann Arbour.

Barnes, G., L. Greenwood, and R. Sommer (1991). 'Courtship violence in a Canadian sample of male college students', *Family Relations* 40: 37–44.

Barnett, O., and A. LaViolette (1993). *It Could Happen to Anyone: Why Battered Women Stay*. Newbury Park: Sage.

Beer, J. (1986). *Peacemaking in Your Neighborhood: Reflections on an Experiment in Community Mediation*. Philadelphia: New Society.

Bowker, L. (1981). 'Women as victims: An examination of the results of L.E.A.A.'s National Crime Survey program', *Women and Crime in America* 158: 164–5.

—— (1983). *Beating Wife-Beating*. Toronto: Lexington.

Breines, W. and L. Gordon (1983). 'The new scholarship on family violence', *Signs: Journal of Women in Culture and Society* 8: 491–553.

Brinkerhoff, M., and E. Lupri (1988). 'Interspousal violence', *Canadian Journal of Sociology* 13: 407–34.

Brown, R. (1990). 'The challenge of family violence: An international review'. In R. Roesch, D. Dutton, and V. Sacco, eds, *Family Violence: Perspectives on Treatment, Research, and Policy*. Burnaby, BC: British Columbia Institute on Family Violence.

Browne, A. (1987). *When Battered Women Kill*. New York: Free Press.

Byles, J. (1980). 'Family violence in Hamilton', *Canada's Mental Health* 28: 4–6.

CDRCP (Community Dispute Resolution Centers Program) (1989). *Annual Report April 1, 1988–March 31, 1989*. Albany, NY: CDRCP.

Cook, R., J. Roehl, and D. Sheppard (1980). *Neighborhood Justice Centers Field Test: Final Evaluation Report*. Washington, DC: US Department of Justice.

Correctional Services of Canada (1988). *Breaking the Cycle of Family Violence*. Ottawa: Ministry of Supply and Services.

Coston, C. (1988). 'The original designer label: Prototypes of New York City's shopping-bag ladies'. Paper presented at the annual meetings of the American Society of Criminology, Chicago.

Crawford, M., and R. Gartner (1992). *Woman Killing: Intimate Femicide in Ontario, 1974–1990.* Report prepared for the Women We Honour Action Committee and the Ontario Women's Directorate, Toronto.

Currie, D., and B. MacLean (1992). 'Women, men, and the police: Losing the fight against wife battery in Canada'. In D. Currie and B. MacLean, eds, *Rethinking the Administration of Justice.* Halifax: Fernwood.

——— (1993). 'Woman abuse in dating relationships: Rethinking women's safety on campus', *Journal of Human Justice* 4: 1–24.

Currie, E. (1985). *Confronting Crime: An American Challenge.* New York: Pantheon.

——— (1989). 'Confronting crime: Looking toward the twenty-first century', *Justice Quarterly* 6: 5–26.

Dankwort, J. (1988). 'Programs for men who batter: A snapshot', *Vis-A-Vis: A National Newsletter on Family Violence* 6: 1–2.

Davis, R., M. Tichane, and D. Grayson (1980). *Mediation and Arbitration as Alternatives to Prosecution in Felony Arrest Cases—An Evaluation of the Brooklyn Dispute Resolution Center* (First Year). New York: Vera Institute of Justice.

DeKeseredy, W. (1988). *Woman Abuse in Dating Relationships: The Role of Male Peer Support.* Toronto: Canadian Scholars' Press.

——— (1992a). *Four Variations of Family Violence: A Review of Sociological Research.* Report prepared for Health and Welfare Canada's Family Violence Prevention Division. Ottawa: Health and Welfare Canada.

——— (1992b). 'Wife assault'. In V. Sacco, ed., *Deviance: Conformity and Control in Canadian Society.* Toronto: Prentice-Hall.

DeKeseredy, W., and R. Hinch (1991). *Woman Abuse: Sociological Perspectives.* Toronto: Thompson Educational Publishing.

DeKeseredy, W., and K. Kelley (1993a). 'The incidence and prevalence of woman abuse in Canadian university and college dating relationships', *Canadian Journal of Sociology* 18: 137–59.

——— (1993b). 'Woman abuse in university and college dating relationships: The contribution of the ideology of familial patriarchy', *Journal of Human Justice* 4: 25–52.

DeKeseredy, W., K. Kelly, and B. Baklid (1992). 'The physical, sexual, and psychological abuse of women in dating relationships: Results from a pretest for a national study'. Paper presented at the annual meeting of the American Society of Criminology, New Orleans.

DeKeseredy, W., and B. MacLean (1990). 'Researching woman abuse in Canada: A left realist critique of the Conflict Tactics Scale', *Canadian Review of Social Policy* 25: 19–27.

————— (1991). 'Exploring the gender, race and class dimensions of victimization: A left realist critique of the Canadian Urban Victimization Survey'. *International Journal of Offender Therapy and Comparative Criminology* 35: 143–61.

DeKeseredy, W., and M. Schwartz (1991). 'British left realism on the abuse of women: A critical appraisal'. In H. Pepinsky and R. Quinney, eds (1991).

————— (1994). 'Locating a history of some Canadian woman abuse in elementary and high school dating relationships', *Humanity and Society* 18: 49–63.

Dobash, R.E., and R.P. Dobash (1979). *Violence Against Wives*. New York: Free Press.

————— (1992). *Women, Violence and Social Change*. London: Routledge.

Dobash, R.P., R.E. Dobash, M. Wilson, and M. Daly (1992). 'The myth of sexual symmetry in marital violence', *Social Problems* 39: 71–91.

Dutton, D. and B. Levens (n.d.). *Crisis Intervention Training for Police: A Prescriptive Package*. Ottawa: Solicitor General of Canada.

Ehrlich, S. (1989). *Lisa, Hedda and Joel: The Steinberg Murder Case*. New York: St Martin's Press.

Ellis, D. (1987). 'Post-separation woman abuse: The contribution of social support', *Victimology* 13.

————— (1989). 'Male abuse of a married or cohabiting female partner: The application of sociological theory to research findings', *Violence and Victims* 4: 235–55.

————— (1990). 'Marital conflict mediation and post-separation wife abuse', *Law and Inequality* 2: 317–39.

Ellis, D., and DeKeseredy, W. (1989). 'Marital status and woman abuse: The DAD model', *International Journal of Sociology of the Family* 19: 67–87.

Ellis, D., J. Ryan, and A. Choi (1987). *Lawyers, Mediators and the Quality of Life Among Separated and Divorced Women*. Report prepared for the Laidlaw Foundation, Toronto. North York, Ont.: York University, LaMarsh Research Programme on Violence and Conflict Resolution.

Ellis, D., and N. Stuckless (1992). 'Preseparation abuse, marital conflict mediation, and postseparation abuse', *Mediation Quarterly* 9: 205–25.

Ellis, D., and L. Wight (1987). 'Post-separation woman abuse: The contribution of lawyers', *Victimology* 13.

Eshleman, J. (1978). *The Family: An Introduction*. Boston: Allyn and Bacon.

Felstiner, W., and L. Williams (1980). *Community Mediation in Dorchester, Massachusetts*. Washington, DC: US Department of Justice.

Finkelhor, D., and K. Yllo (1985). *License to Rape: Sexual Abuse of Wives.* New York: Free Press.

Gaquin, D. (1977–78). 'Spouse abuse: Data from the National Crime Survey', *Victimology* 2: 232–43.

Gelles, R., and C. Cornell (1985). *Intimate Violence in Families.* Beverly Hills: Sage.

Gelles, R., and M. Straus (1988). *Intimate Violence: The Causes and Consequences of Abuse in the American Family.* New York: Simon and Schuster.

Giles-Sims, J. (1983). *Wife Battering: A Systems Theory Approach.* New York: Guilford Press.

Goffman, E. (1961). *Asylums: Essays on the Social Situation of Mental Patients and Other Inmates.* New York: Anchor.

Government of Canada (1993). *Changing the Landscape: Ending Violence— Achieving Equality.* Ottawa: Supply and Services.

Gulliver, P. (1979). *Disputes and Negotiations: A Cross-Cultural Perspective.* New York: Academic Press.

Harman, L. (1989). *When a Hostel Becomes a Home: Experiences of Women.* Toronto: Garamond.

Habermas, J. (1975). *Legitimation Crisis.* Boston: Beacon Press.

Hatt, K., T. Caputo, and B. Perry (1990). 'Managing consent: Canada's experience with neoconservatives', *Social Justice* 17: 30–48.

Hilberman, E., and K. Munson (1977–78). 'Sixty battered women', *Victimology* 2: 460–71.

Hirschel, J., I. Hutchison, C. Dean, and A. Mills (1992). 'Review essay on law enforcement response to spouse abuse: Past, present, and future', *Justice Quarterly* 9: 247–83.

Hornick, J., B. Burrows, J. Hudson, and H. Sapers (1988). 'Summary and future directions'. In J. Hudson, J. Hornick, and B. Burrows, eds, *Justice and the Young Offender in Canada.* Toronto: Thompson Educational Publishing.

Horrocks, R. (1982). 'Alternatives to courts in Canada', *Alberta Law Review* 20: 326–34.

Hotaling, G., and D. Sugarman (1986). 'An analysis of risk markers and husband to wife violence: The current state of knowledge', *Violence and Victims* 1: 101–24.

Jaffe, P., and C. Burris (1984). *An Integrated Response to Wife Assault: A Community Model.* Working paper prepared for the Solicitor General of Canada. Ottawa: Solicitor General of Canada.

Jaffe, P., and J. Thompson (1979). *Family Consultant Service and the London Police Force.* Ottawa: Solicitor General of Canada.

Jaffe, P., P. Wolfe, A. Telford, and G. Austin (1986). 'The impact of police charges in incidents of wife abuse', *Journal of Family Violence* 1: 37–48.

Johnson, H. (1990). 'Wife abuse'. In McKie and Thompson, eds (1990).

Kennedy, L. (1990). *On the Borders of Crime: Conflict Management and Criminology.* Toronto: Longman.

Kennedy, L., and D. Dutton (1989). 'The incidence of wife assault in Alberta', *Canadian Journal of Behavioural Science* 21: 40–54.

Knopp, F. (1991). 'Community solutions to sexual violence: Feminist/ abolitionist perspectives'. In Pepinsky and Quinney, eds (1991).

Last, J. (1983). *A Dictionary of Epidemiology.* New York: Oxford.

Leighton, B. (1989). *Spousal Abuse in Metropolitan Toronto: Research Report on the Response of the Criminal Justice System.* Ottawa: Solicitor General of Canada.

Lerman, L. (1984). 'Mediation and wife abuse: A feminist critique', *Response* 7: 5–6, 12.

Levens, B. (1978). 'Domestic disputes, police response and social agency referral', *Canadian Police College Journal* 2: 13–26.

Levinger, G. (1966). 'Sources of marital dissatisfaction among applicants for divorce', *American Journal of Orthopsychiatry* 36: 804–6.

Lewis, C., R. Agrad, K. Gopic, J. Harding, T. Singh, and R. Williams (1989). *The Report of the Race Relations and Policing Task Force.* Toronto: Solicitor General of Ontario.

Lupri, E. (1990). 'Male violence in the home'. In C. McKie and K. Thompson, eds (1990).

McKie, C., and K. Thompson, eds (1990). *Canadian Social Trends.* Toronto: Thompson Educational Publishing.

MacLeod, L. (1980). *Wife Battering in Canada: The Vicious Circle.* Ottawa: Advisory Council on the Status of Women.

——— (1987). *Battered but not Beaten: Preventing Wife Battering in Canada.* Ottawa: Advisory Council on the Status of Women.

Mallin, D. (1987). 'Sheltering the homeless', *Canadian Home Economics Journal* 37: 114–16.

Mercer, S. (1988). 'Not a pretty picture: An exploratory study of violence against women in high school dating relationships', *Resources for Feminist Research* 17: 15–22.

Merry, S. (1989). 'Myth and practice in the mediation process'. In

M. Wright and B. Galaway, eds, *Mediation in Criminal Justice: Victims, Offenders and Community*. London: Sage.

Messerschmidt, J. (1986). *Capitalism, Patriarchy, and Crime: Toward a Socialist Feminist Criminology*. Totowa, NJ: Roman and Littlefield.

Michalowski, R. (1983). 'Crime control in the 1980s: A progressive agenda', *Crime and Social Justice* 19: 13–23.

O'Brien, J. (1971). 'Violence in divorce-prone families', *Journal of Marriage and the Family* 33: 692–8.

Okun, L. (1986). *Woman Abuse: Facts Replacing Myths*. Albany: State University of New York Press.

Parliament, J. (1990). 'Women employed outside the home'. In McKie and Thompson, eds (1990).

Pepinsky, H. (1991). 'Peacemaking in criminology and criminal justice'. In Pepinsky and Quinney, eds (1991).

Pepinsky, H., and R. Quinney, eds (1991). *Criminology as Peacemaking*. Bloomington: Indiana University Press.

Pizzey, E. (1974). *Scream Quietly or the Neighbors Will Hear*. New York: Penguin.

Podnieks, E. (1990). *National Survey on Abuse of the Elderly in Canada*. Toronto: Ryerson Polytechnical Institute.

Quinney, R. (1991). 'The way of peace: On crime, suffering, and service'. In Pepinsky and Quinney, eds (1991).

Rhen, G. (1985). 'Swedish active labour market policy: Retrospect and prospect', *Industrial Relations* 24.

Rock, P. (1988). 'Governments, victims and policies in two countries', *British Journal of Criminology* 28: 44–66.

Rubin, L. (1976). *Worlds of Pain: Life in the Working Class*. New York: Basic Books.

Russell, D. (1982). *Rape in Marriage*. New York: Macmillan.

Sacco, V., and H. Johnson (1990). *Patterns of Criminal Victimization in Canada*. Ottawa: Statistics Canada.

Schechter, S. (1982). *Women and Male Violence*. Boston: Free Press.

Schwartz, M. (1988). 'Ain't got no class: Universal risk theories of battering', *Contemporary Crises* 12: 373–92.

——— (1989). 'Asking the right questions: Battered wives are not all passive', *Sociological Viewpoints* 5: 46–61.

Schwartz, M., and W. DeKeseredy (1988). 'Liberal feminism on violence against women', *Social Justice* 15: 213–21.

——— (1991). 'Left realist criminology: Strengths, weaknesses and the feminist critique', *Crime, Law and Social Change* 15: 51–72.

Schulman, M.A. (1979). *A Survey of Spousal Violence in Kentucky.* Study No. 79271 conducted for the Kentucky Commission on Women. Washington, DC, US Government Printing Office.

Selva, L., and R. Bohm (1987). 'A critical examination of the informalism experiment in the administration of justice', *Crime and Social Justice* 29: 43–57.

Silverman, R. (1992). 'Street crime'. In V. Sacco, ed., *Deviance: Conformity and Control in Canadian Society.* Scarborough: Prentice-Hall.

Skipper, J. and G. Nass (1966). 'Dating behavior: A framework for analysis and an illustration', *Journal of Marriage and the Family* 28: 412–13.

Smith, M. (1985). *Woman Abuse: The Case for Surveys by Telephone.* LaMarsh Research Programme on Violence and Conflict Resolution, Report No. 12. North York: York University.

——— (1987). 'The incidence and prevalence of woman abuse in Toronto', *Violence and Victims* 2: 173–87.

——— (1989a). *Woman Abuse in Toronto: Incidence Prevalence and Socio-demographic Correlates.* LaMarsh Research Programme on Violence and Conflict Resolution, Report No. 18. North York: York University.

——— (1989b). 'Woman abuse: The case for surveys by telephone', *Journal of Interpersonal Violence* 4: 308–24.

——— (1990a). 'Sociodemographic risk factors in wife abuse: Results from a survey of Toronto women', *Canadian Journal of Sociology* 15: 39–58.

——— (1990b). 'Patriarchal ideology and wife beating: A test of a feminist hypothesis', *Violence and Victims* 5: 257–73.

——— (1991). 'Male peer support of wife abuse: An exploratory study', *Journal of Interpersonal Violence* 6: 512–19.

Snider, L. (1990). 'The potential of the criminal justice system to promote feminist concerns', *Studies in Law, Politics, and Society* 10: 141–69.

Solicitor General of Canada (1983). *Canadian Urban Victimization Survey: Victims of Crime.* Ottawa: Ministry of the Solicitor General.

Spanier, G. (1983). 'Married and unmarried cohabitation in the United States 1980', *Journal of Marriage and the Family* 45: 277–88.

Standing Committee on Health and Welfare, Social Affairs, Seniors and the Status of Women (1991). *The War Against Women.* Ottawa: House of Commons.

Stark-Adamec, C., and P. Adamec (1982). 'Aggression by men against women: Adaptation or aberration', *International Journal of Women's Studies* 5: 42–54.

Statistics Canada (1990). *Conjugal Violence Against Women.* Juristat Service Bulletin. Ottawa: Statistics Canada.

——— (forthcoming). *Violence Against Women Survey.* Ottawa: Canadian Centre for Justice Statistics.

Stets, J., and D. Henderson (1991). 'Contextual factors surrounding conflict resolution while dating: Results from a national study', *Family Relations* 40: 29–36.

Storrie, K, and N. Poon 1991. 'Programs for abusive men: A socialist feminist perspective'. In L. Samuelson and B. Schissel, eds, *Criminal Justice: Sentencing Issues and Reform.* Toronto: Garamond.

Straus, M. (1979). 'Measuring intrafamily conflict and violence: The Conflict Tactics (CT) Scales', *Journal of Marriage and The Family* 41: 75–88.

Strauss, M., and R. Gelles (1986). 'Societal changes and change in family violence from 1975 to 1985 as revealed by two national surveys', *Journal of Marriage and the Family* 48: 465–79.

Straus, M., R. Gelles, and S. Steinmetz (1981). *Behind Closed Doors: Violence in the American Family.* New York: Anchor Books.

Sudermann, M., and P. Jaffe (1993). 'Violence in teen dating relationships: Evaluation of a large scale primary prevention programme'. Paper presented at the annual meeting of the American Psychological Association, Toronto, Ontario.

Sugarman, D., and G. Hotaling (1989). 'Dating violence: Prevalence, context, and risk markers'. In M. Pirog-Good and J. Stets, eds, *Violence in Dating Relationships: Emerging Social Issues.* New York: Praeger.

Volpe, M. (1991). 'Mediation in the criminal justice system: Process, promises, problems'. In Pepinsky and Quinney, eds (1991).

Walker, L. (1979). *The Battered Woman.* New York: Harper and Row.

Chapter Five

VIOLENCE BY AND AGAINST CHILDREN IN CANADA

NATASHA J. CABRERA

The recent stabbing death of a young mother in Edmonton by two youths, aged 15 and 16, during a break and entry (*Maclean's*, 2 May 1994: 25), and the drive-by shooting of a man walking down an Ottawa street by three teenagers (*Maclean's*, 13 June 1994: 14), have served as further catalysts for citizens' and government officials' demands to change Canada's Young Offenders Act, which controls the administration of justice to young people aged 12 to 18. Some of these changes include imposing tougher sentences and lowering the age of young offenders so they can be tried as adults. With the help of the media, the public perception is not only that violence committed by young offenders is on the increase and the sentences have minimal deterrent value, but also that young offenders receive lighter sentences than adults for the same crime and are generally incorrigible (Meloff and Silverman, 1992).

Similarly, the sex slayings of a nine-year-old girl in 1984 (*Globe and Mail*, 26 Sept. 1990: 112), two Ontario schoolgirls in 1991 and 1992 (*Maclean's*, 11 April 1994: 21) and the sex-abuse scandal at an unlicensed day-care in Martensville, Saskatchewan (*Maclean's*, 21 February 1994: 21) contributed to public rage demanding that sex abusers of children serve maximum sentences without parole. Additionally, the case of a 20-month-old child in Alberta who was beaten unconscious at the home of his foster parents and now lies brain-dead in hospital (*Maclean's*, 23 August 1993: 13) has elicited government reports on the state of the country's foster-care programs.

These incidents epitomize the horrific nature of violence by and against children. While the media expose and sensationalize such crimes, academic research on this subject has examined the prevalence, causes, and in some cases the responses to this social and policy problem. Most of this work is concerned with etiological explanations and the implementation and evaluation of therapeutic techniques to help the victims of such tragedies.

Although a number of respected researchers in Canada have focused on the general cause and outcome of child abuse,[1] few have examined the incidence of violence by and against children in this country (e.g., McNight et al., 1966; Cormier, Angliker, Gagné and Markus, 1978). In this chapter I review the literature on this subset of child abuse, focusing on the incidence of violence by and against children, the relationship between the two, and the responses to violence against children. I conclude with recommendations for future research and policy implementation.

Before presenting the data, a few caveats are in order. First, although child abuse is a generic name and covers a wide variety of unacceptable or deviant actions,[2] this discussion will focus on violence by and against children. Violence in this context includes physical and sexual violence but excludes other factors that may lead to physical violence, such as child pornography, psychological abuse, or neglect. This focus implies that the violence committed by children is a consequence of their own experience of emotional, physical, and sexual violence. Hence I treat violence against children as a phenomenon that has far-reaching consequences, including violent behaviour on the part of victims themselves whether as children or as adults.[3]

With respect to age, it is also important to note that in Canada children under 14 are deemed incapable of giving informed consent to sex (Steed, 1994: xiii). However, according to the 1988 amendments to the Criminal Code of Canada (hereafter the Code) and the Canada Evidence Act, the new legal definition of 'sexual exploitation' protects children between the ages of 14 and 18. Hence my discussion of violence against children covers the ages from birth to 18. On the other hand, the discussion of violence by children refers to the ages from 12 to 18, in conformity with the Young Offenders Act. Children under the age of 12 are protected under educational and child-welfare legislation and cannot be tried under the Young Offenders Act.

CANADIAN RESEARCH

Unfortunately, the existing literature on physical and sexual violence by and against children in Canada is limited. Accurate statistics (official or non-official) on the incidence of violence against children are non-existent because most research focuses on one aspect of the problem (e.g., Meloff and Silverman, 1992; Silverman and Kennedy, 1993). For example, Silverman and Kennedy (1993) report incidence rates for first- and second-degree murders by young offenders but make only passing reference to sexual crimes; they focus on child homicide (including family violence and infanticide) but say little about child sexual abuse.

According to Chisholm (1978), this paucity of data can be blamed on a number of factors, including (1) lack of a standard, usable definition of child abuse; (2) variation in reporting systems; (3) lack of consistent procedures in dealing with child abuse; (4) failure to recognize (or perhaps acknowledge) child abuse, which leads to non-reporting; and (5) problems of professional and public education. While all these factors continue to exist today, another problem is that what is considered child abuse varies from province to province; hence the range of behaviour that is tolerated varies as well. This lack of consensus explains the variabilty in what aspects of the incident get reported, what actions constitute child abuse (e.g., emotional and physical neglect and abuse), and what evidence is necessary (e.g., presence of physical injury) (Chisholm, 1978: 318). Although as of 1978 reporting of abuse or ill-treatment of children is mandatory in nine of the twelve provincial or territorial jurisdictions there still exists a public reluctance to acknowledge or report such crimes. Only in Ontario must cases of child abuse be reported to the Children's Aid Society or the Crown Attorney; in the other provinces such reports are directed to the appropriate child-welfare authorities (Johnson and Thompson, 1978: 429).

There may also be unrepresentative reporting of adolescent abuse. Although we rightly focus on young-child abuse, the protection that at least four provinces (Alberta, Manitoba, Quebec, and Yukon) offer adolescents may be actually jeopardizing their well-being. For example, adolescent suicide, often precipitated by the experience of physical or sexual abuse, is fast becoming a serious problem in Canada.

The major problems identified in the literature seem to be the inadequate reporting of child abuse and a general public denial that these acts have occurred. Lay people—even those in professions that have the most contact with minors—sometimes fail to report offences to the proper authorities (Chisholm, 1978; Holmes, 1978). Although we are now more willing than ever before to report such crimes there are still many abuses that go unreported. Even when abused children reach out for help, their efforts are rarely recognized, and when they are, may often be ignored or disbelieved (Steed, 1994; Marron, 1993). On this point Chisholm noted that not only is there a great deal of psychological, sexual, and physical abuse of minors that does not become public, but our society appears to be quite tolerant of it (1978: 319). As Holmes (1978: 419) put it: 'Many thousands of children have been and will continue to be physically maimed, emotionally destroyed and even murdered because otherwise rational, loving and concerned human beings do not report offenses against children.' Although as a society we have made tremendous gains to protect children from abuse, as I show later in the chapter, these gains have not been sufficient.

There are some official and unofficial statistics that testify to the prevalence of violence committed against children. However, official data on sexual abuse may misrepresent the problem, as they are usually collected from self-reports of victimization by inmates in correctional institutions. Such data do not include children who have been sexually abused but who have not been convicted of a criminal offence, or who have not left home and hence are not part of the 'missing children' statistics. Since researchers tend to rely on official data, their results reflect the same problem. Data on physical violence against children are also unreliable. Physical violence, especially by parents, is usually tolerated as an extreme form of discipline and does not come to the public's attention unless homicide is involved. According to Silverman and Kennedy (1993: 183–4), in the period between 1961 and 1990 there were 876 cases of child homicide in Canada; this represents less than 10 per cent of total homicides.

The incidence of violence by children is also difficult to determine with accuracy. From 1987 to 1989, violent offences by youth appear to have risen by about 10 per cent (Marron, 1993: 49). However, a recent study by Meloff and Silverman (1992: 31) suggests that the incidence of homicide by young people is not increasing as suggested by the popular media. There is a paucity of research on the types of homicide committed by youth (e.g., patricide, matricide, or some form of family homicide), and the studies that have been conducted usually deal with a limited number of cases (e.g., Cormier et al., 1971; Cormier et al., 1978). For example, Cormier et al. (1978: 476) reported that of a total of 100 incidents committed by adolescents, included in their study, 14 were matricide, 11 were patricide, and 2 were fratricide. A more extensive study was conducted by Silverman and Kennedy (1993: 164) who report that between 1961 and 1990 there were 794 incidents of murder involving offenders under the age of 18; 18 per cent were committed by youth less than 15 years old; together, these crimes account for 7 per cent of homicides in Canada.

Although other types of violence committed by children, such as sexual violence, receive considerable attention from both the news media and television talk shows, sociological and criminological studies on this type of violence are rare as well. Most of the data come from official statistics or government reports. For example, sexual assaults by youth account for 1.04 per cent of charges laid under the Young Offenders Act, with an annual average of 1,179 (Marron, 1993: 154). From 1961 to 1990, 7 per cent of criminal offences committed by youths aged 15–17 were sexually related; among offenders under 15, 3 per cent of crimes were sexually related (Silverman and Kennedy, 1993: 164–5).

VIOLENCE BY AND AGAINST CHILDREN

VIOLENCE AGAINST CHILDREN

Despite attempts by some of the victims to get help, a paedophile in Kingston, Ontario, a respected choirmaster and élite member of the community, sexually abused approximately 325 choirboys for a period of 12 years before he was charged and convicted (Steed, 1994). In the 1950s and 1960s, 14 Christian Brothers from the Roman Catholic church in Ottawa sexually abused approximately 600 boys. They were convicted of offences ranging from buggery to assault causing bodily harm (Steed, 1994: 42). In Prescott, Ontario, 55 males and females (mostly males) were charged with sexually abusing 225 alleged victims over a period of almost ten years. Countless other anecdotes point to the reluctance of family members, neighbours, and the public at large to believe that a child or adolescent has been sexually or physically abused by someone they know (Steed, 1994; Marron, 1993). Such disbelief and denial allow abuse to continue.

Less sensationalized by the media, unless a death is involved, is physical abuse. Because it is often tied to child discipline, physical abuse is more tolerated and accepted by both the public and the police than sexual abuse. And because the boundary between tolerable and intolerable physical abuse is not clear, it is difficult to identify children at risk until it is too late.

1. Physical Violence
Physical violence against children includes homicide, infanticide, and severe forms of corporal punishment that may result in death or near-death. Documentation of physical violence against children is often embedded in studies dealing with child abuse. For example, Caplan et al. (1984) reviewed 422 cases of child maltreatment, which occurred during 1973–77, found in the files of a child welfare agency and a children's hospital, both located in Toronto. The researchers used the definitions of child abuse employed by both the Hospital for Sick Children (HSC) and the Metropolitan Toronto Children's Aid Society (CAS). These records included both confirmed and suspected cases of physical and sexual abuse as well as neglect. They found 48 per cent confirmed cases of physical abuse and 1 per cent confirmed cases of sexual abuse. However, the authors do not break these aggregates down into subtypes of violence against children; nor do they present profiles of the victims, perpetrators, or families.

With regard to homicide of children aged 0–13, Silverman and Kennedy (1993) found that between 1961 and 1990 (with a total of 876 cases) children under 2 comprised 33 per cent of the victims and older children (2–13) 67 per cent. However, the highest rate of homicide— 4.2 per 100,000 cases—involved children under 2; for children between 2 and 13 the peak was .8. Younger children (under 2) were most likely to be killed by their mothers (46 per cent); fathers or stepfathers were involved in 34 per cent of the cases. Among older children (2–13) 25 per cent were killed by fathers/stepfathers and 29 per cent by mothers. The bulk (67 per cent) of the women charged with infanticide (36 per cent) are declared mentally ill and receive lenient sentences (Silverman and Kennedy, 1993: 155–6). Overall, 86 per cent of younger children and 68 per cent of older children were killed by family members (Silverman and Kennedy, 1993: 185). These researchers found no differences between boys and girls in terms of victimization rates. The overall rate of child homicide fluctuates but has not been shown to go below the rate recorded for 1961 (Silverman and Kennedy, 1983: 183).

In general, theories explaining child abuse fall into four main categories: psychopathological, social-situational, cultural, and social psychological.[4] A brief account of the most common sociocultural explanation follows.

Physical violence is widely seen as an extension of socially acceptable punishment patterns, or as a logical consequence of parental disciplinary actions (Bell, 1975: 417cf; Gil, 1970; Kadushin et al., 1981: 190; Martin, 1983: 59; Paulson and Blake, 1969: Parke and Collmer, 1975; Steinmetz, 1977a; 1977b). Many discipline-related factors have been linked to child abuse, including rigid parenting styles; unrealistic expectations of child development (Gil, 1970; Helfer, 1973; Steele and Pollock, 1974; Galdston, 1975); parents who are physically punished as children (Straus, 1983); high levels of support for corporal punishment (Gray et al., 1976; Schneider et al., 1976); and, using below-average levels of coercion (Burgess et al., 1981). Strauss (1983) has also found that the same causal variables are relevant for ordinary physical punishment as for 'abusive' violence.[5]

To test this hypothesis, Lenton (1990) asked a random sample of families, who had been identified as engaging in child abuse, in the Toronto area about parents' disciplinary techniques. Participation in her study was voluntary, and the selection criterion (i.e., at least one child between the ages of 3 and 17) was met by 117 families of an initial sample of 338 families. Of these, 82 per cent had fathers and of these 76 per cent were interviewed; however, only 50 per cent of fathers responded (Lenton, 1990: 165). Not all the disciplinary items selected were violent. For example, Lenton's categorization of aggressive disciplinary actions includes behaviours that are not in themselves aggressive (e.g., withholding food, withdrawing emotionally) but that could lead to aggressive behaviour. She found three types of discipline: mixed, primarily reactive (e.g., milder reactions, such as yelling, spanking, verbal threats), and positive reactions to both good and bad behaviour on the part of the child (e.g., rewards, emotional support, withholding of privileges, etc.). The violent pattern included the most severe disciplinary reactions (i.e., result in injury to child). And the proactive method included techniques to teach the child (e.g., using positive models, accepting scolding from child for adult aggression, meeting regularly to discuss guidelines for behaviour and parent withdrawal of love). She reported that milder and even more severe aggressive actions are common among all parents. With the exception of withholding food and beating, mothers are somewhat more likely to use violent disciplinary techniques than fathers (Lenton, 1990: 169). A problem with Lenton's findings is her definition of what constitutes aggressive discipline.

Unfortunately, there are few comparative studies across Canada dealing with both physical and sexual violence against children. The need for such studies is obvious; without such data intervention and prevention of child abuse seems a distant goal.

2. Sexual Violence

Although it is generally believed by those working in the field that sexual violation of children is so prevalent as to be a 'normative experience' (Steed, 1994: xiii), the literature on the incidence of sexual violence against children suffers from the same problems as the literature on child abuse in general. For example, Caplan et al. (1984: 345) attributed the low number of sexual abuse cases found in their study (i.e., 1 per cent) to the way their sample was selected and concluded that their result was not a good indicator of actual incidence in the population. Another problem is the willingness by those in charge to report or record such offences. It took three or four generations of native children, who over a period of 100 years or so were sexually abused by Catholic priests and teachers, before this tragedy was acknowledged (Steed, 1994). And Burgess (1988) writes that this crime generally goes unreported, undetected and undisclosed. Of those reported, less than one third of alleged offenders are charged; of these, one third are convicted; and from this subset, only a minority end up incarcerated or in treatment programs (Steed, xii). Nevertheless, Steed suggests that this dismal record is changing—more abusers are now going to jail—although élite sexual abusers' denial is usually believed.

Most accounts of sexual child abuse are case studies highlighted in media reports and journalistic books (e.g., Steed, 1994); there are some official reports, but academic studies are rare. Thus generalization about child abuse is problematic. It is estimated that 42,000 children under the age of 15 are sexually abused by adults every year. In a 1987 study of 12,446 missing children cases reported to police in Metro Toronto, Montreal, Edmonton, and Surrey, BC over a one-year period, 10 per cent were sexually abused and 14 per cent and 12 per cent were physically abused by their father and mother or sibling, respectively (Marron, 1993: 85). In 1992, according to Statistics Canada, 40 per cent of all reported sexual assaults were committed against children aged 11 and under (Steed, 1994: xiii).

The available statistics suggest that females fare worse as victims than males, although this could be a methodological and social artifact. A 1990 study of more than 16,000 high school-aged girls by the Nova Scotia Advisory Council on the Status of Women found that 11 per cent had been sexually abused by their boyfriends, 18 per cent physically assaulted, and 32 per cent emotionally abused; 19 per cent of those who had engaged in sex said they had been forced. Others say that the recent increases in numbers of reported sex crimes are the result of greater vigilance and awareness of sexual victimization.

According to a 1990 report for the Ontario Ministry of Community and Social Services, 82 per cent of inmates at the federal Prison for Women (Kingston, Ontario), which houses all women sentenced in Canada, reported sexual abuse as children. In a 1985 study, Russell found that one in three American females had been sexually abused in childhood; 16 per cent were incest victims. Similar results were found by a 1992 report on a survey entitled Female's Safety, conducted by the Institute of Social Research at York University (cited in Steed, 1994: 131). According to this survey, 43 per cent of females respondents reported sexual abuse in childhood and 17 per cent had experienced incest by the age of 16. Boys, however, are also victims of sexual assault, although there may be a social and personal bias against reporting such crimes. The 1984 Badgley Report to the federal government, based on a four-year task force and 100,000 cases of child sexual abuse, concluded that one in four girls and one in seven boys experienced unwanted sexual acts. More recently, some argue that this pattern is changing, producing a shift in reporting trends; more males are willing to come forward (Steed, 1994: xii).

There are no stereotypes of offenders. Parents, relatives, or trusted friends within 'affinity systems' victimize children (Burgess, 1988). Paedophiles can be male or female, from any socioeconomic background; they can be macho womanizers, saintly priests, selfless teachers; they can be extroverted or introverted, charismatic or passive. Some offenders abuse their own children; others roam the streets. Some work in professions that give them maximum exposure to children; others have minimal contact as a result of their work (Steed, 1994: xiv).

The causes of sexual violence against children are complex and beyond the scope of this chapter. Briefly, it has been associated with a variety of causes/processes. For example, it has been linked to the patriarchal structure of families, where the father, under extreme conditions, is led to believe that he 'sexually owns' the females under his care (Lahey, 1984). In other situations, the adult child abuser has been a victim of abuse as a child. This 'cycle of violence' suggests that early childhood experiences are powerful determinants of later behaviour.

VIOLENCE BY CHILDREN

In 1993 the world was appalled by the brutal abduction and murder of a two-year-old in England at the hands of two 11-year-olds (*Maclean's*, 6 December 1993). Incidents such as this have contributed to the public perception that children and teenagers who commit such crimes do so for thrills, status, or entertainment (Marron, 1993: 29). Too often the social problems associated with violent behaviour are ignored and the justice system is blamed for being too lax.

The incidence of violent crimes committed by youth is plagued with the same problems discussed earlier (e.g., data collection). Nevertheless, it is estimated that the overall rate of violent youth crime has increased tenfold since the early 1960s (Marron, 1993: 52). Youth court statistics show that the proportion of violent offences coming before the court has risen from 11 to 18 per cent in recent years. The total number of such offences rose by 10 per cent over a three-year period (Marron, 1993: 52). Ontario accounted for 40 per cent of all convictions under the Young Offenders Act and had the highest rate of violent offences; this scenario is typical of urban centres (Marron, 1993: 49).

According to the 1990 report for the Ontario Ministry of Community and Social Services (MCSS) responsible for providing services for 12- to 16-year-olds, females are less likely to be charged with violent offences; nine in ten charges are laid against males and the rate of crime is perceived to be increasing at a rapid pace.

1. Physical Violence

The 1990 MCSS reported that the violent offences with which young people were charged included sexual assaults (9 per cent), possession of weapons/explosives (.14 per cent), robberies (13 per cent), murders and attempted murders (.04 per cent) and, finally, non-sexual assaults (more than 60 per cent). There is an average of 40 cases per year of homicides by children and about 60 attempted murders per year. Although the annual murder rate fluctuates, there is no overall rise in violent crime.

There are some studies that deal with a select number of incidents of violence by children. Cormier et al. (1978), for example, performed a longitudinal study of adolescents charged under the Juvenile Delinquents Act (which was replaced by the Young Offenders Act in 1984) with causing the death of an individual. Looking specifically at cases in which the offender was an adolescent and the victim was a family member (parent, brother or sister), they reported that 'the incidence of adolescents who kill a sibling seems low compared to adolescents who kill a parental figure' (Cormier et al., 1978: 466–7). Unfortunately, there is no indication of the size of the sample and what we might expect the incidence to be in the total population.

In a later study, Meloff and Silverman (1992) looked at the incidence of juvenile homicide in Canada between 1961 and 1983. Catego-
rizing their findings according to the victim-offender relationship, they
also noted gender, race, number of offenders (single or multiple), and
means of offence. They found that homicide rates rose with age, from
.29 per 100,000 for 13-year-olds to 2.71 per 100,000 for 17-year-olds. Most
homicides were committed by single offenders and involved one victim.
But probability of being a victim of multiple youth offenders increased
with social distance. Of all crime-based homicide by youth, 70 per cent
were theft-related. In 30 per cent of the cases, homicide occurred as a
result of another crime (theft or sexual crime). The most common
means of homicide (35 per cent) was shooting (mainly with rifles and
shotguns), followed by stabbing (30 per cent) and beating (22 per cent),
with younger offenders (under 15) using guns more frequently (48 per
cent) than older ones (15–17 years) who were more likely to stab their
victims (34 per cent) (Meloff and Silverman, 1992: 20–4).

Of all homicides, 34 per cent involved a family member; the balance are almost equally distributed between acquaintances (35 per
cent) and strangers (32 per cent) (Meloff and Silverman, 1992). But in
crime-related homicides the two parties were rarely acquainted.
Younger offenders are more likely to kill family members than older
ones, but the latter are more likely to be involved in crime-based homicide where the victim is a stranger. Most homicides involved Caucasians
against Caucasians, but in terms of other proportions in the population
aboriginal people were over-represented, and were more likely than
Caucasians to kill someone with whom they had close social relations
(Meloff and Silverman, 1992: 31). In general, males were more likely to
kill either family members or strangers, and more likely to be involved
in crime-based homicide, than were females.

Although their data show general patterns of homicide by juveniles, Meloff and Silverman do not offer comparisons with general populations of juveniles, nor do they report the number of young offenders
involved in homicide during this period, 1961–1983. Because their data
are based on self reports or victimization studies, it is difficult to determine with accuracy the incidence of this type of violence by young
offenders.

When Silverman and Kennedy (1993: 164–5) added seven years to
the data set obtained by Meloff and Silverman (1992), the results were
similar. They report that between 1961 and 1990, there were 794 murders committed by youth under 18 years old. Indian youth comprised
almost 30 per cent of offenders both under 15 and between 15 and 17.
The victims of both the younger (under 15) and the older youth
(15–17), regardless of ethnicity or race, were males in 62 per cent and
73 per cent of the cases, respectively. Younger children killed people

under 18 years of age in approximately 45 per cent of cases; older children's targets seems to be across ages. Shooting was more common among younger offenders, stabbing among older ones. Younger children killed family members in 45 per cent of cases, friends/acquaintances in 31 per cent. Younger children were more likely to kill their parents (18 per cent of cases) than older youth (12 per cent). Although chronic offenders comprised only 6 per cent of the young offenders, they committed half the murders reported (Marron, 1993: 48). These data support Marron's (1993) contention that most crimes committed by youth occur within the family. Such crime may be the result of dysfunctional family dynamics that include sexual, physical or emotional abuse.

Violence leading to murder can be triggered by relatively minor occurrences—for example, a petty dispute over a small drug deal. Unless placed in the context of the young offender's personal, emotional, and intellectual problems, many of the murders appear to be senseless. However, clinical data show that some violent young offenders suffer from some diagnosed mental illness, which may be responsible for senseless 'thrill killings' (Marron, 1993: 161, 162).

One of the best supported psychological views on why adolescents kill is that exposure to chronic violence has a damaging impact on behaviour and can increase the likelihood of engaging in violence (DeAngelis, 1993; Hill, 1993; Ross, 1980). The 1990 report for the Ontario Ministry (MCSS) concluded that victims of child abuse are ten times more likely to commit criminal offences in adolescence than are children who have not been abused. The expression of violence by children who have experienced violence can also be directed toward the self. Ross (1980) reports that in some cases there is a link between child-abuse and self-mutilation (p. 275). Even when children's exposure to violence is indirect—as when they witness shootings, robberies, etc.—they learn to use violence as a problem-solving technique (Slaby, 1993). Slaby (1993: 40) argues that through a process of socialization and development, violence is acquired as the appropriate way to solve interpersonal problems, alleviate frustration and obtain material rewards that are deserved but not obtained. In short, violence by children is a logical consequence of violence against children.

Most children exposed to chronic violence live in environments that are plagued by social problems: child abuse both at home and in the sex trade, poverty, family and community violence. They fall through the cracks of the health and social-services systems, experience isolation or lose community awareness in middle- or upper-class neighbourhoods (Marron, 1993: 34), experience prejudice and discrimination, use drugs or alcohol, and have ready access to guns (Slaby, 1993). Some of these problems such as child abuse and isolation cut across social class (Marron, 1993).

Another important contributing factor to violence by children is exposure to television. Because adolescents who are not protected by their families or societies do not have their developmental needs (i.e., acquiring personal and group identity, self-efficacy and personal power) met in a normal way, Hill (1992) argues, they are more susceptible to the aggressive models abundant in popular culture 'where violence is used as a means of control and power'. Eron (1993) agrees that television has a major impact on the development of youth violence and concludes that 'continued exposure to violence on television affects the attitudes and behaviour of youngsters' both in the present and in their future interactions as adults. A study for the Central Toronto Youth Services concluded that media and other cultural images glorify 'youthful sexuality', tolerate exploitive pornography, and give sexual licence to males (cited in Marron, 1993: 159).

There is plenty of evidence to support the link between television and violence and aggression, especially in children and adolescents (Eron, 1993). This connection has been found across ages, gender, and socio-economic and intelligence levels (Huesmann, 1993). However, younger children seem to be more susceptible (Huesmann and Eron, 1993). The debate seems to centre around the size of the effect, and the mechanism by which televised aggression affects viewers (Wilcox, 1992). Aside from 'copycat' murders, the most significant problem is the effect of television violence in shaping values and attitudes (Eron, 1993). According to Eron, if a child watches two to four hours of televison per day, by the end of elementary school such a child would have 'seen 8,000 murders and more than 100,000 other acts of violence'. Teenagers, on average have seen more than 200,000 violent acts through the media. In addition to time spent watching violent television programs, other factors related to the impact of violent television on aggression include: the imitating ability of children, especially with desirable heroes with whom children can identify; accepting violence as a solution to problems; and being desensitized to television (Huesmann, 1993). Of course, exposure to violence on television has the most severe impact when it is accompanied by other predisposing and precipitating factors such as poverty, poor educational achievement, family violence, and neurophysiological traumas.

2. Sexual Violence

The 1990 report for the Ontario Ministry of Community and Social Services concluded that there was a 160 per cent increase over two years in the number of sexual offenders aged 12–15 recorded by the Ontario Child Abuse Register. Similar increases in offences were found nationally, with male adolescents accounting for about 25 per cent of all sex crimes committed (Marron, 1993: 155).

In one of the few studies available of adolescent sexual offenders, researchers from Central Toronto Youth Services reviewed all cases reported to police in Toronto over a 30-month period: a total of 438 incidents involving 341 males and 8 females and resulting in 288 charges and 164 convictions (cited in Marron, 1993). In 41 cases, the perpetrator was between 5 and 11 years old and could not be charged under the Young Offenders Act. Most victims were friends and acquaintances, 16 per cent were family members. In an earlier study, one-third of victims were relatives; most victims were between 6 and 15 years old, but 15 per cent were children less than 6 years old (cited in Marron, 1993: 156). Native youths are over-represented, according to Canadian aboriginal peoples' advocacy groups. This suggests that there may be a social/ethnic bias, racial prejudice, and sexual stereotyping (Marron, 1993: 47).

Weapons were used only in 5 per cent of the cases, physical force in 43 per cent, and verbal threats in 19 per cent. In one-fifth of the incidents the victims were emotionally traumatized and in 40 per cent of cases there was more than one perpetrator, perhaps indicating gang-style violence (Marron, 1993: 156). Finally, 15 per cent of the incidents occurred inside schools or on school property during regular school hours.

Silverman and Kennedy (1993: 165) found that 7 per cent of sexually-related crimes were committed by youths between 15 and 17, and 3 per cent by youths under 15. Given the limited data available, however, the incidence of sexual violence by children is impossible to determine. Although the majority of sexual assaults against children are committed by males, Becker and Hunter (1994) suggest that the number of juvenile females caught molesting boys and girls is growing. Under-reporting of female perpetrators reflects the general view that sexual abuse is a male-only crime (Becker and Hunter, 1994) and boys tend to keep silent when they have been victimized by females.

There is no reliable profile of the typical young sexual offender. Indeed, it has been argued that because sexuality affects youth in different ways, it is not possible to develop such a profile. In general, though, it appears that young sex offenders do not make good criminals: many are irresponsible, lack foresight and judgement, leave fingerprints, make phone calls from the scene of the crime, or return with friends to show their deed. They also tend to believe that they face only a 3-year maximum sentence (in fact, many are transferred to adult court), have a mistaken belief in their invulnerability, are easily manipulated by others, are immature, and often are victims of child abuse themselves (Marron, 1993: 154).

As mentioned earlier, almost all violent offenders have a background of emotional, physical, or sexual abuse (Marron, 1993: 41). About one-fourth of sexual offenders have prior convictions for non-sexual assaults. Some clinical accounts of sexual offenders suggest that they tend to be loners with poor self-esteem, have antisocial attitudes and poor impulse control, do not believe they can form healthy relationships, have difficulties in school and tend to have low or borderline intelligence. Moreover, their home experiences have taught them that it is normal to make aggressive sexual demands, and that family violence or sexual abuse are not serious problems (Marron, 1993: 157). Both female and male offenders tend to have a history of sexual abuse, suicidal thinking, and attempts at suicide; to be repeat offenders, aggressive, and depressed; and to experience post-traumatic stress disorder (Becker and Hunter, 1994). Relations of power and abuse that children learn when they are subjected to violence by bigger and more powerful adults may prompt them to mimic the behaviour they themselves experienced and to target victims who are even less powerful than they are.

A case study outlined by Becker and Hunter (1994) illustrates the cycle of violence. When E was 6, she was caught having oral sex with her 2-year-old brother; she later molested a 4-year-old girl and a 2-year-old boy; and she engaged in bestiality with a dog. According to these researchers, E's behaviour mirrored her own suffering: she was repeatedly raped by her father, an alcoholic and heroin addict, and physically abused by her mother. She also regularly witnessed her father beating and raping her mother (as reported by Sleek, *APA Monitor*, 1992: 34).

A caveat is in order. The discussion thus far has concentrated specifically on Canada. Although Silverman and Kennedy (1993) make comparisons between American and Canadian crime rates, this approach was not taken here because of the number of factors (e.g., race, culture, legal system, etc.) that make such comparisons speculative at best. Finkelhor (1994: 411) makes a similar point, noting that 'variation in rates between countries probably does not reflect variation in true prevalence'. Even within one country, he writes, wide variations in rates may result from differing survey methodologies and definitions of sexual abuse.

RESPONSES TO VIOLENCE BY AND AGAINST CHILDREN

In the winter of 1994, a woman judge in Quebec ruled that since the offender (an uncle of the victim) had only sodomized his niece, sparing her virginity, he deserved a light sentence. The man was sentenced to 23 months in jail (the prosecution asked for 48 months) after he was convicted of sexual assault, sodomy, and sexual interference (*Maclean's*, 31 January 1994: 17).

In many cases, it has taken suicides, ongoing agony, horror, and ruined lives to bring child molesters to justice (Steed, 1994). 'Left to their own devices, the average paedophile abuses 300–400 children over a 15–20 year period before he's caught—if he's caught' (Detective Wendy Leaver, Metro Toronto Police, Sexual Assault Squad, cited in Steed, 1994: 50).

These incidents suggest that institutional responses to violence against children are rooted in sexism and disbelief. At the same time, such responses make it difficult for perpetrators to get the kind of help they need to break the cycle of violence. Other examples show how society fails to address the social and mental-health problems that give rise to violence among children. A study of children's mental health in Ontario, for example, concluded that 18 per cent of children exhibit significant levels of behavioural and emotional disorder, but fewer than one sixth receive help (Marron, 1983: 55).

In general, the literature on responses to child abuse consists of two approaches: one that focuses on treatment and one that emphasizes punishment and deterrence.

TREATMENT

Given the history and the gravity of the problem, therapeutic treatment for survivors of child sexual abuse has not been the priority of the medical field. Nor is clinical treatment a priority for young people in correctional institutions. Social workers, correctional officers, and psychologists point out that they have limited resources, and that their facilities are overcrowded and understaffed (Marron, 1993: 186).

However, this situation may be changing. Reichert (1994) notes that considerable resources have been devoted to psychotherapy for children who have been abused, including one-on-one and group approaches. And the Beechgrove Children's Centre in Prescott, Ontario, has developed an early-intervention program that is being studied throughout North America (Steed, 1994: 131).

For violent offenders 'scared-straight' and boot-camp programs, which are prevalent in the United States, are being experimented with in Canada. However, there is no evidence to suggest that these programs work, and in fact some have argued that they may make offenders more aggressive or violent (Marron, 1993: 183–4).

The main challenge to implementing treatment is the difficulty of identifying high-risk individuals early enough: most offenders are identified as high risk only when they come to the attention of the courts or the legal system. In 1990 the Ontario Ministry of Community Social Services produced a check-list of all factors that contribute to youth crime, including parenting, early home life (80 per cent of incidents of wife abuse are witnessed by children), influence from peers, personal temperaments and aptitudes, difficulties in school, antisocial attitudes, and psychological and neurological problems. This check-list can be used to identify high-risk children.

The success of prevention programs depends on their ability to deal with poverty, drug addiction, child abuse, difficulties integrating into labour force, discrimination faced by minority youth, and sense of alienation (Marron, 1993). The law and youth system are not as effective as they should be because there is little community support and the government does not adequately finance rehabilitative services (p. 324). Because the problems are so complex, touching all aspects of a child's life, treatment programs must provide intensive health, educational and social services for whole families, not just their children, perhaps even beginning at the prenatal stage. Some observers also suggest that treatment for children with problems should be compulsory (Marron, 1993: 320).

Community support is essential. For example, schools should be at the centre of a co-ordinated system of children's family services, while members of the community, including youth, police, crown attorneys, parents, teachers, and social workers, come together in informal committees to identify and find solutions to common social problems (Marron, 1993: 317). In addition, of course, post-release rehabilitation programs are needed to provide positive role models and expose young offenders to cultural, educational, and recreational opportunities (p. 320).

THE CRIMINAL-JUSTICE SYSTEM

The assumption that punishment is a deterrent is based on the power of rationality. However, most young offenders, who are protected under the Young Offenders Act, do not rationally consider the pros and cons of committing a particular crime (Marron, 1993: 181). Nonetheless, the criminal justice system (e.g., the police, courts, prison and probation) is based on the 'punish them' approach. This argument can also be applied to adults who commit violence against children. Although there are no specific laws dealing with punishing those who commit crimes against children in the Criminal Code of Canada, Holmes (1978: 418) notes that it 'contains numerous laws related to behaviour described in the literature on the abused, neglected or sexually assaulted child . . . Other offenses that are related to the battered child syndrome are described under various headings ranging from assault to murder' (p. 418).

The Young Offenders Act, which replaced the Juvenile Delinquents Act (1908 to 1984), covers youth between 12 and 18 years of age and aims to 'protect' both minors and society (Marron, 1993: 188). It has relatively low penalties (i.e., three years for murder, two for lesser crimes), provides a lawyer free of charge, and deals only with criminal offences. It also provides for 'alternative measures' bypassing the courts and using instead community agencies or probation.

With regard to protecting abused children, all provinces have Child Welfare Acts that authorize police, social workers and welfare officials to remove children from homes where child abuse is suspected. But because there are no clear guidelines regarding responsibility for the investigation and successful resolution of offences pertaining to child abuse, this duty is often problematic for the police to accomplish (Holmes, 1978: 423).

Legislation protecting and punishing children has been criticized by child advocates and those in favour of stiffer sentences for children who commit crimes. Criminal cases of child sexual abuse are problematic to prosecute (e.g., Berliner and Barbieri, 1984). And Martin (1992) argues that victims of familial child abuse may be victimized twice: in the family and by the criminal-justice system. With respect to the latter he suggests that the recent increase in the number of child sexual abuse cases adjudicated through the criminal-justice system has drawn attention to the effects that that system may have on child victims and prompted a search for ways to reduce this traumatic response while guaranteeing the legal rights of the accused (p. 330).

In order to minimize the risk to the children involved, several procedures have been suggested: (1) better training of staff; (2) modifying the criminal-justice system to suit the needs and limitations of child witnesses; (3) providing a court-appointed special advocate; and (4) preventing sexually abused young children from having to testify in open court (Martin, 1992: 332).

Martin's (1992) concerns have been partially addressed by changes to the law. Amendments made to the Criminal Code and the Canada Evidence Act in 1988 allow greater accommodation for children. Three new offences were defined: sexual interference, sexual exploitation, and invitation to sexual touching (Steed, 1994). Police have the authority to charge adults who have sexually molested children by engaging in sexual games or other activities that lead up to but do not necessarily include molestation or penetration. Another important change, especially for sexual crimes, is that children's evidence no longer needs corroboration (Steed, 1994: 119). The courts now accept closed-circuit testimony, and police videotapes of children's statements about abuse are allowed as evidence. In addition, hearsay may be admitted as evidence, and more credence is given to children's testimony as they are now believed to be capable of providing accurate accounts of events. Finally, there is also a victim-witness assistance program that prepares children to testify by explaining to them how the legal system works (Steed, 1994: 120). Nevertheless, some sexually abused children are still retraumatized as they face their abusers in court.

Perceiving that the rate of youth violence is increasing at a disturbing pace, and that the sentences young offenders receive are too light, the public has demanded stiffer penalties and tougher conditions. Recent amendments to the Young Offenders Act include raising maximum sentences from three to five years, making it easier to transfer cases from youth to adult court, and allowing earlier parole if the youth is sentenced as an adult to life in prison (Marron, 1993: 190).

Critics still argue that the act does not go far enough. For example, once released, young offenders cannot be publicly identified. This anonymity, it has been argued, gives offenders a sense of invulnerability and puts the public at risk. In reality, however, the law is much tougher on young offenders than is perceived. For example, custody terms cannot be shortened by early parole, and although young offenders can apply after six months to have their sentences commuted, this is not commonly sought or granted (Marron, 1993: 211, 212). And while conditions vary from province to province, most serious crimes can be transferred to adult court if the offender is over 14 years old and the judge thinks such a move is in the public's best interest (Marron, 1993: 213).

Despite the public's apprehension that the system is too lenient, across the country more young offenders are being placed in custody than ever before (Marron, 1993: 180). Four out of five youths appearing in court are found guilty, and many are given longer jail sentences than adults for similar crimes. One-fifth of those convicted in youth court are sentenced to some form of custody, either secure custody, which resembles an adult prison sentence, or open custody, which is held in community-run groups. Less than 5 per cent of charged youth are acquitted and more than half the cases that come before youth courts result in probation or community-service orders (Marron, 1993: 177–8). And youth court records show that over the past few years about one-third of murder cases have been transferred to adult court (Marron, 1993: 152).

In general, more than 100,000 criminal convictions are registered under the Young Offenders Act each year. There are, however, regional disparities. In Saskatchewan and Manitoba, approximately 7 per cent of youths are arrested each year, compared to less than 5 per cent in Ontario, and less than 4 per cent in Quebec. These discrepancies may be blamed on racial and socio-economic factors. Aboriginal youth and those from poor socio-economic backgrounds are generally over-represented in correctional institutions (Marron, 1993: 46).

A survey of Ontario's 76 court judges found that 74.5 per cent said they had placed more emphasis on punishment since the introduction of the Young Offenders Act in 1984. Most 'custody' sentences are for non-violent property crimes; some youth are put in custody for their own good and receive sentences for crimes for which adults would probably not have been sent to jail (Marron, 1993: 179).

How effective is incarceration as punishment? The available statistics are not very promising. More than 75 per cent of youths who have been in custody offend again when they get out, and there is some evidence that violent crime has risen since more youths have been going to jail (Marron, 1993: 183). Moreover, the 1990 report for the Ontario Ministry concluded that longer and harsher sentences to custody neither reform nor deter, and may even aggravate the problem. This finding is buttressed by federal statistics on repeat offenders, which show that the interval before committing a crime becomes shorter after each sentence (i.e., four months between the first and second offences and one to one-and-a-half between the fourth and fifth) (Marron, 1993: 181).

The failure of the punishment approach is due partly to the inability to deal with underlying causes of crime and partly to the inconsistencies and biases of the legal system. Penalties range from suspended sentences to life in prison. One man received a suspended sentence for sexually molesting boys in the 1960s; another man received two years less a day for sexually abusing a pre-teen boy from 1988 to 1991; in another case, the convicted man received thirty years for sexually assaulting five former stepchildren and one friend between the ages of 7 and 14; and, a convicted paedophile faces a dangerous offender application brought by the Crown prosecutor, which if approved means an indefinite sentence (Steed, 1994: 76).

One problem in dealing with child sexual abuse is that the criminal-justice and child-protection systems often have conflicting goals. The aim of the former is to prosecute and punish the offender rather than to protect the child (Martin, 1992: 331). On the other hand, the child-protection system aims at simultaneously maintaining the family unit (even when the child offender is a family member) and protecting the child. Because the criminal-justice and the child-protection systems have different orientations, the child is interviewed by many people, increasing his or her trauma and confusion (Martin, 1992: 331). With sex crimes, the offence is judged not by the behaviour of the perpetrator but by the response of the victim. If the victims do not come forward right away, or have turned to drugs, become promiscuous, or started lying or stealing (common reactions to sexual abuse), judges tend to be lenient with the offenders, particularly when they are considered valued members of society (Martin, 1992: 77).

Moreover, responses to violence against children are not consistent across the country. Both 'rural and urban police are mandated under provincial laws to report all suspected cases of child abuse and neglect to the proper provincial authorities' (Holmes, 1978: 417). Holmes (1978) reviewed the responses of rural police (in particular, the Royal Canadian Mounted Police) to child abuse. He writes that in rural areas the police are the sole protectors of children when a report of suspect child abuse has been filed (p. 417). Their responses are a function of how well known the accused is and the credibility of source. The majority of cases brought to the attention of police forces fall into three categories: adult survivors who report childhood abuse, current incest violations, and children abused in paedophiliac sex rings including sport teams and choirs (Steed, 1994: xiv).

Most of the research on police responses to sexual abusers of children underlines the need for more resources (e.g., 'our hands are tied') and how much they depend on the public to report the offences. Aside from internal structural inefficiencies to deal with child abuse the police forces, like society in general, have shown denial or negligence in investigating allegations of child abuse. In at least one case, the police refused to investigate or lay charges against an élite member of a community even when the victim lodged a formal complaint.

CONCLUSION

The incidence of violence by and against children in Canada is difficult to determine. Part of the problem is the lack of research in this area, which, in turn, may be due to lack of funding, difficulty in obtaining access to those involved, and the sensitive subject matter itself.

Public responses to violence by and against children tend to be inconsistent. Sensational media coverage of specific cases elicits a visceral response, and outraged demands for drastic measures (e.g., Alberta Premier Ralph Klein has suggested that the death penalty be reintroduced for juveniles who kill). In everyday life, on the other hand, many members of the public still accept all kinds of physical punishments as legitimate disciplinary measures, are reluctant to report child offenders, and do little or nothing to support solutions to the social problems that so often give rise to violence. Turning a blind eye to violence against children has been an important component of violence committed by children. Until we understand that the two often go together, the responses to child abuse provided by the criminal-justice and child-protection services systems may always be too little, too late.

NOTES

Special thanks to Jeffrey Ian Ross and Patti Culross for comments.

The views expressed in this paper are those of the author and not necessarily those of the National Research Council or the National Academy of Sciences.

[1] See, for example, Tree Foundation of Canada (1979).

[2] Child abuse can include physical, sexual, and emotional abuse, physical neglect, and inappropriate or inadequate care. One of the more encompassing definitions is this: 'any act of commission or omission by individuals, institutions or society as a whole, and any conditions resulting from such acts or inaction, which deprive children of equal rights and liberties, and/or interfere with their optimal development, constitute by definition abusive or neglectful acts or conditions' (Gil, 1975).

[3] Another effect of child abuse is their easy induction into Satanic cults (Belitz and Schact, 1994).

[4] See, for example, Lenton (1992) for a review of these theories.

[5] See Lenton (1990) for a review of these studies.

REFERENCES

Adler, Tina (1993). 'Urban youth need haven from increasing violence', *The APA Monitor* 24, 8: 46.

Allan, Letitia J. (1978). 'Child Abuse: A Critical Review of The Research and The Theory.' Pp. 43–79 in J.P. Martin, ed., *Violence in the Family*. New York: Wiley.

Anderson, J.P. et al. (1973). 'Task Force on Child Abuse in Nova Scotia', *Nova Scotia Medical Bulletin* 51, 6: 185–9.

Badgley, R., et al. (1984). *Sexual Offenses against Children*. Canada: Canadian Government Publishing Centre.

Bagley, C. (n.d.). *Child Sexual Abuse in Canada: Further Analysis of the 1983 national survey*. Calgary: University of Calgary.

Bakan, David (1971). *Slaughter of the Innocents: A study of the battered child phenomenon*. Boston: Beacon Press.

Bakan, D., M. Eisner and H. Needham (1976). 'Child Abuse: A Bibliography', Canadian Council on Children and Youth. Toronto.

Becker, J. and John Hunter (1994) (reported by Scott Sleek). 'Girls who've been molested can later become molesters', *The Chronicle of Higher Education* January: 34.

Bell, Norman (1975). 'Reduction of Stress in Child Rearing'. In L. Levi, ed., *Society, Stress, and Disease Vol. 2: Childhood and Adolescence*. New York: Oxford University Press.

Belitz, Jerald and Anita Schacht (1994). 'Satanism as a Response to Abuse: The Dynamics and Treatment of Satanic Involvement in Male Youths', *Family Therapy* 21, 1: 81–98.

Berliner, L. and M.K. Barbieri (1984). 'The testimony of child victims of sexual assault', *Journal of Social Issues* 40: 125–37.

Besherov, Douglas J. (1981). 'Toward Better Research on Child Abuse and Neglect: Making Definitional Issues an Explicit Methodological Concern', *Child Abuse and Neglect* 5: 383–90.

Blackburn, Walter W. (1978). *Report on the Child Abuse Survey.* Toronto: Ontario Minister of Community and Social Services.

Brake, Michael (1985). *Comparative Youth Culure: The Sociology of Youth Cultures and Youth Subcultures in America, Britain, and Canada.* London: Routledge and Kegan Paul.

Burgess, R.L. et al. (1981). 'A Social Interactional Approach to the study of Abusive Families'. In J.P. Vincent, ed., *Advances in Family Intervention Assessment and Theory: An Annual Compilation of Research, Vol. 2.* Greenwich, CT: JAI Press.

Canada (1976). *Child Abuse and Neglect.* Report to the House of Commons, Standing Committee on Health, Welfare and Social Affairs, First Session, Thirteenth Parliament. Ottawa: Supply and Services.

Caplan, Paula J. et al. (1984). 'Toronto Multiagency Child Abuse Research Project: The Abused and the Abuser', *Child Abuse and Neglect* 8: 343–51.

Carter, James E. and Lynne Drescher (1976). 'A Community Response to Child Abuse', *The British Columbia Medical Journal* 18: 45–6.

Child, Youth and Family Policy Research Centre (1991). *The State of the Child in Ontario.* Toronto: Oxford University Press.

Chisholm, Barbara A. (1978). 'Questions of Social Policy—A Canadian perspective'. Pp. 318–28 in John M. Eekelaar and Sanford N. Katz, eds, *Family Violence.* Toronto: Butterworths.

Cook, Joanne and Roy Bowles, eds (1980). *Child Abuse: Commission and Omission.* Toronto: Butterworths.

Corder, B.F. Haizlip. T, and P. DeBoer (1990). 'A Pilot Study for a structured time-limited therapy group for sexually abused, pre-adolescent children', *Child Abuse and Neglect* 14: 243–51.

Cormier, B.M. et al. (1971). 'The Psychodynamics of Homicide Committed in a Specific Relationship', *Canadian Journal of Criminology and Corrections* 13, 1: 1–8.

Cormier, Bruno, C.C.J. Angliker, P.W. Gagné and P. Markus (1978). 'Adolescents Who Kill a Member of the Family'. Pp. 466–78 in J. Eeekelaar and S. Katz eds, *Family Violence: An Interpersonal and Interdisciplinary Study.* Toronto: Butterworths.

Dawson, Ross (1976). 'Current Issues in Child Abuse in Ontario', *Journal of the Ontario Association of Children's Aid Societies* 19 (November: 3).

DeAngelis, Tori (1993). 'It's baaack: TV violence, concern for kid viewers', *The APA Monitor* 24, 8: 16.

———— (1993). 'Despite rise of violence by youth, solutions exist', *The APA Monitor* 24, 10: 40.

Dickens, Bernard M. (1976). *Legal Issues in Child Abuse.* Toronto: University of Toronto Centre for Criminology.

———— (1978). 'Legal Responses To Child Abuse'. In John M. Eekelaar, and Sanford Katz, eds. Pp. 338–62 in *Family Violence: An International and Interdisciplinary Study.* Toronto: Butterworths.

Donovan, Macrina V. 'Sexual Assault of Children: Under Twelve Years of Age,' Masters Thesis, University of Windsor.

Eekelaar, John and Sanford Katz, eds (1978). *Family Violence: An International and Interdisciplinary Study.* Toronto: Butterworths.

Eron, L. (1993: cited in DeAngelis, Tori). 'It's baaack: TV violence, concern for kid viewers', *The APA Monitor* 24, 8: 16.

Finckenauer, James (1982). *Scared Straight! And the Panacea Phenomenon in Corrections.* Englewood Cliffs, NJ: Prentice Hall.

Finkelhor, David (1994). 'The International Epidemiology of Child Sexual Abuse', *Child Abuse and Neglect* 18, 5: 409–17.

Frazer, F.M. (1976). 'How to proceed', *The British Columbia Medical Journal* 2: 53–4.

Frazer, F.M., J.R. Anderson, and K. Burns (1973). *Child Abuse in Nova Scotia: Research Project about Battered and Maternally Deprived Children.* Halifax, N.S.

Friedrich, W. et al. (1992). 'Psychotherapy outcome of sexually abused boys', *Journal of Interpersonal Violence* 73, 3: 396–409.

Galdston, R. (1975). 'Preventing the Abuse of Little Children', *American Journal of Orthopsychiatry* 45: 372–81.

Gil, David G. (1970). *Violence Against Children.* Cambridge, MA: Harvard University Press.

———— (1975). 'Unravelling Child Abuse', *American Journal of Orthopsychiatry* 45, 3: 346–56.

Gil, E. (1991). *The Healing Power of Play: Working with Abused Children.* New York: Guilford Press.

Gray, J., C. Cutler, J. Dean, and C.H. Kempe (1976). 'Perinatal assessment of mother-baby interaction'. In R. Helfer and C.H. Kempe, eds, *Child Abuse and Neglect: The Family and the Community.* Cambridge, MA: Ballinger.

Greenland, C. (1973). *Child Abuse in Ontario.* Toronto: Ministry of Community and Social Services.

Harris, Michael (1990). *Unholy Orders: Tragedy at Mount Cashel.* Markham, ON: Viking Penguin Books Canada Ltd.

Helfer, Ray (1973). 'Etiology of Child Abuse', *Pediatrics* 51: 777–9.

Hill, Hope (1993: cited in DeAngelis, Tori). 'Despite rise of violence by youth, solutions exist', *The APA Monitor* 24, 10: 40.

Holmes, R.C. (1978). 'The Police Role in Child Abuse'. Pp. 417–27 in John M. Eekelaar and Sanford N. Katz, eds, *Family Violence: An International and Interdisciplinary Study.* Toronto: Butterworths.

Huesmann, Rowell (1993: cited in DeAngelis, Tori). 'It's baaack: TV violence, concern for kid viewers', *The APA Monitor* 24, 8: 16.

Johnson, W. and J. Thompson (1978). 'Child Abuse: The Policeman's Role: An Innovative Approach'. Pp. 428–37 in John M. Eekelaar and Sanford N. Katz, eds, *Family Violence: An International and Interdisciplinary Study.* Toronto: Butterworths.

Kadushin, Alfred and Judith C. Martin (with James McGloin) (1981). *Child Abuse: An International Event.* New York: Columbia University Press.

Kweller, R.B and S.A. Ray (1992). 'Group treatment of latency-age male victims of sexual abuse', *Journal of Child Sexual Abuse: Research, Treatment and Program Innovations for Victims, Survivors and Offenders* 1, 4: 1–18.

Lahey, Kathleen A. (1984). 'Research on Child Abuse in Liberal Patriarchy'. Pp. 156–84 in Jill McCalla Vickers, ed., *Taking Sex into Account: The Policy Consequences of Sexist Research.* Ottawa: Carleton University Press.

Le Blanc, Marc, and Marcel Frechette (1989). *Male Criminal Activity from Childhood Through Youth—Multilevel Developmental Perspectives.* New York: Springer-Verlag.

Lenton, Rhonda L. (1989). 'Parental Discipline and Child Abuse', PhD Dissertation, Department of Sociology, University of Toronto.

———— (1990). 'Techniques of Child Discipline and Abuse by Parents', *Canadian Review of Sociology and Anthropology* 27, 2: 157–85.

Leschield, Alan, Peter Jaffe, and Wayne Willis, eds (1991). *The Young Offenders Act: A Revolution in Canadian Juvenile Justice.* Toronto: University of Toronto Press.

Lieber, Harry (1977). *Obstacles to the Identification and Reporting of Child Abuse.* Social Policy and Research, United Way of Greater Vancouver.

MacFarlane, K.J. Waterman, S. Conerly, S. Damon, L. Durfee and S. Long (1986). *Sexual Abuse of Young Children.* New York: Guildford Press.

Maclean's (1993). 'Children at Risk'. 23 August: 13.

Maclean's (1993). 'Unparalleled evil'. 6 December: 32.

Maclean's (1994). 'Judge Under Attack'. 31 January: 17.

Maclean's (1994). 'End of a Sex Scandal'. 21 February: 21.

Maclean's (1994). 'Straight to Trial'. 11 April: 21.

Maclean's (1994). 'Tackling Youth Crime'. 13 June: 14.

Maclean's (1994). 'Outrage over murder'. 2 May: 25.

Mandell, J. and L. Damon (1989). *Group Treatment for sexually abused children.* New York: Guildford Press.

Marron, K. (1993). *Apprenticed in Crime: Young Offenders, the Law, and Crime in Canada.* Toronto: McClelland-Bantam Books.

Martin, Judith (1983). *Gender-Related Behaviours of Children in Abusive Situations.* Saratoga, CA: R. and E. Publishers.

Martin, Michael J. (1992). 'Child Sexual Abuse: Preventing Continued Victimization by the Criminal Justice System and Associated Agencies', *Family Relations* 41: 330–3.

Marvasti, J.A. (1989). 'Play therapy with sexually abused children'. Pp. 1–41 in S. Sgroi, ed., *Sexual Abuse treatment for children, adult survivors, offenders and persons with mental retardation: Vulnerable populations.* Vol 2. Lexington, D.C. Heath and Company.

McCullagh, John, and Mary Greco (1990). *Servicing Street Youth: A Feasibility Study.* Toronto: Children's Aid Society of Metropolitan Toronto.

McNight, C.K. et al. (1966). 'Matricide and Mental Illness', *Canadian Psychiatric Association Journal* 2, 2 (March/April).

Meloff, William and Robert A. Silverman (1992). 'Canadian kids who kill', *Canadian Journal of Criminology* (January): 15–34.

Mohr, J.W. and C.K. McKnight (1971). 'Violence as a Function of Age and Relationship With Special Reference to Matricide', *Canadian Psychiatric Association Journal* 16.

Ontario Ministry of Community and Social Services (1990). *Children First: Report of the Advisory Committee on Children's Services.* Toronto.

Ontario Social Development Council (1988). *YOA Dispositions: Challenges and Choices. A Report of the Conference on the Young Offenders Act in Ontario.* Toronto.

Parke, R.D. and C.W. Collmer (1975). 'Child Abuse: An Interdisciplinary Analysis'. Pp. 509–90 in E.M. Hetherington, ed., *Review of Child Development Research* 5. Chicago: University of Chicago Press.

Paulson, M. and P. Blake (1969). 'The Physically Abused Child: A Focus on Prevention', *Child Welfare* 48: 86–95.

Reichert, Elisabeth (1994). 'Play and Animal-Assisted Therapy: A Group-Treatment Model for Sexually Abused Girls Ages 9–13', *Family Therapy* 21, 1: 55–62.

Ross, R.R. (1980). 'Violence In, Violence Out: Child-abuse and self-mutilation in adolescent offenders', *Canadian Journal of Criminology* 22, 3: 273–87.

Schlesinger, Bernard (1977). *Child Abuse in Canada*. Guidance Centre, Faculty of Education, University of Toronto.

——— (1981). 'Sexual Abuse of Children', Child Abuse Unit, Ministry of Community and Social Services, Toronto.

Schneider, Carol, James Hofmeister, and Ray E. Helfer. 'A Predicting Screening Questionnaire for Potential Problems in Mother-Child Inter-action'. Pp. 393–407 in R. Heefer and C.H. Kempe, eds, *Child Abuse and Neglect: The Family and the Community*. Cambridge, MA: Ballinger.

Slaby, Ronald (1993: cited in DeAngelis, Tori). 'Despite rise of violence by youth, solutions exist', *The APA Monitor* 24, 10: 40.

Sleek, Scott (1994). 'New findings may update treatment for sex abuse', *APA Monitor* 25, 1: 34–5.

Silverman, R. and L. Kennedy. (1993). *Deadly Deeds: Murder in Canada*. Scarborough, ON: Nelson Canada.

Smith, David F. (1976). 'Child Abuse Health Centre for Children OPD', *British Columbia Medical Journal* 2: 47–49.

Smith, Selwyn M. (1975). *The Battered Child Syndrome*. Toronto: Butterworths.

——— (1978). *The Maltreatment of Children*. Baltimore: University Park Press.

Steed, J. (1994). *Our Little Secret*. Toronto: Random House of Canada.

Steele, Brandt, and Carol Pollock (1974). 'A Psychiatric Study of Parents Who Abuse Infants and Small Children'. Pp. 89–133 in Ray Helfer and C. Henry Kempe, (eds), *The Battered Child, 2nd ed.* Chicago: University of Chicago Press.

Steinmetz, Suzanne (1977a). 'The Use of Force for Resolving Family Conflict: The Training Ground for Abuse', *The Family Coordinator* 26: 19–26.

——— (1977b). *The Cycle of Violence*. New York: Praeger.

Stolk, Mary Van (1972). *The Battered Child in Canada*. Toronto: McClelland and Stewart Ltd.

Strauss, Murray A. (1983). 'Ordinary Violence, Child Abuse, and Wife-Beating: What Do They Have in Common?' Pp. 213–34 in David Finkelhor et al., eds, *The Dark Side of Families: Current Family Violent Research*. Beverly Hills: Sage.

Tator, J. and K. Wilde (1979). 'Child Abuse and the Courts', *Canadian Journal of Family Law* 3: 165–205.

Tree Foundation of Canada (1979). 'Inventory of Canadian Research and Demonstration Projects on Child Abuse and Neglect', Research Report prepared by the Tree Foundation of Canada under contract with the Departments of the Solicitor General and National Health and Welfare.

——— (1979). 'Beaten Women, Battered Children', *Children Today*.

Turner, R. Jay, William R. Avison, and Samuel Noh (1982). *Screening for Problem Parenting: An Evaluation of a Promising Measure*, unpublished report. Toronto: Ontario Ministry of Community and Social Services.

Wilcox, Brian L. (1992). *Big World, Small Screen*. Michigan: University of Michigan Press.

Chapter Six

VIOLENCE AND THE ELDERLY

VINCENT F. SACCO

Traditionally, criminological interest in the relationship between age and criminal violence has focused on the teenage years (Hirschi and Gottfredson, 1983; Sampson and Laub, 1992). Accordingly, scholars have invested a great deal of energy in attempting to explain why the risks associated with involvement in violent criminal events, whether as offenders or as victims, are so much greater in late adolescence and early adulthood than at other points in the life-cycle.

Over the last three decades, however, criminal violence in later life has come to be identified as a problem that requires investigation as well. At the same time, the social problem of crime and the elderly has been constructed in several different ways. Among the claims made are that the elderly face particularly high risks of violent victimization; are uniquely affected by the deleterious consequences of criminal violence; are fearful of victimization to a degree that seriously detracts from the quality of their lives; are particularly vulnerable to violence within the family setting; and are themselves involved in violent offending at increasingly alarming rates.

This chapter provides a critical overview of what is known about the problem of violence and the elderly in Canada. Arguments about levels and types of elderly crime and victimization are addressed with reference to the available empirical evidence. It will become evident that what emerges from such a discussion is a significant discrepancy between social-science data and popular rhetoric about violence and the elderly.

THE SOCIAL PROBLEM OF VIOLENCE AND THE ELDERLY

Violence and the elderly emerged as a social problem in North America in the early 1970s. Initially, the construction of the issue emphasized the unique problems faced by the elderly as victims of street crime. Definitions of the seriousness of the problem emerged and diffused in rapid fashion (Karmen, 1990; Cook, 1981; Cook and Skogan, 1990). According to Cook (1981), in the United States in 1970 the issue of crime against the elderly was the subject of only one *New York Times* article, two Law Enforcement Assistance Administration (LEAA) research awards, and one Congressional hearing. Moreover, in that year there were no academic or professional publications that focused on the issue. By 1977, 91 articles about victimization of the elderly had appeared in the *New York Times*, 56 LEAA grants had been awarded, 17 accounts of the problem had appeared in the Congressional Record, and 47 academic and professional books and articles had been written.

According to Cook (1981), the problem emerged in the context of a 'ripe issue climate' that facilitated the convergence of diverse views of the problem as articulated by various interest groups. Generally, the problem of crime against the elderly consolidated a variety of social concerns about the threat of criminal violence, the rights of victims, and the 'greying' of the population. Consequently, attention to the problem reflected diverse interests. The news industry quickly discovered the dramatic value of reports that portrayed the elderly as victims of vicious street predators (Fishman, 1978). Advocacy groups concerned with promoting the interests of the aged derived considerable value from the linkages that could be drawn between the specific problem of crime against the elderly and more general problems associated with aging. Politicians, eager to demonstrate their concern about and commitment to an emerging constituency, happily embraced the issue. Political rhetoric about crime against the elderly, unlike political rhetoric about many other social problems, was unlikely to generate controversy or divisiveness; no legitimate political faction favoured the predatory victimization of older people.

Cook and Skogan (1990) note that with respect to the American scene, the problem of street crime against the elderly had significantly declined in salience by the early 1980s. They suggest that this happened, in large part, because the accumulating body of social-scientific evidence failed to support claims about the seriousness of the problem. Moreover, attempts to reformulate the problem in terms of the consequences of crime, or the fear of crime—rather than simple levels of crime—did not generate widespread public or policy interest. The problem of fear of crime, for instance, was regarded as 'less serious' than the problem of crime itself, particularly when research suggested discrepancies in the social locations of crime and fear. In addition, in the case of fear—unlike crime—it was not easy to determine which state agency should be responsible for handling the problem.

In the 1980s, attention began to shift away from older persons as victims of violent strangers and towards victims of 'elder abuse' in domestic settings (Gordon, 1987; Leroux and Petrunik, 1989; Sacco, 1990; 1993). Like the earlier problem of street crime against the elderly, the problem of elder abuse has gained widespread acceptance in rather rapid fashion.

The current concern over elder abuse integrates earlier concerns about violent street crime and more recent concerns about family violence (Leroux and Petrunik, 1989). Increasingly, since the 1960s, it has been argued that dominant ideological beliefs about the nurturing character of family life have obscured our understanding of the ways in which the organization of familial relations threatens the safety of vulnerable family members. The 'discovery' of child abuse in the 1960s (Nelson, 1984; Pfohl, 1977) and wife assault a decade later (Loseke, 1992; Tierney, 1982) set the stage for public recognition of the risks faced by aged family members. Yet, according to Baumann (1989) the dominant cultural image of old age as a time of peace and serenity continued to hide the problem of elder abuse from public view even while violence against children and wives gained recognition as urgent social issues.

The contemporary construction of the problem of elder abuse combines and extends established images of elderly victims and violent families, serving to legitimate claims about the seriousness of the problem. In the current period, elder abuse is the subject of legislative debates and government task forces and the theme of scholarly conferences. It is also the principal subject matter of at least one scholarly journal (*The Journal of Elder Abuse and Neglect*) and has attracted the interest of researchers from a variety of disciplines.

The decade of the 1980s also witnessed the development of popular and criminological interest in the elderly offender (Feinberg, 1984). In this formulation of the problem, claims-making rhetoric began to emphasize concerns about a 'geriatric crime wave' (Sunderland, 1982) as attention shifted from the role of the elderly as victims of violence to the role of the elderly as perpetrators of violence.

Some writers have questioned whether the focus on elderly offenders represents the 'invention' of a new type of criminal (Cullen et al., 1985). These arguments, summarized by Forsyth and Gramling (1988), suggest that crimes by the elderly came to prominence not because of changes in levels of elderly offending, but because the interests of claims-making groups could be advanced by the promotion of the problem. Criminal-justice bureaucracies, for instance, which justify their existence in terms of the numbers of clients processed, could realize practical advantages by viewing the elderly as an untapped resource. In addition, the style of academic work and the system of academic rewards encourage the discovery of 'new problems' that promise to prove interesting for publication purposes. In a related way, the mass media came to view the elderly offender as representing a new angle on the 'crime-wave' story that has always been so valuable as news commodity.

These various social problem formulations indicate a variety of ways of thinking about the violence in later life. However, the relevant body of social-scientific evidence reveals a picture that is considerably more complicated than many of these earlier formulations would suggest.

SOURCES OF DATA ABOUT VIOLENCE AND THE ELDERLY

Data describing criminal violence among the elderly, like those relating to criminal violence more generally, are derived from three principal sources: the agents of legal control, the victims of violence, and the self-reports of offenders (Fattah and Sacco, 1989; Jackson, 1990). Each data source has several limitations.

Data gathered by policing agencies in connection with the Uniform Crime Reporting (UCR) system provide a continuous time-series that describes Canadian crime trends (Silverman et al., 1991). However, UCR data have traditionally told us relatively little about the age distribution of crime. Until recent revisions to the UCR system, the utility of the information available was compromised by its aggregate character and by the failure to collect detailed data about either offenders or victims (Statistics Canada, 1990). The Homicide Survey is an important exception in that, since 1961, it has collected police-reported data relating to both homicide incidents and the characteristics of victims and offenders (Statistics Canada, 1992).

In 1988, the Canadian Centre for Justice Statistics began to phase in a revised UCR survey (Statistics Canada, 1990). Unlike the survey it replaces, the revised data collection system is 'incident-based', thereby allowing greater flexibility in analyses of criminal events and the characteristics of offenders and victims. Moreover, the range of data elements collected in the survey has been expanded to include several social and demographic characteristics of offenders and victims of violent crimes (Morrison, 1991). Although only preliminary data from the revised UCR are currently available, it is clear that these revisions greatly enhance the value of official data in the investigation of issues relating to crime and aging. However, irrespective of the methods of data collection, or collation, employed, police-level data by their very nature leave unaddressed the large numbers of crimes that never come to the attention of law-enforcement agencies.

Elder-abuse researchers have also made extensive use of data gathered by social-control agencies (Block and Sinnott, 1979; Chen et al., 1981; Lau and Kosberg, 1979; Shell, 1982). Such studies involve the examination of case records relating to abuse, or interviews with physicians, nurses, social workers, police officers, coroners, or others who are likely to be involved in the processing of abuse cases.

Surveys of crime victims offer an alternative procedure for investigating the problem of violence and the elderly. Through the use of general population surveys, these studies allow crime levels to be estimated and the correlates of victimization to be examined in ways that are unaffected by the biases of criminal-justice processing (Fattah, 1991; O'Brien, 1985; Skogan, 1986).

To date, only three major victim surveys have been undertaken in Canada. The first, the Canadian Urban Victimization Survey (CUVS), was conducted in 1982. Approximately 60,000 respondents in seven major metropolitan areas were asked about their experiences with crime during the calendar year 1981 (Solicitor General Canada, 1983). A partial replication of the CUVS was done in one of the original seven cities, Edmonton, in 1985 (Solicitor General Canada, 1987). The second major study, the General Social Survey (GSS) was undertaken in 1988 and asked approximately 10,000 respondents, representative of the non-institutionalized population of the ten Canadian provinces over the age of 15, about their victimization experiences during the calendar year 1987 (Sacco and Johnson, 1990). It is intended that the 'personal risk' cycle of the GSS will be repeated at five-year intervals. Both the CUVS and the GSS survey instruments included questions about three violent offences: sexual assault, robbery, and assault. The third survey, conducted by Statistics Canada on behalf of Health and Welfare Canada, was undertaken in 1993. Approximately 12,300 women, 18 years of age or over, were interviewed about their experiences with violence and about their perceptions of personal safety (Statistics Canada, 1993).

The general limitations of victimization surveys have been extensively documented and need not be elaborated here (e.g., Block and Block, 1984; Fattah, 1991; Skogan, 1986). However, as methodologies for investigating the criminal victimization of the elderly, these surveys pose some unique problems. Most notably, serious violent victimization incidents are relatively rare among members of this population. This means that extremely large samples are necessary if the data are to have any analytical value. In the absence of large samples, it is impossible to provide statistically reliable estimates of elderly victimization levels or to perform sophisticated multivariate analyses of the data. These problems are compounded when interest centres on the victimization experiences of elderly sub-populations (e.g., distinct ethnic or racial groups).

It should be noted that victim accounts have also been used, to a somewhat lesser extent, in the investigation of abuse and neglect of the elderly by informal caregivers in the home (Pillemer and Finkelhor, 1988; Block and Sinnott, 1979). A national study of elder abuse was funded by Health and Welfare Canada in 1989 (Podnieks, 1990). The study collected data about physical abuse (as well as material abuse, chronic verbal aggression, and neglect) through a random-sample telephone survey of 2,000 elderly persons living in private dwellings.

Finally, data about violence may be generated by self-report studies of offenders (O'Brien, 1985; Nettler, 1984). Because such studies have usually been conducted with juvenile offenders, their findings are of limited relevance to questions about violence and the aged. However, research into elder abuse and neglect by domestic caregivers is one exception to this pattern (Anetzberger, 1987; Steinmetz, 1983). In such investigations efforts are made to gather data from individuals who are caregivers of elderly persons in order to determine the characteristics of those who are involved in abusive relationships as well as to yield estimates of the frequency and intensity of the abusive behaviour itself. Like all self-report research, these studies risk unrepresentative samples and have the potential to confuse offenders' stated reasons for their actions with the causes of these behaviours (Nettler, 1984).

These data sources differ quite markedly with respect to the kinds of information they collect and the operational assumptions from which they proceed. Significant methodological differences exist regarding the ways in which violence is defined and the ways in which acts of violence are counted. Nor is there consistency in the ways in which 'the elderly' are defined for research purposes (Sacco, 1993; Wolf and Pillemer, 1989). While most writers employ a chronological definition of the group in question, the age that should serve as the cut-off point between the elderly and the non-elderly is to a large extent an arbitrary matter (Fattah and Sacco, 1989; Silverman and Kennedy, 1993). Most studies focus on those individuals over the ages of 60 or 65, but consensus does not exist on this matter (Pillemer and Suitor, 1988).

ELDERLY VICTIMIZATION

RISKS

The findings of victimization surveys consistently show that, for the offences routinely measured in such surveys, risks decline with age. Contrary to popular rhetoric, which pictures the elderly as facing the highest risks of crime, the available data indicate that they face the lowest risks. This is an extremely robust finding. It holds for a variety of violent and non-violent crimes, in several different countries, and for at least the last several decades—the period during which valid victimization data have been generated. Risks of violent victimization, like risks of violent offending, tend to be greatest in early adulthood and to decline thereafter (Fattah and Sacco, 1989; Yin, 1985).

By way of illustration, Table 6.1 describes aggregate data from the 1988 General Social Survey. For the personal offences (sexual assault, robbery, assault, personal theft) and household (break and enter, motor vehicle theft, theft of household property, and vandalism) covered by the survey, the risks of victimization can be seen to decline steadily with age. While only 8% of Canadians over the age of 65 reported one or more victimizations, 37% of those between the ages of 15 and 24 did so.

The general pattern of an age-decline in victimization emerges even more sharply when violent offences are considered. Table 6.2 presents findings from the 1982 Canadian Urban Victimization Survey. For

Table 6.1: **Frequency of Victimization by Age**
General Social Survey, 1988

| | Not victimized (%) | Victimized by frequency | | | |
		Total (%)	One (%)	Two or more (%)	Not stated (%)
All ages	75	24	15	8	1
15–24	63	37	20	16	—
25–44	72	27	18	9	1
45–64	83	15	11	4	2
65 or over	90	8	7	1	1

SOURCE: Sacco and Johnson (1990: 32).

total counts of violent incidents, as well as for each specific violent offence (sexual assault, robbery, and assault), the rates of elderly victimization are substantially lower than the rates for younger segments of the population. The overall rate for those between the ages of 16 and 24 is 13 times greater than the elderly rate. The victimization level for the youngest members of the sample exceeds the elderly level by factors of 5 and 16 for robbery and assault respectively. In the case of sexual assault, the number of reported incidents involving the elderly is too low to allow a statistically reliable estimate to be made. The 1993 national survey of violence against women found 27% of women aged 18 to 24 had experienced violence in the previous 12 months, as compared with 2% of women 55 years of age or over (Statistics Canada, 1993).

Although general population surveys provide the best information about the age-decline in victimization risk for a range of criminal offences, the recent revisions to the UCR survey, as previously stated, will no doubt increase the value of police data for research into victim characteristics. These data seem to support much of what is already known

Table 6.2: **Rates of Violent Victimization by Age** (rates per 1,000 population)
Canadian Urban Victimization Survey, 1982

| | Total violence | Incident type | | |
		Sexual assault	Robbery	Assault
All ages	70	3.5	10	57
16–24	154	9	21	123
25–39	74	3	9	62
40–64	25	1[a]	5	20
65 or older	12	—[b]	4	8

[a]Because of low incident count, caution is required in interpretation of rate.
[b]Actual incident count is too low to allow statistically reliable estimate to be made.
SOURCE: Solicitor General Canada (1985b: 2).

about the relative degree of involvement of elderly people in violent criminal events. Trevethan (1992), who examined new UCR data collected from 13 police departments between 1988 and 1992, reports that only 3% of the 43,299 violent incidents involved elderly victims (over age 60). When compared to the relative size of the elderly population, this figure suggests a significant under-representation of older people as victims of violent crime.

Because of the sample size, the CUVS and the GSS have been able to uncover only a relatively small number of victimization incidents involving the elderly. As a result, detailed analysis of these events is difficult. The much larger American National Crime Victimization Survey (NCVS) program has permitted a more extensive investigation of the nature of elderly victimization (Antunes et al., 1977; Bachman, 1992; Hochstedler, 1981; Whitaker, 1987). Many of these findings are consistent with the more limited Canadian UCR and victimization data (Trevethan, 1992; Solicitor General Canada, 1985b). Among the more significant findings of the NCVS are the following:

1. The 'mix' of crimes differs for elderly and non-elderly victims. While elderly victims are particularly susceptible to crimes of economic predation, non-elderly victims are more likely to be subjected to violence. Aggregated NCVS data from 1987 through 1990 reveal that while those under 65 are almost four times more likely to be victimized by an assault than by a robbery, for elderly victims the likelihood of assault is 1 1/2 times that of robbery (Bachman, 1992). In general, it appears that 'elderly victims are more likely to be preyed upon than to be victimized with the intent to do personal injury; younger victims are more likely to be treated violently than to be preyed upon' (Cook et al., 1981: 231).
2. Rates of robbery and assault are higher for males than for females. Higher risks of violent victimization are also associated with measures of social or economic disadvantage, urban residence, and marital estrangement (i.e., divorce/separation).
3. In comparison to non-elderly victims, victims of violence who are elderly are more likely to be victimized by a stranger, alone when victimized, victimized at or near the home, and victimized during the day.

HOMICIDE

In 1991, 56% of Canadian homicide victims were between the ages of 18 and 39 (Statistics Canada, 1992). Homicide victims 60 years of age or over accounted for only about 10% of the total—a figure that suggests a slight under-representation of this group in the homicide-victim population as compared to the Canadian population as a whole.

Patterns of elderly homicide in Canada have been extensively studied by Silverman and Kennedy (1993: 188–200). Through an analysis of homicide incidents occurring in Canada between 1961 and 1990, they note that while those 65 years of age and over account for 8 per cent of homicide victims (the lowest proportion for any age group), this figure is directly proportional to the size of this age group in the general population. Moreover, over the study period, the data indicate no general upward trend in rates of elderly homicide victimization.

Silverman and Kennedy also found that, when compared to younger age groups, elderly victims of homicide were more likely to be killed in their own homes; fully 75% of homicides occurred there. As in the case of other age groups, the elderly are more likely to be murdered by someone they know than by a stranger. However, the number who were killed by a stranger (43%) was higher for the elderly than for any other age group.

Consistent with the finding from victimization surveys that older victims are more likely to be preyed upon than treated as objects of violence *per se*, these researchers found that the elderly are more than twice as likely (41%) as others to be victims of theft-based murder. Another 4% of elderly homicides resulted from sex-related offences. Similar patterns are revealed by American homicide data (Bachman, 1992; Messner and Tardiff, 1985).

INTERPRETING ELDERLY VICTIMIZATION

The levels and types of risks of violent crime experienced by the elderly may be understood with reference to the concepts and models associated with lifestyle (Hindelang et al., 1978) and routine-activity (Cohen and Felson, 1979) theories of crime. These analytical frameworks stress an understanding of the ways in which everyday patterns of behaviour affect levels of probabilistic exposure to criminal harm. For example, lifestyle determines the extent to which people engage in high-risk activities (evening leisure activities outside of the home); frequent those settings (such as taverns) in which violent victimizations more frequently occur; or associate with others whose risks of criminal offending are high.

Data on elderly lifestyles indicate that older people engage in evening activities outside of the home less frequently than younger people; and that when they do, their preference is for 'low-risk' (e.g., visiting friends or family) rather than 'high-risk' (e.g., drinking at bars) activities (Golant, 1984). Data from the CUVS revealed that only 10% of elderly people reported more than 20 evening activities outside of the home per month, compared to approximately 45% for those between the ages of 25 and 39, and 70% for those under 25 (Solicitor General Canada, 1985b: 2).

Notably, attempts to demonstrate that age differences in victimization risk are attributable to variations in exposure to danger, as measured by, for instance, evening activities outside of the home, have produced inconsistent results (Corrado et al., 1980; Lindquist and Duke, 1982; Miethe et al., 1987; Skogan, 1980; Stafford and Galle, 1984). Sizable variations across age groups persist even when such activity variables are taken into account. Data from the CUVS (Table 6.3) suggest that young people between the ages of 16 and 24 who are in the lowest activity category have a rate of violent victimization approximately 4 times greater than elderly people who report between 20 and 29 evening activities per month.

Popular arguments about the 'special vulnerability' of older people would seem to suggest that if their levels of exposure to risk approached the levels of exposure associated with younger people, elderly rates of violent crime would be similar to the rates for more youthful members of the population. This argument proceeds from the view that offenders may be encouraged to seek out older victims because of their diminished physical strength and agility, and their lessened ability to protect themselves or resist a motivated offender.

However, the research on this issue is equivocal. Data from the CUVS, for instance, suggest that while elderly people were less likely to frequent high-risk locations, they were more likely than others to be victims of robbery when they did so (Solicitor General Canada, 1985b). In contrast, data from the 1982 British Crime Survey indicate that differences between age groups in the levels of risk associated with 'street crimes' changed very little when different patterns of going out— including frequency, means of travel, destination, and activity—are taken into account (Clarke et al., 1985).

In addition to activity patterns, the segregation of age groups in Canadian society contributes to lower elderly-victimization risks. The

Table 6.3: **Rates of Violent Victimization by Age and by Average Number of Evening Activities Outside the Home per Month** (rates per 1,000 population)
Canadian Urban Victimization Survey, 1982

| Age | Evening activities | | | |
	0–9	10–19	20–29	30 or more
16–24	86	92	122	206
25–39	35	57	71	122
40–64	20	21	28	47
65 or over	10	13	22	—[a]

[a]Actual incident count is too low to allow statistically reliable estimate to be made.
SOURCE: Solicitor General Canada (1985b: 2).

overall effect of such segregation is to minimize interaction between the elderly and those groups in which criminal offending is most heavily concentrated (i.e., young males). Moreover, as Antunes et al. (1977: 324) note, 'the elderly typically live alone, and have fewer opportunities to become involved in rancorous intra-familial disputes.'

Lifestyle factors are useful in understanding not only the levels but also the character of elderly victimization. Because the locus of much elderly activity is the home and its immediate vicinity, this is the setting for a large number of victimization incidents (Massey and McKean, 1985). For older people, there are fewer occupational constraints to structure how time is spent and they are somewhat freer than younger members of the population to engage in leisure activities or do chores outside the household in daytime. This pattern is reflected in the greater number of incidents that occur during the day. Older people are also more likely to live alone, and not surprisingly to be alone when victimized.

Much of the violence that is directed toward older people seems to emerge as a by-product of opportunistic predatory offending. In the context of such events, the violence is not an end itself but rather a means to an end. The finding that large numbers of stranger homicides involve elderly victims and take place in the home in connection with a theft-related crime is consistent with this interpretation (Fox and Levin, 1991). Silverman and Kennedy (1993: 197) argue that many such crimes occur when an elderly resident confronts an intruder involved in breaking and entering.

THE AFTERMATH OF VICTIMIZATION

An analysis by Trevethan (1992) of revised UCR data from 13 reporting jurisdictions in 1991 revealed that for the aggregate category of violent crime, the level of physical injury among elderly victims is not significantly different from the level among younger victims. As the data in Table 6.4 illustrate, approximately equal proportions of both age groups experienced minor and major injuries. However, while those under age 60 are more likely to be injured in police-recorded assaults, elderly victims are more apt to experience injury in robbery events.

Victimization-survey data indicate that with respect to the types of crimes measured, elderly victims experience relatively low rates of injury (Bachman, 1992; Cook et al., 1978; Cook et al., 1981; Hochstedler, 1981; Solicitor General Canada, 1985b). The CUVS survey results suggest that the elderly were no more likely than others to report having been injured, although the consequences of their injuries were typically more serious (Solicitor General Canada, 1985a). Elderly victims who were injured were twice as likely as younger victims to require medical or dental attention. Pooled American National Crime Victimization Survey

Table 6.4: **Level of Injury in Violent Crime by Age**[a]
Revised Uniform Crime Report Data

	Level of injury (%)			
	None	Minor	Major	Fatal
All ages	45	47	7	1
Under 60	45	47	7	1
60 or over	45	42	8	4
Assault	37	56	7	—
Under 60	37	56	7	—
60 or over	46	47	7	—
Robbery	75	22	4	—
Under 60	76	20	3	—
60 or over	57	35	9	—
Other violence	63	23	8	6
Under 60	64	23	7	5
60 or over	17	35	14	33

[a]Data are based on 39,549 incidents from 13 police jurisdictions, 1988–91.
SOURCE: Trevethan (1992: 7).

data from the period 1987–90 suggest that about the same percentage of elderly (33%) and non-elderly (31%) victims reported physical injuries. However, among injured victims, 9% of the elderly reported 'serious' injuries such as broken bones, loss of teeth, or internal injuries, compared to 5% of those under 65. In addition, 14% of elderly victims who were injured required hospital care, compared to 8% of the younger victims (Bachman, 1992). Such data imply that while older people are not necessarily more likely to be injured in the context of a victimization incident, they suffer more from their injuries (Muram et al., 1992).

It can be argued that the data on physical injuries normally collected in victimization surveys leave several issues unaddressed (Fattah and Sacco, 1989: 204). These data do not, for instance, describe age variations in periods of recovery (Skogan, 1977). Although the physical effects of victimization may erode over time, there is reason to believe that these processes may occur less rapidly for older than for younger victims (Burt and Katz, 1985).

Second, the physical effects of violent victimization may include not only such obvious manifestations as broken bones or lost teeth. Injuries may complicate existing health problems and reduce the ability to function independently (Burt and Katz, 1985). Feinberg's (1981) study of elderly victims referred to a victim-compensation program in which it was found that in addition to direct and obvious injuries, some victims reported a worsening of problems such as heart ailments or hypertension, and greater difficulty in carrying out daily activities such as shopping or cooking.

Finally, it should be noted that the physical effects of victimization may be bound up in complex ways with the other problems created by the incident. The victimization may contribute to feelings of depression (Sykes and Johnson, 1985), nervousness and sleeplessness (Feinberg, 1981), and other emotional problems (Solicitor General Canada, 1987); in turn, such psychological distress may exacerbate physical problems or impede recovery.

The degree to which individuals can rely on the assistance of supportive interpersonal networks may play an important role in mediating the physical and psychological costs of violent victimization (Janoff-Bulman and Frieze, 1983; Ruback et al., 1984). Yet, because the elderly are more likely to live alone (Brillon, 1987) and in many cases to experience greater social isolation (Rathbone-McCuan and Hashimi, 1982), many may find that such support is not readily available.

The research indicates that in the aftermath of the victimization episode, elderly victims are somewhat more likely than others to report the incident to the police (Brillon, 1987; Yin, 1985). According to the American NCVS data for the period 1987–90, 60% of elderly victims of violence reported the event to the police, compared with 47% of non-elderly victims. Similarly, the CUVS data reveal that elderly victims of violence are about as likely as victims aged 40–64 to report the crime to police, but more likely than younger victims to do so (Solicitor General Canada, 1985b).

The data on police-reporting decisions by elderly and non-elderly victims support the view that the decision to contact the police reflects a crude cost-benefit analysis of the situation in which victims find themselves (Gottfredson and Gottfredson, 1980). When victims who have not reported violent crimes to the police are asked about their failure to do so, they typically state that the event was 'too minor' to warrant such action or that the 'police couldn't do anything anyway' (Sacco and Johnson, 1990; Solicitor General Canada, 1984). In addition, the probability of reporting is related to offence characteristics that are indicative of legal seriousness (Gottfredson and Hindelang, 1979: 16; Skogan, 1976: 120–1). Incidents are more likely to be reported when they involve serious physical injury or financial loss, the use of a weapon, or victimization by a stranger, or when they occur at or around the home.

It appears that victims weigh the advantages and disadvantages associated with reporting and act accordingly. If the crime is particularly serious or particularly threatening, the victim is more likely to report it than if the crime is of a more minor nature. With respect to the elderly specifically, it may be that their generally high regard for the police increases the likelihood that crimes will be reported (Solicitor General Canada, 1985b); in general, however, perceptions of the police and criminal justice system have been shown to have weak predictive utility with respect to such decisions (Gottfredson and Gottfredson, 1980).

VIOLENT VICTIMIZATION AND THE FEAR OF CRIME

One of the most consistently reported findings in the criminological literature is the high level of fear of victimization among the elderly (Baldassare, 1986). According to many writers, it is the fear of crime, as distinct from crime itself, that is the real problem for older people (Baumer, 1978; Cook et al., 1981).

Several studies done in this country, the United States, and elsewhere support the conclusion that age status is related to the concern for personal safety (Clemente and Kleiman, 1976; DeFronzo, 1979; Garofalo, 1981; Hindelang et al., 1978; Sacco and Johnson, 1990; Skogan and Maxfield, 1981; Solicitor General Canada, 1985b; Toseland, 1982). However, several studies find the relationship between age and fear to be small or negligible (Braungart et al., 1980; Burt and Katz, 1985; Yin, 1985), or in some cases negative rather than positive (Gomme, 1988; Sacco and Glackman, 1987).

Even in those studies that do find a high level of fear among the elderly, age does not generally emerge as the most significant discriminator between more and less fearful segments of the population. In general, differences between men and women exceed those between the elderly and non-elderly in the context of both bivariate and multivariate analyses (DeFronzo, 1979; Garofalo, 1979; Skogan and Maxfield, 1981; Toseland, 1982).

Other factors that are correlated with fear of violent crime in the elderly population are substantially similar to those associated with fear among the non-elderly. Thus the concern about the possibility of victimization is greater for ethnic minorities and the poor (Baumer, 1978; Braungart et al., 1980; Lee, 1983), urban residents (Sacco, 1985; Sacco and Johnson, 1990; Sundeen and Mathieu, 1976), residents of high-crime, socially disorganized, and age-integrated communities (Akers et al., 1987; Lawton and Yaffe, 1980; Lee, 1983; Maxfield, 1984), and people who have already been victims of violent or serious property crimes (Fattah and Sacco, 1989; Sacco and Johnson, 1990).

The inconsistency between high levels of measured fear and low levels of measured victimization among the aged has been interpreted by some as evidence of the irrationality of elderly concerns about crime (Jaycox, 1978). The apparently paradoxical nature of the relationship between elderly victimization and elderly fear has attracted considerable research scrutiny, and several resolutions of this paradox may be offered.

First, as was discussed previously, some researchers have argued that elderly levels of victimization are in fact not lower when differences in levels of exposure are taken into account. Thus, if older people perceive (accurately) their risks of victimization to be as high or higher than those of the rest of the population when they expose themselves to risk, their fears may not be disproportionate (Stafford and Galle, 1984; Lindquist and Duke, 1982).

Second, it has been suggested that rather than view a high level of fear as an irrational response to low levels of victimization, it may make more sense to argue that the concern for personal safety, and its associated behavioural restrictions, may be causally prior to the low victimization rate (Baumer, 1978; Hindelang et al., 1978). This implies that if the fear of crime keeps older people home, it lowers their risk such that the level of elderly victimization will be below that experienced by younger people whose fear of crime is less and whose exposure to risk is higher. Despite its intuitive appeal, this argument is not supported by the available empirical evidence (Balkin, 1979; Garofalo, 1981). Instead, it appears that it is not fear of crime, in any simple or direct sense, but rather the general content of their lifestyles that keeps elderly people away from high-risk situations or settings.

A third resolution of the paradox of higher fear and lower victimization levels among the elderly contends that it may be a mistake to assume that risk, rather than vulnerability to risk, is the central element of elderly fear. In other words, to argue that elderly fears are excessive, in the presence of risks that are lower than those faced by other members of the population, is to presuppose that older people do not differ from younger ones in their perceptions of the gravity of the consequences associated with victimization. By contrast, it might be argued that elderly fear is high not because older people believe that their chances of victimization are high, but because they believe that they will be less able than others to cope effectively with the effects of any victimization that might occur (Warr, 1984). Perhaps the elderly are more afraid not because they inaccurately assess their chances of being victimized, but because they do accurately assess their greater vulnerability to the adverse effects of victimization.

Finally, LaGrange and Ferraro (1987; 1989) have argued that the apparent paradox between levels of victimization and fear may result from the use of inadequate measures of fear of crime. A review of the literature on fear of crime makes it clear that researchers disagree regarding the most appropriate operationalization of this construct (Fattah and Sacco, 1989; Gibbs et al., 1987). However, most attempts to investigate this issue, in the context of survey research, have employed similar questions asking respondents about their feelings of safety while alone in the neighbourhood at night. One standard item asks, 'How safe do you feel or would you feel walking alone in your neighbourhood at night? Would you say that you feel very safe, somewhat safe, somewhat unsafe or very unsafe?' A variation on this theme asks respondents to reply in dichotomous fashion to the question, 'Is there any place around here where you feel unsafe walking alone at night?' Although literally hundreds of thousands of people in Canada, the United States, and Great Britain have been asked these questions in victimization and crime-perception surveys, many researchers have expressed skepticism regarding the validity of these measures (Clarke, 1984; Garofalo, 1979; 1981; Gibbs et al., 1987; Yin, 1980).

Notably, it is when such measures are used that the elderly appear particularly afraid. LaGrange and Ferraro (1987) argue that questions asking about feelings of safety while alone on neighbourhood streets at night are largely irrelevant to the everyday lives of most elderly people, who rarely find themselves in such situations. For older respondents, such questions are too hypothetical and abstract, and their use for the investigation of age differences in levels of fear 'has the effect of exaggerating fear of crime among the elderly and perhaps even underestimating the level of fear among younger respondents' (LaGrange and Ferraro, 1987: 186).

Data addressing this issue are presented in Tables 6.5, 6.6, 6.7, and 6.8. Table 6.5 presents 1988 GSS data on feelings of safety while walking alone in the neighbourhood at night. The pattern revealed by the data is consistent with previous research. For the sample as a whole, the proportion that reports feeling (somewhat or very) unsafe is greater among elderly than non-elderly respondents. It will also be noted that females report more fear than males, irrespective of age category, and that the increase in fear with the advent of old age is much more pronounced for males than for females (who are generally more fearful at all stages of the life-cycle).

Other data from the GSS provide a somewhat different picture (Table 6.6). When asked to compare their own neighbourhood to other areas in Canada, elderly Canadians were no more likely than younger people to characterize local crime levels as 'higher'. Nor are they

Table 6.5: **Feelings of Safety by Age and Gender**
General Social Survey, 1988
(% 'unsafe' walking alone in neighbourhood at night)

	Both gender groups	_Male_	_Female_
All ages	25	11	39
Under 65	24	10	37
65 or over	37	22	49

SOURCE: Sacco and Johnson (1990: 62–3).

Table 6.6: **Perceptions of Crime**
General Social Survey, 1988

	Perceived level of crime in neighbourhood compared to other areas in Canada (%)			
	Higher	About the same	Lower	Don't know/not stated
All ages	8	29	57	6
Under 65	8	29	57	5
65 or over	7	32	51	10

	Perceived change in level of crime in neighbourhood in 1987 (%)			
	Increased	Decreased	Same	Don't know/not stated
All ages	20	8	62	9
Under 65	20	8	61	9
65 or over	20	6	64	10

	Crime of most concern (%)			
	Attack or threat	Theft	Deliberate damage	Something else/ not stated
All ages	42	36	15	7
Under 65	43	36	15	6
65 or over	37	36	16	11

SOURCE: Sacco and Johnson (1990: 59, 60, 64).

Table 6.7: **Proportion of Women Who Felt Worried in Specific Situations, by Age Group**
Violence Against Women Survey

		Age group	
	Total[a]	Under 65	65 and Over
Walking alone in area after dark	60	61	52
Waiting for/using public transportation alone after dark	76	71	51
Walking alone to car in parking garage	83	85	62
Home alone in the evening	39	42	26

[a]Excludes women who are never in these situations.
SOURCE: Statistics Canada (1993).

more likely to perceive changes in neighbourhood crime as having 'increased' during 1987. When asked about the crime that is of 'most concern' to them, elderly respondents were not more likely to choose the most serious offence type: 'attack or threat of attack'. These data, in contrast to those on safety alone at night, provide little reason to identify the elderly as most fearful. Similarly, data from the 1993 'violence against women' survey (Table 6.7) suggest that when respondents are asked about a variety of social situations, the non-elderly are more likely to provide fearful responses.

The findings of the 1984 Vancouver Urban Survey provide further support for the view that empirical findings about elderly fear are item-specific (Table 6.8). This survey asked a sample of 489 Vancouver respondents about the extent to which they 'worry' about the possibility of victimization with respect to several specific offence categories (Sacco and Glackman, 1987). The items used an eleven-point scale with the end points '0' and '10' labelled 'never worry' and 'worry a great deal' respectively. Table 6.8 suggests that the use of such measures provides a markedly distinct image of the age distribution of fear of crime for offences that involve violence or the threat of violence. Consistent with the findings of studies employing 'safe alone at night' measures, women are more likely to report that they worry about the possibility of victimization for all three offences and for both age groups. However, it is also clear that, for all three offences, the mean level of worry for the elderly is lower and not higher than for those under 65 years of age. Similar findings have been generated by other researchers who have employed crime-specific rather than global measures (LaGrange and Ferraro, 1987).

Table 6.8: **Worry About Crime** (mean levels)
Vancouver Urban Survey, 1984

	Both gender groups	Male	Female
Break and enter while home			
All ages	2.96	2.28	3.46
Under 65	3.12	2.44	3.65
65 or over	2.03	1.12	2.53
Use weapon to take something			
All ages	3.40	3.06	3.66
Under 65	3.53	3.14	3.85
65 or over	2.66	2.54	2.72
Sexual assault			
All ages	3.03	1.10	4.47
Under 65	3.19	1.20	4.75
65 or over	2.11	.35	3.09

SOURCES: Vancouver Urban Survey Data.

For many elderly people, the fear of crime and violence is no doubt a serious problem. In its extreme forms this fear isolates older people and reduces the quality of their lives. However, efforts to characterize the elderly in general as a group consumed by worry about personal safety are probably exercises in hyperbole. It seems clear that our estimates of the problem are sensitive to the types of measures employed. In the absence of a clear and consensual judgement about how the fear of crime should be measured, definitive statements are impossible.

ELDER ABUSE

As was stated at the beginning of this chapter, the problem of abuse of the elderly in domestic settings has recently begun to attract the attention of researchers, activists, and policy-makers. Although this problem is usually 'typified' in terms of extreme physical violence or cruelty, the concept of elder abuse is not synonymous with physical violence. Rather, it is usually employed in a way that encompasses a broad range of forms of mistreatment. Johnson's (1986) exhaustive review of research definitions and clinical protocols concludes that the number of distinct categories of abuse identified by analysts usually ranges from 2 to 6, and that the '[c]ommon constitutive elements include physical abuse, psychological abuse, material abuse, exploitation and neglect' (Johnson, 1986: 177). However, the gap between the ways in which the problem is typified and the manner in which it is operationally defined no doubt confuses the meaning of popular estimates suggesting, for instance, that 4% of all elderly Canadians (98,000) have been abused since age 65 (Health and Welfare Canada, 1990).

The available research literature suggests agreement regarding a relatively small number of correlates of elder abuse, despite significant disparities in the ways in which abuse is defined for research purposes (Pillemer and Frankel, 1991). Most researchers contend that elderly women are at greater risk of various types of abuse than elderly men, and that, within the elderly population, the risk of abuse increases with age (Anetzberger, 1987; Brillon, 1987; Fattah and Sacco, 1989; Shell, 1982). The existence of gender differences in abuse victimization could be deduced from knowledge of the gender imbalance of the elderly population. Several studies also find that the victim of abuse is typically someone who suffers from a physical or functional impairment (Brillon, 1987; Pillemer and Finkelhor, 1988; Quinn and Tomita, 1986). Again, however, some recent research disputes the correlational significance of such impairment (Pillemer, 1985; Wolf, 1986).

Baumann (1989) has described how inadequate research designs and ageist assumptions about the elderly have resulted in the widespread acceptance of a 'conventional wisdom' about the causes of elder abuse.

This conventional wisdom portrays the abuse victim as an elderly parent who is functionally impaired and dependent on her adult children for the basic necessities of life (O'Malley et al., 1983). This dependency is said to upset the family dynamics of the adult offspring. In the context of these 'generationally-inverse families' parent and child roles are reversed, and the strain toward abuse and neglect is seen to arise quite logically from the stress of the caregiving situation (Steinmetz, 1981; 1983).

These dominant theoretical constructions have recently been called into question by more rigorous research studies (Wolf, 1988). Community studies, for instance, indicate that the stereotyped image of elders being abused by their adult offspring may apply to a smaller proportion of cases than was previously thought. In fact, much of what we call elder abuse involves the mistreatment of one spouse by another (Mastrocola-Morris, 1989; Pillemer and Finkelhor, 1988; Podnieks, 1990). Recent research also indicates that the image of the abusive caregiver as a well-meaning individual who is overcome by the stresses of caring for a dependent elder may be inaccurate. A growing body of literature points to a link between various forms of abuser psychopathology (including substance abuse) and mistreatment of the elderly (Pillemer, 1986; Quinn and Tomita, 1986).

As well, the prevailing view that dependency contributes to abuse by raising stress levels and placing the elder in a position of extreme powerlessness relative to the abuser, may be misleading (Pillemer, 1985; Wolf, 1986). Using data from three American 'model projects', a comparison of a sample of abused elderly with a sample of non-abused controls reveals that abuse victims were not more likely to be dependent on their caregivers than were the controls. Importantly, this analysis also indicated that in many cases the abused elderly were more likely to describe their caregivers as being dependent on them for, among other things, housing or financial assistance. In such cases, the abuser may be a dependent offspring who, because of mental impairment or other personal problems, is unable to separate from the elder. This research suggests that it may be the dependency of the abuser rather than the abused that culminates in mistreatment.

More generally, the theoretical significance of caregiver stress to elder abuse has itself been called into question. Many more caregivers define their situations as stressful than engage in abusive conduct. Moreover, the empirical correlation of stress with abuse is not unequivocal. Stress itself may in some cases be a reaction to the guilt and anxiety that mistreatment produces in the caregiver. Taken together, these problems suggest that the general tendency to argue that the elder is abused because he or she creates stress for an otherwise benevolent caregiver is at best an over-simplification and at worst a particularly pernicious form of victim-blaming (Sacco, 1990).

As has been stated, only one major investigation of elder abuse has been undertaken in Canada. In 1989, Health and Welfare Canada funded a national telephone survey of 2,008 elderly persons (65 years of age or over) living in private dwellings. The study focused on four types of abuse: material abuse, chronic verbal aggression, physical violence, and neglect. To be sure, the method of data collection and some of the measures employed in the study are problematic. (The sample, for instance, is restricted to those with telephones, and it is possible that many types of abuse are not addressed by the questions asked.) However, the results provide the only national data relating to the prevalence and correlates of abuse of the elderly.

Physical violence was operationalized using a modified form of the Conflict Tactics Scale (Straus and Gelles, 1992). With respect to CTS behaviours involving a spouse, one co-resident child, or one other social-network member, respondents were asked about victimizations that had occurred since they had turned 65. The study revealed a physical violence prevalence rate of 5 per 1,000 elderly persons living in private dwellings, or about 0.5% of the sample. Given the sample size, the number of cases available for analysis is small. Proportionately, however, the physical violence revealed by the survey was quite severe. In nearly two-thirds of the cases, the victim had been slapped, grabbed, or shoved. In more than one-third of the cases, the victim had been threatened with a knife or a gun during the previous year.

Consistent with research discussed above, the survey found that a majority of abusers were spouses of the victims. Victims were also no more likely than non-victims to report that they were in poor health, or that they experienced problems in performing everyday activities. Compared to the spouses of non-victims, spouses who were physically abusive were more likely to be reported to have a range of physical and emotional problems and to be dependent on the victim for financial support.

Quite clearly, data on elder abuse in Canada are just beginning to accumulate, and it is difficult at this stage to determine whether the concern about this problem will go the way of earlier moral panics about the victimization of the elderly (Cook and Skogan, 1990; Leroux and Petrunik, 1989). What is equally clear is that despite claims that the concept of elder abuse sensitizes the research community to empirical distinctions that might otherwise go unnoticed, it may also be the case that the concept creates distinctions that obscure our understanding. As we have seen, some studies show that what we are calling elder abuse may be recognized as spousal abuse among aging husbands and wives. To the extent that such abuse represents the continuation of a pattern that begins in young adulthood or middle age, it would seem that the introduction of a new label adds little of substance.

With respect to the other major manifestation of elder abuse—the victimization of aging parents by adult children—a similar point can be made. American national self-report data indicate, for instance, that the annual rate of physical abuse of parents by adolescents is between 5% and 9% (Agnew and Huguley, 1989; Peek et al., 1985). If such patterns of abuse continue over the life cycle, it is not evident how the problem is illuminated by terming it 'elder abuse' when the victim turns 65. In short, there may be no more compelling reason to talk about elder abuse than there is to talk about 'middle-age abuse'.

Even though much of what is written about elder abuse focuses on caregiver relationships, it also seems to be the case that abuse may occur outside such relationships (Pillemer and Suitor, 1988). The Canadian national survey revealed, for instance, that 40 per cent of the cases of material abuse involved friends, acquaintances, or neighbours (Podnieks, 1990). Moreover, if elder abuse is constructed as caregiver abuse, the age of victims ceases to be highly relevant since anyone with diminished physical or mental capacity may be susceptible to abuse, irrespective of age.

At a minimum, theoretical and empirical refinements await resolution of ambiguities in the way the concept is defined for research purposes. These ambiguities involve inconsistencies in the definition of the elderly; uncertainty regarding the nature and number of forms that abuse may take; and the widespread tendency to confuse abuse as a behaviour with its physical and emotional consequences (Sacco, 1993).

THE ELDERLY OFFENDER

Offender data further support the contention that the elderly are infrequent participants in violent criminal events (Flowers, 1989). Much of the concern expressed in popular media about a 'geriatric crime wave' has quite evidently overstated both the nature and the magnitude of the problem.

Analyses of US arrest data by Cullen et al. (1985) indicate that those over the age of 65 constitute less than 1% of the total arrestee population for violent crimes. According to Wilbanks (1984a), the ratio of non-elderly to elderly people arrested for violent crimes is approximately 17 to 1. When older offenders are arrested it is likely to be for non-violent, alcohol-related offences or for various forms of theft.

Nor do the data support the conclusion that the degree of elderly involvement in violent crime has changed dramatically in recent years. Those changes that have occurred involve a large percentage increase and relatively small raw numbers (Cullen et al., 1985), and some real growth in the rate of theft rather than any significant increase in levels of violent offending (Fattah and Sacco, 1989; Burnett and Ortega, 1984).

In Canada, because detailed information on offender characteris-tics is less available, we restrict attention to the crime of homicide. Silver-man and Kennedy's (1993) analysis of homicide trends over the period 1961–90 allows for the comparison of 245 homicides involving elderly offenders with homicides involving younger offenders. Homicides by elderly offenders accounted for only 2.3% of the total, which—given that those over age 65 constitute about 8% of the Canadian population—sug-gests a significant under-representation of older offenders.

Thirty-five per cent of the victims of elderly offenders were male and 65 per cent were female. These figures suggest a reversal of the pat-tern for those under age 65. Of the nine elderly female offenders, all but one killed a male. Although both elderly and non-elderly homicides are more likely to involve male than female offenders, the gender gap is even greater for those over 65 than for younger offenders. All of the elderly homicide offenders, for the period in question, acted alone. The data revealed no overall trend suggestive of an increase in the rate at which homicides by elderly offenders are occurring.

The data analysed by Silverman and Kennedy suggest that offend-ing, like victimization, reflects patterns of routine activities. Murders involving older offenders typically involve a victim who is a family mem-ber, friend, or acquaintance; stranger homicide and murder in the con-text of another crime (such as robbery or sexual assault) are both extremely rare. Not surprisingly, the victim also tends to be older. Homi-cides committed by older offenders typically occur in the home of either the victim (73 per cent) or the home of the offender (14 per cent), and only rarely in public places (about 4 per cent). These find-ings are largely consistent with American data (Kratcoski, 1990; Krat-coski and Walker, 1988).

More generally, theoretical interest in elderly offending has tended to focus on two major issues. The first concerns the relatively low rate of violent offending among the elderly as compared to the rest of the population. Stated simply, why are elderly rates of violent crime as low as they are? Part of the answer can be found in the gender ratio of the elderly population and the lower rates of female offending, irre-spective of age level. In addition to demographic structure, however, several factors have been suggested to explain the decline in criminality with advancing age. These include the decline in physical strength and ability, the decrease in the volume of social interaction, changes in the direction of aggressive tendencies, the weakening of criminal motiva-tion, and the reduction in occupationally-related or other criminal opportunities (Fattah and Sacco, 1989).

It may be argued, however, that there are few compelling reasons to focus theoretical attention on crime-rate differences between the elderly and the non-elderly. The low rates of elderly offending do not represent a pattern that begins at age 65 but rather one that begins in early adulthood and continues into old age (Hirschi and Gottfredson, 1983). The factors that link aging to a reduction in criminal behaviour find their origins much earlier in the life cycle.

The second major issue focuses theoretical attention on the occurrence of elderly offending. Again, the literature offers no shortage of explanations (McCarthy and Langworthy, 1988; Fattah and Sacco, 1989; Newman et al., 1984; Wilbanks and Kim, 1984). Many of these attempt to identify factors that are thought to be unique to older people, such as senile dementia or other functional impairments, a reduced probability of arrest or conviction, disengagement from social roles, or the presence of economic or other stressors associated with later life (Jackson, 1981; Mizurchi et al., 1982; Moberg, 1953; Whiskin, 1968). However, this line of inquiry is also problematic. Wilbanks (1984b) argues that theories about elderly offenders implicitly tend to regard such offenders as a homogeneous category, when in fact levels of offending differ significantly across gender and racial groups.

It may also be argued that 'special' theories focusing on the elderly offender are unnecessary. If the objective of scientific theory is increased generalizability, the proliferation of new explanations for phenomena that may be adequately explained by existing theories is counter-productive. Opportunity theories of victimization and offending, for example, are just as applicable to criminal events involving the elderly as the non-elderly (Kennedy and Silverman, 1990; Kratcoski and Walker, 1988; Messner and Tardiff, 1985).

This last argument has been forcefully made by Akers et al. (1988), who suggest that the dominant theories of offender motivation that emphasize social learning, social bonds, or anomie and strain are adequate to the task of explaining crimes by the elderly. While in each case the theoretical statement may require modifications to take account of the unique character of elderly offending, the theories are not so limited that they are unable to provide an interpretive framework for understanding the older criminal.

CONCLUSION

The data reviewed in this chapter provide a portrait of elderly involvement in violent criminal events that is in sharp contrast with much of what is popularly believed about the issue. The evidence suggests that elderly victimization rates are relatively low, and that while the crimes that victimize the elderly are predatory in nature, they are not particularly violent in either their content or their consequences. In addition, claims about the ways in which the concern for personal safety has made the elderly 'prisoners of fear' are not consistently supported by the available research. Domestic violence directed against the elderly appears to be statistically rare, as does violent offending by the elderly.

In the aggregate, the material reviewed in this chapter would seem to suggest that 'violence and the elderly' is not a problem requiring serious attention. However, the intention here is not to be dismissive. It is quite possible that glib conclusions about low levels of elderly crime problems may prove, in the long run, as unproductive as glib conclusions about high levels of such problems.

Over the past twenty-five years, academic and popular discourse about violence and the elderly has swung, like a pendulum, between two extreme positions. One of these positions has maintained that the elderly experience frequent and serious problems with violence. The other contends that these problems relating to street crime, fear of crime, or domestic abuse are not really problems after all. While adherents of the latter position have made important contributions in debunking outlandish claims about the amount of violence that involves the elderly—as victims or as offenders—it appears that as this pendulum swings, we risk losing sight of some of the more basic and intractable issues that confront the elderly in Canadian society.

The discovery of low rates of victimization among the elderly was quite rightly interpreted by most observers as 'good news'. Yet it is important to remember the nature of the social forces, including age segregation and the restricted mobility of older people, that keep these rates low. Similarly, low rates of domestic violence reflect, in part, the fact that elderly people are more likely to live alone. It may be that the absence of anyone to perform the caregiving role, rather than the presence of someone who performs this role in an abusive fashion, is the real dilemma facing many seniors. The suggestion that 'safe alone at night' measures do not properly assess elderly fear because older people do not use the streets at night, and cannot even accurately picture themselves doing so, likewise necessitates careful scrutiny. In general, much of the 'good news' about violence and the elderly requires cautious interpretation.

References

Agnew, R. and S. Huguley (1989). 'Adolescent violence toward parents', *Journal of Marriage and the Family* 51: 699–711.

Akers, R.L., A.J. La Greca, C. Sellers, and J. Cochran (1987). 'Fear of crime and victimization among the elderly in different types of communities', *Criminology* 25, 3: 487–505.

Akers, R.L., A.J. La Greca and C. Sellers (1988). 'Theoretical perspectives on deviant behavior among the elderly'. Pp. 35–50 in McCarthy and

Langworthy, eds, *Older Offenders: Perspective in Criminology and Criminal Justice*. New York: Praeger.

Anetzberger, C.J. (1987). *The Etiology of Elder Abuse by Adult Offspring*. Springfield, IL: Charles C. Thomas.

Antunes, G.E., F.L. Cook, T.D. Cook, and W.G. Skogan (1977). 'Patterns of personal crime against the elderly: Findings from a national survey', *The Gerontologist* 17: 321–7.

Bachman, R. (1992). *Bureau of Justice Statistics Special Report: Elderly Victims*. Washington: US Department of Justice.

Baldassare, M. (1986). 'The elderly and fear of crime', *Sociology and Social Research* 70, 3: 218–21.

Balkin, S. (1979). 'Victimization rates, safety and fear of crime', *Social Problems* 26: 343–58.

Baumann, E.A. (1989). 'Research rhetoric and the social construction of elder abuse'. Pp. 55–74 in J. Best, ed. *Images of Issues*. New York: Aldine De Gruyter.

Baumer, T.L. (1978). 'Research on fear of crime in the United States', *Victimology* 3: 254–64.

Block, C.R. and R.L. Block (1984). 'Crime definition, crime measurement, and victim surveys', *Journal of Social Issues* 40: 137–60.

Block, M.R., and J.D. Sinnott (1979). 'Methodology and results'. Pp. 67–84 in Block and Sinnott, eds, *The Battered Elder Syndrome*. College Park: University of Maryland Center on Aging.

Braungart, M.M., R.G. Braungart, and W.J. Hoyer (1980). 'Age, sex and social factors in fear of crime', *Sociological Focus* 13: 55–65.

Brillon, Y. (1987). *Victimization and Fear of Crime Among the Elderly*. Toronto: Butterworths.

Burnett, C., and S.T. Ortega (1984). 'Elderly Offenders: A Descriptive Analysis'. Pp. 17–40 in Wilbanks and Kim, eds, *Elderly Criminals*. New York: Lanham.

Burt, M.R., and B.L. Katz (1985). 'Rape, robbery, and burglary: Responses to actual and feared criminal victimization, with special focus on women and the elderly', *Victimology* 10: 325–58.

Chen, P.N., S.L. Bell, D.L. Dolinsky, J. Doyle, and M. McDunn (1981). 'Elder abuse in domestic settings: A pilot study', *Journal of Gerontological Social Work* 4: 3–17.

Clarke, A.H. (1984). 'Perceptions of crime and fear of victimisation among elderly people', *Aging and Society* 4: 327–42.

Clarke, R., P. Ekblom, M. Hough, and P. Mayhew (1985). 'Elderly victims of crime and exposure to risk', *Journal of Criminal Justice* 24: 1–9.

Clemente, F., and M.B. Kleiman (1976). 'Fear of crime among the aged', *The Gerontologist* 16: 207–10.

Cohen, L.E., and M. Felson (1979). 'Social change and crime rate trends: A routine activity approach', *American Sociological Review* 44: 588–608.

Cook, F.L. (1981). 'Crime and the elderly: The emergence of a policy issue'. Pp. 123–47 in D.A. Lewis, ed. *Reactions to Crime*. Beverly Hills: Sage Publications.

Cook, F.L., and W.G. Skogan (1990). 'Agenda setting and the rise and fall of policy issues: The case of criminal victimization of the elderly', *Environment and Planning C: Government and Policy* 8: 395–415.

Cook, F.L., W.G. Skogan, T.D. Cook, and G.E. Antunes (1978). 'Criminal victimization of the elderly: The physical and economic consequences', *The Gerontologist* 18: 338–49.

Cook, T.D., J. Fremming, and T.R. Tyler (1981). 'Criminal victimization of the elderly: Validating the policy assumptions'. Pp. 223–51 in Stephenson and Davis, eds, *Progress in Applied Social Psychology*. New York: John Wiley and Sons.

Corrado, R.R., R. Roesch, W. Glackman, J.L. Evans, and G.L. Leger (1980). 'Life styles and personal victimization: A test of the model with Canadian survey data', *Journal of Crime and Justice* 3: 189–301.

Cullen, F.T., J.F. Wozniak, and J. Frank (1985). 'The rise of the elderly offender—Will a "new" criminal be invented?' *Crime and Social Justice* 23: 151–65.

DeFronzo, J. (1979). 'Marital status, sex and other factors affecting the fear of crime', *Western Sociological Review* 10: 28–39.

Fattah, E.A. (1991). *Understanding Criminal Victimization*. Scarborough: Prentice-Hall.

Fattah, E.A., and V.F. Sacco (1989). *Crime and Victimization of the Elderly*. New York: Springer.

Feinberg, G. (1984). 'White haired offenders: An emergent social problem'. Pp. 83–101 in Wilbanks and Kim, eds, *Elderly Criminals*. New York: Lanham.

Feinberg, N. (1981). 'The emotional and behavioral consequences of violent crime on elderly victims', *Victimology* 6: 355–7.

Fishman, M. (1978). 'Crime waves as ideology', *Social Problems* 25: 531–43.

Flowers, R.B. (1989). *Demographics and Criminality*. New York: Greenwood Press.

Forsyth, C.J., and R. Gramling (1988). 'Elderly crime: Fact and artifact'. Pp. 3–13 in B. McCarthy and R. Langworthy, eds. *Older Offenders: Perspective in Criminology and Criminal Justice*. New York: Praeger.

Fox, J.A., and J. Levin (1991). 'Homicide against the elderly: A research note', *Criminology* 29, 2: 317–27.

Garofalo, J. (1979). 'Victimization and the fear of crime', *Journal of Research in Crime and Delinquency* 16: 80–97.

——— (1981). 'The fear of crime: Causes and consequences', *The Journal of Criminal Law and Criminology* 72: 839–57.

Gibbs, J.J., E.J. Coyle, and K.J. Hanrahan (1987). 'Fear of crime: A concept in need of clarification'. Paper presented at the Annual Meetings of the American Society of Criminology, Montreal.

Golant, S.M. (1984). 'Factors influencing the nighttime activity of old persons in their community', *Journal of Gerontology* 39: 485–91.

Gomme, I. (1988). 'The Role of experience in the production of the fear of crime: A test of a causal model', *Canadian Journal of Criminology* 30: 67–76.

Gordon, R.M. (1987). 'Financial abuse of the elderly and state "protective services": Changing strategies in the penal-welfare complex in the United States and Canada', *Crime and Social Justice* 26: 116–34.

Gottfredson, M.R., and D.M. Gottfredson (1980). *Decisionmaking in Criminal Justice*. Cambridge, MA.: Ballinger Publishing.

Gottfredson, M.R., and M.J. Hindelang (1979). 'A study of the behavior of law', *American Sociological Review* 44: 3–18.

Health and Welfare Canada (1990). 'Elder Abuse'. Information sheet.

Hindelang, M., M.R. Gottfredson, and J. Garofalo (1978). *Victims of Personal Crime: An Empirical Foundation for a Theory of Personal Victimization*. Cambridge, MA: Ballinger Publishing.

Hirschi, T., and M. Gottfredson (1983). 'Age and the explanation of crime', *American Journal of Sociology* 89: 552–84.

Hochstedler, E. (1981). *Crimes Against the Elderly in 26 Cities*. Washington, DC: US Department of Justice.

Jackson, M. (1981). 'Criminal deviance among the elderly', *Canadian Criminology Forum* 4, 1: 45–53.

Jackson, P.G. (1990). 'Sources of data'. Pp. 21–50 in K.L. Kempf, ed. *Measurement Issues in Criminology*. New York: Springer-Verlag.

Janoff-Bulman, R., and I.H. Frieze (1983). 'A theoretical perspective for understanding reactions to victimization', *Journal of Social Issues* 39: 1–17.

Jaycox, V.H. (1978). 'The elderly's fear of crime: Rational or irrational?' *Victimology* 3: 329–34.

Johnson, T. (1986). 'Critical issues in the definition of elder mistreatment'. Pp. 167–96 in K.A. Pillemer and W.S. Wolf, eds. *Elder Abuse: Conflict in the Family*. Dover, MA: Auburn Publishing.

Karmen, A. (1990). *Crime Victims: An Introduction to Victimology*. Second ed. Pacific Grove, CA: Brooks/Cole.

Kennedy, L.W., and R.A. Silverman (1990). 'The elderly victim of homicide: An application of routine activity theory', *Sociological Quarterly* 31, 2: 305–17.

Kratcoski, P.C. (1990). 'Circumstances surrounding homicides by older offenders', *Criminal Justice and Behavior* 17, 4: 420–30.

Kratcoski, P.C., and D.B. Walker (1988). 'Homicide among the elderly: Analysis of the victim/assailant relationship'. Pp. 62–75 in McCarthy and Langworthy, eds, *Older Offenders: Perspective in Criminology and Criminal Justice*. New York: Praeger.

LaGrange, R.L., and K.F. Ferraro (1987). 'The elderly's fear of crime', *Research on Aging* 9, 3: 372–91.

——— (1989). 'Assessing age and gender differences in perceived risk and fear of crime', *Criminology* 27, 4: 697–719.

Lau, E.E., and J.I. Kosberg (1979). 'Abuse of the elderly by informal care providers', *Aging* 299: 10–15.

Lawton, M.P. and S. Yaffe (1980). 'Victimization and fear of crime in elderly public housing tenants', *Journal of Gerontology* 35: 768–79.

Lee, G.R. (1983). 'Social integration and fear of crime among older persons', *Journal of Gerontology* 38: 745–50.

Leroux, T.G., and M. Petrunik (1989). 'The construction of elder abuse as a social problem: A Canadian perspective', *International Journal of Health Services* 20, 4: 651–63.

Lindquist, J.H., and J.M. Duke (1982). 'The elderly victim at risk: Explaining the fear-victimization paradox', *Criminology* 20: 115–26.

Loseke, D.R. (1992). *The Battered Woman and Shelters*. Albany: State University of New York Press.

Massey, C.R., and J. McKean (1985). 'The social ecology of homicide: A modified lifestyle/routine activities perspective', *Journal of Criminal Justice* 13: 417–28.

Mastrocola-Morris, E. (1989). *Woman Abuse: The Relationship Between Wife Assault and Elder Abuse*. Ottawa: National Clearinghouse on Family Violence, Health and Welfare Canada.

Maxfield, M.G. (1984). 'The limits of vulnerability in explaining fear of crime', *Research in Crime and Delinquency* 21: 233–50.

McCarthy, B., and R. Langworthy (1988). *Older Offenders.* New York: Praeger.

Messner, S.F., and K. Tardiff (1985). 'The social ecology of urban homicide: An application of the "routine activities" approach', *Criminology* 23, 2: 241–67.

Miethe, T.D., M.C. Stafford, and J.S. Long (1987). 'Social differentiation in criminal victimization: A test of routine activities/lifestyle theories', *American Sociological Review* 52: 184–94.

Mizurchi, E.J., B. Glassner, and T. Pastorello (1982). *Time and Aging.* Bayside, NJ: General Hall Inc.

Moberg, D. (1953). 'Old age and crime', *Journal of Criminal Law, Criminology and Police Science* 43: 773–5.

Morrison, P. (1991). 'The future of crime statistics in Canada: The revised uniform crime reporting system'. Paper presented at the Annual Meetings of the Canadian Sociology and Anthropology Association.

Muram, D., K. Miller, and A. Cutler (1992). 'Sexual assault of the elderly victim', *Journal of Interpersonal Violence* 7, 1: 70–6.

Nelson, B.J. (1984). *Making an Issue of Child Abuse.* Chicago: University of Chicago Press.

Nettler, G. (1984). *Explaining Crime.* Third ed. New York: McGraw-Hill.

Newman, E., D. Newman, and M. Gewirtz (1984). *Elderly Criminals.* Cambridge: Oelgeschlager, Gunn and Hain.

O'Brien, R.M. (1985). *Crime and Victimization Data.* Beverly Hills, CA: Sage Publications.

O'Malley, T.A., D.E. Everitt, and H.C. O'Malley (1983). 'Identifying and preventing family-mediated abuse and neglect of elderly persons', *Annals of Internal Medicine* 98: 998–1005.

Peek, C.W., J.L. Fischer, and J.S. Kidwell (1985). 'Teenage violence toward parents: A neglected dimension of family violence', *Journal of Marriage and the Family* 47: 1051–8.

Pfohl, S. (1977). 'The discovery of child abuse', *Social Problems* 24: 310–23.

Pillemer, K.A. (1985). 'The dangers of dependency: New findings on domestic violence against the elderly', *Social Problems* 33: 146–58.

——— (1986). 'Risk factors in elder abuse: Results from a case-control study'. Pp. 239–63 in K.A. Pillemer and W.S. Wolf, eds. *Elder Abuse: Conflict in the Family.* Dover, MA: Auburn Publishing.

Pillemer, K.A., and D. Finkelhor (1988). 'The prevalence of elder abuse: A random sample survey', *The Gerontologist* 28: 51–7.

Pillemer, K.A., and S. Frankel (1991). 'Violence against the elderly'. Pp. 158–83 in M.L. Rosenberg and M.A. Fenley, eds. *Violence in America: A Mental Health Approach.* New York: Oxford University Press.

Pillemer, K.A., and J. Suitor (1988). 'Elder abuse'. Pp. 247–70 in V.B. Hasselt, R.L. Morrison, A.S. Bellack and M. Hersen, eds. *Handbook of Family Violence.* New York: Plenum.

Podnieks, E. (1990). *National Survey on Abuse of the Elderly in Canada.* Toronto: Ryerson Polytechnical Institute.

Quinn, M.J., and S.K. Tomita (1986). *Elder Abuse and Neglect: Causes, Diagnosis and Intervention Strategies.* New York: Springer Publishing.

Rathbone-McCuan, E., and J. Hashimi (1982). *Isolated Elders.* Rockville, MA: Aspen Systems Corporation.

Ruback, R.B., M.S. Greenberg, and D.R. Westcott (1984). 'Social influence and crime-victim decision making', *Journal of Social Issues* 40: 51–76.

Sacco, V.F. (1985). 'City size and perceptions of crime', *Canadian Journal of Sociology* 10: 277–93.

———— (1990). 'Elder abuse policy: An assessment of categoric approaches'. In R. Roesch, D.G. Dutton and V.F. Sacco, eds. *Family Violence: Perspectives on Treatment, Research and Policy.* Vancouver: British Columbia Institute of Family Violence.

———— (1993). 'Conceptualizing elder abuse: Implications for research and theory'. In W. Bilsky et al. eds. *Criminal Victimization and Fear of Crime Among the Elderly—Survey Research: Past, Present, and Future.* Stuttgart: Enkie Verlag.

Sacco, V.F. and W. Glackman (1987). 'Vulnerability, locus of control and worry about crime', *Canadian Journal of Community Mental Health* 6: 99–111.

Sacco, V.F., and H. Johnson (1990). *General Social Survey Analysis Series: Patterns of Criminal Victimization in Canada.* Ottawa: Ministry of Supply and Services.

Sampson, R.J., and J.H. Laub (1992). 'Crime and deviance in the life course', *Annual Review of Sociology* 18: 63–84.

Shell, D.J. (1982). *Protection of the Elderly: A Study of Elder Abuse.* Winnipeg: Manitoba Council on Aging.

Silverman, R., and L. Kennedy (1993). *Deadly Deeds.* Scarborough, ON: Nelson Canada.

Silverman, R.A., J.J. Teevan, and V.F. Sacco (1991). *Crime in Canadian Society.* Fourth ed. Toronto: Butterworths.

Skogan, W. (1976). 'Citizen reporting of crime: Some national panel data', *Criminology* 13: 535–49.

—— (1977). 'Policy problems in criminal justice: The case of the elderly victim of crime'. Paper presented at the Annual Meetings of the American Society for Public Administration.

—— (1980). 'Adjusting rates of victimization for exposure to risk, to understand the crime problems of the elderly'. Unpublished manuscript. Evanston, IL: Northwestern University.

—— (1986). 'Methodological issues in the study of victimization'. Pp. 53–79 in E.A. Fattah, ed. *From Crime Policy to Victim Policy*. London: Macmillan Press.

Skogan, W.G. and M.G. Maxfield (1981). *Coping with Crime*. Beverly Hills, CA: Sage Publications.

Solicitor General Canada (1983). *Canadian Urban Victimization Survey Bulletin 1: Victims of Crime*. Ottawa: Ministry Secretariat/Programs Branch.

—— (1984). *Canadian Urban Victimization Survey Bulletin 2: Reported and Unreported Crimes*. Ottawa: Ministry Secretariat/Programs Branch.

—— (1985a). *Canadian Urban Victimization Survey Bulletin 5: Cost of Crime to Victims*. Ottawa: Ministry Secretariat/Programs Branch.

—— (1985b). *Canadian Urban Victimization Survey Bulletin 6: Criminal Victimization of Elderly Canadians*. Ottawa: Ministry Secretariat/Programs Branch.

—— (1987). *Canadian Urban Victimization Survey Bulletin 8: Patterns in Violent Crime*. Ottawa: Ministry Secretariat/Programs Branch.

Stafford, M., and O.R. Galle (1984). 'Victimization rates, exposure to risk, and fear of crime', *Criminology* 22: 173–85.

Statistics Canada (1990). 'The future of crime statistics from the UCR survey', *Juristat* 10, 10.

—— (1992). 'Homicide in Canada', *Juristat* 12, 18.

—— (1993). 'The violence against women survey', *The Daily*, 18 November.

Steinmetz, S.K. (1981). 'Elder abuse', *Aging*, January/February: 6–10.

—— (1983). 'Dependency, stress and violence between middle-aged caregivers and their elderly parents'. Pp. 134–49 in J.I. Kosberg, ed. *Abuse and Mistreatment of the Elderly: Causes and Interventions*. Littleton, MA: John Wright.

Stephenson, G. M., and J. M. Davis (1981). *Progress in Applied Social Psychology*. New York: John Wiley and Sons.

Straus, M.A., and R.J. Gelles (1992). *Physical Violence in American Families.* New Brunswick, NJ: Transaction Publishers.

Sundeen, R.A., and J.T. Mathieu (1976). 'The fear of crime and its consequences among elderly in three urban communities', *The Gerontologist* 16: 211–19.

Sunderland, G. (1982). 'Geriatric crime wave: The great debate', *The Police Chief* 49: 40, 42, 44.

Sykes, G.W., and K.W. Johnson (1985). 'The aftermath of criminal victimization'. Paper presented at the Annual Meetings of the American Society of Criminology. San Diego, California.

Tierney, K.J. (1982). 'The battered women movement and the creation of the wife beating problem', *Social Problems* 29: 207–20.

Toseland, R.W. (1982). 'Fear of crime: Who is most vulnerable?' *Journal of Research in Crime and Delinquency* 10: 199–209.

Trevethan, S. (1992). 'Elderly victims of crime', *Juristat Service Bulletin.* 12, 16.

Warr, M. (1984). 'Fear of victimization: Why are women and elderly more afraid?' *Social Science Quarterly* 65: 681–702.

Whiskin, F. (1968). 'Delinquency in the aged', *Journal of Geriatric Psychiatry* 1: 243.

Whitaker, C.J. (1987). *Bureau of Justice Statistics Special Report: Elderly Victims.* Washington, DC: US Department of Justice.

Wilbanks, W. (1984a). 'The elderly offender: Placing the problem in perspective'. Pp. 1–15 in Wilbanks and Kim, eds. (1984).

——— (1984b). 'The elderly offender: Sex and race variations in frequency and pattern'. Pp. 41–52 in Wilbanks and Kim, eds. (1984).

Wilbanks, W. and P. Kim (1984). *Elderly Criminals.* New York: University Press of America.

Wolf, R.S. (1986). 'Major findings from three model projects on elder abuse'. Pp. 218–38 in K.A. Pillemer and W.S. Wolf, eds. *Elder Abuse: Conflict in the Family.* Dover, MA: Auburn Publishing.

——— (1988). 'Elder abuse: Ten years later', *Journal of the American Geriatrics Society* 36: 758–62.

Wolf, R.S., and K.A. Pillemer (1989). *Helping Elderly Victims: The Reality of Elder Abuse.* New York: Columbia University Press.

Yin, P.P. (1980). 'Fear of crime among the elderly: Some issues and suggestions', *Social Problems* 27: 492–504.

——— (1985). *Victimization of the Aged.* Springfield, IL: Charles C. Thomas.

Chapter Seven

HOMICIDE IN CANADA

ROSEMARY GARTNER

The reasons people kill each other in Canada are no different from the ones that prompt citizens of other countries to kill. Interpersonal conflicts over status, resources, control, and reputation produce the vast majority of criminal homicides in Canada, as elsewhere. If this is so, why is it important to look at the details of Canadian homicides? It is important because the incidence and characteristics of homicide in a society provide insights into the distinctive features of that society, including its historical development, systems of stratification, institutions, and values. Moreover, changes in the rates and characteristics of homicide convey information about more general processes of change. Homicide rates are indicators of the quality of life that a society provides to its members. Trends in the distribution of these rates—over time, across space, and among social groups—are linked to the distribution of other social disadvantages and benefits.

This chapter depicts the incidence and characteristics of homicide in Canada by focusing on three sources of variation: temporal, spatial, and social. It begins by tracing trends in Canadian homicide rates from the 1920s through the 1980s. This allows us to evaluate recent concerns over rising levels of homicide from the perspective of trends over several decades. We turn next to a discussion of spatial variation in homicide rates: the distribution of homicide across regions and communities of different sizes. Following this, we examine the distribution of homicide among social groups distinguished by gender, race, and age. The final section addresses the growing fears of Canadians that patterns of homicide in Canada are coming to resemble those in the United States—not just in levels, but also in some characteristics.

DEFINITIONS AND DATA SOURCES

Homicide is defined, both in dictionaries and in the Canadian Criminal Code, as the killing of a human being, directly or indirectly, by another. The term encompasses a wide range of behaviours, and on its own it indicates nothing about criminal responsibility. Studies of homicide could, then, examine both criminal and non-criminal acts ranging from planned, purposeful murders to killings during war or legal executions, to deaths caused by the negligence of physicians, police officers, vehicle operators, or employers.[1] In practice, however, most research is restricted to acts falling within the narrower legal designation of culpable homicide.

LEGAL DEFINITIONS AND CLASSIFICATIONS

The law in Canada regarding culpable homicide has changed little since the 1892 Criminal Code defined it as the criminal offence of either murder or manslaughter. According to the Code, culpable homicide is murder if the offender intends to cause the death of the person killed; intends to cause bodily injury that the offender knows is likely to cause death; or, in either of these situations, accidentally or mistakenly kills another person. A murder is also committed if, during the commission of certain crimes, an offender causes the death of another person, whether or not that death, or the injury leading to it, was intended.[2] Until 1948, the only other type of culpable homicide was manslaughter, defined as culpable homicide involving sufficient provocation. In 1948, infanticide was added as a separate offence; it is referred to as the killing of a newborn child by its mother 'not fully recovered from the effects of giving birth'.[3]

Over the last century, then, amendments to the Code have altered slightly the legally defined types of culpable homicide. The punishments assigned to these legal categories have also changed. The most important changes have involved the classifications of murder. Initially, all murders were capital offences and carried a mandatory death sentence.[4] In 1961 murder was divided into capital and non-capital offences, and in 1967 the former was limited to the murder of an on-duty law-enforcement or prison officer. With the abolition of the death penalty in 1976, two categories of murder, first- and second-degree, were established. 'First-degree murder' refers to planned and deliberate murders, murders of police or prison officers, and murders committed in the course of hijacking, hostage-taking, kidnapping, or sexual assault.[5] All other murders are considered second-degree.

OTHER DEFINITIONS AND CLASSIFICATIONS

Legally, some homicides are non-culpable and exempt from criminal penalties. Even so, many of these non-criminal homicides share important characteristics with criminal homicides. Some argue that the distinctions between criminal and non-criminal homicide are often arbitrary or politically-based, and hence that research focusing only on legally designated homicides is fundamentally flawed (Lenton, 1989a; Taylor, 1983). These critics argue that the exclusion from research of deaths due to the actions of corporations, government officials, or private institutions substantially limits both estimates of the incidence of homicide and explanations of its causes.

Even so, the behaviours and situations that are subsumed within legal definitions of homicide are remarkably diverse. Yet, perhaps by necessity, legal definitions rely on relatively few criteria in constructing classifications of culpable homicide. To understand and explain homicide as social behaviour, however, it is necessary to classify homicides according to more detailed non-legal criteria. For this reason, some Canadian researchers separate criminal homicides into different subtypes—for example, differentiating homicides according to the prior relationship between victim and offender, the social roles or demographic characteristics of victims and offenders, or the features of the precipitating incident (Chimbos, 1978; Gillis, 1986; Jayewardene, 1975; Kennedy and Silverman, 1990; Langevin and Handy, 1987; Silverman and Kennedy, 1988, 1993; Silverman and Mukherjee, 1987; Silverman, Reidel, and Kennedy, 1990; Wilson and Daly, 1987).

This chapter draws on both legal and non-legal criteria in its analysis of homicide in Canada. It follows conventional practice by examining behaviours that fall within the legal definition of culpable homicide. Deaths caused by actions that currently are not defined as criminal homicide are not included. Its focus is on lethal interpersonal violence by persons with no official mandate to use violence, and the term 'homicide' should be read as 'criminal homicide' for the remainder of the chapter. Its goal is to describe these legally designated behaviours according to a series of social classifications and correlates.

SOURCES OF DATA ON CRIMINAL HOMICIDE

There are two primary sources of official statistics on homicides in Canada: public-health and criminal-justice agencies. These institutions differ somewhat in their measurement and reporting procedures and in the purposes for which they gather data on homicides. To adequately portray the complex phenomenon of homicide in Canada, data from both sources are necessary.

Medical examiners, acting as public-health officials, determine the cause of death of all Canadians who die both in and outside Canada. They record this information on certificates that are submitted to the federal government, entered into the Mortality Data Base, and published annually in vital statistics reports. Police investigators, typically working in conjunction with medical examiners, also record deaths that are determined to be homicides and report these to the Canadian Centre for Justice Statistics.[6] Only homicides occurring in Canada, regardless of the nationality of the victim, appear in police statistics. This information is used to construct the Uniform Crime Reporting Data Base and the Homicide Data Base, and is the basis for Statistics Canada's annual reports on homicides known to police in Canada.

Choosing to study only officially designated homicides has several advantages for researchers. Perhaps most significantly, the costs of collecting large amounts of data on an annual basis are borne by the government, which compiles and makes these data available to researchers. Nevertheless, reliance on official statistics has its costs. The application of legal definitions to particular acts and persons is neither straightforward nor unproblematic. It is often said that homicides are the most reliably reported and recorded crimes, and thus that official statistics on homicides are relatively untainted by error compared to other crimes (Archer and Gartner, 1984; Gurr, 1989; Monkkonen, 1989). Yet for any homicide to appear in official statistics, a number of decisions must be made by a variety of actors, each of whom may introduce error into the recording process. Moreover, some homicides never appear in official statistics because they are filtered out by decision-makers early on in the recording process. Legal definitions are ultimately only abstractions; they cannot provide definitive boundaries for all real-world events. Inevitably there is slippage between these definitions and the evidence available to apply them.

As a result, homicides are under-reported to some extent in all official statistics. An unknown number of people who go missing, or who perish in automobile crashes, house fires, or hospitals and nursing homes, are victims of criminal homicides, but their deaths are not reported in official statistics on homicide because bodies cannot be found or the mode of death is either incorrectly attributed or impossible to determine.[7] Over the last century, advances in medical technology have probably increased the likelihood of detecting deaths due to homicide. Still, some types of deaths remain particularly difficult to classify. For example, my own examination of medical examiners' files suggests that infant deaths, where obvious severe injuries are not present, may frustrate classification efforts.[8]

The processes of defining some (but not all) homicides as criminal actions and applying this definition to particular deaths produce criminal-justice data on a smaller and more select group of events than that encompassed by the term 'homicide'. The under-counting resulting from these processes will inevitably affect descriptions of the characteristics of homicide. For example, the exclusion of workplace deaths due to employer negligence will change descriptions of victims, offenders, and precipitating incidents. The misclassification of homicides in hospitals or nursing homes can also alter the portrayal of the situations and persons involved in criminal homicide. By comparing characteristics of these excluded cases of homicide with attributes of homicides that appear in official statistics, we could determine how under-counting affects portrayals of homicide based on official statistics. But this would be a monumental, if not impossible, task. Consequently, this chapter is limited to a description of officially recognized and recorded homicides.

THE DISTRIBUTION OF HOMICIDE OVER TIME

In the early 1970s the violent-crime rate in virtually every Western country surged upwards. This crime wave challenged scholars for an explanation and encouraged a popular perception—fostered by media commentary—that unprecedented levels of mayhem are an inescapable product of post-industrial society. In fact, criminal violence in Western Europe and the United States has undergone a long-term decline (Gurr, 1989). Despite this evidence of the importance of a historical perspective, most research on crime continues to confine its focus to recent and relatively short time spans. In Canada, the ubiquitous rise and plateauing of homicide rates since the early 1970s is thoroughly documented (Boyd, 1988; Brantingham and Brantingham, 1984; Johnson, 1987; Reed, Bleszynski, and Gaucher, 1978). How current levels and patterns of Canadian homicide rates compare with those in earlier decades of the twentieth century is less well-known.

TRENDS IN THE TOTAL RATE OF HOMICIDE

Sufficiently reliable data on homicides for the country as a whole are not available from either public-health or police agencies prior to the 1920s. Since 1921, the numbers and rates of deaths due to homicide have been collected by public-health officials and published annually in vital statistics reports. These data are based on determinations of medical examiners, and are *victim-based* measures of homicide, rather than *offender-* or *incident-based* measures (see, e.g., Reed et al., 1978). Undercounting of deaths due to homicide was probably more prevalent in earlier years, especially in remote and rural areas.

The reason police statistics on homicide in the early years of the century do not provide a full count of homicides in Canada is that only a limited number of departments reported regularly to the Dominion Bureau of Statistics.[9] Over the years, the number of police departments participating in the national reporting system increased, but variations in reporting procedures increased as well. In 1962, the Uniform Crime Reporting System was established, which standardized definitions and reporting procedures for all police forces in Canada.

Because medical examiners and police officials differ both in their methods and purposes of investigation, and in their units of measurement (i.e., victims, offenders, or incidents), some discrepancies in the homicide data from these two sources are inevitable. Even so, comparison of their respective rates shows that these differences are minimal and do not affect estimates of the trend in homicide rates. The mean homicide rate for Canada during the years 1954–90 was 1.88 (per 100,000 population) according to Vital Statistics figures and 2.01 according to police figures reported to the Dominion Bureau of Statistics and the Canadian Centre for Justice Statistics. The correlation between the two rates for these years is .98. This suggests that we can be reasonably confident in using statistics from both sources to discuss trends in homicides over time.

Rates of death due to homicide, as reported in *Vital Statistics* for 1921–90, are plotted in Figure 7.1. Quite apparent is the dramatic increase in the rate beginning in the early 1970s. The highest homicide rate for the period was recorded in 1975, and the mean annual rate during the 1970s was higher than that experienced in any other decade. These rates were not entirely unprecedented, however. In 1930, the homicide rate exceeded 2 per 100,000, a level unsurpassed until the early 1970s and higher than some years in the 1980s.[10] After peaking in 1930, the rate declined through the Depression years and stabilized at annual rates of between 1 and 1.5 per 100,000 from the beginning of the Second World War until the mid-1960s.[11]

TRENDS IN RATES OF SPECIFIC TYPES OF HOMICIDE
Once the Uniform Crime Reporting System was established, data on the characteristics of homicide victims, offenders, and situations began to be systematically compiled. However, from 1961 through 1973, detailed data were collected and reported only on first- and second-degree murders; data on the characteristics of manslaughters and

Figure 7.1: **Trends in Canadian Homicide Rates, 1921–1990**

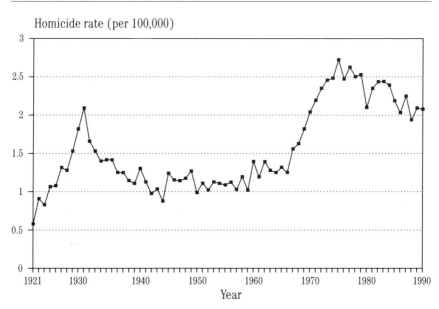

SOURCE: Vital Statistics

infanticides were not. In 1974, the Canadian Centre for Justice Statistics began reporting data on all murders, manslaughters, and infanticides in Canada. These data, spanning almost thirty years, are the basis for the following examination of levels, trends, and patterns in homicide rates.

Social scientists view homicides as events developing out of the dynamics of particular social relationships. Hence they consider the relationship between the victim and the offender to be one of the most important features of a homicide. The motivations of offenders, the events precipitating the incident, and the personal characteristics of victims and offenders vary depending on the nature of this relationship (Daly and Wilson, 1988; Jayewardene, 1975; Silverman and Kennedy, 1987; Silverman and Mukherjee, 1987).[12]

Over thirty different victim-accused relationships are presently distinguished on the Statistics Canada reporting forms used by the police.[13] Most official and scholarly reports combine these into a few categories representing degrees of intimacy in the relationship. The four relationship categories typically used are spouses (legal and common-law), family members, friends or acquaintances, and strangers. But other classifications also have been proposed. For example, Crawford and Gartner (1992) argue that the category 'intimate partners'—which includes current and former spouses, lovers, fiancés, and so on—is more meaningful for some purposes than the narrower category 'spouses'.

Most homicides in Canada occur in domestic settings and between persons who know each other well. Between 1961 and 1990, intimate partners and other family members were *each* responsible for 17% of all homicides (Table 7.1). Another one-third of all homicides were committed by friends or acquaintances of the victims. Only 19% of homicides were committed by strangers, and 15% remained unsolved. Counting only solved homicides, intimate partners and family members accounted for over 40% of the killings.

Canadians' fears over escalating rates of homicide are focused largely on random and unpredictable violence by strangers. If this fear has a basis in fact, we should see disproportionate increases in stranger and unsolved homicides during the 1970s and 1980s. Evidence for such a trend is mixed, as the figures in Table 7.1 indicate. The average annual homicide rate in the 1970s and 1980s was twice the rate of the 1960s, but the proportion of homicides accounted for by each of the relationship types was relatively stable over time. This means that each type of homicide increased at a similar pace. However, there was a slight shift, especially in the 1970s, towards less-intimate victim–offender relationships and unsolved homicides. The greatest increase in rates occurred for unsolved homicides, which accounted for only 9% of all homicides in

Table 7.1: **Homicides of Different Victim–Offender Relationship Types, Canada, 1961–1990**

	Total homicides	Partner homicides	Other family homicides	Acquaintance homicides	Stranger homicides	Unsolved homicides
1961–69						
Rate[a]	1.26	.29	.27	.37	.23	.10
Average annual no. of victims	249	56	54	72	45	22
% of all victims	100%	22%	22%	29%	18%	9%
1970–79						
Rate[a]	2.56	.38	.41	.84	.49	.44
Average annual no. of victims	641	98	101	209	121	112
% of all victims	100%	15%	16%	33%	19%	17%
1980–90						
Rate[a]	2.57	.45	.43	.76	.52	.41
Average annual no. of victims	579	102	98	175	117	87
% of all victims	100%	18%	17%	30%	20%	15%

[a]Rates are calculated per 100,000 population

NOTE: Data prior to 1974 exclude manslaughter and infanticide.

SOURCE: Canadian Centre for Justice Statistics.

the 1960s but 17% in the 1970s. Acquaintances and strangers also have accounted for a larger proportion of homicides in recent years. Even so, in the 1980s homicides by intimate partners and other family members still accounted for 40% of all solved homicides.

A longer-term view of changes in victim-offender relationships can be gained from data for Canada's largest city, Metropolitan Toronto.[14] Both the rate and the characteristics of homicide in Toronto are quite similar to those for the country as a whole. For the years 1921–90, Toronto's annual homicide rate averaged 1.34 per 100,000 and ranged from 0 to 2.67. Canada's rate, according to data from *Vital Statistics*, averaged 1.55 and ranged from .57 to 2.70. The correlation between the two rates is .86, indicating that trends in the two rates were similar. The

distribution of Toronto homicides among the four relationship categories and unsolved homicides is shown in Table 7.2. Except for a somewhat larger proportion of partner homicides in Toronto, this
distribution is quite similar to that for Canada (Table 7.1).[15] In other

Table 7.2: **Homicides of Different Victim–Offender Relationship Types,
Toronto, 1920–1990**

	Total homicides	*Partner homicides*	*Other family homicides*	*Acquaintance homicides*	*Stranger homicides*	*Unsolved homicides*
1920–39 Average annual no. of victims	4.4	1	.9	1.2	.7	.6
% of all victims	100%	23%	20%	27%	16%	14%
1940–59 Average annual no. of victims	9.1	1.9	2.5	2.3	1.4	1.1
% of all victims	100%	21%	27%	25%	15%	12%
1960–69 Average annual no. of victims	21.0	6.2	4.2	3.8	4.0	2.8
% of all victims	100%	30%	20%	18%	19%	13%
1970–79 Average annual no. of victims	45.4	12.1	5.2	13.0	8.6	6.5
% of all victims	100%	27%	12%	29%	19%	14%
1980–90 Average annual no. of victims	52.9	12.5	5.5	21.7	7.6	5.6
% of all victims	100%	23%	11%	41%	14%	11%

SOURCE: Metropolitan Toronto Police Department

words, long-term patterns in homicide in Toronto may well be representative of those in the country as a whole.

These long-term patterns reveal that since 1921 the proportions of all homicides accounted for by different types of victim-offender relationships have changed only slightly. Unsolved homicides and homicides by strangers constituted about 30% of all Toronto homicides before the Second World War and through the 1950s and 1960s, just as they have in the most recent decades. Similarly, homicides between intimates or family members have consistently accounted for between 40 and 50% of all homicides. The most variable component of the total rate has been homicides by acquaintances and friends. These accounted for as little as 18% of all homicides in the 1960s and as much as 34% in the 1980s. Since 1961, trends in the rates of all five types have paralleled the trend in the total homicide rate in Toronto, as in Canada as a whole. Despite substantial variations in the levels of Canadian homicide over time, then, the victim-offender relationships that make up the total rate appear to have changed little over the last several decades.

THE DISTRIBUTION OF HOMICIDE OVER SPACE

Within a country, homicide rates typically vary a great deal from place to place. This means that rates aggregated at the national level can obscure substantial spatial differences in the risks of homicide. One type of spatial variation is regional. For example, in the United States homicide rates in the southern and southwestern states are over ten times those in north central states.[16] A second type of spatial variation in homicide rates occurs between urban and rural areas. In most countries, homicide rates in the largest cities (and sometimes in the most rural areas) are higher than those in smaller cities and towns (Archer and Gartner, 1984). Canada is no exception to this pattern of significant spatial variation in homicide rates.

PROVINCIAL AND REGIONAL VARIATION IN HOMICIDE RATES

Provincial homicide rates have consistently shown a distinct east-to-west upward trend throughout the twentieth century (Table 7.3). Over the last several decades, the mean annual homicide rate has been lowest in Newfoundland and highest in British Columbia (and, in recent years, Manitoba). This east-to-west trend shifts to a south-to-north variation when the Yukon and Northwest Territories are included. Homicide rates in the territories are two to three times those in British Columbia, and well over ten times the rates in Newfoundland and PEI. Trends over time in rates within provinces have varied somewhat. Even so, the rank order correlations of provincial rates average .88 over the last seven decades. In other words, regional differences in homicide are remarkably stable and have characterized periods of economic boom and bust, war and peace, population growth and decline, immigration and emigration.[17]

Efforts to explain regional differences have focused on spatial variations in the composition (e.g., age, ethnicity), distribution (rural-urban), and mobility of provincial populations; in economic well-being; and in family structure (Chappell and Hatch, 1986; Kennedy, Forde, and Silverman, 1989; Kennedy, Silverman, and Forde, 1991; Lenton, 1989a,b).[18] These characteristics are typically treated as elements of Canada's social structure—the institutionalized patterns and processes that organize interactions and relationships among people. However, the persistence of regional variations in homicide suggests that relatively enduring cultural differences among the regions of Canada also need to be taken into account. The absence of attention to cultural factors—that is, the accumulated traditions and shared experiences distinctive to people of different regions that shape their values and beliefs—may help to explain the limited success of existing accounts of regional differences in homicide rates.[19]

Regions differ not only in their homicide rates, but also in the character of their homicides. For example, over 40% of homicides in the Atlantic provinces, Ontario, the Prairie provinces, and the Territories occur between intimate partners or family members. In contrast, less than 25% of homicides in Quebec and less than 33% of those in British Columbia are committed by partners or family (Table 7.4). What set BC and particularly Quebec apart are the relatively large proportions

Table 7.3: **Provincial Homicide Rates,[a] by Decade**

	Mean rate, 1921–89	1920s	1930s	1940s	1950s	1960s	1970s	1980s
Newfoundland	.49				.37	.54	.51	.45
PEI	.70	.13	.44	.94	.75	1.03	1.03	1.03
Nova Scotia	1.17	.73	1.06	.97	.88	1.18	1.75	1.56
New Brunswick	1.10	.95	.80	.74	.76	.57	1.92	1.94
Quebec	1.41	1.01	1.12	.67	.85	1.34	2.46	2.27
Ontario	1.47	1.32	1.38	1.32	1.19	1.29	1.99	1.84
Manitoba	1.94	1.51	1.60	1.40	1.01	1.49	3.24	3.24
Saskatchewan	1.76	1.17	1.38	1.17	.95	1.68	3.02	2.74
Alberta	1.98	1.97	2.29	1.27	1.51	1.59	2.73	2.49
British Columbia	2.63	2.67	2.63	2.02	1.67	2.39	3.71	3.06
Yukon	8.70				3.94	9.45	11.69	6.79
NWT	7.36				3.61	4.27	9.41	10.28
Canada	1.56	1.15	1.42	1.13	1.09	1.41	2.42	2.23

[a]Rates are calculated per 100,000 population

SOURCE: Vital Statistics

of their homicides that are unsolved (15 and 30 per cent, respectively). Unsolved homicides are more likely to be committed by strangers or casual acquaintances than are solved homicides.[20]

In BC and Quebec, then, homicides have a less intimate character than homicides in other provinces. But this does not mean that the *rate* of partner and family killings in these two provinces is necessarily lower than elsewhere. In BC, these rates are actually well above the national average. In Quebec, however, rates of intimate partner and family killings are lower than anywhere else in Canada. Compared to other Canadians, then, Québécois are less likely—both in absolute and in relative terms—to kill intimates or kin.[21]

URBAN AND RURAL VARIATIONS IN HOMICIDE

Conventional wisdom, both popular and academic, portrays urban settings and interactions as more dangerous, conflict-ridden, and anomic than those in smaller communities. Not surprisingly, then, fear of crime is much higher among city residents than residents of small towns and rural areas (Johnson and Sacco, 1990). One does not have to look far for support for these fears. In the United States, cities like Miami, Detroit, Washington, DC, and New York have rates of homicide over three times the national average. This pattern is repeated throughout the world. In most countries, the largest cities have rates of homicide higher than those for the country as a whole (Archer and Gartner, 1984). This suggests that within the east-to-west patterning of homicide in Canada lies another type of spatial variation associated with community size.

Table 7.4: **Regional Homicide Rates[a] by Different Victim–Offender Relationship Types, 1961–1990**

	Average no. of victims annually	Total homicide rate	Partner homicide rate	Other family homicide rate	Acquaintance homicide rate	Stranger homicide rate	Unsolved homicide rate
Atlantic provinces	29	1.35	.24	.31	.43	.28	.09
Quebec	142	2.26	.24	.30	.62	.42	.68
Ontario	141	1.72	.38	.33	.52	.33	.16
Prairie provinces	103	2.62	.54	.54	.91	.49	.15
British Columbia	76	3.10	.52	.48	1.06	.59	.45
Territories	7	10.89	2.79	2.76	3.39	1.70	.24
Canada	498	2.16	.38	.37	.67	.42	.32

[a]Rates are calculated per 100,000 population in province in 1981.
NOTE: Data prior to 1974 exclude manslaughter and infanticide.
SOURCE: Canadian Centre for Justice Statistics.

Figure 7.2: **Mean Homicide Rates, by Community Size, 1978–1990**

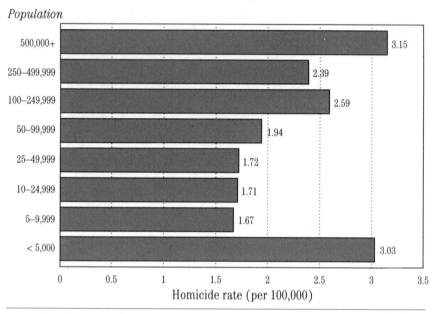

Population

SOURCE: Canadian Centre for Justice Statistics

The relationship between homicide rates and community size is not a simple linear one. The largest communities (i.e., those with populations of 500,000 or more) are indeed characterized by the highest rates of homicide in Canada (Figure 7.2). But these rates do not decline steadily as community size decreases. On average, homicide rates in communities of between 250,000 and 499,000 residents are slightly lower than those in areas with populations between 100,000 and 249,000. Most striking is the rate for the most rural areas of Canada, which is only negligibly below that for the largest communities. This apparent anomaly is not unprecedented: in the United States, homicide rates for the most rural areas of the country tend to be higher than for small-to-medium sized cities (i.e., those between 10,000 and 100,000 in population) (Archer and Gartner, 1984: 104). In Canada, however, the rural contribution to homicide rates is clearly greater and the urban contribution less than is the case in the United States.

Another way to illustrate this complex relationship between community size and homicide rates is to compare the rates of major Canadian cities and the provinces in which they are located (Table 7.5). Of 13 major cities, fewer than half have homicide rates at least 5 per cent higher than the rate for their respective provinces; four have rates essentially the same as the provincial rates, and in three cases the city

Table 7.5: **Average Homicide Rates[a] for Major Cities, and Corresponding Provinces, 1981–1990**

	City rate	Provincial rate	% of provincial rate
St John's, Nfld	.94	.84	112
Halifax, NS	1.89	1.63	116
Saint John, NB	2.60	1.96	133
Quebec City, Que.	1.99	2.84	71
Montreal, Que.	3.56	2.84	125
Ottawa, Ont.	1.94	2.00	97
Toronto, Ont.	2.02	2.00	101
Winnipeg, Man.	3.32	3.66	91
Regina, Sask.	4.32	3.01	144
Saskatoon, Sask.	2.11	3.01	70
Edmonton, Alta	3.42	2.82	121
Calgary, Alta	2.33	2.82	83
Vancouver, BC	3.50	3.47	101

[a]Rates are calculated per 100,000 population and based on figures for Census Metropolitan Areas.

SOURCE: Canadian Centre for Justice Statistics

rates are lower. The three latter cities are on the Prairies, indicating that homicide is a more rural phenomenon in the middle of the country than elsewhere. In contrast, in Quebec homicide is more concentrated in urban areas.

Homicide rates for the major cities do not display the clear east-to-west pattern of provincial rates. Moreover, cities within the same region can vary widely in their rates. For example, between 1981 and 1990 Edmonton's homicide rate was 50% higher than Calgary's, and Regina's was twice as high as Saskatoon's. Apparently characteristics of particular communities can override factors responsible for regional differences in homicide rates. Some of these community characteristics are economic, some are institutional or cultural, and others emerge from the social groups that compose a community's population.

THE DISTRIBUTION OF HOMICIDE AMONG SOCIAL GROUPS

The risks of being involved in homicide, either as a victim or an offender, are unevenly distributed among social groups. In virtually all modern societies, the highest rates of victimization and offending occur among persons who are disadvantaged in status, power, and economic resources (Curtis, 1974; Daly and Wilson, 1988; Nettler, 1982). Often these disadvantages are associated with characteristics such as age, race or ethnicity, and gender. These same personal characteristics are also linked to activity patterns and lifestyles that provide varying degrees of exposure to or protection from potentially violent interactions.[22] Through a complex set of processes, then, the risks of homicide come to be differentially distributed by gender, race, and age, among other characteristics. Consequently, in Canada as elsewhere, members of certain social groups are exposed to a number of social disadvantages, including higher risks of homicide.

VARIATION IN HOMICIDE BY GENDER

In some respects, females are an exception to the typical link between social disadvantage and risk of homicide. Despite their deficiencies in social and economic power, women are much less likely than men to be involved in homicide, either as victims or offenders. This apparent gender benefit for females, however, obscures a less obvious inequity. Women are much more likely (by a factor of three) to be victims than offenders, whereas men are more likely to be offenders than victims. Thus, whatever the factors are that insulate females from homicide, they are less effective at reducing their chances of being targets, rather than perpetrators, of aggression (see DeKeseredy and Ellis, this volume).

How large is the gender gap in homicide victimization in Canada? Because Vital Statistics reports sex-specific homicide rates, the difference between female and male rates can be calculated for the period 1921–90. During these years, women accounted for 36% of all homicide victims known to authorities. The gender gap was quite stable over time because the trends in female and male victimization rates are very similar (Figure 7.3); the correlation between the two rates for these 68 years is .90. In recent years, however, the gap has widened, as Figure 7.3 indicates. When homicide rates increased in the 1970s, the male victimization rate rose faster than the female one.[23] This pattern, observed in several societies, means that the most volatile component of the homicide rate is homicides by and against males (Daly and Wilson, 1988; Gartner, 1990).

This growing difference between female and male victimization rates has occurred as women's lives and daily activities have become less centred around the home and family. This change, according to the opportunity model of victimization, should increase women's risks of victimization. The opportunity model views activities that occur outside the home, away from the 'guardianship' of family members, in isolated public places, and at night as highly risky (Cohen and Felson, 1979; Hindelang, Gottfredson, and Garofalo, 1978). Yet women's risks have not increased relative to men's as their daily activities have become more similar.

One reason for the inaccuracy of the opportunity model in this instance is its inattention to distinctive features of female victimization (Gartner and McCarthy, 1991). The opportunity model applies primarily to victimization in public places and by non-intimates. Women, however, are much more likely to be killed by persons they are related to or know intimately. Between 1961 and 1990, over half of all female victims were killed by intimate partners or family members, compared to less than a quarter of male victims (Table 7.6).[24] Female victimization rates are lower than male rates in every category of victim-offender relationship except intimate-partner killings, where women are the victims almost four times more often than men. The victimization of males, in contrast, fits the opportunity model: over three-quarters of male victims are killed by acquaintances, strangers, or unknown assailants.

Changes over time in relationships between female victims and their killers are more consistent with the opportunity model (Table 7.6). Prior to the 1970s, 36 per cent of women were killed by non-intimates (i.e., acquaintances and strangers) or unknown assailants. Subsequently, the proportions of females killed by non-intimates and unknown assailants rose to 46% in the 1970s and 49% in the 1980s. These decades saw increasing numbers of women in the labour force

Figure 7.3: **Trends in Canadian Homicide Victimization Rates: by Gender, 1921–1990**

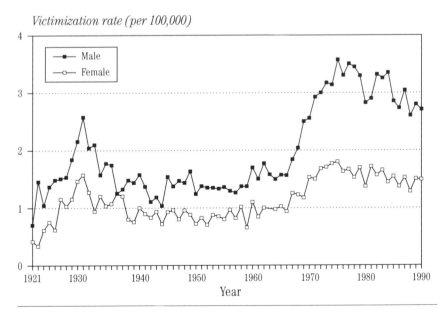

SOURCE: Vital Statistics

Table 7.6: **Sex-Specific Victimization Rates for Different Victim–Offender Relationship Types, Canada, 1961–1990**

	All homicides	Partner homicides		Other family homicides		Acquaintance homicides		Stranger homicides		Unsolved homicides	
	Rate[a]	Rate	%[b]	Rate	%	Rate	%	Rate	%	Rate	%
1961–69											
Female	1.04	.47	45	.20	19	.20	19	.11	11	.06	6
Male	1.49	.07	5	.36	24	.53	36	.36	24	.17	11
1970–79											
Female	1.80	.70	39	.28	16	.30	17	.32	18	.20	11
Male	3.32	.20	6	.60	18	1.24	37	.70	21	.58	17
1980–90											
Female	1.87	.58	32	.34	19	.38	21	.26	14	.26	14
Male	3.28	.20	6	.50	15	1.26	38	.68	21	.64	20
1961–90											
Female	1.57	.59	38	.28	18	.30	19	.23	15	.17	11
Male	2.74	.16	6	.49	18	1.03	38	.59	22	.47	17

[a]Rates are calculated per 100,000 female (or male) population.
[b]Percentage of all female (or male) victims.

NOTE: Data prior to 1974 exclude manslaughter and infanticide.

SOURCE: Canadian Centre for Justice Statistics (unpublished statistics).

and living outside traditional family structures (Jones, Marsden, and Tepperman, 1990). According to the opportunity model (Cohen and Felson, 1979; Hindelang et al., 1978), these changes should raise women's risks of acquaintance and stranger homicides. (Note that the relationships between male victims and their killers has changed little over time; this fits with the absence of major shifts in the lifestyles and activity patterns of men.) In sum, female victimization has not increased relative to male victimization as gender differences in lifestyles have diminished; however, it has become more diversified, occurring across a wider variety of relationships.[25]

The gender gap in offending is much greater than that in victimization. Since at least 1961, female and male offending rates have exhibited similar trends.[26] Women account for 13% of homicide suspects and their rate of offending (.5 per 100,000 female population) is one-seventh of the male rate (Table 7.7). As with victimization, the post-1970 surge in homicide was disproportionately due to male offenders (Figure 7.4). Thus the absolute difference in female and male offending rates increased through the mid-1970s.[27] However, both male and female offending rates increased at similar rates, more than doubling from the 1960s to 1970s; the correlation between the two rates for the years 1961–88 is .94.

Table 7.7: **Sex-Specific Offending Rates[a] for Different Homicide Types, 1961–1990**

| | All homicides | Domestic homicides | | Homicides during other crimes | | Other homicides | |
	Rate	Rate	%[b]	Rate	%	Rate	%
1961–69							
Female	.26	.21	80	<.01	3	.05	18
Male	2.04	.75	37	.41	20	.88	43
1970–79							
Female	.60	.38	63	.05	8	.18	30
Male	4.17	1.22	29	.73	18	2.23	53
1961–90							
Female	.50	.32	64	.03	6	.15	30
Male	3.47	1.05	30	.67	19	1.75	51

[a]Rates are calculated per 100,000 female (or male) population.
[b]Percentage of all female (or male) suspects.
NOTE: Data prior to 1974 exclude manslaughter and infanticide. (These categories differ from those in Table 7.6 because they are taken from published material, rather than from data provided to the author.)
SOURCE: Canadian Centre for Justice Statistics.

Figure 7.4: **Trends in Canadian Homicide Offending Rates: by Gender, 1961–1991**

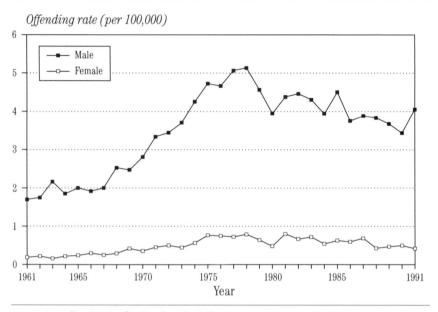

SOURCE: Canadian Centre for Justice Statistics

There is little evidence that the major changes in women's lives occurring since 1961 have altered their likelihood of offending (relative to males)—which parallels the pattern for victimization. However, the character of women's offending (again, as with their victimization) did change after the 1960s (Table 7.7). Whereas in the 1960s, 80% of women offenders were involved in domestic homicides, by the 1980s domestic homicides accounted for only 55% of killings by females. While rates of both domestic and non-domestic homicide by women increased, the latter rose more than the former. A similar but much less pronounced shift occurred among male offenders. Thus the growth in the proportion of homicides among strangers and acquaintances, noted earlier, is a consequence of shifts in the patterns of *both* female and male offending.

With one exception there are few regional differences in the gender gap in victimization and offending. In Quebec, compared to the national average, women are consistently under-represented among both victims and offenders. In the 1970s and 1980s in Quebec, women accounted for only 33% of homicide victims and just under 10% of offenders. In all other provinces women accounted for 36 to 38% of the victims and 13 to 15% of the offenders.

VARIATION IN HOMICIDE BY RACE

There is enormous ambivalence in Canadian society about discussing differences among racial and ethnic groups in involvement in crime. Partly as a consequence, statistics documenting such variations are only sporadically published by Statistics Canada.[28] This approach appears to be a compromise between those who argue such statistics are too easily misinterpreted, especially when presented with little comment and out of context, and those who believe that without such information, a major consequence of racial inequalities (i.e., criminal victimization and offending) cannot be adequately documented and addressed. Clearly, official statistics on racial differences in homicide cannot capture social and cultural differences in the experiences, causes, and consequences of homicide. They can, however, take the first step towards documenting an important source of the inequities experienced by disadvantaged racial and ethnic groups.[29]

In Canada, the risks of homicide victimization are disproportionately felt by aboriginal Canadians (see Long, this volume).[30] Indigenous peoples (including Inuit and Métis) constitute about 2% of the total population, but 15% of all homicide victims. During the last two decades, the homicide victimization rate for aboriginal Canadians has been approximately 20 per 100,000 aboriginal population— nine times the non-aboriginal rate.[31] The over-representation of native people among homicide victims has been relatively stable over time (Moyer, 1992). Aboriginal Canadians accounted for 17% of homicide victims between 1961 and 1970 (Jayewardene, 1975) and 15% of victims between 1972 and 1987 (Statistics Canada, 1987; Kennedy et al., 1989).

Because most homicides are intra-racial (about 85 per cent of aboriginal victims are killed by aboriginal offenders), a disproportionate number of suspects are aboriginal as well. Native people account for about 18% of all persons arrested for homicide. Their rate of offending (approximately 20 per 100,000 aboriginal population) was about ten times the non-aboriginal rate in the 1970s and 1980s (Silverman and Kennedy, 1993).

Homicides involving aboriginal people are more likely to take place in family and kin networks than are non-aboriginal homicides (Boyd, 1988; Jayewardene, 1975; Jilek and Roy, 1976; Langevin and Handy, 1987; Moyer, 1992; Silverman and Kennedy, 1993). For example, between 1962 and 1984, 52% of aboriginal victims were killed by offenders to whom they were related (Moyer, 1992). In contrast, homicides between strangers or in the course of another criminal act made up a smaller proportion of aboriginal than non-aboriginal homicides—probably because the life circumstances of aboriginals, especially on reserves, makes contact with strangers less likely.

Because of the concentration of aboriginal people within and across certain regions, aboriginal homicides have a distinct spatial distribution. Thus most homicides involving aboriginal Canadians occur in rural areas, and over 80% occur in the provinces west of Ontario, because this is where aboriginal communities are concentrated. Even so, *rates* of aboriginal homicide (calculated per 100,000 aboriginal population) appear to follow the east-to-west pattern observed for total homicide rates (Table 7.8).[32] In 1984, British Columbia had the highest rates of both victimization and offending among aboriginal people. Aboriginal homicide rates in the Yukon and the Northwest Territories were lower than in the Prairie provinces and BC. However, it is the aboriginal contribution to the homicide rate in the Territories that raises the rates in the far north far above the national average for all Canadians.[33]

Explanations of the disproportionate risks of homicide (and violent death generally) faced by aboriginal Canadians emphasize the social and economic dislocation, the cultural insecurity, and the various forms of discrimination they face (LaPrairie, 1987; Shkilnyk, 1985)—all factors attributed by some to the colonization of aboriginal societies by the majority culture (Havemann, Couse, Forster, and Matonovich, 1985).[34] The distribution of homicide across other racial groups in Canada lends credence to accounts based on material conditions rather than particular racial or cultural factors. For example, black Canadians, who also face a number of social, cultural, and economic disadvantages, appear to be over-represented among homicide victims and offenders as well. Black Canadians constitute less than 1% of the population but 3% of homicide victims and offenders. In contrast, Asian Canadians as a group[35] are less economically disadvantaged than other racial groups; they also appear to be under-represented as homicide victims and offenders.

VARIATION IN HOMICIDE BY AGE

Regardless of gender or race, age will shape the likelihood of involvement in homicide either as victim or as offender, though in somewhat

Table 7.8: **Native Victimization and Offending Rates for Different Regions, 1984**

	Atlantic provinces	Quebec	Ontario	Prairie provinces	British Columbia	Yukon and NWT
Victimization rate[a]	20.5	10.7	13.1	23.5	37.1	17.4
Number of victims	3	5	11	41	24	5
Offending rate[a]	20.5	4.3	14.3	32.1	31.9	13.9
Number of offenders	3	2	12	56	20	4

[a]Rates are calculated per 100,000 Native population.
SOURCE: Canadian Centre for Justice Statistics.

different ways. The source of this association between age and criminal violence remains a subject of much controversy (Greenberg, 1985; Hirschi and Gottfredson, 1983). While most academics would agree that the association is ubiquitous (if not universal), fewer agree on why this is so. Physiological, psychological, and sociological factors surely all play roles, but how they combine to produce the age effect remains unclear.

The age distribution of homicide in Canada exhibits an inverted U-shape, peaking in the young adult years. In general, this pattern corresponds to the patterns in most countries (Curtis, 1974; Gartner, 1990; Wallace, 1986). The ages with the highest (age-specific) rates of victimization also have the highest rates of offending, and this has altered only slightly over the last few decades (Table 7.9). Between 1961 and 1989, persons aged 20–29 were more likely to commit as well as more likely to die from homicide than those in any other age group. For offending, however, the age risks have shifted downwards since the 1960s. Age-specific offending rates were higher for those aged 30–39 than for those aged 16–19 before 1970, but not after. In contrast, victimization rates remained higher among both the 30–39 and 40–49 age groups than among those aged 16–19.

Age may have played a role in the crime wave of the 1970s through the aging of the baby-boom cohort.[36] This unusually large group reached the peak ages for criminal offending in the early 1970s in

Table 7.9: **Age-Specific Rates (per 100,000 population) of Victimization and Offending, Canada, 1961–1990**

	0–15	*16–19*	*20–29*	*30–39*	*40–49*	*50–59*	*60 and older*
1961–69							
Victimization rate	.46	.99	1.65	1.80	1.61	1.47	1.19
Offending rate	.40	1.98	2.58	2.37	1.29	.80	.44
1970–79							
Victimization rate	.89	2.64	3.73	3.52	3.24	2.62	2.13
Offending rate	.73	4.58	5.60	3.87	2.27	1.27	.58
1980–90							
Victimization rate	1.19	2.58	4.20	3.69	3.01	2.53	1.84
Offending rate	.85	4.72	5.97	3.62	2.23	1.20	.53
1961–90							
Victimization rate	.85	2.07	3.19	3.00	2.62	2.20	1.72
Offending rate	.66	3.76	4.72	3.29	1.93	1.09	.52

NOTE: Data prior to 1974 exclude manslaughter and infanticide.
SOURCE: Canadian Centre for Justice Statistics.

several Western countries. For example, between 1961 and 1976, the proportion of the population aged 15–24 increased from 14 to 19% in Canada. Even if age-specific crime rates remained stable, this change in the composition of the population would have raised the total homicide rate. However, more was changing than the age distribution of the population. Age-specific rates of victimization and offending increased for all age groups in the 1970s, although the largest rises occurred for the 16–19 and 20–29 age groups (Maxim and Keane, 1992). In other words, homicide rates increased not only because more persons were in the high-risk age groups, but also because the rate at which high-risk age groups committed homicide increased.

Offending is more strongly associated with age than is victimization. Consequently, the age distribution of offenders is more peaked than that of victims. In contrast, risks of victimization are more evenly spread over the life course, and are higher than rates of offending except during the late-teen and young adult years. One of the inequities faced by Canadians aged 60 and older is a rate of victimization that is over three times their rate of offending. Members of no other age group are so much more likely to be victims than victimizers.

The types of relationships that are most risky also vary by age, but in a complex fashion (Table 7.10). Domestic homicides claim almost 75% of child victims, but only 18% of those victims aged 16–19. Acquaintances and strangers are by far the most common killers of those aged 16–19 and 60 and older. The relatively high proportion of

Table 7.10: **Distribution of Victim–Offender Relationship Types Within Age Groups, Canada**

	0–15	16–19	20–29	30–39 (%)	40–49	50–59	60 and older
Victims							
% domestic homicides	75	18	27	34	41	34	27
% other homicides	24	67	55	48	46	53	59
% unsolved homicides	5	15	18	17	13	13	14
Offenders							
% domestic homicides	31	20	25	41	54	59	60
% other homicides	69	80	75	59	46	41	40

NOTE: Percentages calculated on the basis of figures reported for 1961–74, and 1978–82.
SOURCE: Canadian Centre for Justice Statistics.

non-domestic homicides among older victims is due to theft-related killings of older Canadians (Kennedy and Silverman, 1990; Sacco, this volume). For offenders, the likelihood of killing in a domestic relationship increases steadily from the teen years onward. At the peak ages of victimization and offending, the majority of homicides occur between persons who do not know each other intimately.

Regional variations in the age distribution are difficult to document, since the necessary statistics are rarely reported. For the years 1983–1984, age distributions of victims and offenders were quite similar in the Atlantic provinces, Ontario, and British Columbia. Compared to the rest of the country, however, the age distributions of both victims and offenders were older in Quebec and younger in the Prairie provinces. In Quebec only 38% of the victims and 41% of the offenders were under age 30, whereas in the Prairie provinces 51% of the victims and 67% of the offenders were under age 30.

THE AMERICANIZATION OF CANADIAN HOMICIDE?

Canadians pride themselves on being law-abiding and non-violent. Much of this perception comes from comparisons with citizens of the United States, who kill each other at a per capita rate more than three times that of Canadians. Suggestions that this picture might be changing, and that the differences between Canadian and US homicide rates are diminishing, have caused considerable concern among the Canadian public and some debate among scholars (Hagan, 1989; Kennedy et al., 1989; Lenton, 1989a,b).[37] The weight of the evidence indicates that the gap between Canadian and US rates has been remarkably persistent over time, and is far from closing (Hagan, 1989). Canadian-US differences in homicide rates are most pronounced for urban residents: rates for the five largest cities in the United States are, on average, about 10 times greater than those for the five largest cities in Canada (Table 7.11).

This may do little to reassure Canadians concerned about changes in the character, not just the level, of homicide. Many fear that

Table 7.11: **Homicide Rates (per 100,000 population) for the Five Largest Canadian[a] and US Cities, 1990**

Toronto	1.9	New York City	30.7
Montreal	3.4	Los Angeles	28.2
Vancouver	3.5	Chicago	30.5
Ottawa-Hull	1.5	Houston	34.8
Edmonton	3.5	Philadelphia	31.7

[a]Rate calculated for the Census Metropolitan Area.

SOURCE: Canadian Centre for Justice Statistics; Federal Bureau of Investigation.

homicides associated with robbery, sexual assault, strangers, guns, and drugs as well as unsolved killings—all features associated with violent crime in the US—are becoming more common in Canada (de Villiers, 1991).

These concerns receive only limited support from homicide statistics (Table 7.12). For example, the proportion of homicides committed with firearms is lower now than in the 1960s, before gun-control legislation was introduced (Sproule and Kennett, 1988; 1989). However, the proportion of homicides committed with handguns, which remained stable during the last three decades, did rise sharply in 1991.[38] The proportion of homicides occurring during robberies increased only slightly over time (from 9% in the 1960s and 1970s to 12% in the 1980s), but the proportion involving sexual assaults has remained stable at between 3 and 5% of all homicides. Consistent with public fears, the percentage of homicides that remain unsolved has risen substantially since the 1960s, reaching a high of 23% in 1991. However, the proportion of stranger homicides has not increased relative to other types of victim-offender relationships.

The role of drugs and the drug trade in homicide is much more difficult to establish definitively with existing statistics. Until recently, the homicide reporting form included a relatively ambiguous category for alcohol or drug 'involvement', which appears to have been reserved for cases where the victim or suspect had recently used drugs. As Table 7.12 indicates, the proportion of homicides with 'drug-involvement' thus defined has been relatively stable over the last two decades. In revisions of the reporting form in 1991, two different and more specific measures of drug-relatedness were included. One measures 'evidence of drug trafficking or settling of drug related accounts' and the other measures evidence of alcohol and/or drug consumption

Table 7.12: **Selected Characteristics of Homicides in Canada, 1961–1991**

	1961–69	1970–79	1980–89	1990	1991
% of homicides:					
Committed with firearms	44	41	33	30	36
Committed with handguns	11	11	10	10	18
During robberies	9	9	12	10	11
During sexual assaults	3	4	4	5	3
Involving drugs	1	4	3	—	—
Committed by strangers	18	19	20	19	10
Unsolved	9	17	15	22	23

NOTE: Data prior to 1974 exclude manslaughter and infanticide.
SOURCE: Canadian Centre for Justice Statistics.

by victims and suspects. Obviously, making these determinations is not always straightforward and the results are not always accurate.

Even less can be said about trends in other types of homicides that figure prominently in public concern. As with drug homicides, documenting the rates of serial murders or gang killings reliably over time would be a formidable task. Information on these relatively rare types of homicide is largely confined to case studies or analyses of official statistics for limited periods of time (Boyd, 1988; Langevin and Handy, 1987; Reed et al., 1978). Mass murders, which can be identified from official statistics, are not becoming more common relative to other killings. Statistics Canada figures indicate that the percentage of homicides with multiple victims has been stable at about 7% since the 1960s. The majority of these events are intimate-partner and family killings (Silverman and Kennedy, 1993).

At least through the late 1980s, then, the character of Canadian homicides had changed only slightly in the direction feared by the public. Memory is short and often selective, so that reconstructions of the past are often shaded by nostalgia. For example, the tendency to believe that earlier decades of the twentieth century experienced little violence of the type we fear today is not supported by data on homicides in Toronto since 1921. As the figures in Table 7.2 indicated, the proportions of stranger and unsolved homicides varied over time in Toronto, but did not follow a clear upward trend. The same is true for homicides in the course of robberies or sexual assaults (Table 7.13). The proportion of firearm homicides was lower in the 1980s than at any other time except from 1940 to 1959. The proportion of handgun homicides declined through the 1960s and increased slightly thereafter; handguns were used as often in Toronto homicides in the 1980s as in the 1940s and 1950s, and less often than in the 1920s and 1930s.

Table 7.13: **Selected Characteristics of Homicide in Toronto, 1920–1990**

	1920–39	1940–59	1960–69	1970–79	1980–90
% of homicides:					
Committed with firearms	43	22	26	28	23
Committed with handguns	39	12	4	9	13
During robberies	13	10	12	10	14
During sexual assaults	3	3	3	3	6
Committed by strangers	15	14	19	18	14
Unsolved	15	12	13	14	11
Number of homicides	90	180	210	454	582

SOURCE: Metropolitan Toronto Police Department

We should be cautious in drawing conclusions from this evidence. More recent data are needed to assess the validity of concerns over, for example, the role of drugs or illegal handguns in homicide. At the same time, short-term trends should not be interpreted as signalling permanent shifts or the start of longer-term tendencies in homicide rates. Homicides remain relatively rare events in Canada, and as such they are subject to occasional sharp but random fluctuations in their levels or characteristics. For example, from 1985 to 1986 the number of homicide victims dropped from 704 to 569, decreasing the homicide rate by 20%. In 1987, however, 642 persons were killed, increasing the rate by 13%. In other words, recent data can tell us only about short-term changes. Long-term data are needed to judge whether such changes are chance fluctuations or indicators of more lasting transformations in homicide rates. Understandably, however, the caution typically urged by scholars in interpreting statistics on crime can exasperate policy-makers and law-enforcers, as well as the public.

CONCLUSION

Canadians show a greater tendency to kill one another than do citizens of most Western industrialized democracies, according to data from the World Health Organization.[39] Canada's homicide rate of 2.2 per 100,000 for the years 1951–84 placed it third among 18 developed democracies, behind the United States (8.9 per 100,000) and Finland (2.7 per 100,000), and just ahead of Australia (1.7 per 100,000) (WHO, various years). At the other end of the range were Ireland and the Netherlands, with rates averaging .7 per 100,000. Given the similarities among these countries in economic structures, cultural systems, and social and legal institutions, the magnitude of the differences in risks of homicide is remarkable, and it has prompted a number of efforts at explanation (Gartner, 1990).

Comparing homicide rates for different countries can illuminate nuances in national character and provide insights into the values and norms of a society. But highly aggregated analyses also obscure significant differences in the risks of violent death, and thus the quality of life, within countries. As this chapter has shown, the risks of homicide within Canada vary across time, space, and demographic groups in ways that call for explanation. Some of this variation is not unique to Canada. For example, variations in homicide over time, between women and men, among age groups, and among disadvantaged minority groups appear to be broadly similar for a number of countries (Curtis, 1974; Gurr, 1989; Gartner, 1990). To explain these similar patterns, researchers need to look at social structures and processes common across countries. Other types of variation are more specific to Canada: for example, the east–west regional patterning of homicide rates and the pronounced differences in the characteristics of homicide in Quebec compared to other provinces. These features of Canadian homicide will require more attention both to particular historical developments and to cultural and institutional contexts that are distinctive to Canada.

Whatever the reasons, Canadians as a group have been spared the levels of lethal interpersonal violence that characterize the United States, and they appear likely to preserve this relative advantage. This protection is not equally distributed among Canadians, however. Understanding why this is so is the first step towards providing equal protection to all Canadians.

NOTES

[1] Rates of criminal and non-criminal homicide are positively related; in other words, where rates of non-criminal homicides are high, rates of criminal homicides also tend to be high (Archer and Gartner, 1984; Bowers, 1984; Williams and Flewelling, 1988). This suggests at least one reason why research should pay more attention to the full range of homicides, rather than focus only on criminal homicide.

[2] The provision that a person is a murderer by doing something 'for an unlawful object' that the person 'knows or ought to know is likely to cause death, and thereby causes death' has been used to convict persons who did not kill, but were engaged in crimes with offenders who did kill. In 1987, in R. v. Vaillancourt, the Supreme Court ruled that although such acts are culpable homicide, to amount to murder there must be proof beyond a reasonable doubt of 'subjective foresight of death' on the part of the accused.

[3] Other homicide offences include causing death by criminal negligence, dangerous operation of a motor vehicle, and impaired driving causing death.

[4] Capital murder was defined as the planned and deliberate killing of a person, or the killing of an on-duty police officer or other official of the criminal justice system. Conviction for capital murder required the imposition of a death sentence, although this sentence was not inevitably carried out.

[5] Prior to 1985, a murder committed by a person who had previously been convicted of either first- or second-degree murder also was automatically defined as first-degree murder.

[6] Prior to 1971, this information was collected by the Judicial Statistics Division of the Dominion Bureau of Statistics.

[7] Between 1976 and 1985, an average of 4,813 persons were killed annually in traffic 'accidents' and an average of 4,752 other 'accidental' deaths were recorded each year. If 6 per cent of these deaths were actually

homicides, the estimate of the number of homicides in Canada during these years would double.

8 Ironically, advances in medical technology may compound this problem. A series of infant deaths in the coronary care unit of a Toronto hospital in 1981 led to the filing of murder charges against a nurse employed in the unit. These charges were subsequently dismissed on the basis of new evidence questioning not only the nurse's involvement but the determination that the deaths were homicides. The case has led to considerable debate in the medical community over the medical evidence used in the criminal investigation and in the determination of the cause of death. (See, for example, a series of letters in *The New England Journal of Medicine* [1986].)

9 Official statistics on homicide prior to the 1920s are limited to a small number of cities whose municipal police forces reported statistics to the federal government.

10 Given the likelihood of significant under-reporting for the earliest years, it is possible that the homicide rates of the 1920s and 1930s were not substantially different from those of the 1960s and 1980s.

11 Unlike most other nations that fought in the Second World War, Canada did not experience significant increases in its homicide rate in the postwar period relative to pre-war levels (Archer and Gartner, 1984).

12 For a critique of efforts to classify homicides according to presumed conceptually meaningful categories, see, for example, Nettler (1982).

13 These include legal spouse, common-law spouse, estranged legal or common-law spouse, parent, child, sibling, other family member, various step-relationships, common-law family member, boy/girlfriend, lovers' triangle, close acquaintance, casual acquaintance, business relationship, roommate, neighbour, criminal contact, police officer, stranger, and unknown relationships. Statistics Canada publications typically combine these into three major categories of victim-offender relationship: 'domestic relationships' (immediate family, common-law family, and other kin), 'acquaintances', and 'strangers'.

14 These data were collected by Professor Bill McCarthy and the author, with the co-operation of the Homicide Division of the Metropolitan Toronto Police Department.

15 Because of the small number of homicides in each relationship category, within-category rates per 100,000 population are not calculated for Toronto.

16 For documentation of these regional differences, see the *Uniform Crime Reports* issued annually by the US Federal Bureau of Investigation. For analyses of the causes of this regional variation, see the research reviewed by Harries (1990: 62–83).

17 Boyd (1988) cites reports from the Dominion Bureau of Statistics that indicate these differences existed in the late nineteenth century as well.

18 Hackler and Don (1990) have examined whether the regional variation in violent and property crime rates in part may be due to differences in

screening, recording, and reporting practices of different police agencies. As they note, such system characteristics are not likely to exert a noticeable influence on homicide rates.

[19] Unfortunately, measuring cultural differences is notoriously difficult, especially in quantitative analysis. Some researchers have used indirect measures, such as firearm ownership, to capture differences in attitudes, norms, and values about violence (Dixon and Lizotte, 1987); but this practice has been strongly criticized. To further complicate this issue, some measures rejected as inappropriate proxies for cultural differences, such as ethnic composition of the population, are used instead to measure structural causes of homicide (Lenton, 1989a). Clearly, the fit between available measures and underlying cultural and structural factors is far from ideal, as is the assumption that any one measure represents only a structural or only a cultural factor.

[20] Homicides in the course of other criminal acts and gangland homicides probably are over-represented among unsolved homicides (Statistics Canada, 1976). This finding suggests that homicides in British Columbia and Quebec are more often related to criminal activities and relationships than are homicides in other provinces.

[21] To my knowledge, there has been no research addressing why Quebec has lower rates of intimate partner and family killings than the rest of Canada.

[22] Of course, the association between certain personal characteristics and lifestyles or activity patterns is in large part due to the uneven distribution of social and economic advantages on the basis of these characteristics.

[23] Between 1969 and 1977, the female rate increased by 67%; however, the male rate increased by 91%, widening the gender gap. Using a different series of data and analysis, Maxim and Keane (1992) also found no evidence of a convergence in gender-specific rates of homicide for the years 1950–1986.

[24] The data in Tables 6 and 7 were made available to the author by the Canadian Centre for Justice Statistics and do not appear in this form in their annual homicide reports. Unfortunately, such detailed data were not available for the other social groups discussed in this section.

[25] A longer-term view might portray a different picture for the nation as a whole, however. Data on female victimization in Toronto suggest that in the 1950s and 1960s the proportion of females killed by intimates and family members was higher than at any other point in the century. Moreover, killings of females by acquaintances and strangers accounted for similar proportions of female victimizations prior to the Second World War and after 1970. In other words, female victimization may not have consistently shifted from more to less intimate victim-offender relationships over the last century.

[26] Annual sex-specific data on offending are available from Statistics Canada, but not Vital Statistics, and have been published only since 1961.

[27] However, the proportion of offenders who were female actually increased from 11% in the 1960s to 13% in the 1970s. Absolute and proportional differences can portray different patterns of change, and this is a source of criticism of both measures (Preston, 1976).

[28] Some have asserted that even when such statistics are reported they must be evaluated with great caution. Block, McKie, and Miller (1983: 24), for example, state that data on the race of victims or offenders collected by Statistics Canada 'might be charitably described as inadequate from a [sic] ethnological point of view . . . [and] are to be regarded as suspect'.

[29] For a thorough review of the debate over collecting race and crime statistics, see Doob (1991).

[30] Much of the data reported in this section are taken from Silverman and Kennedy (1993); these researchers were given access to detailed homicide data from the Canadian Centre for Justice Statistics.

[31] Estimates of the rates of aboriginal victimization and offending vary considerably; for example, Moyer (1992) cites an aboriginal victimization rate of 12 per 100,000 in the early 1980s. Differences in rates appear to be due to use of different estimates of the size of the aboriginal population. My figures are taken from publications of the Canadian Centre of Justice Statistics.

[32] Because Statistics Canada publishes these regional figures only for 1984 and the numbers of aboriginal victims and offenders in some regions are quite small, this conclusion is made cautiously. See Silverman and Kennedy (1993: 213–15) for a discussion of rural-urban differences in aboriginal homicide rates.

[33] As Kennedy et al. (1989) note, the greater remoteness of aboriginal communities probably leads to under-reporting of their homicides. Under-reporting may also result from problematic relationships between residents of aboriginal communities and law enforcement officials. Both of these factors may mean aboriginal homicides in the Territories are more likely to be under-reported than those in the provinces. Thus the apparently lower homicide rates for aboriginals in the Territories compared to some provinces must be interpreted cautiously.

Whether rates of Aboriginal homicides on reserves are higher than non-reserve rates cannot be determined from available data. In addition, whether under-reporting or misclassification is more likely for homicides on reserves requires investigation. (See Long, this volume.)

[34] The oft-cited association between alcohol abuse and homicides among aboriginal peoples has sometimes been presented as an explanation of their homicide rates. On its own, alcohol abuse is not an explanation of homicide, however, and seems likely to be a spurious correlate. Understanding the role of alcohol in aboriginal homicides requires contextualizing the use and abuse of alcohol within aboriginal communities and social relations (Fisher, 1987; Shkilnyk, 1985).

[35] I use the phrase 'as a group' cautiously, intending to highlight the point that variation within races is often as great as variation among races in all

of the relevant variables noted here. For example, the risks of homicide vary greatly among different aboriginal communities, as do the forms and extent of disadvantage faced by members of these communities. This intra-racial variation is as crucial as inter-racial variation in understanding the distribution of homicide among racial groups. At minimum, the former rules out many types of biological and cultural explanations of the distribution.

[36] For evidence from Canada and the US that challenges aspects of this demographic explanation, see Block, McKie, and Miller (1983).

[37] Some scholars have predicted declining Canadian–US differences in crime rates and other measures of social behaviour because of an 'Americanization' of Canada (Horowitz, 1973; Lipset, 1990). According to this argument, the economic and political dominance of the United States will ultimately eradicate most cultural and structural differences between the two countries.

[38] An interesting feature of firearm homicides is that they are about equally spread across each of the victim-offender relationship types. Thus, about 40% of firearm homicides were 'domestic' killings; two-thirds of these were committed with long guns. Handguns tend to be used more often the more distant the victim-offender relationship. About half of all firearm homicides by strangers are committed with handguns.

[39] Nevertheless, homicides account for less than 1% of all criminal violence known to police. Homicides are also not a major cause of death for any demographic group in Canada. Annually, traffic accidents claim about eight times as many lives and suicides claim about six times as many lives as do homicides.

REFERENCES

Archer, Dane and Rosemary Gartner (1984). *Violence and Crime in Cross-National Perspective*. New Haven: Yale University Press.

Avio, Kenneth (1979). 'Capital punishment in Canada: A time-series analysis of the deterrent hypothesis', *Canadian Journal of Economics* 12: 647–76.

Block, Carolyn R., Craig McKie, and Louise S. Miller (1983). 'Patterns of change over time in Canadian and United States homicide', *Policy Perspectives* 3: 121–80.

Bowers, William J. (1984). *Legal Homicide*. Boston: Northeastern University Press.

Boyd, Neil (1988). *The Last Dance: Murder in Canada*. Scarborough, ON : Prentice-Hall.

Brantingham, Paul, and Patricia Brantingham (1984). *Patterns in Crime*. New York: Macmillan.

Chappell, Duncan, and Alison Hatch (1986). 'Violent crime in Canada: An assessment of current knowledge'. Pp. 228–37 in Robert A. Silverman and James J. Teevan, eds, *Crime in Canadian Society.* Toronto: Butterworths.

Chimbos, Peter D. (1978). *Marital Violence: A Study of Interspousal Homicide.* San Francisco: R & E Research Associates.

Cohen, Lawrence E., and Marcus Felson (1979). 'Social change and crime rate trends: A routine activities approach', *American Sociological Review* 44: 588–608.

Crawford, Maria, and Rosemary Gartner (1992). *Woman Killing: Intimate Femicide in Ontario, 1974–1990.* Toronto: Women We Honour Action Committee.

Curtis, Lynn (1974). *Criminal Violence: National Patterns and Behavior.* Lexington, MA: D.C. Heath.

Daly, Martin, and Margo Wilson (1988). *Homicide.* Hawthorne, NY: Aldine de Gruyter.

de Villiers, Marq (1991). 'Is our city still safe?' *Toronto Life,* June: 31–7.

Dixon, Jo, and Alan Lizotte (1987). 'Gun ownership and the "Southern subculture of violence"', *American Journal of Sociology* 93: 383–405.

Dominion Bureau of Statistics (1921–1966). *Vital Statistics.* Ottawa: Health and Welfare Division.

——— (1965–1970). *Causes of Death, Canada.* Ottawa: Health and Welfare Division.

Doob, Anthony (1991). *Workshop on Collecting Race and Ethnicity Statistics in the Criminal Justice System.* Toronto: Centre of Criminology, University of Toronto.

Fisher, A.D. (1987). 'Alcoholism and race: The misapplication of both concepts to North American Indians', *Canadian Review of Sociology and Anthropology* 24: 81–96.

Gartner, Rosemary (1990). 'The victims of homicide: A temporal and cross-national comparison', *American Sociological Review* 55: 9–23.

Gartner, Rosemary, and Bill McCarthy (1991). 'The social distribution of femicide in urban Canada, 1921–1988', *Law and Society Review* 25: 801–25.

Gillis, A.R. (1986). 'Domesticity, divorce, and deadly quarrels: An exploration of integration-regulation and homicide'. Pp. 133–48 in Tim Hartnagel and Robert Silverman, eds, *Critique and Explanation: Essays in Honor of Gwynn Nettler.* New Brunswick, NJ: Transaction Books.

Greenberg, David (1985). 'Age, crime, and social explanation', *American Journal of Sociology* 91: 1–21.

Gurr, Ted Robert (1989). 'Historical trends in violent crime: Europe and the United States'. Pp. 21–54 in Gurr, ed., *Violence in America*. Newbury Park, CA: Sage.

Hackler, Jim and Kim Don (1990). 'Estimating system biases: Crime indices that permit comparisons across provinces', *Canadian Journal of Criminology* 32: 243–64.

Hagan, John (1989). 'Comparing crime and criminalization in Canada and the U.S.A.', *Canadian Journal of Sociology* 14: 361–71.

Harries, Keith D. (1990). *Serious Violence: Patterns of Homicide and Assault in America*. Springfield, IL: Charles Thomas.

Havemann, Paul, Keith Couse, L. Forster, and Rae Matonovich (1985). *Law and Order for Canada's Indigeneous People*. Regina: School of Human Justice, University of Regina.

Higginbottom, Susan F., and Edward Zamble (1988). 'Categorizations of homicide cases: Agreement, accuracy, and confidence of public assignments', *Canadian Journal of Criminology* 30: 351–66.

Hindelang, Michael J., Michael R. Gottfredson, and James Garofalo (1978). *Victims of Personal Crime: An Empirical Foundation for a Theory of Personal Victimization*. Cambridge, MA: Ballinger.

Hirschi, Travis, and Michael R. Gottfredson (1983). 'Age and the explanation of crime', *American Journal of Sociology* 89: 552–84.

Horowitz, Irving Louis (1973). 'The hemispheric connection: A critique and corrective to the entrepreneurial thesis of development with special emphasis on the Canadian case', *Queen's Quarterly* 80: 327–59.

Jayewardene, C.H.S. (1975). 'The nature of homicide: Canada 1961–1970'. Pp. 267–89 in Robert A. Silverman and James J. Teevan, eds, *Crime in Canadian Society*. Toronto: Butterworths.

Jilek, Wolfgang, and Chunilal Roy (1976). 'Homicide committed by Canadian Indians and non-Indians', *International Journal of Offender Therapy and Comparative Criminology* 20: 201–16.

Johnson, Holly (1987). 'Homicide in Canada', *Canadian Social Trends*, Winter: 2–6.

Johnson, Holly, and Vincent F. Sacco (1990). *Patterns of Criminal Victimization in Canada*. General Social Survey Analysis Series. Ottawa: Statistics Canada.

Jones, Charles, Lorna Marsden, and Lorne Tepperman (1990). *Lives of Their Own*. Toronto: Oxford University Press.

Kennedy, Leslie W., David R. Forde, and Robert A. Silverman (1989).

'Understanding homicide trends: Issues in disaggregation for national and cross-national comparisons', *Canadian Journal of Sociology* 14: 479–86.

Kennedy, Leslie W., and Robert A. Silverman (1990). 'The elderly victim of homicide: An application of the routine activity approach', *Sociological Quarterly.* 31: 307–19.

Kennedy, Leslie W., Robert A. Silverman, and David R. Forde (1991). 'Homicide in urban Canada: Testing the impact of economic inequality and social disorganization', *Canadian Journal of Sociology* 16: 397–410.

Langevin, Ron, and Lorraine Handy (1987). 'Stranger homicide in Canada: A national sample and a psychiatric sample', *Journal of Criminal Law and Criminology* 78: 398–429.

LaPrairie, Carol (1987). 'Native women and crime: A theoretical model', *Canadian Journal of Native Studies* 7: 121–37.

Layson, Stephen (1983). 'Homicide and deterrence: Another view of the Canadian time-series evidence', *Canadian Journal of Economics* 16: 52–73.

Lenton, Rhonda (1989a). 'Homicide in Canada and the U.S.A.: A critique of the Hagan thesis', *Canadian Journal of Sociology* 14: 163–78.

——— (1989b). 'Conflict over consensus: Canadian and American homicide reconsidered', *Canadian Journal of Sociology* 14: 372–6.

Lipset, Seymour Martin (1990). *Continental Divide.* New York: Routledge.

Maxim, Paul S., and Carl Keane (1992). 'Gender, age, and risk of violent death in Canada, 1950–1986', *Canadian Review of Sociology and Anthropology* 29: 329–45.

Monkkonen, Eric H. (1989). 'Diverging homicide rates: England and the United States 1850–1875'. Pp. 80–101 in T.R. Gurr, ed., *Violence in America.* Newbury Park, CA: Sage.

Moyer, Sharon (1992). 'Race, gender, and homicide: Comparisons between aboriginals and other Canadians', *Canadian Journal of Criminology*, July-Oct.: 387–402.

Nettler, Gwynn (1982). *Killing One Another.* Cincinnati: Anderson.

New England Journal of Medicine (1986). 'Mysterious clusters of deaths in hospitals'. 314: 382–85.

Preston, Samuel (1976). *Mortality Patterns in National Populations.* New York: Academic Press.

Reed, Paul, Teresa Bleszynski, and Robert Gaucher (1978). 'Homicide in Canada: A statistical synopsis'. Pp. 178–208 in M.A. Beyer Gammon, ed., *Violence in Canada.* Toronto: Methuen.

Shkilnyk, Anastasia M. (1985). *A Poison Stronger than Love: The Destruction of an Ojibwa Community*. New Haven: Yale University Press.

Silverman, Robert A., and Leslie Kennedy (1987). 'Relational distance and homicide: The role of the stranger', *Journal of Criminal Law and Criminology* 78: 272–308.

———— (1988). 'Women who kill their children', *Violence and Victims* 3: 113–27.

———— (1993). *Deadly Deeds: Murder in Canada*. Scarborough, Ont.: Nelson Canada.

Silverman, Robert A., and S.K. Mukherjee (1987). 'Intimate homicide: An analysis of violent social relationships', *Behavioral Sciences and the Law* 5: 37–47.

Silverman, Robert A., Marc Reidel, and Leslie W. Kennedy. (1990). 'Murdered children: A comparison of racial differences across two jurisdictions', *Journal of Criminal Justice* 18: 401–16.

Sproule, Catherine F., and Deborah J. Kennett (1988). 'The use of firearms in Canadian homicide: The need for gun control', *Canadian Journal of Criminology* 30: 31–7.

———— (1989). 'Killing with guns in the USA and Canada 1977–1983: Further evidence for the effectiveness of gun control', *Canadian Journal of Criminology* 31: 245–51.

Statistics Canada (1971–1988). *Causes of Death, Canada*. Ottawa: Health and Welfare Division.

———— (1973b). *Murder Statistics, 1961–1970*. Ottawa: Judicial Division.

———— (1973a). *Murder Statistics, 1971*. Ottawa: Judicial Division.

———— (1976). *Homicide in Canada: A Statistical Synopsis*. Ottawa: Justice Statistics Division.

———— (1978, 1983, 1984, 1986, 1987, 1988). *Homicide in Canada*. Ottawa: Canadian Centre for Justice Statistics.

———— (1986). *Homicide in Canada, 1976–1985: An Historical Perspective*. Ottawa: Canadian Centre for Justice Statistics.

———— (1987). *Historical Homicide Data and Other Data Relevant to the Capital Punishment Issue*. Ottawa: Canadian Centre for Justice Statistics.

Taylor, Ian (1983). *Crime, Capitalism, and Community: Three Essays in Socialist Criminology*. Toronto: Butterworths.

Wallace, Allison (1986). *Homicide: The Social Reality*. New South Wales: Bureau of Criminal Statistics and Research, Department of the Attorney General.

Williams, Kirk, and Robert Flewelling (1988). 'The social production of criminal homicide: A comparative study of disaggregated rates in American cities', *American Sociological Review* 53: 421–31.

Wilson, Margo, and Martin Daly (1987). 'Spousal violence in Canada'. Paper presented at the Third National Family Violence Research Conference, University of New Hampshire.

World Health Organization (1951–1988). *World Health Statistics Annual: Vital Statistics and Causes of Death*. Geneva: WHO.

Chapter Eight

VIOLENCE BY MUNICIPAL POLICE IN CANADA: 1977–1992

JEFFREY IAN ROSS

In general, three organizations of the modern state exert violent coercive power: the military, national security organizations, and various police agencies.[1] Of all these groups, municipal police engage in the most acts of physical violence. This is largely a result of their function, which brings them into far more frequent contact with other citizens than is the case for employees of the state's other coercive agencies.[2]

Police violence has been defined in various ways. Most definitions, however, treat it as a type of misconduct and deviance. The term is used to cover a wide range of phenomena. Depending on the context, violent police behaviours are variously referred to as police abuse, brutality, extra-legal or excessive force, riots, torture, shootings, death squad activity killings and deadly force.[3]

The first police officer in Canada appeared on the streets of Quebec City in 1651. Most municipal police forces, however, were not established until the mid-1800s, when communities developed substantial populations.[4] Since this time, police agencies and practices have evolved and, in some cases, police departments have amalgamated with others in neighbouring jurisdictions (Loreto, 1984). Currently, urban police forces are the largest law-enforcement organizations in Canada, accounting for approximately 55 per cent of all police personnel in the country (approximately 58,000 uniformed officers) (Sewell, 1985: 33) and 'serving and protecting' about 51 per cent of Canadian citizens (Loreto, 1990: 211). Of the 588 municipalities with police forces in 1994, 191 contracted their services from the RCMP and 397 had their own forces (Griffiths and Verdun-Jones, 1994: 64).[5] The largest police forces are those for the cities of Toronto, Montreal, and Vancouver.

Municipal police forces are established and regulated under provincial legislation (usually called Police Acts), which require cities and towns to furnish adequate policing for their communities (Hann, McGinnis, Stenning, and Farson, 1985; Stenning, 1981). They enforce the relevant laws in the geographical area in which they patrol: federal and provincial statutes, and the particular bylaws of the city (Griffiths and Verdun-Jones, 1994: 64). Despite these fundamental similarities, however, there are considerable differences in the ways communities are policed.

Now that the definitions of police violence, the history and context of municipal policing have been discussed, the rest of the chapter will briefly survey the literature on the causes of police violence, examine the prevalence of police violence in Canada, review existing controls on police behaviour, and make a number of recommendations for the future.

THE LITERATURE ON POLICE VIOLENCE[6]

A number of studies dealing with police violence, in the general sense of the term, have been conducted. This research consists of descriptions of police violence, discussions about the causes of police violence in general or specific types (e.g., police use of deadly force), and analyses of the effects of police violence. By far the lion's share of this research has focused on the causes of police violence.

Most studies of police violence are descriptive (e.g., Reiss, 1968). A number of studies have examined police violence, particularly its causes. These include many of the same factors articulated in more general studies of police behaviour,[7] misconduct,[8] deviance,[9] and complaints against the police.[10] They may be classified as individual, situational, organizational, community, and legal.[11] Although some researchers (e.g., Feld, 1971; Manning, 1980; Westley, 1953, 1970) examined the general causes of police violence, most focus on single factors, which are often classified into internal and external factors (e.g., Stark, 1972). The former includes such influences as individual personality, attitudes and values; working environment; police culture; relationship to the courts; and professionalization (e.g., Kania and Mackay, 1977). The latter usually encompass community structure and social polarization (e.g., Feld, 1971). General studies have not demarcated the important contribution that different influences have in causing police violence. Often ignored, for example, is the relationship between police violence and frequency of street stops, the incidence of crime in a community, the number of police deployed in a particular area, and the number and type of arrests.[12] In general, the higher any of these numbers are, the more opportunities police have to engage in violence.

Several individual, situational, organizational, community, and legal variables have been posited, some of which have been tested, as causes leading police to use violence. However, because this literature is primarily American in focus, its generalizability beyond the US is problematic. In addition, no theories have been developed or analyzed. The data are limited in scope, usually ahistorical and collected in the context of observational studies and often not comparable among jurisdictions. Finally, none of these analyses examines efforts to remove the presumed causes of police violence.[13]

Only five specific types of police violence have been investigated in any great detail: police torture, police death squad activity, deaths in police custody, police riots, and use of deadly force. Most studies have focused on the last of these. In general, this literature concentrates on ten areas of explanation: the sources of information on this activity, the actions it includes, the types of political systems it takes place in, geographical locations, perpetrators, victims; causes; purposes, effects, and data quality.

Although the literature on general and specific types of police violence has added considerably to our understanding, it has several drawbacks.

(1) Since violence committed by the police and by other coercive agencies of the state is not clearly distinguished, it is unclear whether the same causes apply to all state agencies that use violence; (2) the abundance of definitions makes distinctions among the various subtypes of police violence difficult; (3) there is little research that evaluates methods of reducing violence;[14] (4) few researchers make recommendations for change; (5) ideological biases hamper the objectivity of many studies; (6) questionable research methods are used (e.g., victims' self-reports); (7) much of this research is ahistorical, outdated, and limited to one police organization or a handful of police forces; (8) only a few studies examining some sub-types of police violence have outlined a theory, developed a model, or tested the relative influence of posited causal factors; and, finally, (9) few researchers have tracked individual instances of police violence in their entirety, from allegation to conviction of officers or dismissal of charges against them. When outcomes are addressed they tend to be narrowly framed in the context of 'control mechanisms' instituted by the public, government, and/or the police to affect future acts of police violence.[15] Until these shortcomings are addressed, understanding the causes and effects of police violence, and ultimately significantly reducing the incidence of police violence will be difficult at best.

DOCUMENTING POLICE VIOLENCE

Data on police violence, whether in Canada or elsewhere, are scarce.[16] Information on violent practices short of deadly force consists largely of idiographic studies conducted by the media. In the main, no organizations or individuals, public or private, gather comprehensive data on police violence in Canada. There are, however, some statistics that do touch, in whole or in part, on police violence.

The first are statistics on citizens' complaints. In general, these are of two types: those compiled by individual police departments and those collected by independent citizens' organizations reviewing police activity. In both cases access to these figures is problematic,[17] and the information they provide is rarely detailed enough to test hypotheses on the process of police violence. Yet citizens' complaints of assault make up the largest category of complaints against the police.[18] As with the reporting of crime in general, not all citizens who have been assaulted by the police will report it; hence complaints against law enforcement officers are underestimated in official and unofficial sources of data.[19] Finally, data collected privately by organizations such as the Citizens Independent Review of Police Archives (CIRPA) can be biased, as these groups have their own axes to grind.

The crucial issue is to determine the proportion of these violent actions that are unjustified (i.e., not legally permissible). This is impossible to gauge accurately from all types of data because they are incomplete and it is commonly recognized that suspected officers, with the collusion of their peers and supervisors, often cover up or destroy incriminating evidence. In addition, the criminal-justice system often affords police officers a protective shield that is virtually impenetrable (Binder and Scharf, 1980; Fyfe, 1982, 1988; Sherman and Langworthy, 1979).

The only analysis of complaints statistics for Canada was done by Henshel (1983). He compared the statistics from CIRPA with the statistics produced in the very first years of the Office of the Public Complaints Commissioner for Ontario (1982–1983). Henshel found that different types of persons complained to the two different organizations. He made a number of recommendations for the Public Complaints Office: no suggestions were made for controlling police more effectively.

The second type of statistics are what might be labelled events data on police use of deadly force. In Canada, such information is available only from Statistics Canada's 'health and mortality' rates (also known as vital statistics) under the heading 'death by legal intervention'. According to these data, such homicides (which include and do not separate killings by both police officers and prison guards) number only about ten per year. Of all deaths by legal intervention between 1970 and 1981, 95 per cent (119) were caused by firearms, and only 5 per cent by other means (Canada, 1981).

Vital statistics 'provide scarce demographic or situational data with respect to police use of deadly force'. Only the province where the deaths occurred, and the gender and age of the victims, are evident. The bulk of these events took place in Quebec (37.0 per cent) followed by Ontario (27.7 per cent), and British Columbia (11.8 per cent) (Chappell and Graham, 1985: 9). In general, these statistics were in proportion to provincial populations during that time. No national studies are available of police use of firearms.[20] The only available 'national' figures on non-fatal shootings by Canadian police were published by the Ministry of the Solicitor General in 1976 and cover a five-year period (1970 to 1974) (Canada, 1976); these statistics probably understate the number of incidents, as complete data were not available for Saskatchewan, Quebec, and the Atlantic provinces.

Finally, three studies examined police use of deadly force. First, Abraham et al. (1981) analyzed inquest proceedings related to seven shootings by the Metropolitan Toronto Police, from 1978 to 1980, in an effort to determine some of the situational variables associated with such deaths. The bulk of these deadly force incidents took place in 'confrontation situations' between police and 'armed' citizens. Only one event came to trial and ended with the acquittal of two officers on charges of manslaughter.

Second, Chappell and Graham (1985) examined the use of deadly force by police in British Columbia between 1970 and 1982. They '[r]elied upon newsclipping services and newspaper indices, [and] reports of fourteen deaths by police firearms' (1985: 92). By supplementing their research with coroner's files they were able to identify demographic and situational variables. Among their most interesting findings was that, despite a number of irregularities in police procedure, no officers were dismissed from their force; the coroners did not waive an inquest; and all officers 'were found to have acted in the line of duty' (1985: 108).

Third, Bernheim (1990) in perhaps the most comprehensive treatment reviews the incidence of police use of deadly force in Canada focusing on the years 1961–86, the province of Quebec, and two deadly-force situations in the cities of Montreal and Sherbrooke that have since been referred to as the Griffin/Gosset and Rock Forest incidents respectively. Bernheim blames the judicial system, the Criminal Code, and politicians for creating a climate in which deadly force is considered permissible. He also recommends tighter regulations governing the use of guns; changing the police uniform; the use of specialized squads for intervening in violent situations; and general disarming of police to decrease the possibility of their using deadly force. Although these studies constitute a good start, none of them develops or tests any hypotheses or theories, creates models, or mentions the effects of deadly-force situations.

The above discussion suggests that what is needed is a data set of police violence that covers a broader range of types of police violence and a wider geographical base than previous studies. To this end, the following section will present an events data methodology based on newspaper reports.

METHODOLOGY

Each act of police violence is an event, similar to those measured in conflict processes literature, consisting of a series of stages, actions, or effects. Ideally, the scope, intensity, and frequency of each act of police violence should be analyzed. This is not easy to accomplish. Among other difficulties, a long time usually elapses between the initial allegation and the final decision as to the event's legality (in Toronto, for example, the August 1978 shooting of Andrew [Buddy] Evans was determined to be a clean shoot as a result of a coroner's inquest which ended November 1979). In order to accommodate for these problems, the method used here combines events data, case studies, and the comparative approach.

METHOD

1. Events Data Set

A data set was created following the methodology used in Ross (1988; 1992a; 1993; 1994): creation of a detailed chronology, coding of these events on a series of relevant variables, and running of frequency distributions.

A chronology was constructed based on articles referring to acts of municipal police violence in Canada, located from citations of *Globe and Mail* newspaper articles listed in the *Canadian News Index*.[21] All citations that appeared to relate to police violence were identified; then separate case studies of the incidents were constructed and assembled into a chronology.

2. Time Frame

This chronology begins with events starting in 1977 and ends in 1992; that is, if an event took place before 1977 but was reported in or after that year, it was omitted. This starting point, 1977, was chosen for three major reasons. These are from least to most important: 1977 corresponds with the beginning of what some researchers consider as the post-industrial era characterized by particular social problems; this time frame encompasses considerable variation in structural features of society; and, the *Canadian News Index* did not start cataloguing newspaper articles until 1977.

3. Events Included

All clearly identified incidents of real or alleged, justified or unjustified, physical and/or sexual violence committed by on-duty municipal police officers were included. Omitted were incidents in which officers fired their guns in the air; assaults committed by a number of officers from combined forces in which the officer responsible was not clearly identified; violent actions by police dogs; and violence committed by police vehicles in car chases.

In the main, news items that could be interpreted as police violence or responses to police violence were recorded in a chronological fashion, coded, and statistically analyzed.

4. Limitations

One must consider the following caveat: many incidents of police violence are never reported in the press. This may reflect the ability of police actors to conceal their activities; journalistic/editorial constraints; or distorted coverage or dissemination through other formal or informal mediums of communication. In general, the present data set is limited to cataloguing a subset of what has been identified as 'public police violence': those acts of police violence that are detected by the police hierarchy or citizen actors (e.g., the media). It is argued that public police violence is the most important type of extra-legal violence to force changes in police department policies and practices (Ross, 1992b).

Since several incidents of police violence stretch over a number of years,[22] it was necessary to track each individual event over a long time period: from allegation, to charge, to trial, to outcome. This can be a resource intensive process.

Finally, most cases that appear in the newspapers consist only of allegations of police abuse: some are founded, others are not. Many citizens charged or convicted of an offence will lie about their treatment by police. Thus all possible efforts were made, within the confines of media reports, to determine the authenticity of each allegation.

RESULTS

In all, 18 variables were coded. They refer to the characteristics of each event: year, month, and day event took place, province where incident took place, police force responsible for real or alleged violence, most severe type of violence, race or ethnicity of victim/s, race or ethnicity of police officer/s, age of victim/s, age of police officer/s, gender of victim/s, gender of police officer/s, number of victim/s involved in event, number of police officer/s involved in action, and most severe outcome or sanction meted out to police officer.

1. Year

Over the 16 years for which data were collected, there was a total of 114 acts of public police violence. Police violence took place in almost all years, the exception being 1986. Three years had the highest numbers of incidents: 1977, 1978, and 1991. The 1977–78 totals were related to

Table 8.1: **Year Incident Took Place**

Year	Frequency	%	Year	Frequency	%
1977	9	7.9	1986	0	0.0
1978	10	8.8	1987	4	3.5
1979	10	8.8	1988	7	6.1
1980	8	7.0	1989	9	7.9
1981	5	4.4	1990	9	7.9
1982	6	5.3	1991	16	14.1
1983	7	6.1	1992	7	6.1
1984	3	2.6			
1985	4	3.5	Total	114	100.0

reports of real or alleged police brutality by the Toronto police and the 1991 total included a series of shootings by Toronto and Montreal police departments (see Table 8.1).

2. Month
Every month of the year was represented. Incidents per month ranged from a low of 4 to a high of 16. The summer months of May to September accounted for close to half (47 per cent) of all reported incidents of police violence. This finding might be explained by the fact that during the summer months more 'street' crime is reported and people have more contact with police authorities (see Table 8.2).

3. Day
Police violence took place on almost every day of the month, and the number of acts did not increase as the month developed. It ranged from a low of 1 to a high of 10 incidents. This finding does not support the hypothesis that police violence might increase with the numbers of police arrests/citations which tend to increase towards the beginning and the end of the month, as police allegedly attempt to meet formal or

Table 8.2: **Month Incident Took Place**

Year	Frequency	%	Year	Frequency	%
January	5	4.4	August	16	14.0
February	9	7.9	September	8	7.0
March	7	6.1	October	9	7.9
April	4	3.5	November	10	8.8
May	8	7.0	December	10	8.8
June	8	7.0	Missing	6	5.3
July	14	12.3	Total	114	100.0

Table 8.3: **Day Incident Took Place**

Day	Frequency	%	Day	Frequency	%
1	5	4.4	18	2	1.8
2	2	1.8	19	5	4.4
3	2	1.8	20	2	1.8
4	5	4.4	21	2	1.8
5	3	2.6	22	2	1.8
6	4	3.5	23	3	2.6
7	2	1.8	24	3	2.6
8	2	1.8	25	1	.9
9	10	8.8	26	4	3.5
10	2	1.8	27	2	1.8
11	6	5.3	28	3	2.6
12	2	1.8	29	4	3.5
13	2	1.8	30	3	2.6
14	6	5.3	31	2	1.8
15	3	2.6	Missing	16	14.0
16	2	1.8			
17	2	1.8	Total	114	100.0

informal quotas (see Table 8.3). The distribution of incidents per quartile fluctuated with a peak of 30 during the second quartile (8th day to the 14th) to a low of 18 during the third quartile (15th day to the 21st). No immediate explanation can be given for this result (see Table 8.3).

4. Province
Most incidents (85; 74.6 per cent) took place in Ontario; Quebec followed with 15 events (13.2 per cent). The remaining acts took place in only five other provinces (Nova Scotia, Manitoba, Saskatchewan, Alberta, and British Columbia). Thus approximately half of all the provinces were represented (see Table 8.4).

Table 8.4: **Province Where Incident Took Place**

Province	Frequency	%
Ontario	85	74.6
Quebec	15	13.2
Saskatchewan	4	3.5
British Columbia	4	3.5
Nova Scotia	3	2.6
Manitoba	2	1.8
Alberta	1	.9
Total	114	100.0

Table 8.5: **Police Force of Accused Officer**

City	Frequency	%	City	Frequency	%
Vancouver, BC	4	3.5	Peel Regional, Ont.	4	3.5
Lethbridge, Alta	1	.9	Smiths Falls, Ont.	1	.9
Martinsville, Sask.	1	.9	Strathroy, Ont.	1	.9
Regina, Sask.	2	1.8	Thunder Bay, Ont.	1	.9
Saskatoon, Sask.	1	.9	Tillsonburg, Ont.	3	2.6
Winnipeg, Man.	2	1.8	Toronto, Ont.	51	44.7
Chatham, Ont.	1	.9	Waterloo Regional, Ont.	4	3.5
Coburg, Ont.	3	2.6	Windsor, Ont.	2	1.8
Durham, Ont.	3	2.6	Montreal, Ont.	13	11.4
Halton Regional, Ont.	5	4.4	Quebec City, PQ	1	.9
Hamilton Wentworth, Ont.	2	1.8	Sherbrooke, PQ	1	.9
Ingersoll, Ont.	1	.9	Halifax, NS	1	.9
Kitchener, Ont.	1	.9	New Victoria, NS	1	.9
London, Ont.	1	.9	New Waterford, NS	1	.9
Niagara Regional, Ont.	1	.9			
Ottawa, Ont.	3	2.6	Total	114	100.0

5. Police Force

The majority of incidents (51; 44.7 per cent) took place in Toronto; Montreal followed a distant second, with 13 (11.4 per cent). Otherwise the majority of events took place in cities in southern Ontario. This finding probably reflects both the geographical bias of *The Globe and Mail* and the fact that this area is one of the most densely populated areas in Canada (see Table 8.5).

6. Type of Violence[23]

The bulk of incidents (67 of 114; 58.8 per cent) involved beatings or assaults. The second most commonly reported type of event (39; 34.2 per cent) was police use of deadly force leading to either wounding or death. The balance was divided among cases of abuse (1), death in police custody (5), and sexual assault (2) (see Table 8.6).

7. Race/Ethnicity[24]

The majority of both victims and police officers involved were of white Anglo-Saxon Protestant or European background: 32.5 and 31.6 per cent, respectively. The second most common victim group were individuals of African origin, accounting for 20.2 per cent of the incidents (see Table 8.7).

Table 8.6: **Type of Real or Alleged Police Violence**

Type	Frequency	%
Beating/assault	67	58.8
Use of deadly force	39	34.2
Deaths in police custody	5	4.4
Sexual assault	2	1.8
Abuse	1	.9
Total	114	100.0

8. Age[25]

The youngest victim was 16 years of age and the oldest 65, but most victims tended to be under 30 years of age. On the other hand, in 54.4 per cent of the cases the age of the victim was not reported. Likewise, in 92.1 per cent of incidents the police officer's age was not available. In cases where both ages could be identified, officers tended to be older than victims (see Table 8.8).

9. Gender

In most incidents of violence both the victim and police officer were males: 85.1 per cent of victims, and 75.4 per cent of officers (see Table 8.9).

10. Numbers of Victim/s and Police Officer/s

In 79.8 per cent of the events, only one victim was involved. However, the number of police officers per incident was greater than the number of victims. In only 34.2 per cent of the cases was there only one officer (see Table 8.10).

Table 8.7: **Race/Ethnicity of Real or Alleged Victim/s and Police Officer/s**

Type	Victim/s		Police Officer/s	
	Frequency	%	Frequency	%
WASP/European Origin	37	32.5	36	31.6
African	23	20.2	1	.9
Native American	4	3.5	0	0.0
Asian	3	2.6	0	0.0
Francophone	3	2.6	7	6.1
Hispanic	2	1.8	0	0.0
South East Asian	1	.9	0	0.0
Mixed	1	.9	0	0.0
Missing	40	35.1	70	61.4
Total	114	100.0	114	100.0

Table 8.8: **Age of Real or Alleged Victim/s and Police Officer/s**

	Victim/s		Police Officer/s	
Age	Frequency	%	Frequency	%
16	1	.9	0	0.0
17	7	6.2	0	0.0
18	1	.9	0	0.0
19	6	5.3	0	0.0
20	1	.9	0	0.0
21	1	.9	0	0.0
22	4	3.5	0	0.0
23	3	2.6	0	0.0
24	4	3.5	2	1.8
25	0	0.0	0	0.0
26	2	1.8	1	.9
27	0	0.0	0	0.0
28	2	1.8	0	0.0
29	1	.9	1	.9
30	3	2.6	0	0.0
31	0	0.0	1	.9
32	4	3.5	0	0.0
33	1	.9	1	.9
34	0	0.0	0	0.0
35	2	1.8	1	0.0
41	1	.9	1	.9
44	1	.9	1	.9
45	1	.9	0	0.0
46	1	.9	0	0.0
48	1	.9	0	0.0
49	1	.9	0	0.0
59	2	1.8	0	0.0
65	1	.9	0	0.0
Missing	62	54.4	105	92.1
Total	114	100.0	114	100.0

Table 8.9: **Gender of Real or Alleged Victim/s and Police Officer/s**

	Victim/s		Police Officer/s	
	Frequency	%	Frequency	%
Male	97	85.1	86	75.4
Female	6	5.3	1	.9
Mixed[a]	6	5.3	1	.9
Missing	5	4.4	26	22.8
Total	114	100.1	114	100.0

[a]Events in which the victim/s or officer/s consisted of both males and females.

Table 8.10: **Number of Victim/s and Police Officer/s Per Incident**

	Victim/s		Police Officer/s	
Number	Frequency	%	Frequency	%
1	91	79.8	39	34.2
2	5	4.4	24	21.1
3	2	1.8	5	4.4
4	0	0.0	9	7.9
6	1	.9	0	0.0
7	1	.9	0	0.0
12	1	.9	0	0.0
28	1	.9	0	0.0
29	1	.9	0	0.0
53	0	0.0	1	.9
200	0	0.0	1	.9
286	1	.9	0	0.0
Missing	10	8.8	35	30.7
Total	114	100.0	114	100.0

11. Outcomes[26]
Of the 31 different outcomes resulting from these incidents, the most common were charges of assault (12.3 per cent), cases settled in court (7.9 per cent), and miscellaneous investigations (7.0 per cent). It is important to note, however, that in 17.5 per cent of these cases information on this variable was missing (see Table 8.11).

12. Summary
The majority of incidents involved assault, took place during the summer months, in Ontario, and most likely in Toronto. Both victims and officers tended to be males, and officers were usually older than victims.

CONTROLLING POLICE VIOLENCE

The problem of controlling police officers' use of excessive force is like that of adjusting brakes on a car: make them too loose and you risk crashing, too tight and you might not be able to back out of the driveway. That is, too little control may leave police too ready to use violence in a coercive fashion, and too much control may put police themselves at risk. Controlling police violence is part of a larger debate about the autonomy and control of government organizations.[27] Control is often discussed in research on public administration, street-level bureaucrats, and the police in particular. Individuals (e.g., Ackroyd, 1975; Bayley, 1979; 1985: Chapter 5) have advanced lists of factors believed to be important in

Table 8.11: **Outcomes or Most Severe Sanctions of Case**

	Frequency	%
Appeal to police commission	1	.9
Complaint launched with provincial police commission	3	2.6
Investigations		
Police investigation took place	4	3.5
Miscellaneous investigation took place	8	7.0
Investigation by provincial police commission	4	3.5
A coroner/s inquest takes place	6	5.3
Provincial Police investigation	2	1.8
Public complaints commission investigation	1	.9
Investigation by Special Investigations Unit (Ontario)	6	5.3
Mediation with police department	1	.9
Charges		
Officer/s charged with assault under the Police Act	3	2.6
Officer/s charged with assault	14	12.3
Officer charged with careless use of a firearm	1	.9
Officer/s charged with criminal negligence causing bodily harm	2	1.8
Victim/s sue police in civil court	4	3.5
Convictions		
Officer convicted of assault causing bodily harm	5	4.4
Officer/s convicted under Police Act of using excessive force	2	1.8
Police chief fired	1	.9
Officer convicted of forcible confinement	1	.9
Officer/s found guilty of misconduct by public complaints commission	1	.9
Acquittals		
Case settled in civil court	9	7.9
Officer cleared of wrongdoing by provincial police commission	1	.9
Provincial court overturns public complaints board decision	2	1.8
Provincial police commission recommends no internal discipline to be taken	1	.9
Coroner's inquest absolves the officer/s of wrongdoing	2	1.8
Officer acquitted of manslaughter	2	1.8
Officer acquitted of careless use of a firearm	1	.9
Officer acquitted of attempted murder	1	.9
Officer given conditional discharge	1	.9
Special Investigations Unit determines clean shoot	3	2.6
No charges are laid	1	.9
Missing	20	17.5
Total	114	100.0

controlling police in general, or specifically 'deviant' actions such as undercover operations (e.g., Marx, 1988), corruption (e.g., Sherman, 1978), and use of deadly force (e.g., Fyfe, 1980). The notion of controlling police is covered by studies that develop typologies, analyze police reform (and change), review discretion, and study deviance.

Although considerable work has been done in this area, most of it has focused on defining and classifying types; description; case-study analysis; one narrow type of police violence (namely, use of deadly force); and the American setting. It does not develop a theory or model. When relationships are identified and tested, the findings have untested applicability to other contexts of reform, discretion, and deviance such as police violence. This section will review the literature on controlling police violence in order to demonstrate its contributions and shortcomings. Beginning with a definition of 'control' in this context, it moves on to examine various types of control relevant to police, how they may be used to control police use of violence, and experiments with violence-reduction programs.

TYPES OF CONTROL

In any organization, the principle of control arises from the need for members to perform their duties in accordance with some set of standards. Such control should be an ongoing process, not simply a response to some specific wrongdoing.

Whatever the organization, control mechanisms may be either internal or external. Internal controls include hiring policies, training, supervision, hierarchy, disciplinary codes, policy manuals, collective agreements, internal review boards, and intra-agency competition. External controls include external review boards, legislation, and extra-agency competition. Both kinds of control mechanisms may include powers of review and sanction (e.g., suspension, dismissal).

Controls may also differ on an inclusivity/exclusivity dimension. According to Marx (1988),

> Civilian review boards in the United States, for example, deal single-mindedly with police; legislatures, on the other hand, regulate the police as part of a larger mandate to regulate governmental processes generally.

Internal and external types of control may be further classified as 'institutional/formal' (e.g., legislation, legislative oversight, congressional committees, courts, advisory boards, review boards, ombudsmen, ethics committees, commissions of inquiry, governmental regulation, monetary appropriations, prosecutors, inter-agency competition, etc.), 'informal' (e.g., public opinion, media attention, public protest, education activities, lobbying, critical international attention, etc.). The former are bureaucratic solutions, while the latter are more unstructured and spontaneous. Informal controls are often the last resort for citizens and usually have some influence on other forms of control. As used by citizens, these mechanisms can be ordered along a continuum from low-intensity (e.g., letters to elected officials) to high-intensity (e.g., riots, armed attacks, assassinations). In sum, institutional controls are primarily conventional and legislated, whereas informal controls are mostly unconventional and non-legislated.[28]

Police and their respective departments are subject to all the above types of control. The relative influence, however, varies with police departments, units in the police organization, individual police officers, and the many different actions that officers engage in. Despite the energy devoted to developing typologies of control, no research exists that definitively identifies which types have the most effect on police use of violence as a whole.

CONTROLLING POLICE ORGANIZATIONS

Four major internal institutions and actors exert control in police organizations: (1) recruitment divisions screen applicants; (2) personnel training provides education and socialization; (3) policy manuals and standing orders outline guidelines and standard operating procedures; (4) supervisors and administrators oversee, inspect, and exercise authority through sub-bureaus, and disciplinary and review boards (e.g., internal affairs departments, Trials departments etc.).

A variety of external mechanisms exert control over the police through federal, provincial, and some municipal constitutions, statutes, and laws that specify the situations in which force (deadly or otherwise) may be used. The courts may impose special standards or initiate injunctions against the police. Medical examiners or coroners may inspect victims of police use of force. Legislative bodies may exercise some control through the passage of statutes, oversight hearings, appropriations, and the ratification of appointments, while executive-branch authorities, such as premiers, mayors, city managers, agency heads, and police commissions may use their powers of appointment and resource allocation, suasion, and policy directives. Finally, review boards (civilian, partially civilian, or partisan) can provide analyses of police violence and recommendations for improvement.

Bayley (1985) goes one step further, noting that '[s]ome processes within the police are designed explicitly for control; others assist in controlling, but that is not their primary function.' Bayley refers to the latter type of control as 'implicit'. This classification is similar to formal and informal types of control. Thus he categorizes and describes the devices for promoting control according to four types: external-exclusive, external-inclusive, internal-explicit, and internal-implicit. He concedes, however, that in practice police and their communities will rely on several types of control simultaneously (Bayley, 1985: 171). Although he makes a series of informal propositions, Bayley does not construct a theory. He also neglects to discuss the effect that these controls have on police. As he rightly points out,

> [f]ormal description . . . is only the first step. It is necessary to go further and determine whether mechanisms in place are actually used. . . . Studies of police control must start, not stop with descriptions of mechanisms. They must describe the actual operation. (Bayley, 1985: 171–2)

In sum, these mechanisms and processes of control have neither been assembled into a theory nor analyzed to explain the process and/or utility of various controls on police violence.[29]

CONTROLLING POLICE VIOLENCE

One of the most comprehensive and sophisticated analyses of control over police use of violence is Manning's (1980). He classifies control mechanisms into three 'potentially conflicting' kinds: community (public standards shaped by public opinion; mass media attitudes); political/legal (politicians' statements and reactions to incidents of violence that come to public attention); and occupational (official departmental standards, which sometimes include a clear statement of conditions under which force will be employed; responses and reactions within the police culture). In general, Manning believes that occupational controls provide the most powerful means of controlling the police. He also points out at least three ways we can improve control of police violence: increasingly move the police into a regulatory mode, disarm the police, and 'chang[e] the reward structure that serves to define and reinforce role priorities' (Manning, 1980: 139).

Although Manning's work is commendable, it is not a theory; nor has it been implemented in an applied setting. His examples lack generalizability beyond the United States, and, like many researchers, he focuses primarily on police use of deadly force. Although there are good reasons for this focus, deadly force is merely the tip of the iceberg; other types of police violence such as assault are more frequent.

IMPROVING CONTROL OVER POLICE VIOLENCE

The paucity of theory has not stopped government agencies and police administrators from introducing new policies and procedures, many of which have been successful, to control police violence. New external mechanisms range from community police boards and police monitoring units to police commissions, citizen advisory boards, and complaints bureaus. In Canada, numerous commissions and inquiries initiated by cities (e.g., Metropolitan Toronto Board of Commissioners, 1970) and provinces (e.g., Ontario, 1972, 1975, 1976; Quebec, 1977; Saskatchewan, 1965) have investigated real or alleged acts of police violence. The majority of these forums have documented actual or suspected incidents of police violence and have suggested a variety of changes. Although many of these recommendations have been implemented, others have fallen by the wayside. Likewise, a series of internal mechanisms have been experimented with and in some cases provisionally implemented. For example, Toch (1977: Chapter 7) identifies seven internal control mechanisms: better selection procedures and methods of dismissing violent police officers; alternative administrative controls; enhanced police-community relations; peer review panels; organizational changes; improved skills in family crisis intervention; and increased use of women police officers. But empirical studies of these mechanisms in action are rare.

Since police forces in Canada are usually supervised by municipal and provincial police commissions or boards the literature on controlling police generally focuses on these oversight bodies (e.g., Hann et al., 1985). But research in this area is scant.[30] Most of it has concentrated on cataloguing organizational relationships; examining the importance of professionalism in freeing police forces from political domination; reviewing the roles and autonomy of police chiefs; and analyzing the relations between police boards and chiefs.

In perhaps the most thorough study, Stenning (1981) found that police boards varied considerably in composition, mandate, assumed role, authority, status and level of activity in municipal police governance. That is, there was neither a typical police board nor a typical style of governing authority.

Canadian police forces have the same traditional mechanisms for controlling police violence that are found in other Western democracies. Although the provinces have greater legislative power to place restrictions on the police than does the federal government, they usually do not use this power. Thus the use of force by Canadian police is governed by Section 25, Subsection 1 of the Criminal Code, which allows officers to use 'as much force as is necessary' to effect an arrest. Moreover, Subsections 3 and 4 of the code permit a police officer to use lethal force to apprehend a fleeing suspect when other procedures have failed. Understandably, this section of the Code is highly controversial (Pavlich, 1981; Griffiths and Verdun-Jones, 1994: 113–14).

At the individual level, citizens can deal with police violence by filing a formal complaint, and police forces maintain internal procedures for dealing with such problems. In addition, the provinces have their own mechanisms to provide for independent investigation of citizens complaints.

In Ontario, for example, the Special Investigations Unit (SIU)—established in 1991 under the former Liberal government's Ontario Police Services Act, largely in response to a series of Toronto area police shootings—is an independent civilian body that investigates serious incidents involving the police.

CONCLUSIONS AND FUTURE RESEARCH

Although the data set presented in this chapter provides an introduction to the problem of public police violence in Canada, there are various factors that make the chronology a limited source for coding events.

First, the range of sources should be expanded to include (in order of increasing importance) case studies of police organizations, governmental reports (e.g., royal commission reports, etc.), reports of groups, public and private, that attempt to assert control on the police, articles from other newspapers (besides *The Globe and Mail*), and, most important, police incident reports.[31]

Measuring effective and successful control of police violence will no doubt be difficult. Measures of success might include positive actions that the police organization takes after the initial event (illegal police violence) has occurred and the time period between successive acts of illegal police violence.

Second, although frequency distributions are fine for initial descriptions, they say nothing about the causal underpinnings of any socio-political process. A more telling method of statistical analysis would be to examine the patterns in which the various outcomes (control initiatives) occur. This would entail the use of dynamic (e.g., panel, event-count, event sequence, or event history) as opposed to static statistical models (e.g., basic regression models or cross-sectional models). Both those tasks (expanded sources and more sophisicated statistical tests) would be aided by appropriate resources.

NOTES

Special thanks to Natasha J. Cabrera for comments.

[1] Many of the issues discussed in this section are treated in greater detail in Ross (1995).

[2] Many scholars have emphasized the coercive aspect of policing or the special function of the police to use legitimized coercion (American Bar Association, 1972; Bayley, 1979; Bent, 1974: Chapter 1; Bittner, 1970; 1974; Goldstein, 1977; Manning, 1977; Muir, 1977; Rumbaut and Bittner,

1979). Others, the minority, argue that most police work is based on legitimate coercive power (French and Raven, 1959; Sykes and Brent, 1983). According to these authors, 'citizens usually obey police because they recognize the right of police to take charge in disordered situations' (Sykes and Brent, 1983).

[3] For a review of the history of policing in Canada see, for example, Kelly and Kelly (1976). For a content analysis of literature on the history of municipal policing in Canada see Ross (1995a).

[4] 'Many municipalities, rather than establishing and maintaining their own police forces, have chosen to contract with the provincial police force for municipal policing services. In all provinces except Quebec, provincial police forces are involved in municipal policing. In Ontario, policing services in some communities are provided by the Ontario Provincial Police (OPP) under contract, while in the remaining provinces, the RCMP, acting as the provincial police force, contracts to provide municipal policing services' (Griffiths and Verdun-Jones, 1994: 64–5). For a review of contemporary policing in Canada see, for example, Ross (1995b).

[5] Thus this field of study excludes both police actions against violence and violence against police, focusing on violence committed by police. See Sherman (1980) for a distinction among the three.

[6] This section is expanded on in Ross (1993b).

[7] Some of the research on police behaviour includes Galliher (1971); Goldstein (1967); Lundman (1980); and Mastrofski and Parks (1990); Sherman (1980).

[8] See, for example, Broadaway (1974); Lundman (1974); and Blau (1986).

[9] See, for example, Barker and Carter (1986); Kotecha and Walker (1976); Punch (1985); and Stoddard (1968).

[10] See, for example, Beral and Sisk (1963); Box and Russell (1975); Brown (1987); Hudson (1970); Regan (1971); Russell (1976).

[11] Two sets of variables have been found to be important in police use of deadly force. 'One is environmental and lies beyond the direct control of police administrators; the other is internal and is subject to control by police chiefs. The former category includes such variables such as the level of violence among the constituencies of the police and the extent of lawful police authority to use deadly force. Included in the second category are variables such as general police operating philosophies and specific policies, both formal and unstated' (Fyfe, 1988: 180).

[12] Likewise, number of arrests is related to type of shift (e.g. time, location patrolled, etc.). See Watchorn (1966) for an early treatment of this perspective.

[13] For a more comprehensive treatment of the causes of specific types of police violence see Ross (1993: 19–25).

[14] Although no studies investigating the removal of the possible causes of police violence exist, there has been some research designed to help police reduce their use of violence (e.g., Brinegar, 1986).

[15]See, for example, Ross (1992b).

[16]This argument is based on examination of the Inter-University Consortium for Political and Social Research's *Guide to Resources and Services 1986–1987*.

[17]The author wrote a number of governmental and non-governmental organizations asking if they collected data on police violence or if they knew who did. Organizations consulted included the International Association on Civilian Oversight of Law Enforcement, the Citizens Independent Review of Police Activities (Toronto), the Office of the Public Complaints Commissioner (Toronto), the Canadian Civil Liberties Association, and Amnesty International.

[18]See Henshel (1983) or Ontario (1987).

[19]See Box (1983: 100–1) for an assessment of the futility of this method as a means of control.

[20]That is, situations in which the police discharged their firearms but the suspect was not necessarily killed (sometimes referred to as 'shots fired').

[21]*The Globe and Mail* is widely considered to be Canada's national newspaper and is published simultaneously across Canada.

[22]For instance, an allegation of police abuse often takes a number of years before it comes to trial, if it comes to trial at all.

[23]The most severe form of police violence was coded. For example, if a police assault took place at the same time as a shooting, only the shooting was coded.

[24]If the race or ethnicity was not given, it was inferred from situational factors including the victim/s or police officer/s last name. The author recognizes the unreliability of this process.

[25]If more than one victim or police officer was involved an average age was taken.

[26]This variable was coded on most severe sanction meted out.

[27]For control of governmental organizations see Dimock (1935/1968); Hage (1980): March and Simon (1958); Pfeffer and Salanick (1978); Simon (1976); Tannenbaum (1968); Van Gusteven (1976). For early discussions of internal and external controls on the police see, for example, Cooper (1975); Hudson (1972); Moodie (1972); Stark (1972); and White (1972).

[28]These are also referred to as citizen-oriented or community controls. There is also the distinction among legal, organizational, and political constraints. The difference between internal and external controls with respect to the police is made by several scholars (e.g., Grant, 1975; Sherman, 1974b; Watchorn, 1966).

[29]Three other research topics that are relevant to the control of police violence are police reform and change, controlling police discretion, and controlling police deviance.

[30]Notable exceptions include Grosman (1975), Stenning (1981), Tardiff (1974), and a variety of federal and provincial commissions of inquiry

into police wrongdoing. For a more in-depth review of these books and commission reports see Hann et al. (1985).

[31]Gamson (1975), for example, in his study of social-reform groups, limited his sample to groups that functioned prior to 1945 to be able to ascertain whether the groups had achieved their objectives.

REFERENCES

Abraham, John D. et al. (1981). 'Police use of deadly force: A Toronto perspective', *Osgoode Hall Law Journal* 19, 2: 199–236.

Ackroyd, Jack W. (1975). 'Rejoinder to Grant, Alan, "The Control of Police Behaviour"'. Pp. 111–16 in W.S. Tarnopolsky, ed., *Some Civil Liberties Issues of the Seventies*. Toronto: Osgoode Hall Law School.

American Bar Association (1972). *The Urban Police Function: Report of an Advisory Committee on the Police Function, Frank J. Remington, Chairman*. Chicago: American Bar Association.

Barker, Thomas, and David L. Carter (1986). 'Introduction'. Pp. 1–7 in Thomas Barker and David L. Carter, eds, *Police Deviance* Cincinnati: Pilgrimage.

Bayley, David H. (1979). 'Police function, Structure, and control in Western Europe and North America'. Pp. 109–44 in Norval Morris and Michael Towry, eds, *Crime and Justice: An Annual Review of Research*, Vol. 1. Chicago: University of Chicago Press.

———— (1985). *Patterns of Policing: A Comparative International Analysis*. New Brunswick, NJ: Rutgers University Press.

Bent, Alan Edward (1974). *The Politics of Law Enforcement: Conflict and Power in Urban Communities*. Lexington, MA: Lexington Books.

Beral, Harold, and Marcus Sisk (1963). 'The administration of complaints by civilians against the police', *Harvard Law Review* 77 (January): 499–519.

Bernheim, Jean-Claude (1990). *Police et pouvoir d'homicide*. Montréal: Méridien.

Binder, Arnold and Peter Scharf (1980). 'The violent police-citizen encounter', *Annals of the American Political and Social Science* 452 (November): 111–21.

Bittner, Egon (1970). *The Functions of the Police in Modern Society*. Rockville, MD: National Institute of Mental Health.

———— (1974). 'Florence Nightingale in pursuit of Willie Sutton: A theory of the police'. Pp. 17–44 in Herbert Jacob, ed., *The Potential for Reform in Criminal Justice*, Vol. 3.

Box, Steven (1983). *Power, Crime, and Mystification.* London: Tavistock.

Box, Steven, and Ken Russell (1975). 'The politics of discreditability: Disarming complaints against the police', *Sociological Review* 23, 2: 315–46.

Brinegar, Jerry Lee (1986). *Breaking Free From Violence.* New York: Gardner Press.

Broadaway, Fred (1974). 'Police misconduct'. *Journal of Police Science and Administration* 2, 2 (June): 210–18.

Brown, David (1987). *The Police: Complaints Procedure: A Survey of Complainants' Views.* London: Her Majesty's Stationery Office.

Canada, Statistics Canada (1970–1982). 'Causes of death'. Annual Catalogue #84–203.

——— Ministry of the Solicitor General (1976). *Statistics Handbook Selected Aspects of Criminal Justice,* 8 March: 128.

Chappell, Duncan, and Linda P. Graham (1985). *Police Use of Deadly Force: Canadian Perspectives.* Toronto: University of Toronto Centre for Criminology.

Cooper, Lynn (1975). 'Controlling the Police'. Pp. 141–8 in Emilio Viano and Jeffrey Reiman, eds, *The Police in Society.* Lexington, MA: Lexington.

Dimock, Marshall E. (1935/1968). 'Forms of control over administrative action'. Pp. 287–321 in Charles G. Haine and Marshall E. Dimcock, eds, *Essays on the Law and Practice of Governmental Administration.* New York: Greenwood Press.

Feld, Barry C. (1971). 'Police violence and protest', *Minnesota Law Review* 55, 4 (March): pp. 731–78.

French, John R., and Bertram H. Raven (1959). 'The basis of social power'. Pp. 150–67 in D. Cartwright, ed., *Studies in Social Power* Ann Arbor: University of Michigan Press.

Fyfe, James (1988). 'Police use of deadly force', *Justice Quarterly* 5, 2 (June): 165–205.

Fyfe, James J., ed. (1982). *Readings on Police Use of Deadly Force.* Washington, DC: Police Foundation.

Galliher, John F. (1971). 'Explanations of police misconduct: A critical review and analysis', *Sociological Quarterly* 12, 3 (Summer): 308–18.

Gamson, William A. (1975). *The Strategy of Protest.* Homewood, IL: Dorsey.

Goldstein, Herman (1967). 'Administrative problems in controlling the exercise of police authority', *Journal of Criminal Law, Criminology, and Political Science* 58: 160–72.

——— (1977). *Policing a Free Society.* Cambridge, MA: Ballinger.

Grant, Alan (1975). 'The control of police behaviour'. Pp. 75–110 in Walter Tarnopolsky, ed., *Some Civil Liberties Issues of the Seventies* Toronto: Carswell.

Griffiths, Curt T., and Simon N. Verdun-Jones (1994). *Canadian Criminal Justice* Second Edition. Toronto: Butterworths.

Grosman, Brian (1975). *Police Command: Decisions and Discretion.* Toronto: Macmillan.

Hage, Jerald (1980). *Theories of Organizations: Form, Process, and Transformation.* New York: John Wiley.

Hann, Robert G., James H. McGinnis, Philip Stenning, and A. Stuart Farson (1985). 'Municipal police governance and accountability in Canada: An empirical study', *Canadian Police College Journal* 9, 1: 1–85.

Henshel, Richard (1983). *Police Misconduct in Metropolitan Toronto: A Study of Formal Complaints.* Report No. 8. LaMarsh Research Programme on Violence and Conflict Resolution, North York, ON: York University.

Hudson, James R. (1970). 'Police-citizen encounters that lead to citizen complaints', *Social Problems* 18, 3: 179–93.

———— (1972). 'Organizational aspects of internal and external review of police', *Journal of Criminal Law, Criminology and Political Science* 63, 3: 427–33.

Kania, Richard E., and Wade C. Mackay (1977). 'Police violence as a function of community characteristics', *Criminology* 15, 1: 27–48.

Kelly, William, and Nora Kelly (1976). *Policing in Canada.* Toronto: Macmillan of Canada.

Kotecha, K.C., and J. Walker (1976). 'Police vigilantes', *Society* 13, 3: 48–52.

Loreto, Richard Anthony (1984). 'Reorganizing municipal forces in Ontario: The convergence of functional and local reform interests', PhD dissertation, University of Toronto.

———— (1990). 'Policing'. Pp. 207–39 in Richard A. Loreto and Trevor Price, eds, *Urban Policy Issues: Canadian Perspectives.* Toronto: McClelland and Stewart.

Lundman, Richard J. (1974). 'Domestic police citizen encounters', *Journal of Police Science and Administration* 2, 1: 22–7.

Lundman, Richard J., ed. (1980). *Police Behaviour.* New York: Oxford University Press.

Manning, Peter K. (1977). *Police Work.* Cambridge, MA: MIT Press.

———— (1980). 'Violence and the police role', *Annals of the American Academy of Political and Social Science* 452 (November): 135–44.

March, James and Herbert Simon (1958). *Organizations.* New York: John Wiley and Sons.

Marx, Gary T. (1988). *Undercover: Police Surveillance in America.* Berkeley: University of California Press.

Mastrofski, Stephen, and Roger B. Parks (1990). 'Improving observational studies of police', *Criminology* 28: 475–96.

McMahon, Maeve W., and Richard V. Ericson (1984). *Policing Reform: A Study of the Reform Process and Police Institution in Toronto.* Toronto: Centre of Criminology, University of Toronto.

Metropolitan Toronto Board of Commissioners of Police. 1970. 'Report of an inquiry into allegations made against certain members of the Metropolitan Toronto'. Judge C.O. Bick, Chair. Toronto.

Moodie, Peter (1972). 'The use and control of police'. Pp. 231–47 in Robert Benewick and Trevor Smith, eds, *Direct Action and Democratic Politics.* London: Allen and Unwin.

Muir, William Ker, Jr (1977). *Police: Streetcorner Politicians.* Chicago: Aldine Publishing.

Ontario (1972). 'Royal Commission of Inquiry in Relation to the Conduct of the Public and the Metropolitan Toronto Police Report'. Judge Vannini, Chair. Toronto: Queen's Printer.

——— (1975). 'Royal Commission on the Conduct of Police Forces at Fort Erie the 11th of May, 1974 Report' (Pringle Report). Toronto: Queen's Printer.

——— (1976). 'Royal Commission into Metropolitan Toronto Police Practices: Report' (Morand Report). Toronto: Queen's Printer.

——— (1987). 'Fifth Annual Report of the Office of the Public Complaints Commissioner'. Offices of the Public Complaints Commissioner.

Pavlich, D.J. (1981). 'Law and Arrest', in J. Atrens, P.T. Burns, and J.P. Taylor, eds, *Criminal Procedure: Canadian Law and Practice*, III–1 211, Vancouver, Butterworths.

Pfeffer, Jeffrey, and Gerald R. Salanick (1978). *The External Control of Organizations: A Resource Dependence Perspective.* New York: Harper and Row.

Punch, Maurice (1985). *Conduct Unbecoming.* London: Tavistock Press.

Quebec (1977). 'Rapport d'enquête sur la conduite des membres du corps de police de la ville de Montreal, relativement à des incidents survenus le 24 juin 1974'. Quebec City: Commission de Police du Quebec.

Regan, D.E. (1971). 'Complaints against the police', *Political Quarterly* 4 (October/December): 402–13.

Reiss, Albert Jr (1968). 'Police brutality: Answers to key questions', *Trans-Action*, July-August: 10–19.

Ross, Jeffrey Ian (1988). 'Attributes of domestic political terrorism in Canada, 1960–1985', *Terrorism: An International Journal* 11, 3 (Fall): 213–33.

—— (1992a). 'Contemporary radical-right wing violence in Canada', *Terrorism and Political Violence* 4, 3: 72–101.

—— (1992b). 'The outcomes of public police violence: A neglected research agenda', *Police Studies: The International Review of Police Development* 15, 1 (Autumn): 163–83.

—— (1993). 'The politics and control of police violence in New York City and Toronto'. PhD dissertation, University of Colorado.

—— (1994). 'Low-intensity conflict in the peaceable kingdom: The attributes of international terrorism in Canada, 1960–1990', *Conflict Quarterly* 14, 3 (Summer): 36–62.

—— (1995a). 'Municipal policing in Canada: A historical approach', *Urban History Review* (forthcoming).

—— (1995b). 'Contemporary municipal policing in Canada', *Police Studies: The International Review of Police Development* (forthcoming).

Ross, Jeffrey Ian, ed. (1995). *Controlling State Crime.* New York: Garland Publishing.

Rumbaut, Reuben G., and Egon Bittner (1979). 'Changing perceptions of the police role'. Pp. 239–88 in Norval Morris and Michael Tonry, eds, *Crime and Justice: An Annual Review of Research* Vol. 1. Chicago: University of Chicago Press.

Russell, Ken (1976). *Complaints Against the Police: A Sociological View.* Leicester: Oldham and Manton.

Saskatchewan (1965). 'Royal Commission to Inquire into Allegations of Misconduct on the Part of Certain Police Officers of the City of Saskatchewan Report'. Regina.

Sewell, John (1985). *Police: Urban Policing in Canada.* Toronto: James Lorimer and Company.

Sherman, Lawrence W. (1974). 'Who polices the police: New York, London, Paris?' Pp. 13–22 in Donal E.J. MacNamara and Marc Riedel, eds, *Police: Perspectives, Problems, Prospects.* New York: Praeger.

—— (1978). *Scandal and Reform: Controlling Police Corruption.* Berkeley: University of California Press.

—— (1980). 'Causes of police behavior: The current state of quantitative research', *Journal of Research in Crime and Delinquency* 17, 1: 69–100.

Sherman, Lawrence W., and Robert H. Langworthy (1979). 'Measuring homicide by police officers', *Journal of Criminal Law and Criminology* 70, 4: 546–60.

Simon, Herbert (1976). *Administrative Behavior: A Study of Decision-Making Processes in Administrative Organization*, Third Ed. New York: Free Press.

Stark, Rodney (1972). *Police Riots*. Belmont, CA: Wadsworth Publishing.

Stenning, Philip C. (1981). *Police Commissions and Boards in Canada*. Toronto: Centre of Criminology, University of Toronto.

Stoddard, Ellwyn R. (1968). 'The "informal code" of police deviancy: A group approach to "blue coat crime"', *Journal of Criminal Law, Criminology and Police Science* 59, 2: 201–13.

Sykes, Richard E., and Edward E. Brent (1983). *Policing: A Social Behaviorist Perspective*. New Brunswick, NJ: Rutgers University Press.

Tardiff, Guy (1974). *Police et politique au Québec*. Montreal: Editions de L'Aurore.

Tannenbaum, Arnold Sherwood (1968). *Control in Organizations*. New York: McGraw Hill.

Toch, Hans J. (1977). *Peacekeeping: Police, Prisons and Violence*. Toronto: Lexington Books.

Van Gunsteven, Herman R. (1976). *The Quest for Control: A Critique of the National-Central-Review Approach in Public Affairs*. New York: Weber.

Watchorn, D.J. (1966). 'Abuse of police powers: Reasons, effect and control', *University of Toronto Faculty of Law Review* 24: 48–69.

Westley, William A. (1953). 'Violence and the police', *American Journal of Sociology* 59, 1: 34–41.

———— (1970). *Violence and the Police: A Sociological Study of Law, Custom and Morality*. Cambridge, MA: MIT Press.

White, Susan O. (1972). 'Controlling police behavior'. Pp. 23–34 in Donal E.J. MacNamara and Marc Riedel, eds, *Police: Perspectives, Problems, and Prospects*. New York: Praeger.

Chapter Nine

A Sociopolitical Approach to the Reproduction of Violence in Canadian Prisons

Michael Welch

In terms of imprisonment rates (adults and juveniles combined) Canada ranks second among North American and European nations (including Australia), surpassed only by the United States (csc, 1991). Contrary to the popular myth that Canada is a 'peaceable kingdom', then, crime and violence remain serious social problems (Torrance, 1975). Indeed, some of the most violent and criminogenic environments in Canadian society are situated within its prisons. According to Cooley (1992), the victimization (robbery, sexual assault, and assault) rate of men in prison stands at 538 per 1,000, compared to 90 per 1,000 for males in society at large. Other studies reveal that male prisoners also stand a greater risk of being murdered within prison than do men in the community (Porporino, Doherty, and Sawatsky, 1987). Specifically, Jayewardene and Doherty (1985) determined that inmates in Canadian penitentiaries are, on average, 14 times more at risk for murder than males in the general population.

It is ironic, as Porporino (1986: 213) notes, that 'the most violent individuals in society, once apprehended and convicted, are isolated within settings where violence is especially commonplace'. Moreover, violence is continually perpetuated, or reproduced, in prisons. As Lowman and MacLean (1991: 130) point out: 'Prison seems to either produce or reinforce the very behaviour it is supposed to "correct".'

This chapter examines the contradictory nature of the reproduction of violence in Canadian prisons, beginning with a brief overview of the historical developments that have led to the present crisis. It then introduces the motives underlying aggressive behaviour in the prison setting, before examining a variety of violent manifestations in the contemporary prison system. The chapter concludes with a discussion of the policies and strategies currently used to control prison violence, and their limitations. Finally it should be noted that the focus of this chapter is violence in men's prisons, not only because violence is more prevalent there than in women's institutions, but because it is far more severe.

A BRIEF HISTORY OF CORRECTIONS IN CANADA

A historical examination of punishment in Canada must take into account the numerous social forces and social movements that help situate corrections in its proper social context. In particular, it is important to address the social, cultural, political, and economic influences that have shaped (and continue to influence) the course of correctional policy in Canada.

In the early 1700s, punishment in Canada paralleled penal practices in Western Europe, England, and colonial America. Corporal punishments (e.g., whipping) and public humiliation (e.g., the use of pillories and stocks) were common, as were transportation, banishment, and fines (Coles, 1979). Both the rationale for and the harshness of early punishments were rooted in English criminal law, and were enforced in Upper and Lower Canada. However, the Act of 1800 enacted in Upper Canada reduced the severity of many punishments; for example, convicted felons were subject to fines instead of whipping or having a hand burned (Baehre, 1977).

Mounting criticisms of corporal punishments and dissatisfaction with transportation and banishment led to the emergence of incarceration, which in the eighteenth century was rarely used as a form of punishment. The early penal institutions in Canada, as well as in Western Europe, England, and colonial America, were workhouses (also known as Houses of Correction or Bridewells). In 1754, the first Canadian workhouse was constructed in Nova Scotia: along with serious criminals it housed vagrants, beggars, prostitutes, drunks, orphans, and runaway youth. Like workhouses elsewhere, Canadian institutions were criticized for their horrific conditions, poor food, lack of security and segregation, and the brutality of their keepers (Phillips, 1991). The manifest goal of the workhouse was to instil discipline and promote the Protestant work ethic; its latent purpose, however, was to control the growing urban underclass (Fingard, 1984, 1989; Houston, 1972, 1974; Welch, 1994, 1996a).

The popularity of combining punishment with labour generated the construction of a new workhouse in Halifax in 1818. However, as the work performed inside the institution became more skilled, labour organizers petitioned the government to cease the practice, arguing that prison labour unfairly competed with the labour of workers in society at large. As a consequence, prisoners were restricted to rigorous forms of work that were dispiriting and relatively unproductive (breaking stones, pumping water, or walking the treadmill or 'stepping mill') (Coles, 1979; Palmer, 1980).

One of the most significant developments in Canadian correctional history took place between 1830 and Confederation, in 1867. According to Ekstedt and Griffiths (1988), during this period, public and political attention shifted to crime in Canadian society, which led to the construction of Canada's first penitentiary, in Kingston, Ontario, in 1835. However, other historians present different interpretations. Bellomo (1972), for example, asserts that the Kingston penitentiary was constructed in response to several social and institutional problems, including overcrowding in the local gaols as well as an increase in crime. Conversely, Beattie (1977) notes that serious crime was not widespread during this era, although the perception that crime was rampant did fuel the penitentiary movement. At a deeper level of analysis, Beattie points out that crime was viewed as a major threat to the stability of society, a threat against which the penitentiary stood as a powerful defence.

Penitentiaries gained further social and political support as a result of demographic changes in society at large. Between 1820 and 1850, Canadian society was composed largely of settlers who were also landowners; but as the ranks of landless labourers (both skilled and unskilled) grew, so too did social and political tensions (Chunn, 1981; Ekstedt and Griffiths, 1988). Urbanization and industrialization led to the emergence of increasing numbers of unemployed workers. Penal institutions served as a primary defence against crime and disorder, and the threat posed by the 'dangerous class' (Taylor, 1979; for criticism of this thesis see Phillips, 1991).

More radical-élitist perspectives concerning the emergence of the penitentiary in Canada are found in the work of Gosselin (1982) and Smandych and Verdun-Jones (1982). These authors challenge the liberal-pluralist notion that the penitentiary was a product of good intentions and benevolence. Rather, Gosselin (1982) suggests that the penitentiary served (along with the courts, the police, and the army) as one component in a 'web of coercion', thereby functioning as a mechanism of physical and psychological control over the working class.

Smandych and Verdun-Jones (1982) offer a similar interpretation, tracing the rise of the penitentiary to economic concerns. In this view, not only was the penitentiary an economically effective and self-sustaining institution, but the practice of institutionalization was thought to have economic benefits for society as well.

The Kingston penitentiary emerged as a powerful symbol based on 'moral architecture' exhibiting the features of order and morality (Taylor, 1979: 407). Baehre (1977: 199) reinforced this theme by noting that the Kingston penitentiary not only served as a model for its prisoners, but as a model for society as well.

By 1867, provincial penitentiaries were located in Kingston, Saint John, and Halifax. With Confederation they were brought under the legislative authority of the Parliament of Canada. The first Penitentiary Act (1868) led to the establishment of the federal penitentiary system as well as the Department of Justice.

The 1870s saw further expansion of the federal penitentiary system: institutions were built in Montreal (1873), Stony Mountain, Manitoba (1876), and New Westminster, BC (1878). In 1880 the penitentiaries in Saint John and Halifax were closed, and a new institution was constructed at Dorchester, New Brunswick (Ekstedt and Griffiths, 1988).

Although these penitentiaries were newly constructed, reports soon surfaced condemning their horrific conditions, including lack of segregation, use of corporal punishment, and tendency to function as 'schools of corruption' (see the Moylan reports cited in Edmison, 1970). Attempts at reform continued through the early twentieth century (see the Penitentiary Act of 1906, and the Reports of the Fourth [1928] and Fifth [1931] Inspector of Penal Institutions), but most either failed or had a minimal impact (Ekstedt and Griffiths, 1988; Gosselin, 1982; Skinner, Dreidger, and Grainger, 1981). Nevertheless, during this period in Canada (as well as in the United States), a major development in correctional ideology occurred. That is, the institutionalization of offenders as a primary mechanism of punishment had become widely and uncritically accepted by both citizens and governmental leaders (Welch, 1996a).

After the Second World War, Canadian prisons were further transformed as they adopted the treatment model recommended in the 1949 *Annual Report of the Commissioner of Penitentiaries* (1950). Rehabilitation efforts were identified in various types of intervention: education, vocational training, and therapeutic techniques. The medical approach to corrections met with considerable support and fanfare and lasted until the late 1960s, by which time the treatment model failed to change the attitudes and behaviours of criminals. Though the defeat of rehabilitation is often attributed to the rise of the 'law and order' conservatives, it should be noted that the liberal-oriented medical model also was criticized by radicals. Radicals argued that the application of medical techniques and technology by 'experts' to the criminal population represented a subtle form of repression over the lower classes (Gosselin, 1982).

THE CONTEMPORARY CANADIAN PRISON SYSTEM

Responsibility for corrections in Canada is shared by the federal, provincial, and territorial governments. Provincial governments are responsible for offenders serving sentences of less than two years, those sentenced to probation, and young offenders. The Correctional Services of Canada (CSC), an agency of the Ministry of the Solicitor General, administers sentences of two years or more. This responsibility includes the management of correctional institutions and the supervision of offenders who have been conditionally released by the National Parole

Board, as well as those released by law on mandatory supervision. Of the 225 correctional facilities in Canada, 167 are provincial and territorial and 58 are federal (CSC, 1991).

According to its mission statement, the Correctional Services of Canada 'contributes to the protection of society by actively encouraging and assisting offenders to become law-abiding citizens, while exercising reasonable, safe, secure, and humane control' (CSC, 1991: 6). As part of its mission, the CSC promotes five core values:

> Core Value 1: We respect the dignity of individuals, the rights of all members of society, and the potential growth and development.

> Core Value 2: We recognize that the offender has the potential to live as a law-abiding citizen.

> Core Value 3: We believe that our strength and our major resource in achieving our objectives is our staff and that human relationships are the cornerstone of our endeavour.

> Core Value 4: We believe that the sharing of ideas, knowledge, values and experience, nationally and internationality, is essential to the achievement of our Mission.

> Core Value 5: We believe in managing the Service with openness and integrity and we are accountable to the Solicitor General (CSC: 1991: 7).

In a nation of more than 26 million citizens (approximately 20 million of them adults), Canada's adult prisoner population exceeds 29,000. These figures translate to an adult imprisonment rate of 151 per 100,000. As Table 9.1 illustrates, Canada's total imprisonment rate

Table 9.1: **Rates Expressed per 100,000 Total Population (Adults and Juveniles)**

United States	426.0	Austria	77.0
Canada	112.7	Spain	75.8
United Kingdom	97.4	Denmark	68.0
Turkey	95.4	Italy	60.4
West Germany	84.9	Sweden	56.0
Portugal	83.0	Norway	48.4
France	80.3	The Netherlands	40.0
Australia	78.7		

SOURCE: CSC (1991)

(adults and juveniles combined) is second only to that of the US among North American and European nations (including Australia) (CSC, 1991).

Canada's correctional population grew from 10,651 in 1984–85 to 12,357 in 1992–93. Table 9.2 documents the population figures nationally, regionally, and according to security level.

Almost half of all inmates—approximately 49 per cent—serve their time in medium-security institutions; roughly 25 per cent are confined to maximum-security and 13 per cent to minimum-security institutions; the remaining inmates are serving time in community correctional centres or provincial institutions (CSC, 1991). The typical prisoner is a young (20–34 years), single, white male serving a first penitentiary term of less than six years for either a robbery, a non-violent offence, or a break and enter conviction (see Table 9.3). It should be emphasized, however, that aboriginal offenders are disproportionately

Table 9.2: **Average Actual Count of Federal Inmate Population: Fiscal Years 1984–85 to 1992–93**

Fiscal Years	1984- 1985	1985- 1986	1986- 1987	1987- 1988	1988- 1989	1989- 1990	1990- 1991	1991- 1992	1992- 1993
National	10,651	11,213	11,104	10,584	11,064	11,447	11,290	11,781	12,357
Atlantic region	1,111	1,118	1,100	974	963	1,024	978	1,058	1,168
Quebec region	2,971	3,159	3,239	3,137	3,328	3,370	3,271	3,431	3,659
Ontario region	2,774	2,947	2,964	3,883	3,011	3,137	3,178	3,343	3,565
Prairie region	2,312	2,387	2,219	2,039	2,164	2,269	2,291	2,370	2,417
Pacific region	1,484	1,601	1,582	1,551	1,595	1,646	1,571	1,579	1,548
Maximum security	3,540	3,649	3,471	3,343	3,555	3,769	3,680	3,475	3,429
Medium security	5,604	5,995	6,053	5,706	6,047	6,185	6,006	6,563	6,717
Minimum security	1,261	1,323	1,285	1,211	1,163	1,200	1,288	1,450	1,891
C.C.C.[a]	246	246	295	324	300	293	316	293	321

[a](C.C.C.) Community Correction Centre
[aa]SOURCE: Research and Statistics Branch

Table 9.3: **Profile of an On-Register Male Offender**

Profile	Number of offenders[a]	%
Age 20–34 yrs	8,301	61.5
Single[b]	8,192	60.7
Common-law	3,635	27.0
Married	1,675	12.4
Serving first penitentiary term	8,090	60.0
Serving a sentence of less than six (6) years	7,775	57.6
Serving a sentence for:		
Homicide	1,661	12.3
Attempted murder	258	1.9
Manslaughter	604	4.5
Sexual offences	1,712	12.7
Other violent offences	880	6.5
Robbery	3,123	23.1
Other non-violent offences	2,073	15.4
Break and enter	2,029	15.0
Drugs	1,162	8.6

[a]Profile based on an on-register male population of 13,502. The on-register population includes federal offenders incarcerated in provincial institutions and provincial offenders incarcerated in federal institutions under federal/provincial exchange of services agreements. It includes offenders on federal day parole.
[b]Includes offenders who are separated, divorced, widowed and not stated.
SOURCE: CSC (1991)

represented in the correctional population (see Table 9.4 and Figure 9.1 and Long, this volume). Another pertinent characteristic of Canadian prisoners is their educational background: approximately 65 per cent of new offenders tested below the grade-eight level in mathematics and language (CSC, 1991). (Education particularly is important with respect to economic opportunity outside the penitentiary.)

MOTIVES AND GOALS OF PRISON VIOLENCE

In order to identify the various types of prison violence, it is important to understand why and how violence emerges in the prison setting. Just as forms of violence differ, so too do the motives or goals behind it. In general, these motives and goals are characterized as either *instrumental* or *expressive* (Bowker, 1985). These two kinds of violence can be traced to two particular forms of aggression. Instrumental violence stems from

Table 9.4: **On-Register Offender Population Profile by Race**

Race	M^a	F^b
Caucasian	11,082 (81.1%)	218 (68.8%)
Aboriginal	1,513 (11.2%)	49 (15.4%)
Black	505 (3.7%)	28 (8.8%)
Asiatic	110 (0.8%)	5 (1.6%)
Other	292 (2.2%)	17 (5.4%)
Total	13,502 (100%)	317 (100%)

[a]Male offender population
[b]Female offender population

Figure 9.1: **Distribution of Visible Minorities Amongst Federal Inmate Population, 1990–1991**

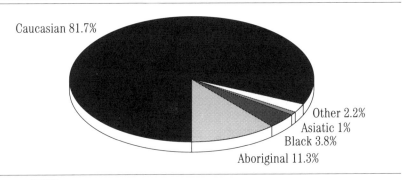

Caucasian 81.7%

Other 2.2%
Asiatic 1%
Black 3.8%
Aboriginal 11.3%

SOURCE: CSC (1991)

incentive-motivated aggression, whereas expressive violence is rooted in *annoyance-motivated aggression* (Porporino and Marton, 1983; Zillman, 1978). Each of these forms of aggressive behaviour serves a function: the first, 'to attain various rewards or incentives'; the second, 'to deal with annoyance (e.g., frustration, mistreatment, provocation)' (Porporino and Marton, 1983: 9). The former is known as incentive-motivated aggression and the latter as annoyance-motivated aggression.

INSTRUMENTAL VIOLENCE AND INCENTIVE-MOTIVATED AGGRESSION

Instrumental violence is regarded as rational or calculative because it sets out to achieve a particular goal (Bowker, 1985); because it is often planned, instrumental violence typically emerges from incentive-motivated aggression (Porporino and Marton, 1983). This is especially true of cases in which inmates threaten or physically/sexually assault other prisoners for the purpose of garnering power, enhancing status, or promoting a particular self-image within the prison society. In these efforts to dominate fellow prisoners, inmates may employ violence (or the threat of violence) to obtain what they want: a more desirable living situation, sexual contact, commodities (cigarettes, junk-food, sneakers), contraband (drugs, weapons), or various other services (laundry tasks and paper work for legal matters) (Bowker, 1985; Ellis, Grasmick, and Gilman, 1974; Porporino and Marton, 1983; Toch, 1977). Instrumental violence is not restricted to individual violence; it also is evident in collective actions (riots, disturbances, hostage-takings), especially when goals are set and demands are formally pronounced.

EXPRESSIVE VIOLENCE AND ANNOYANCE-MOTIVATED AGGRESSION

Expressive violence is not necessarily rational, insofar as it does not serve a conscious purpose. Rather, violence of this type tends to be impulsive and emotionally expressive, characterized by a spontaneous release of tension (Bowker, 1985). Expressive violence stems from annoyance-motivated aggression, which in turn reflects an urge to 'escape, to reduce, or terminate acute or chronic annoyance' (Porporino and Marton, 1983: 10). Given the annoyances associated with prison environments—overcrowding, lack of privacy, idleness, incessant noise—even seemingly minor irritations can precipitate violence.

Expressive violence is apparent in both individual outbursts of violence and the kind of collective disturbances characterized by a 'mob mentality'. In either case, expressive violence requires a psychological state of readiness coupled with a conducive situation or precipitating event (Bowker, 1985).

It must be emphasized that instrumental and expressive violence are not mutually exclusive; many violent incidents involve a combination of the two. For instance, inmates may sometimes consciously engage in assaults so that others will perceive them as savagely violent. Such brutal displays of expressive violence are instrumental because they bolster an inmate's reputation, thereby enhancing his power and status among his peers. Moreover, riots and disturbances commonly feature both expressive and instrumental violence: although riots may be instrumental and goal-oriented, they also serve as opportunities for inmates to ventilate pent-up rage over prison conditions and practices.

Porporino and Marton (1983: 11) point out that distinguishing between incentive-motivated (instrumental) violence and annoyance-motivated (expressive) violence is crucial to institutional management: 'Misreading the type of violence which is occurring could actually serve to aggravate the situation.' Given the impulsive nature of annoyance-motivated aggression, for instance, punitive measures are ineffective and may even exacerbate the situation. Rather, if corrections officials detect an increase in annoyance-motivated aggression among inmates, they should attempt to reduce the sources of irritation (e.g., crowding, idleness) and develop programs or activities that will help to reduce tension (Porporino and Marton, 1983).

SOURCES OF PRISON VIOLENCE

Of course there are many sources of prison violence. Three of the most common, however, are violent inmates, the social climate of violence, and overcrowding.

VIOLENT INMATES

Prisons house violent offenders: hence it stands to reason that they are violent places. This is especially true of maximum-security penitentiaries, which hold the most violent criminals. As frequent as violent incidents are in such settings, however, violence also occurs in medium- and, occasionally, minimum-security facilities (Porporino, 1986). According to the CSC (1992: 3), 63 major assaults on inmates were reported in 1991–92. Of these, 26 (41.3 per cent) occurred in 4 of 43 institutions. Three of these institutions were medium-security and only one was maximum-security. Since maximum-security facilities are not the source of most violent acts, then, we must examine other sources of violence besides violent offenders themselves.

THE SOCIAL CLIMATE OF VIOLENCE

As we have seen, inmates may resort to violence, either instrumental or expressive, because of features in their environment. For example, Toch (1985) examined the social climate of violence in prisons and concluded that although the situational context is not the sole producer of violence, it may enhance or reduce the likelihood of its occurrence. Toch identifies a number of contextual factors that contribute to prison violence: (1) Violent behaviour gains 'pay-offs' such as peer admiration and fear, which may serve as a form of protection. (2) Victims generally don't 'rat' on aggressors. (3) The institutional routine and internal architecture of prisons make it easy to plan assaults for times when the risk of being caught is minimal and places where the attack will not be seen. (4) The prevailing climate of violence offers numerous temptations, challenges, and provocations to attack other inmates who are seen as 'deserving' such treatment. (5) The fact that inmates themselves see violence as the norm in prison provides justification.

OVERCROWDING

As correctional populations grow, institutional resources, programs, and services predictably fail to keep pace with demand. The overcrowding that results places enormous strain on the institution as a whole, as well as on prisoners. Moreover, overcrowding is an interactive variable insofar as it exacerbates existing institutional problems and makes prison life even more irritating for inmates (Clements, 1979). One institutional task that is particularly strained by overcrowding is the placement procedure, which often results in mismatching of offenders with facilities and programs (Porporino, 1986). Moreover, inmate transfers necessitated by the arrival of new prisoners can lead to increased violence by destabilizing inmate social networks (Porporino, 1986).

Ellis (1984) supports this argument, stating that inter-institutional movement limits the social-control process that ordinarily functions to suppress violence. A stable prison environment is characterized by networks of ties between inmates; by contrast, a transient population with a continuing influx of relative strangers places enormous strain on inmate society, increasing the number of abrasive interactions through the breakdown of the sub-rosa prison economy. The effect is destabilization, leading to aggression and violence (Ellis, 1984; Porporino, 1986).

Despite some advances in our understanding of the relationship between inmate movement and violence, the overall interaction between overcrowding and violence remains to be clearly delineated. Again, overcrowding serves as an interactive variable; that is, other factors must also be taken into account. And even when other variables are carefully controlled (e.g., age), contradictory results are common. And without clear findings, it is difficult to develop an effective policy (Porporino, 1986; also see Porporino and Dudley, 1984; Porporino and Marton, 1983).

RIOTS AND VIOLENCE IN CANADIAN PRISONS

The year 1971 was a benchmark for corrections in North America because of major riots at two prisons: Attica in New York State and its Canadian counterpart, the Kingston penitentiary in Ontario. The legacy of Attica continues to remind us of the oppression inherent in corrections, but we should not forget the lessons learned at Kingston either. Erupting on 14 April, the large-scale violence persisted for 96 hours: two prisoners were murdered; 16 sex offenders were stalked, bound, and beaten; several correctional officers were taken hostage; and major sections of the institution were destroyed. Prison officials sought assistance from other governmental leaders, and the Canadian Army was called in to quell the uprising (Lowman and MacLean, 1991: 131).

It should be noted that prison violence is often characterized by a contagion effect: although it may be temporarily controlled or contained, violence can spread—even to other institutions. Such an effect was evident in the aftermath of the Kingston riot, when 400 prisoners were transferred to the new maximum-security penitentiary at Mill-haven. Instead of stretching over several months, which might have served as a sufficient 'cooling-out' period, the transfers were completed in only four days. Still outraged over the Kingston riot, the guards at Millhaven retaliated against the transferred inmates; for example, prisoners were forced to run a gauntlet in which they were beaten by clubs. The momentum of this violence persisted for the next six years, during which time Millhaven recorded 19 major disturbances (MacGuigan, 1977). Prison violence continued to plague other Canadian institutions in the 1970s, peaking in 1975–76 with 69 'major incidents', including 39 hostage-takings. By contrast, only 65 'major incidents' had occurred between 1932 and 1974 (MacGuigan, 1977).

In response to the growing violence in Canadian prisons, the Sub-Committee on the Penitentiary System (the MacGuigan Commission) convened in 1977. The Commission's report was a scathing indictment of government and corrections officials, blaming them for creating a crisis in the Canadian penitentiary system. It recommended sweeping changes in the administrative regime and the classification system, as well as improved educational and vocational training for inmates.

Yet major disturbances continued. In the most comprehensive examination to date of prison violence in Canada, Culhane (1985) chronicles major disturbances both before and after the MacGuigan Commission. The following account draws heavily on Culhane's work.

• Oakalla (also known as the Lower Mainland Regional Correctional Centre) is the largest of five provincial facilities in British Columbia in which inmates serve sentences of less than two years. Oakalla has a long history of non-violent demonstrations, inmate fasts, and suicides, as well as riots. In the course of these protests against institutional conditions; prisoners have demanded freedom of speech, the right to be treated as human beings, the abolition of isolation, the development of educational programs, and the right to participate in administrative decision-making.

In 1980, 'in response to an alarming number of reports of violent confrontations between guards and prisoners, of harsh and arbitrary use of discipline and a general atmosphere of tension and hostility' (*Vancouver Free Press*, 18 January 1980), the Attorney-General's Department agreed to investigate. In November 1983, Oakalla 'came down': it was 'a full-blown riot in which rocks were thrown, fixtures ripped out, and cells and furniture smashed and burned' (Culhane, 1985: 32).

• At the British Columbia Penitentiary, in June 1975, prisoners held 15 hostages for 41 hours. The incident ended when the tactical squad stormed the prison, firing on both hostages and inmates. One officer was shot to death and one of the hostage-takers was seriously wounded. A series of hostage-takings followed. In July 1975, a prisoner held a prison barbering instructor hostage for eight hours; in February 1976, two inmates held two guards hostage for 15 hours; in April 1976, four prisoners held three officers for 13 hours, and two prisoners were found dead; in June 1976, there was a botched attempt to take two guards hostage who escaped with minor injuries; in August 1976, an officer was held hostage for 10 minutes; in September 1976, a prisoner (sex offender) was stabbed to death; in the same month during a 12-day state of emergency declared when officers refused to work overtime, three inmates were found dead. Thus in a period of six months six prisoners died (Culhane, 1985: 35–6). After years of institutional conflict, in 1980 the BC Penitentiary was closed.

- Opened in 1966 as one of five Canadian treatment centres for criminal drug addicts, the facility at Matsqui, BC, was transformed into a medium-security prison in 1972 and abandoned its original program. Shortly thereafter, Matsqui began admitting inmates transferred from the soon-to-be-closed British Columbia Penitentiary.

  In 1976 inmates at Matsqui and other Canadian prisons (along with prisoners in the United States, France, and Belgium) began observing National Prison Justice Day each August 10. The purpose of these peaceful, non-violent, observances is to remember and pay tribute to those who have died unnatural deaths in prison. National Prison Justice Day also gives families and supporters outside of prison the opportunity to hold vigils and demonstrations aimed at raising public consciousness of the injustices which occur behind prison walls.

  In the late 1960s and early 1970s, a prisoners'-rights movement began to develop in Canada, paralleling movements in the United States and Western Europe. With the emergence of political consciousness among Canadian prisoners various formal organizations were created, including the Prisoners' Rights Group (PRG). In addition to challenging institutional conditions and the mistreatment of prisoners, the PRG formally addresses issues of basic human rights, including freedom of speech and assembly, in an effort to make the conditions of incarceration more just and humane.

  In 1978, prisoners at Matsqui, along with 3,500 other inmates across Canada, peacefully observed National Prison Justice Day with a 24-hour fast and work stoppage. As was their custom, the PRG had notified prison officials in advance as to the nature of the demonstration, and requested that they avoid reprisals against inmates who participated. Nationwide, most prison officials agreed. At Matsqui, however, officials punished the inmates by cancelling institutional social events, including the monthly open-house family day (Culhane, 1985).

Feeling unjustly penalized for participating in peaceful demonstrations, inmates at Matsqui accused prison officials of becoming
increasingly repressive. Tensions continued to grow until 1981, when
300 inmates took control of the institution for several hours, smashing furniture and setting fire to much of the prison. The next morning, some 200 RCMP officers, 180 army troops, 20 Matsqui police
officers, and six dogs were called in, along with 14 ambulances, in a
massive show of force. Rifles, shotguns, clubs and other riot gear
were prominently displayed, and the prisoners surrendered. The
precipitating factors of the riot were assumed to include the working conditions of the kitchen, compounded by other issues, such as
the mandatory-supervision system and changes in the pay system
(Culhane, 1985).

- When the Kent Maximum Security Institution (near Vancouver in the
Fraser Valley) opened in 1979, with a capacity for 192 inmates, prison
officials boasted of its humane conditions, progressive programming,
and secure environment. Nevertheless, only two months after its opening, a fire was set and a riot ensued. Taking an officer hostage, inmates
protested against the suspension of a rehabilitation program and
demanded an end to unnecessary body searches, denial of visiting privileges, and the use of solitary confinement for minor rule violations.

  Following two years of protests, hunger strikes, boycotts, and other
forms of conflict, the atmosphere at Kent was characterized by anger
and distrust. Finally, in 1981 the prison 'came down': 'Over 100 prisoners were involved in a burning and smashing spree resulting in an
estimated $100,000 damage' (Culhane, 1985: 67).

- The Maximum Security Prison at Archambault, north of Montreal,
opened in 1969, and was designed to house 429 inmates. By 1976,
non-violent work stoppages lasting several months had been organized by prisoners protesting unreasonable visitation and correspondence rules and demanding improvements in health care, working
conditions, food services, and the right to participate in administrative decisions by way of a Prisoner's Committee.

  In 1982, an escape attempt by two prisoners 'escalated into a major
incident': three guards were killed and the two would-be escapees
were found dead, 'having taken cyanide capsules in what was later
recognised as a suicide pact' (Culhane, 1985: 70).

  Later reports revealed that several forms of harassment used by
some guards against inmates had contributed to the high level of tension at Archambault. According to Kolb (1982), inmates accused a
minority of guards with persistent harassment amounting in some
cases to torture, including: keeping prisoners from sleeping by

banging on their cells; use of a detention cell (the 'hole') in which conditions were inhumane; cruel use of tear gas (one inmate was reported to have been restrained by two guards while being shot with tear gas in the mouth at point-blank range); spraying of tear gas onto inmates' food and urinating on their sandwiches; and numerous assaults and beatings of inmates.

Most of these riots and disturbances have represented a form of collective violence that is instrumental, calculated, and aimed at achieving institutional reform, especially in cases in which inmate representatives have presented formal demands. Indeed, many of these incidents have reflected the emerging political consciousness among prisoners. However, the incidence of expressive violence cannot be dismissed, insofar as many prisoners involved in these disturbances were undoubtedly venting their anger over unjust and barbaric treatment.

OTHER SECURITY INCIDENTS IN CANADIAN PRISONS

The Correctional Services of Canada attempts to record all security incidents. Though official reports and state-level data provide some of the documentation needed to assess the extent of violence in correctional institutions, they are not without serious limitations. According to Porporino and Marton (1983: 4), official records may not accurately reflect the actual incidence of violence: 'Some incidents may not be detected and others are handled informally and not officially recorded.' These limitations mean that trends are difficult to determine (Porporino and Marton, 1983).

Security incidents are categorized as either minor or major. Because it is sometimes difficult to distinguish between the two, the CSC has established definitions of major security incidents (see Table 9.5). Incidents that do not meet the 'major' definition are generally classified as minor. The limitations of official records become an issue here too. Porporino and Marton (1983: 4) argue that because incidents are simply listed as either major or minor and classified under one of several descriptive categories, 'the relative seriousness of incidents within a particular category is not assessed'.

Another factor that serves to limit the accuracy of reports is the subculture of violence, which inhibits inmates from reporting violent incidents to corrections staff. Indeed, 'under-reporting . . . is the norm' since victims who 'rat' will be subject to reprisals. Even when assailants are charged, 'convictions are rarely obtained since reliable testimony is unavailable' (Porporino, Doherty, and Sawatsky, 1987: 125).

Limitations of official records restrict and impair our knowledge and comprehension of prison violence. Therefore, '[S]ystematically

Table 9.5: **Definitions of Major Security Incidents**

Murder
Death other than natural, accidental or suicide. There is clear evidence of foul play.

Hostage-Taking
The unlawful seizure and confinement of person(s) against their will and normally entailing demands for concessions made through a third party.

Suicide
The deliberate taking of one's life.

Assault on Staff
A deliberate attack on an employee, either contract, term or indeterminate.

Assault on Inmate
A deliberate attack on an inmate or inmates (victim).

Inmate Fight
A mutual physical altercation between two or more inmates where an instigator cannot be clearly identified. It is not an assault in such a case. Both parties are instigators. There are no victims in a fight.

Major Disturbance—Riot / Smash-Up
An incident that greatly disrupts the daily activities of an institution due to violence or other behaviour and requires the lock-up of the whole inmate population. For example, riots resulting in extensive property damage, large groups of inmates refusing to work or refusing to return to their cells.

Escape from Medium or Higher Security
The unlawful departure from the confines or property of an institution of medium or higher security level.

Escape from CSC Escort
The unlawful flight of an inmate from the custody of a person lawfully escorting the inmate for CSC during an authorized absence from the institution.

Major
There is clear evidence that the instigator caused serious bodily harm to the victim. Injury to the victim is of a serious nature (e.g. unconsciousness, broken bones, knife wounds, cuts requiring numerous sutures, internal injuries, etc.). The victim requires medical treatment and is unable to continue normal routine for any period of time. The injury may result in death or long-term disability.

SOURCE: CSC (1992) *Definitions of Major Security Incidents*. Ottawa: Correctional Services of Canada.

improving the quality of information which is recorded must be a first step in advancing our understanding of violence in prisons' (Porporino and Marton, 1983: 5). Unfortunately, despite these limitations, official government data are still the only sources of information available to researchers.

As indicated in Table 9.6, major security incidents, including murders, major assaults on staff or inmates, and fights, appear to be relatively rare. The national totals for 1992–93 show 6 murders, 6 major assaults on staff, 53 major assaults on inmates, and 11 major fights. Nevertheless, inmates still face a higher risk of being murdered inside prison than outside. Furthermore, according to Porporino, Doherty, and Sawatsky (1987: 133), 'this risk seems to have increased over time and is not showing any evidence of diminishing.'

Table 9.7 presents the national totals of minor security incidents, for 1984–93, including minor assaults on staff or inmates and minor fights. Official statistics show that much of the violence in prisons takes the form of minor security incidents. In 1992–93, the totals were 134 minor assaults on staff, 206 assaults on inmates, and 202 minor fights.

According to the csc (1992: 3), 'The good news is that violence directed toward staff has been decreasing steadily over the last few years; the bad news is that violence directed toward inmates has not.' csc officials note that 28.6 per cent of the assaults against inmates were drug-related (e.g., drug debts, under the influence, etc.), and 19 per cent were retaliatory in nature (reacting to a previous incident of physical or verbal abuse). However, official statistics greatly underestimate the extent of victimization. In an attempt to determine more accurately the incidence of assaults on inmates, Cooley (1992) initiated the Prison Victimization Project. This survey reveals that the incidence rate for assaults (excluding threats) was approximately six times higher than reported in the official statistics (see Figure 9.2) (Cooley, 1992).

Cooley's survey not only provides crucial data about the prevalence of assaults in prison, but also introduces valuable qualitative information about the nature of prison victimization. In particular, he tested the popular notion of the inmate code outlined by Sykes and Messinger (1960), who suggested that inmates conform to a set of behavioural rules. These rules—and their enforcement—are assumed to be deeply ingrained in the prison culture. According to Sykes and Messinger, the following maxims are the most pronounced features of the inmate code:

(1) Don't interfere with others.
(2) Refrain from arguments with fellow prisoners.
(3) Don't exploit inmates.
(4) Don't weaken.
(5) Don't give respect to guards or the world they represent.

Table 9.6: **Major Security Incidents — National Totals**

	1984–85	1985–86	1986–87	1987–88	1988–89	1989–90	1990–91	1991–92	1992–93
Murders – Staff[a]	2	0	0	0	0	0	0	0	0
Murders – Inmates[a]	8	5	11	4	5	2	5	4	6
Hostage-taking[a]	10	6	6	1	3	7	4	4	2
Suicides[a]	21	18	15	10	12	10	11	16	10
Major assaults – Staff[a]	8	10	4	1	4	3	4	2	6
Major assaults on inmates[a]	43	48	36	36	27	37	45	63	53
Major fights[a]	7	7	5	1	2	4	5	7	11
Major disturbances	1	7	3	11	3	0	4	5	6
Escapes – Major security	3	0	2	0	2	1	3	0	0
Escapes – Medium security	27	25	17	10	8	9	11	6	6
Escapes from escorts – Maximum Security	3	3	5	5	2	3	5	2	0
Major security incidents – Totals	133	129	104	79	68	76	97	109	100
Major violent incidents – Totals	99	94	77	53	53	63	74	96	88

[a]Major Violent Incident: This sub-category of major security incidents includes: murders of staff, murders of inmates, hostage-takings, suicides, major assaults on staff, major assaults on inmates, and major fights between inmates.

SOURCE: CSC (1993) *Major Security Incidents National Trends*. Ottawa: Correctional Services of Canada.

Table 9.7: **Minor Security Incidents in Federal Institutions — National Totals**

	1984–85	1985–86	1986–87	1987–88	1988–89	1989–90	1990–91	1991–92	1992–93
Death – Natural causes	15	9	11	8	15	11	10	22	11
Minor disturbance	202	171	127	128	254	193	209	166	54
Minor assault – Staff	127	117	147	129	132	101	127	101	134
Minor assault – Inmate	212	184	218	217	211	257	276	233	206
Minor fight – Inmate	150	179	217	212	234	267	210	235	202
Attempted suicide	77	51	49	53	64	44	54	52	46
Self-inflicted injury	382	229	292	244	267	254	277	192	225
Hunger strike	24	30	63	36	46	45	58	46	18
Walkaway from minimum	142	104	124	106	89	96	120	160	159
Walkaway from CCC	21	5	4	3	8	1	14	11	13
Escape, escort medium	17	15	19	9	18	12	7	12	11
Escape, escort minimum	10	13	8	8	7	8	8	4	10
Escape plot preparation	7	14	12	15	9	5	6	15	10
Attempted escape (ml-max)	10	7	9	6	7	8	6	5	3
Attempted escape (med)	40	25	17	17	13	19	13	17	8
Fire	102	76	103	78	79	62	74	60	64
Totals	1542	1231	1423	1272	1454	1384	1474	1337	1178

SOURCE: CSC (1993) *Minor Security Incidents in Federal Institutions*. Ottawa: Correctional Services of Canada.

Other rules of the inmate code were said to include 'don't break your word', 'don't steal', and 'never rat'. Sykes and Messinger (1960) argued that adherence to this code promotes solidarity among inmates, and that this cohesion leads to greater stability and less violence among prisoners.

However, the Prison Victimization Project found little evidence of the traditional inmate code. Rather, it detected a different set of informal rules of social control. Although these informal rules borrowed from the traditional code, new themes were also evident.

Unlike the traditional code, which was assumed to solidify the inmate society, the informal rules discerned in these institutions exhibited dialectical tendencies. According to Cooley (1992: 33), 'Each element of the informal rules of social control brings the prison population toward social cohesion and, at the same time, separates and atomizes them.' Thus one effect of the informal rules is to create an inmate society that is 'partially unstable' (p. 33).

Inmates reported feeling alienated because of the contradictory nature of the informal rules. For example, they are expected to keep to themselves and 'do their own time'. Yet the resulting isolation curtails communication, and discourages inmates from seeking the assistance of others. Further alienation stems from the informal rules to 'not trust anyone', 'avoid the prison economy', and 'show respect'. Moreover,

Figure 9.2: **Comparison of Survey and Official Data on Assault Rates per 1,000 Inmates**

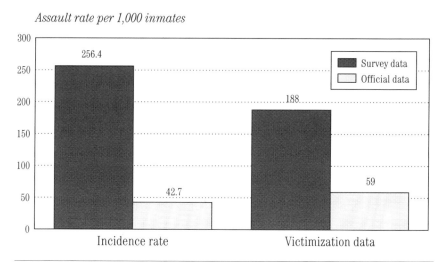

NOTE: Data exclude threats.

SOURCE: Cooley (1992).

violation of the informal rules leads to greater alienation because the brutal nature of enforcement 'tends to destabilize and atomize prisoners' (Cooley, 1992: 34). These conclusions are consistent with Porporino, Doherty, and Sawatsky's (1987) study, which detected a shift in the motives of prison homicide. That is, recent inmate murder victims are killed more often for revenge, or because of some involvement in drug trafficking (especially default on debts) within the prison. Moreover, Porporino et al. note that, owing to the drug trade inside institutions, these murders are more 'calculated and focused' (1987: 134) than in previous years. This finding suggests an increase in instrumental violence and incentive-motivated aggression at the individual level.

Increasing fragmentation of the inmate society leads to isolation, alienation, suspicion, and fear, all of which contribute to the reproduction of violence. Moreover, such fragmentation is perpetuated by the brutality that permeates the underground economy based on drugs and other contraband. Like its counterpart outside, the drug trade inside prisons has not only economic but political and ideological components as well. The economic aspect is obvious: the goal is the accumulation of profit and related material gain. In its political aspect, drug trafficking is a means of enhancing power and social status within the inmate society. Finally, there is an ideological dimension to the drug trade in that misbehaviour—defaulting on debts, or invading someone else's 'turf'—is regarded as so contemptible that violent retaliation appears justified. In fact, it is hardly surprising that the violent, predatory nature of the drug market inside prison mirrors the one outside, since many inmates have been intimately involved with the drug trade in the 'free world'.

Again, however, it is important to emphasize that rates of violence inside prison exceed those outside. Cooley compares the rates of victimization in five prisons and in the community as reported by the General Social Survey (Statistics Canada, 1990):

> The General Social Survey reported an overall rate of personal victimization (for robbery, sexual assault and assault, including threats) of 90 per 1,000 males over the age of 15. The rate for males aged 15 to 24 was 214 per 1,000. The comparable rate for similar personal victimizations in the five prisons was dramatically higher at 538.46 per 1,000. (Cooley, 1992: 32)

Moreover, as we have seen, the risk of being murdered is far greater for male inmates than for men in the community (Porporino, Doherty, and Sawatsky, 1987: 133; Jayewardene and Doherty, 1985).

Why does violence continue to be reproduced in Canadian prisons? The answer lies not only in institutional problems but in the sociopolitical forces at work in the larger society.

A SOCIOPOLITICAL APPROACH

Taking a sociopolitical approach to the reproduction of prison violence requires that we acknowledge the longstanding contradictions evident in both society as well as in correctional institutions. At the societal level, the contradictions become clearer when a sociopolitical comparison between Canada and similar advanced capitalist democracies is made. The renewed war on crime in the United States, for instance, is taking place 'in the absence of either social programs to deal with the immediate casualties of [US] capitalism or political strategies to change the social structures that spawn them . . .' (Lowman and MacLean, 1991: 134–5). Even though Canada faces different social-structural conditions, and its prison population is growing at a slower rate than in the United States, Lowman and MacLean (1991) profess that the same fundamental contradictions exist. Further, both the United States and Canada compound these contradictions by imposing increasingly punitive sanctions on offenders and by utilizing incarceration as a crime control strategy. The problem here is that imprisonment rates fluctuate independent of crime rates.

In recognizing such contradictions at the institutional level, Lowman and MacLean (1991: 130) assert: 'Prison seems either to produce or reinforce the very behaviour it is supposed to "correct".' This means that policies and strategies often fail to correct the contradictions that result in the reproduction of violence in prison. However, before we address the institutional contradictions, let us first elaborate on the sociopolitical aspects of the social order as they pertain to crime control.

During the 1980s, a significant response to the deeper social, political, and economic crises in the United States and Britain was the evolution of the law-and-order campaign. Several observers tracked the emergence of the law-and-order movement, noting that it represents the rise of the New Right in advanced capitalist nations (Horton, 1981; Ratner and McMullen, 1983). 'Their argument is that issues surrounding crime and punishment have been mobilized by the New Right to generate an "authoritarian consensus" that legitimates a more repressive and "exceptional" response by the state to the problems created by the global crisis of capitalism' (Comack, 1990: 71).

In the United States and Britain, the rise of the New Right took the form of Reaganism and Thatcherism, respectively. Whether the New Right and the law-and-order movement achieved the same level of dominance in Canada continues to be debated. Taylor (1987, 1985, 1983) is not convinced that Canada has experienced a similar 'shift to the Right'. However, Comack (1990, 1987, 1983) contends that Taylor's analysis is based on a 'British model' of capital-labour and state relations. 'Consequently, when Taylor addresses the Canadian situation there is a tendency to look for similar types of expressions as found in Britain. Unable to find them, he concludes that they are dwarfed, moribund, or retarded, when in fact they are *different* rather than *absent*' (Comack, 1990: 92).

With this mind, let us elaborate on the sociopolitical approach as it relates to hegemony and the maintenance and reproduction of capitalist social relations. In the work of Gramsci (1971), Hall (1979), and Hall, Critcher, Jefferson, and Roberts (1978), it is proposed that advanced capitalist nations structure the social order by relying on a mode of hegemonic control. However, when normal mechanisms for securing consent grow weary, due to economic crisis, the state resorts to more coercive and repressive mechanisms. Nevertheless, the state cannot simply resort to 'naked force' in achieving this 'shift to the Right'; rather, consent is manufactured so that increasingly repressive measures appear legitimate (Comack, 1990: 73).

The mode of hegemonic control in the United States and Britain must be viewed in its proper context—that is, in terms of economic crisis. The global crisis of capitalism is characterized by high rates of unemployment and inflation, and economic stagnation exacerbated by a world-wide recession. In response to this, the New Right reveals its economic and political agenda. Borrowing from Horton (1981) and Dixon (1981), Comack summarizes: '*Economically*, the New Right is associated with the policies of "austerity capitalism"; a stepped up exploitation of labour and a reduction of the standard of living in order to improve opportunities for capital accumulation' (1990: 74). In the pursuit of capital accumulation, the state not only abandons its responsibility to the subordinate classes, but with paradoxical compliance (via manufactured consent) expands its repressive apparatus (i.e., the criminal justice system) to control the working and lower classes.

To varying degrees, Ratner and McMullen (1983) note that all three countries—Canada, the United States, and Britain—have experienced a crisis of hegemony and turned toward more coercive and repressive mechanisms of social control. Yet, Ratner and McMullen, as well as Taylor (1987, 1985, 1983), propose that Canada departs from the United States and Britain with respect to the use of law-and-order propaganda for ideological purposes.

Canada, indeed, has become more conservative over the past several decades; 'shifts to the Right' (Ross, 1992) have taken place gradually without a polarizing political movement. According to Panitch and Swartz (1988), after World War II, organized labour entered into an agreement with the state that marked their participation as subordinate players in Canada's capitalist democracy. In return for abdicating much of their power, organized labour believed they would obtain security for workers needed for years to come. However, in the mid-1960s, an economic crisis forced the state to reconsider its promise to organized labour. Since labour leaders had previously surrendered much of their leverage decades earlier, they were held at a distinct disadvantage, which marked a shift from consent to coercion. As a result, the state became more coercive in attempts to subordinate labour, while expanding its repressive apparatus as well.

Contrary to Taylor's depiction of Canada as a secure, quintessentially bourgeois social formation, Panitch and Swartz emphatically declare that Canada *has* mediated the capital-labour relation. Because such realignments took place years before the emergence of Reaganism and Thatcherism, it may appear to some observers that a 'shift to the Right' had not occurred at all. Comack (1991: 95) concludes that 'it would seem that the Canadian case is not so much the "anomaly" that it first appeared. Like other nation-states, Canada has been confronted with the dilemma of maintaining the hegemonic control of capital under increasing economic restraints.' Moreover, much of the sociopolitical realignment occurred without salient law-and-order references, though one of the consequences was an expansion of the criminal justice system.

A sociopolitical approach also must recognize that an expansion of the criminal justice system (and support for reinstating the death penalty) is very often approved by the general population. The preponderance of support stems from the lower-middle, working, and lower classes—sectors of the population which are the most socially and economically insecure, in times of economic crisis. Taylor (1983) and Comack (1990) suggest that such support is metaphorical in nature, reflecting their general anxiety of social and economic insecurity more than their fear of violent crime. This consent, however, reveals significant aspects of hegemonic control insofar as expansion of the criminal justice system (and more punitive sentences) are viewed by the masses as 'common-sensical'. That is, imposing increasingly punitive sanctions against criminals seems practical and just. Such consent not only adds legitimacy to the state, but also deflects attention away from more structural problems related to the political economy (Ratner and McMullen, 1983). This political diversion is functional insofar as it deters citizens from questioning the fundamental tendencies and problems of advanced capitalism.

The fundamental tendencies of advanced capitalism are deeply entrenched in contradictions, especially with regard to unemployment and the growth of the surplus population. For instance, a close look at advanced capitalism reveals that unemployment is an expected part of its normal operations:

> As capitalism ages, technological advancements render certain forms of labor obsolete. As higher profits are sought in production, labour saving technology is employed which frees individuals from the workplace, thus swelling the size of the surplus

population. Under these circumstances, economic growth creates unemployment, and unemployment increases both crime and imprisonment. (Lynch and Groves, 1989: 121; see also Michalowski, 1985)

In sum, the expansion of the state's social control apparatus involves strengthening the criminal justice and correctional systems in order to regulate the surplus population—in particular, those who have been economically marginalized by the normal operations of advanced capitalism. Additionally, there are significant cultural and ideological features of capitalist society which serve to further deflect serious questioning of the prevailing economic order. That is, both success (employment, prosperity, wealth and other material accumulation) and failure (unemployment, poverty, homelessness, substance abuse, and resorting to street crime) are defined in highly individualistic terms: people are perceived to succeed or fail in life due to their own efforts and merit. Such an individualistic approach avoids references to the existing social order and how it facilitates opportunities for the upper classes while obstructing opportunities for the middle and lower classes.

Turning to contradictions at the institutional level, it is fitting that we once again acknowledge the point offered by Lowman and MacLean (1991) who argue that prisons tend to reinforce the very behaviour they are designed to reverse. As discussed earlier, violence in prisons is attributed to several sources: the drug traffic, violent offenders, the importation of violent behaviour, the conditions of confinement which foster violence, etc. In light of these sources of violence it is also useful to apply the sociopolitical approach to institutional violence.

Much of the crime and violent victimization in society generally takes place among those occupying the same social class, with a disproportionate number of incidents occurring among members of the lower classes. Instead of directing violence vertically at the upper classes, this pattern of victimization maintains a horizontal trajectory by directing violence against those in the same social class (or those in slightly more elevated social strata). According to Spitzer (1975), this form of criminal victimization is *counter-revolutionary* insofar as antagonism is directed at those who occupy the same social class.

Inmate-inmate violence in prison generally conforms to this pattern of counter-revolutionary victimization. Only in cases of large scale disturbances and riots do such forms of violence (or the threat of violence) constitute a form of revolutionary activity. And in these cases, it is important that relevant social and institutional demands be specified (i.e., the conditions of confinement, improved services), thereby initiating institutional reform.

Regarding the reproduction of violence in Canadian prisons, the work of Spitzer (1975) also adds critical insight. At the societal level, Spitzer notes: 'Victimization is permitted and even encouraged, as long as the victims are members of an expendable class' (1975: 645). Similarly, at the institutional level, Culhane (1985: 50) quotes a statement from the Coalition for Prisoners' Rights, Santa Fe: 'Violence and tension between prisoners is encouraged by prison managers as a tool to control and distract prisoners from the conditions of their confinement.'

POLICIES AND STRATEGIES DESIGNED TO CONTROL PRISON VIOLENCE

Over the past several decades, the Correctional Services of Canada has implemented an elaborate classification system. A major feature of this system is a strategy known as *cascading*: 'the gradual reclassification of prisoners downward through a series of security levels' (Lowman and MacLean, 1991: 144). Understandably, the possibility of being transferred to a lower-security facility provides a significant incentive for inmates to comply with prison rules. Thus cascading serves as another form of prisoner control, enhancing security and reducing the potential for violence.

This system works two ways, however. Indeed, it tends to ensure that every new classification of lower security is balanced by one of greater security. As Lowman and MacLean (1991: 145) point out:

> The logic is that there must always be a more restrictive set of conditions into which a prisoner can be thrust when she or he does not 'respond well' in a less restrictive setting. Seen from this perspective, what appears to be a move toward less restrictive prison regimes and more humane settings is actually complemented by a move toward more restrictive regimes and less humane settings.

In addition, during the 1970s and 1980s the CSC attempted to improve prisoner control by bolstering its restrictive regimes. In particular, it increased its reliance on administrative segregation of inmates (a trend also taking place in American prison systems), introducing 'super' maximum-security facilities (at Millhaven and Quebec) and Special Handling Units (SHUs). In practice, however, these new facilities have aggravated the very problems they were designed to avoid (Lowman and MacLean, 1991: 146). For example, if Special Handling Units are supposed to reduce the incidence of rule-violations and disruptions, then one would expect that over time fewer inmates would have to be held in them. Yet just the reverse has taken place: 'The proportion of the population housed in higher-security institutions is proof enough of this' (Lowan and MacLean, 1991: 146). Moreover, 'Conflict over rules, harassment, and physical conditions ensure that once there, prisoners are likely to remain for a long time . . .' (Lowman and MacLean, 1991: 147).

The procedures by which prisoners are assigned to SHUs have also shifted toward greater repression. Initially, a committee reviewed such transfers which were usually justified on the grounds that an inmate had become incorrigible, had seriously assaulted or murdered another person, had escaped, or had been involved in some other major incident. More recently, a *proactive* strategy has been implemented whereby a prisoner may be perceived as a threat and transferred without having committed a serious violation (Lowman and MacLean, 1991). The SHUs impose solitary confinement upon inmates by caging them in cells approximately 6 by 11 feet for 23½ hours per day; the stay may last weeks, months, and in some cases, years. Confinement in SHUs, even those more modern in construction, has been described by inmates as 'being buried alive in an all-steel pressure-cooker' (Culhane, 1985: 21). Prisoners often are denied adequate meals and sufficient exercise while subjected to the psychological and emotional torment of isolation. Culhane (1985: 18) has cited numerous abuses in 'the hole' over the years, and reports that in many instances (at the British Columbia penitentiary, for instance) inmates were 'hosed down and deprived of food, clothing, and heat' (see also Lowman and MacLean, 1991). In sum, such conditions perpetuate conflict between prisoners and their keepers (see Lowman and MacLean, 1991: 146).

As another form of inmate control, the CSC has expanded its use of protective custody for inmates convicted of sex offences, informants, prisoners who have accrued substantial gambling and drug debts, and those who feel ill-equipped to defend themselves. The use of protective custody divides the inmate population into two antagonistic groups that take out their hostilities on one another rather than on the guards whose behaviour is usually responsible for their anger (Lowman and MacLean, 1991: 151). This 'divide and conquer' strategy not only prevents the development of solidarity among inmates, but, as Culhane (1985: 169) points out, strengthens control by 'relegating an entire section of the prison population to the most despised status of rapists and informers'.

However, Lowman and MacLean suggest that such a manipulation of prisoner society still has the potential ultimately to produce solidarity leading to revolutionary violence:

> at some point, prisoners must become conscious of the way in which their self-classification is manipulated by prison authorities as a form of control. Thus, while the expansion of protective custody may be seen as a divisive policy aimed at inhibiting the

development of a prisoner culture based on solidarity, it may potentially create such prisoner solidarity. If and when this occurs, one might predict that a new wave of militant, violence resistance to the oppressive nature of control practices in Canadian prisons will be directed outwardly toward the prison regime rather than inwardly toward the prison culture. (1991: 151)

Another violence-control strategy that has been criticized is the practice of moving disruptive inmates from one institution to another rather than dealing with the conditions that lead to violent behaviour (Porporino, 1986: 234). Pointing to the failure of the traditional policies of segregation and surveillance, Porporino (1986: i) recommends that 'counter-measures' be implemented that would make violence less necessary, useful, and acceptable. To promote positive inmate behaviour, peaceful conflict resolution, and less stressful interactions between prison staff and inmates, he suggests the following: conflict management, crisis intervention training for staff members, reducing transiency by improving classification and matching of inmates with prison environments and sub-environments, anger-management training for violence-prone inmates, and development of a prison disruption index to monitor the tension levels in institutions.

In sum, the prevailing practice of incarceration is contradictory. Because of the overarching antagonism between the keepers and the kept, and the way institutional practices reinforce such hostility, it is unlikely that an increasingly repressive prison regime can contribute to the CSC's goal of protecting society 'by actively encouraging and assisting offenders to become law-abiding citizens while exercising reasonable, safe, secure, and humane control' (1991: 6). Moreover, since most prisoners eventually do return to society, the larger correctional enterprise is inherently self-defeating insofar as it fails to prepare them to lead law-abiding lives upon release.

Finally, however, the only effective solution lies in correcting the larger social conditions that serve to marginalize large segments of the general population, leaving them at the mercy of the state's social control apparatus (i.e., the criminal justice system): for example, the economic arrangements that continue to force large numbers of young single men into unemployment.

CONCLUSION

The purpose of this chapter was to take a sociopolitical approach to the reproduction of violence in Canadian prisons. In doing so, several key points were made. Collective violence (riots and disturbances) tends to be instrumental (based on incentive-motivated aggression) insofar as such incidents are typically goal-oriented, usually toward institutional reform. Moreover, incidents of collective violence (as well as peaceful demonstrations) which were motivated by efforts of institutional reform often result from prisoner solidarity. One must not overlook the sociopolitical context of the civil rights and prisoners' rights movement which emerged in the early 1970s. Such a movement was emblematic of rising political consciousness among prisoners, prison reformers, and their supporters.

Individual violence among inmates (assaults and other types of victimization), however, stem from the fragmentation of the prisoner society which is commonly related to the underground economy; in particular, to the violent drug market. Individual violence, too, is instrumental insofar as assaults based on revenge (due to a defaulted drug debt or to defend commercial territory or 'turf') are planned, calculated, and focused. The drug market in the 'free world' shares common sociopolitical forces with the drug market inside prison. The drug market in the 'free world' is, in part, a symptom of social inequality and diminishing opportunity for legitimate economic survival. Indeed, similar financial motives for engaging in the underground economy exist in prison.

Nevertheless, both collective and individual violence are produced and reproduced by repressive prison practices. Such correctional practices are dialectically contradictory and self-defeating, meaning that they tend to reinforce or reproduce the very behaviour which they set out to correct (see Welch, 1996a; 1996b).

Reiman (1995) raises several questions about the role of corrections in society, and in the context of prison violence, he helps us identify and confront institutional conditions and the negative effects of incarceration. He proposes that prisons should be both *civilized* and *civilizing*. One can hardly conclude that violent prisons are civilized, a point which should concern us since most inmates eventually return to society. If prisoners do not become more civilized during their incarceration, how can citizens feel safe when inmates are released back into society?

NOTE

The author gratefully acknowledges the assistance of Marie Mark and Carrissa Griffing in preparing the final version of this manuscript.

REFERENCES

Abbott, Jack Henry (1981). *In the Belly of the Beast: Letters from Prison.* New York: Vintage Books.

American Correctional Association (1991). *Riots and Disturbances in Correctional Institutions.* College Park, MD: American Correctional Association.

Annual Report of the Commissioner of Penitentiaries, 1949 (1950). Ottawa: King's Printer.

Attica: The Official Report of the New York State Commission (1972). New York: Bantam Books.

Baehre, R. (1977). 'Origins of the Penitentiary System in Upper Canada', *Ontario History* 69: 185–207.

Beattie, John M. (1977). *Attitudes towards Crime and Punishment in Upper Canada, 1830–1850: A Documentary Study.* University of Toronto, Criminology.

Bollomo, J.J. (1972). 'Upper Canadians' attitudes towards crime and punishment, 1832–1851', *Ontario History* 64: 11–26.

Bowker, Lee (1985). 'An essay on prison violence'. In M. Braswell, S. Dillingham, and R. Montgomery, eds, *Prison Violence in America.* Cincinnati: Anderson.

Chunn, D.E. (1981). 'Good men work hard: Convict labour in Kingston Penitentiary, 1835–1850'. *Canadian Criminology Forum* 4: 13–22.

Clements, Carl B. (1979). 'Overcrowded prisons: A review of the psychological and environmental effects', *Law and Human Behaviour* 3, 3: 217–25.

——— (1982). 'The relationship of offender classification to the problem of prison overcrowding', *Crime and Delinquency* 28: 72–81.

Clemmer, Donald (1940). *The Prison Community.* New York: Holt, Rinehart, and Winston.

Cloward, Richard (1969). 'Social control in prison'. In L. Hazelrigg, ed., *Prison Within Society.* New York: Doubleday.

Cohen, Albert K. (1976). 'Prison violence: A sociological perspective'. In Cohen, G.F. Cole, and R.G. Baily, eds, *Prison Violence.* Lexington, MA: Lexington Books.

Coles, D. (1979). *Nova Scotia Corrections—An Historical Perspective.* Halifax Communications Project in Criminal Justice, Correctional Services Division.

Comack, Elizabeth (1990). 'Law-and-order issues in the Canadian context: The case of capital punishment', *Social Justice* 17, 1: 70–97.

Cooley, Dennis (1992). 'Prison victimization and the informal rules of social control', *Forum on Corrections Research* 4, 3: 31–6.

Correctional Services of Canada (1991). *Basic Facts About Corrections in Canada, 1991.* Ottawa: Correctional Service of Canada.

————— (1992). 'Violence and suicide in Canadian institutions: Some recent statistics', *Forum on Corrections Research* 4, 3: 3–5.

Culhane, Claire (1985). *Still Barred From Prison.* Vancouver: Black Rose Books.

Dixon, Marlene (1981). 'World capitalist crisis and the rise of the right', *Contemporary Marxism* 4 (Winter).

Eckstedt, John W., and Curt Griffiths (1988). *Corrections in Canada: Policy and Practice,* 2nd ed. Toronto: Butterworths.

Edmison, J.A. (1970). 'Perspective in corrections', *Canadian Journal of Corrections* 12: 534–48.

Ellis, Desmond (1984). 'Crowding and prison violence: Integration of research and theory', *Criminal Justice and Behaviour* 11: 277–308.

Ellis, Desmond, H. Grasmick, and B. Gilman (1974). 'Violence in prisons: A sociological analysis', *American Journal of Sociology* 80: 16–34.

Fingard, J. (1984). 'Jailbirds in mid-Victorian Halifax'. Pp. 81–102 in T.G. Barnes et al., eds, *Law in a Colonial Society: The Nova Scotia Experience.* Toronto: Carswell.

————— (1989). *The Dark Side of Life in Victorian Halifax.* Porter's Lake, NS: Pottersfield Press.

Gladstone, Jane, Richard V. Ericson, and Clifford D. Shearing (1991). *Criminology: A Reader's Guide.* Toronto: Centre of Criminology.

Gosselin, Luc (1982) *Prisons in Canada.* Montreal: Black Rose Books.

Gramsci, Antonio (1977). *Selections From the Prison Notebooks.* New York: International Publishers.

Griffiths, Curt, J.F. Klein, and S.N. Verdun Jones (1980). *Criminal Justice in Canada: An Introductory Text.* Vancouver: Butterworths.

Griffiths, Curt and Simon Verdun-Jones (1989). *Canadian Criminal Justice.* Toronto: Butterworths.

Gurr, Ted Robert (1989). *Violence in America,* 3rd ed. Newbury Park, CA: Sage.

Hall, Stuart (1977). *Drifting Into A Law and Order Society.* Great Britain: Cobden Trust.

Hall, Stuart, Chas Critcher, Tony Jefferson, and Brian Roberts (1978). *Policing the Crisis: Mugging, the State and Law and Order.* London: Macmillan.

Horton, John (1981) 'The rise of the right: A global view', *Crime and Social Justice* 15: 7–17.

Houston, S.E. (1972). 'Politics, schools and social change in Upper Canada', *Canadian Historical Review* 53: 249–71.

——— (1974). 'The impetus to reform: Urban crime, poverty and ignorance in Ontario, 1850–1875'. PhD thesis, University of Toronto.

Hylton, J.H. (1981). 'The growth of punishment: Imprisonment and community corrections in Canada', *Crime and Social Justice* 15: 18–28.

Jackson, Margaret A. and Curt T. Griffiths (1991). *Canadian Criminology: Perspectives on Crime and Criminality.* Toronto: Harcourt Brace Jovanovich.

Jayewardene, C., and P. Doherty (1985). 'Individual violence in Canadian penitentiaries', *Canadian Journal of Criminology* 27, 4 (October): 429–39.

Kolb, Charles E.M. (1982). *A Report to the International Human Rights Law Group.* Washington, DC: International Human Rights Group.

Lowman, John, and Brian MacLean (1991). 'Prisons and protest in Canada', *Social Justice* 18, 3: 130–54.

Lynch, Michael J., and W. Byron Groves (1989). *A Primer in Radical Criminology*, 2nd ed. New York: Harrow and Heston.

MacGuigan, M. (Chair) (1977). Sub-Committee on the Penitentiary System in Canada. *Report to Parliament.* Ottawa: Ministry of Supply and Service.

McMahon, Maeve (1992). *The Persistent Prison.* Toronto: University of Toronto Press.

Palmer, B.D. (1980). 'Kingston mechanics and the rise of the penitentiary, 1833–1836', *Social History* 13: 7–32.

Panitch, Leo, and Donald Swartz (1988). *Assault on Trade Union Freedoms.* Toronto: Garamond Press.

Phillips, Jim (1991). 'The history of Canadian criminal justice, 1750–1920'. Pp. 65–124 in J. Gladstone, R. Ericson, and C. Shearing, eds, *Criminology: A Reader's Guide.* Toronto: Centre of Criminology, University of Toronto.

Porporino, Frank J. (1986). 'Managing violent individuals in correctional settings', *Journal of Interpersonal Violence* 1, 2: 213–37.

Porporino, Frank J., Phyllis D. Doherty, and Terrence Sawatsky (1987). 'Characteristics of homicide victims and victimizations in prisons: A Canadian historical perspective', *International Journal of Offender Therapy and Comparative Criminology* 31, 2: 125–35.

Porporino, Frank J., and Kimberly Dudley (1984). *An Analysis of the Effects of Overcrowding in Canadian Penitentiaries.* Ottawa: Correctional Services of Canada.

Porporino, Frank J., and John P. Marton (1983). *Strategies to Reduce Prison Violence.* Ottawa: Correctional Services of Canada.

Ratner, R.S., and John McMullen (1983). 'Social control and the rise of the "exceptional state" in Britain, the United States, and Canada', *Crime and Social Justice* 19: 31–43.

Reiman, Jeffrey (1995). *The Rich Get Richer and the Poor Get Prison*, 4th ed. New York: Macmillan.

Ross, Jeffrey Ian (1992). 'Contemporary radical right-wing violence in Canada: A quantitative analysis', *Terrorism and Political Violence* 4, 3: 72–101.

Skinner, S.J., M. Dreidger, and B. Grainger (1981). *Corrections: An Historical Perspective of the Saskatchewan Experience*. Regina: Canadian Plains Research Centre, University of Regina.

Smandych, Russel C., and Simon N. Verdun Jones (1982). 'The evolution of institutional mechanisms of social control in Ontario: An examination of the evidence and interpretations'. Unpublished paper. Burnaby, BC: Department of Criminology, Simon Fraser University.

Spitzer, Steven (1975). 'Toward a Marxian theory of deviance', *Social Problems* 22: 638–51.

Statistics Canada (1990). 'Patterns of victimization in Canada', *General Social Survey Series*. Ottawa: Statistics Canada.

Sykes, Gresham (1958). *The Society of Captives: A Study of a Maximum Security Prison*. Princeton, NJ: Princeton University Press.

Sykes, Gresham and Sheldon L. Messinger (1960). 'The inmate social system'. In R. Cloward et al., eds, *Theoretical Studies in the Social Organization of the Prison*. New York: Social Science Research Council.

Taylor, C.J. (1979). 'The Kingston, Ontario penitentiary and moral architecture', *Social History* XII: 385–408.

Taylor, Ian (1983). *Crime, Capitalism and Community: Three Essays in Socialist Criminology*. Toronto: Butterworth.

——— (1987). 'Theorizing the crisis in Canada'. In R. Ratner and J. McMullen, eds, *State Control: Criminal Justice Politics in Canada*. Vancouver: UBC Press.

——— (1985). 'Criminology, the unemployment crisis and the liberal tradition in Canada: The need for socialist analysis and policy'. In T. Fleming, ed., *The New Criminologies in Canada*. Toronto: Oxford.

Toch, Hans (1977). *Living in Prison*. New York: Free Press.

——— (1985). 'Social climate and prison violence'. In M. Braswell, S. Dillingham, and R. Montgomery, eds, *Prison Violence in America*. Cincinnati: Anderson Publishing.

Torrance, Judy (1975). 'Cultural factors and the response of government to violence'. PhD dissertation, York University.

Welch, Michael (1994). 'Jail overcrowding: Social sanitation and the ware-housing of the urban underclass'. Pp. 249–74 in A. Roberts, ed, *Critical Issues in Crime and Justice.* Thousand Oaks, CA: Sage.

—— (1996a). *Corrections: A Critical Approach.* New York: McGraw-Hill.

—— (1996b). 'Prison violence in America: Past, present, and future'. In R. Muraskin and A. Roberts, eds, *Visions for Change: Crime and Justice and the Twenty-First Century.* Englewood Cliffs, NJ: Prentice-Hall.

Zillman, D. (1978). *Hostility and Aggression.* Hillsdale, NJ: Lawrence Earlbaum Associates.

Chapter Ten

TERRORISM IN CANADA, 1960–1992

ANTHONY KELLETT

Terrorism is a highly publicized form of political action, but it does not appear to be correspondingly well-understood. In May 1984, a headline in the Ottawa *Citizen* proclaimed: 'Every terrorist group here: Kaplan' (quoting the then Solicitor General). Four months later a story in *The Globe and Mail* was headlined 'Canada rates low in survey of terror' (*Citizen*, 12 May 1994, 10; *Globe and Mail*, 22 Sept. 1984: N11). If experts seem divided as to the nature and extent of terrorism in Canada, it is small wonder that the Canadian public appears confused. Public perceptions of terrorism in this country seem to be influenced by a belief that 'it can't happen here', a view reflective not only of the 'peaceable kingdom' myth, but more importantly of an absence of data on the Canadian variety of this global phenomenon.

To rectify the latter source of confusion, this chapter will examine data from a new, open-source database developed by the National Security Coordination Centre (NSCC) of Solicitor General Canada, and from a variety of secondary sources. The discussion will be divided into two main sections, the first treating domestic incidents and the second dealing with events occurring here but relating (mainly in their targeting) to conflicts in other countries. As a means of shedding further light on the nature and extent of terrorism in Canada, the penultimate section will examine the experience of other countries.

'THE PEACEABLE KINGDOM'

There has been a persistent view in modern Canada that this country is a 'peaceable kingdom', largely immune from the civil violence that has characterized other countries (Kellett, 1988: 91). In the 1980s, however, the claim of civil tranquillity increasingly came under critical examination (Torrance, 1986). Yet as evidence accrues that Canada has been less peaceable than is widely believed, one element of modern conflict in Canada still has not received the critical scrutiny needed for public understanding: terrorism. Political, public, media, and even academic knowledge of the extent of this phenomenon in Canada has until very recently been limited. In the absence of information, it becomes easy to assume that few terrorist incidents have occurred in Canada. Thus, in its

1987 report, the Senate Special Committee on Terrorism and the Public Safety (Kelly Committee) observed that in its hearings it 'heard many explanations for Canada's relative freedom from terrorist attack. The explanations largely encompassed what is referred to as the "peaceable kingdom theory" . . .' (Kelly, 1987: 13).

On the other hand, a dearth of data on the incidence of terrorist violence in Canada can lead to exaggeration as well. In 1986 two Canadian participants at a conference on terrorism held at Saint-Jean caused a furore with claims that an extensive left-wing terrorist network existed in Canada, and with predictions of the occurrence of major terrorist attacks in Canada within five years (*The Globe and Mail*, 25 April 1986, A2).

If people somewhat familiar with the phenomenon disagree as to its scope, it is not surprising that Canadian public opinion can be volatile. A poll of Canadians conducted for the Department of External Affairs in July 1985 (shortly after the crash of Air India Flight 182, which was widely attributed to terrorism) found that terrorism ranked fourth among world problems, being cited by 7% of respondents.[1] Another survey for the department, conducted in April 1987, showed that just 1.4% of respondents cited terrorism as the most pressing world issue (Stone, 1988).

THE DATA REQUIREMENT

In 1982 a Canadian authority on terrorism complained that the lack of reliable statistical data made it 'difficult, if not impossible, to derive an accurate picture of the incidence of various forms of terrorism' in Canada (Mitchell, 1982: 5). Several years later, the first Kelly Committee was surprised to discover that 'no department or agency of the federal government maintained an accurate or up-to-date inventory of terrorist incidents for trend analysis purposes, or otherwise to assist policy makers' (Kelly, 1989: 8). However, Canada has not been unique in lacking reliable evidence as to the nature and extent of indigenous terrorism (Schmid and Jongman, 1988: 174).

The operational utility of the kinds of data to which Mitchell referred is obvious. In complementing intelligence and underwriting analysis, such data can facilitate and enrich both threat assessment and incident management by identifying underlying patterns and causes; making it possible to estimate the probabilities of future terrorist activities; and responding to specific queries about terrorist activities. They can identify the individuals and property most at risk, and may influence the deployment of counter-terrorism resources. By identifying patterns of demands, methods, and so on, they can improve decision-making during incidents.

Another important role for accurate data is in public education. Not only does public opinion tend to be volatile, but much terrorist activity is designed to exploit public fears. Thus the potential exists for over-reaction to terrorist attacks. Much of the anti-terrorism legislation in Europe followed in the wake of particularly shocking incidents.[2] Given that these attacks all occurred in the midst of long and lethal terrorist campaigns, the heightened powers assigned to the police in response to them should not be seen in the light of particular incidents alone. Nonetheless, they do indicate the pressures that governments face when public opinion is aroused.

Thus, when a spectacular attack occurs in a country (such as Canada) where the incidence of terrorism has hitherto been relatively low, observers should place the event in the context of the historical scale of terrorist action before concluding that it is necessarily the harbinger of increased terrorism. The same is true of threats of a campaign of terrorism, such as those made by Saddam Hussein during the Gulf War of 1991, which can evoke enormous apprehension in an inadequately informed public.

The absence of the kind of information needed to educate the public as to the nature and scope of the terrorist threat has recently been remedied with the publication of several chronologies or statistical tables. The earlier ones tended to concentrate on the incidence of international terrorism in Canada (in other words, terrorism related to conflicts external to this country) (Kellett, 1981, 1988; Charters, 1986b). The first Canadian database to include incidents of both domestic and international terrorism was produced by Jeffrey Ian Ross; data drawn from it have been reported in several sources (e.g., Kelly, 1987: 7; Ross, 1988; Ross and Gurr, 1989). By far the most extensive database yet constructed of terrorism in Canada is one developed by the research unit of the NSCC; a chronology derived from the database was published at the beginning of 1992 (Kellett et al., 1992, hereafter cited as NSCC 1992). Unless otherwise stated, the statistics reported here are derived from the NSCC database.

METHODOLOGY

At the time of publication of NSCC 1992, the database comprised 428 incidents of terrorism, along with 511 'excluded' events and 93 terrorist support activities. All entries are for the period 1 January 1960 to 31 December 1989, and relate to incidents occurring within Canada. Events that may have originated inside Canada but actually occurred outside the country, such as the bombing at Narita Airport in Japan (23 June 1985), have been excluded.

In Canada terrorism is not defined in any statute, and terrorist acts are treated as criminal behaviour. The NSCC study defined terrorism as comprising acts of serious violence, planned and executed clandestinely, and committed with a clear intention to achieve political ends. Its primary aims are to extort, intimidate, disrupt, publicize, and communicate demands. Thus a terrorist act may involve one or more targets: the physical target(s), the target(s) of demands, and the wider audience. Terrorism is frequently compounded by the threat, implied or explicit, of further violence.

Each apparent incident that met the criteria in this definition was classified as being either domestic or international, depending on the locus of the conflict (Canada or another country) to which it related.

Events were then coded to give an identity to the attackers. The authorship or motivation of an event may be inferred from claims of responsibility, from the tactics and targets selected, and from a variety of contextual factors (such as anniversary dates). A taxonomy of six group-types was thus developed: Left-Wing, Right-Wing, Religious, National-ist/Separatist, Single-Issue, and Emigré. 'Religious' attacks in Canada have been largely perpetrated by the Sons of Freedom Doukhobors (SOF or Freedomites), 'Nationalist/Separatist' ones by the Front de Libéra-tion du Québec (FLQ) and similar groups. 'Single-Issue' events are vio-lent acts by groups focusing on specific issues (such as animal rights or abortion), and 'Emigré' incidents are those carried out by expatriates with reference to conflicts in their former homelands. 'Left-Wing' and 'Right-Wing' attacks are largely self-explanatory.

The tactics used in an incident are coded according to 12 types (not all 12 are reported in the tables, in the absence of qualifying events; see Table 10.4). The classification of terrorist tactics is based on the practice used in other chronologies and on the Criminal Code of Canada. Threats and hoaxes are not included. The targets referred to in the database are the physical objects of attack, of which 19 possible types are identified (see Table 10.5).

Each entry contains information on the date and location of an incident and, where known, such other details as time, damage, casual-ties, materials used, claims, convictions, and so on. The entries were compiled from open public sources: books, newspaper articles, judicial records, journals, chronologies, and so forth.

'Excluded' entries have not been quantified, and represent inci-dents in which the definitional standards for inclusion were not met, primary source corroboration was lacking, there was insufficient infor-mation to establish the identities or motives of the perpetrators, or essential factors such as date and location could not be determined. Support activities consist of actions (such as bank robberies, arms thefts, the establishment of training camps, and the dissemination of propa-ganda) intended to enhance group capabilities.[3]

DOMESTIC TERRORISM IN CANADA, 1960–1989

INCIDENCE AND LOCATION
Between 1960 and 1989 there were 366 incidents of domestic terrorism in Canada, of which 246 occurred in the 1960s, 64 in the 1970s, and 56

in the 1980s. As Table 10.1 shows, the most prolific periods were 1961–63 and 1968–71; the most tranquil was the period 1973–76.

Two hundred (54.6%) of the domestic incidents occurred in Quebec, and another 157 (42.9%) in British Columbia (BC); 7 took place in Ontario, and 1 each in Alberta and New Brunswick. Virtually all BC and Quebec incidents (96.3% and 90.1% respectively) were of the domestic variety; the opposite was true of Ontario, where 82.5% of all incidents were international. With the exception of the SOF incidents in BC, almost all of which took place in the Kootenays, domestic attacks tended to occur in the major urban centres. For example, 178 (or 89%) of the domestic incidents in Quebec occurred in Montreal, with a further 9 (4.5%) taking place in Quebec City; only 13 (6.5%) happened elsewhere in the province. All 7 of the domestic incidents in Ontario occurred in Ottawa and Toronto. By contrast, only 13 (8.3%) of the 157 BC incidents happened in Vancouver—a testimony to the rural basis of the SOF.

Despite the high number of terrorist events, the casualty rate has remained fairly small, as Table 10.2, comprising both domestic and international incidents, demonstrates.

Clearly Nationalist/Separatist[4] terrorism has been the deadliest type in absolute terms, but relative to the number of attacks perpetrated by each group (reported in Table 10.3), the Emigré group has been the most lethal.[5] As will be seen, the Emigré group is unique in its resort to assassination, which largely accounts for its greater relative deadliness.

Table 10.1: **Terrorist Incidents in Canada, 1960–1989**

Year	Domestic	International	Year	Domestic	International
1960	10	–	1975	1	1
1961	52	–	1976	1	–
1962	45	–	1977	2	2
1963	35	–	1978	4	–
1964	11	1	1979	3	–
1965	9	3	1980	11	2
1966	7	1	1981	14	1
1967	2	5	1982	5	6
1968	38	18	1983	6	–
1969	37	1	1984	6	–
1970	32	3	1985	3	1
1971	19	3	1986	5	4
1972	2	7	1987	2	–
1973	–	1	1988	–	1
1974	–	–	1989	4	1

Table 10.2: **Casualties, by Group Type and Target 1960–1989**

	Left-Wing	Right-Wing	Religious	Nat/Sep.	Single-issue	Emigré
Business	10w			1k,37w		1w
				1tk	1tw	
Clubs						
Public place						
Private citizens		3k				1k
Media						1k,1w
Religious						
Communications						
Transportation						
Educational						
Energy						
Medical						
Diplomatic						3k,6w
Foreign						
Postal			1tk,4tw	3w		
Military	1k			2k,4w		
Political				1k,4w		
Criminal justice			1w			
Other government				1w		

Abbreviations: w = wounded   k = killed   t = terrorist

By contrast, the Religious group has been more dangerous to itself, where casualties are concerned, than to others. Individuals caught in attacks (mostly by Nationalist/Separatist terrorists) on business targets have suffered the highest casualty rate.

GROUPS

As Table 10.3 shows, the two most prolific group types in the domestic field have been the Nationalist/Separatist category, with 200 incidents (54.6% of the total), and the Religious one, with 143 attacks (39.1%). A distant third was the Single-Issue category (9 incidents, or 2.5%).

Nationalist/Separatist

The FLQ burst on the Quebec scene with dramatic suddenness in 1963, with 34 incidents in a single year. After this impetuous start it was battered by arrests in June 1963, but minor incidents continued in the name of the Armée de libération du Québec (ALQ). Following a fresh series of arrests in April 1964, the ALQ was effectively dismantled, only to be succeeded by the more militarily-oriented Armée révolutionnaire du Québec (ARQ), which remained active until mid-1965. Thereafter the number of incidents declined dramatically, to just two in 1967. As we

Table 10.3: **Perpetrators, by Motive Type, 1960–1989**

Group Type	Domestic	International
Left-Wing	6	23
Right-Wing	7	–
Religious	143	–
Nationalist/Separatist	200	3
Single-Issue	9	1
Emigré	1	35

shall see, the movement took a different ideological turn in the mid-1960s, reflecting the new influence of its two left-wing theorists Pierre Vallières and Charles Gagnon (Laurendeau, 1974: 54–6, 60–9). No doubt the FLQ reached its apogee with the 'October Crisis' of 1970; but the government counter-attack did not, as is sometimes implied, succeed in completely smashing it (Charters, 1986a: 56). In fact, one of its most prolific cells was active in 1971, when 20 attacks were launched. However, by 1972 the FLQ remnant was so penetrated by the police as to suggest that it had become 'a security service colony' (Crelinsten, 1987: 60). In December 1971 Vallières renounced the use of violence, and apparently the majority of remaining activists followed his example, abandoning the armed struggle (Fournier, 1984: 316).

In addition to its attacks on a wide range of targets, the FLQ undertook a number of activities—robberies, credit card fraud, propaganda work, and the establishment of training camps—intended to increase its operational capabilities. Thus, in the first four years of its existence, the FLQ was involved in nearly three dozen robberies, some of them armed (in one incident two employees of a firearms store died[6]).

The FLQ was not as large as the frequency of its attacks might suggest, numbering perhaps somewhat over one hundred active members. To these activists might be added a number of sympathizers who lent assistance of some sort—one historian of the FLQ stated that 'some hundreds of persons were implicated in it, in one way or another, either closely or distantly,' adding that its strength on the eve of the October Crisis was about 35 (Fournier 1988: 333). The membership tended to be young and single, with varied backgrounds (a fairly high proportion were students).

As we have seen, although the title FLQ was used generically to refer to the perpetrators of terrorist acts in Quebec between 1963 and 1972, different 'waves' of the movement[7] adopted different names: FLQ, ALQ, ARQ. Thus the 'FLQ' title does not necessarily indicate the endurance of a single terrorist organization over the whole period: 'different groups may adopt the same name at different times, without any central command structure or any coherence in objectives, strategies or tactics' (Crelinsten, 1987: 81). Ideologically, for example, the early FLQ was nationalist and anti-colonialist in both its targeting and its rhetoric; after 1966, by contrast, the FLQ's attacks were made 'in defence of the workers', and the rhetoric was revolutionary. Although some cells may have specialized in particular functions (propaganda, finance, and so on), on the whole they probably normally operated autonomously, conducting their own recruiting, fund-raising, and operations. Nonetheless, there were contacts between cells. After mid-1970, for example, the two cells involved in the October Crisis (the Chenier and Libération cells) 'were essentially one' (Crelinsten, 1987: 67), although they went their separate ways during the October events.

Since the apparent demise of the FLQ in 1972 a few minor incidents have been claimed in its name. The FLQ slogan was used in a bomb threat during the 1976 Olympic Games, and the group title was resurrected in arson and firebomb attacks in Montreal in December 1986 and August 1989. However, the police assessed the incidents as the work of a few crackpots, and discounted the possibility of a resurgent FLQ. A number of other attacks having nationalist motivations occurred between 1972 and 1989, most notably during the 1980 referendum (police detected some technical skill in a series of five minor bombings in a week) and again in 1983.

Religious

As was noted above, incidents of 'Religious' terrorism in Canada have been largely the work of the Sons of Freedom Doukhobors. The Doukhobor community is a pacifist Christian sect which originated in Russia and whose members first came to Canada (originally Saskatchewan and later BC) in 1898–99 with the assistance of Leo Tolstoy. The central tenet of Doukhobor belief is the rejection of temporal authority in favour of the divine spirit, which Doukhobors believe lies within each individual. A major characteristic of the community is its dismissal of the material possessions associated with modern life. In their denial of secular authority, the Doukhobors refused to register their homesteads, and thus land ownership became a major source of friction between the government and the community.

The Doukhobors are composed of three groups: Orthodox, Independent, and Sons of Freedom (SOF). Founded in 1902, the SOF first began their protest activities in the early 1920s, with the destruction of all schools accessible to Doukhobor children. The Orthodox and Independent groups have been involved in the 'black work' of terrorism as victims rather than as perpetrators (Woodcock and Avakumovic, 1968: 311, 325–6). In fact, as a result of the advocacy and use of violence among some Freedomites, the SOF group was officially expelled from the Union of Spiritual Communities of Christ (USCC, the Orthodox body). Even within the radical SOF, the individuals who have engaged in 'black work' have constituted a small minority, and Woodcock and Avakumovic (1968: 327–8) contend that no organized conspiracy existed among the Freedomites. According to these authors, '[t]he real terrorists, who destroyed public property and attempted to instil fear into other Doukhobors, probably numbered no more than two hundred' (Woodcock and Avakumovic, 1968: 333). In general, the violent acts committed by Freedomites represented an attempt to preserve Doukhobor culture against the encroachments of modern society and to discourage assimilation among those Doukhobors who were more receptive to Canadian life.

When negotiations began in 1960 to enable the USCC to buy back land foreclosed in 1939, the Freedomites were bitterly opposed to the move, and there was an upsurge of terrorism. Directed against government, transportation, business, and communications, this wave of violence also targeted Orthodox communities. Altogether there were 107 incidents of SOF terrorism in the space of three years (1960–2). In addition numerous incendiary acts were committed during this period that constituted protest rather than terrorism, in that SOF activists frequently burned their own property as a gesture of abnegation (Woodcock and Avakumovic, 1968: 311, 328, 333).

The number of SOF incidents fell with dramatic suddenness after 1962. In that year many arrests were made after police received numerous confessions spurred by a prophecy that foretold Doukhobor 'migration through the prisons'.[8] The building of a prison for SOF offenders at Agassiz prompted a mass march from the Kootenays to the prison, via Vancouver, in the late summer of 1962. This contact with the outside world, novel for many Freedomites, led to predictions of the 'end of an era' for SOF violence (Woodcock and Avakumovic, 1968: 332). Whether the reason was indeed this contact, or simply the incarceration of the more adept bomb-makers, the number of SOF attacks fell to 13 between 1963 and 1979. However, the optimistic predictions of the late 1960s have not been borne out by more recent events: between 1980 and 1986 there were 23 SOF attacks, and more have occurred since.

Other Groups

Between them, the Nationalist/Separatist and Religious categories accounted for 93.7% of domestic attacks, leaving all other groups responsible for only a tiny proportion of total incidents. Nonetheless, at least one Left-Wing group achieved a measure of notoriety, becoming the subject of a television film. Direct Action, a short-lived BC group of five people sometimes known as the Squamish Five, was responsible for two spectacular bombings in 1982—at a hydro substation on Vancouver

Island and at Litton Industries' Toronto plant—and was caught while preparing to carry out further attacks. In addition, two members were implicated in the firebombing of three Vancouver video stores in November 1982. Direct Action was also involved in a series of thefts (weapons, explosives, vehicles, radio and mountaineering equipment, tools, and money) intended to increase its capabilities.

In March 1983, two months after the arrest of the Squamish Five, a series of minor attacks began in Montreal for which responsibility was claimed in the names of Groupe action directe and Friction directe. The left-wing and nationalistic rhetoric of these claims was reminiscent of the FLQ, and in fact (as one claim letter pointed out) the first two incidents, both firebomb attacks on militia armouries, took place on the twentieth anniversary of FLQ attacks on Montreal armouries in the first wave of terrorism. After two months and five incidents the attacks ceased.

Because many of the issues that appeal to leftist groups have strong international dimensions, only a small proportion (6 incidents, or 20.7%) of Left-Wing attacks have been domestic ones. By contrast, the Single-Issue category has proved largely domestic in focus, as has the Right-Wing one. Despite the burgeoning of right-wing groups in Canada in the 1970s and 1980s (Barrett, 1987: 29), the half-dozen incidents that corresponded to the NSCC definition of terrorism (as opposed to random racist violence) were not clearly attributable to any particular group.

TACTICS

Canadian groups have shown themselves to be tactically conservative, rarely straying far from the traditional terrorist predilection for bombs. As Table 10.4 shows, the international form of terrorism in Canada has shown slightly more tactical variation than the domestic form.

On the domestic front, explosive and incendiary bombings, both successful and unsuccessful, constituted 85.8% of all incidents. Not surprisingly, given the incendiarism of the SOF and the large number of their attacks, arson has featured fairly prominently among terrorist tactics in this country, comprising 13.7% of all incidents. Assassination, a traditional tactic of terrorism, has not been used as an intentional tactic of domestic terrorism in Canada (the murder of Pierre Laporte during the 1970 October Crisis was not a planned part of the original kidnapping). Similarly, the various types of hostage-taking, while common enough in non-political criminal acts in Canada, are rare, comprising 0.3% of attacks.

As Table 10.4 shows, success has been most likely with arson (88% success), followed by bombing (68.3%); failure has been most likely with assassination attempts (50% failure), followed by firebombing (40.7%). The highest success rate was attached to attacks on

Table 10.4: **Terrorist Tactics in Canada, 1960–1989**

Tactic		Domestic	International
Bombing	– Successful[a]	179	30
	– Failed	83	14
Firebombing	– Successful	29	6
	– Failed	23	1
Arson	– Successful	44	–
	– Failed	6	–
Assassination	– Successful	–	3
	– Failed	–	3
Assault		1	1
Kidnapping	– Successful	1	1
	– Failed	–	1
Hostage-taking		–	1
Hijacking		–	1

[a]Success represents ignition, failure non-ignition, in the case of bombing, fire-bombing, and arson; wounding is deemed failure in an assassination attempt, while a failed kidnapping is one in which the intended victim is not taken.

energy targets (such as hydro poles), the lowest to strikes against military and postal targets. The group with the lowest success rate (65%) was the Nationalist/Separatist category, perhaps because it often chose to firebomb militia armouries (nearly three-quarters of such attacks failed).

Bombing has been so prevalent in terrorist incidents in Canada that it tends to overshadow the relatively limited resort to other methods. Nevertheless, the use of particular tactics does provide a clue to terrorist capabilities. While some incendiary devices have been fairly sophisticated, many have been crude Molotov cocktails, well within the technical and logistical capability of most would-be terrorists. Explosive bombs are generally more technically demanding, and often evoke considerable ingenuity (as in the abortive use of wood-block timers in a series of SOF attacks in 1961). A lack, or loss, of bomb-makers therefore can affect a group's tactics. As was noted above after the mass arrests of 1962, when many of the SOF bomb-makers were imprisoned, there were just three SOF bombings between 1963 and 1965. Even that capability seems to have dried up between 1966 and 1979, when arson was the only tactic used. Then from 1980 to 1986 explosives came back into vogue, with 17 out of 23 SOF incidents (73.9%) being bombings.

Despite such variations over time, some tactics are more characteristic of one group type than another. As noted, the Freedomites were predisposed to use arson. Thus, while it comprised 13.7% of all domestic incidents, arson constituted 25.2% of all Religious attacks. By contrast, Nationalist/Separatist terrorists greatly favoured bombs: 83.7% of all such attacks employed explosive devices. And despite the periodic loss of bomb-makers, FLQ bombs became bigger and more sophisticated with time, although the movement did not resort to plastic explosives until January 1972.

An important reason for the low casualty rate of Canadian terrorism is the fact that bombs have generally been placed at night, when few people might be expected to be in the vicinity. Of the 157 successful bombings (domestic and international) for which timings could be established, 140 (89.2%) occurred at night. When bombs were deliberately set to explode in busy places during daylight hours, however, they could produce multiple casualties (an example being the FLQ bombing of the Montreal Stock Exchange in 1969).

TARGETS

While the choice of targets in part derives from practical considerations—a group's capabilities, the availability of targets, the ease or difficulty posed by a particular object of attack—it also reflects the attacker's motives and goals. The range of targets is much greater than that of tactics, and the distinction between domestic and international incidents is far clearer with respect to the former than the latter, as Table 10.5 demonstrates.

Because timing devices allow bombs to be planted well in advance of their intended activation, and hence reduce the risks to the bombers, bombs lend themselves to secondary goals (publicity) as well as to primary ones (coercion). Thus bombing often has a symbolic component, particularly where it is the work of a fledgling group that seeks to attract publicity and recruits. This pattern was evident in the activities of the FLQ. In the first three years of FLQ activity, attacks were largely aimed at military, police, and government buildings, statues, the wealthy English district of Westmount, and so on. With time the FLQ's targeting switched, and by 1968 it was clear that the group's message had become as much socialist as nationalist, its actions being intended to exploit a climate of increasing labour strife. Of 88 Nationalist/Separatist attacks between 1968 and 1971, 49 (55.7%) were directed against business targets, many of them involved in strikes.

The Freedomites' rejection both of modern life and of the state was evident in their attacks. Besides setting fire to their own property, the SOF used firebombs and arson against the property of other Doukhobors in a bid to reverse their assimilation into Canadian society. In addition, the sect's pacifism is reflected in the low level of lethality of its bombings. Against targets other than fellow Doukhobors—the BC Land Settlement Board, railways, hydro lines, gas pipelines, and

Table 10.5: **Terrorist Targets in Canada, 1960–1989**

Target	Domestic	International
Business	75	20
Clubs	3	–
Public place	10	–
Monuments	9	–
Private citizens	24	2
Media	1	3
Religious	20	–
Communications	11	–
Transportation	48	1
Educational	9	–
Energy	42	–
Medical	2	–
Diplomatic	–	30
Foreign	–	3
Postal	35	1
Military	23	2
Political	16	–
Criminal justice	12	–
Other government	26	–

schools—the SOF resorted to bombs. The CPR has been a favourite target, along with some of its subsidiaries; the company was linked in some minds with the 1924 death, in a train explosion of undetermined cause, of the Doukhobor leader of that time.

INTERNATIONAL TERRORISM IN CANADA, 1960–89

INCIDENCE AND LOCATION

Although most terrorism in Canada has been Canadian in focus, between 1960 and 1989 there were 62 incidents having an international dimension. With the exception of a single year (1968), international terrorism has been rather more evenly distributed throughout the period than has domestic terrorism.[9]

Table 10.6 shows that international terrorism has been an urban phenomenon, with just two exceptions (both in BC,[10] where incidents overwhelmingly occurred outside the major centres). No doubt this is because high-profile foreign targets tend to be found in the large cities. Perhaps surprisingly, given its concentration of lucrative diplomatic targets, Ottawa has not been the primary venue of international terrorism, or even of anti-diplomatic incidents: in both cases Montreal has been

Table 10.6: **International Terrorism, by Group Type, Tactic, and Target, 1960–1989**

	Quebec	Montreal	Ottawa	Toronto	Edmonton	Vancouver	Other
1960							
1961							
1962							
1963							
1964		EBF					
1965		NBD		EBD	LBM		
1966			EBD				
1967		EBB EBD	2EBD	EBD			
1968	LBF	4LBB		13LBB			
1969						SFD	
1970		2NKD		LFD			
1971		EFF EFD	EBD				
1972		EFD 2EBD EBB	3EBD				
1973		EBPc					
1974							
1975			LBM				
1976							
1977			EFD			EAPc	
1978							
1979							
1980		2EBD					
1981						EBD	
1982		EBF	2EAD	EBMd EBD LBB			
1983							
1984							
1985			EHD				
1986		EAtD		EAMd			LFP EAD
1987							
1988						EAMd	
1989			EHT				

Abbreviations:

Groups	Tactics	Targets
E = Emigré	A = Assassination	B = Business
L = Left-Wing	At = Assault	D = Diplomatic
N = Nationalist/Separatist	B = Bombing	F = Foreign
S = Single Issue	F = Firebombing	M = Military
	H = Hostage-taking	Md = Media
	K = Kidnap	P = Postal
		Pc = Private Citizens
		T = Transportation

preferred. Since anti-diplomatic attacks tend to be low-risk, and are often the work of groups with limited capabilities, it may be that missions in the national capital are seen as too well protected for attackers to risk; for this reason some incidents may have been deflected towards consular premises elsewhere.

Table 10.6 indicates the main difference between domestic and international terrorism: the most prolific groups on the domestic scene are virtually absent from the international one, where the Nationalist/Separatist group accounted for only three incidents (4.8%), and the Religious group for none. The table further shows that the most common event type (apart from the pipe-bomb incidents of 1968) is the bomb attack by Emigrés against diplomatic targets. The 16 such events (over one-quarter of the total) are clustered in the period 1965 to 1982, and took place in Montreal (5), Ottawa (7), Toronto (3), and Vancouver (1).

GROUPS

Emigré

The most prolific, as well as the deadliest, of the group types on the international scene is the Emigré category. As a type, Emigré attacks have grown in relative importance: of the 33 international incidents that occurred in the 1970s and 1980s, 27 (81.8%) involved émigrés. Their attacks have come in waves of increasing lethality.

The first wave comprised attacks by Cuban and Yugoslavian émigrés. After the Bay of Pigs episode in April 1961, anti-Castro Cubans based largely in the US began to attack targets associated with Castro's regime. Between 1964 and 1980 there were 11 attacks of Cuban provenance, eight of them in Montreal; one person was killed and two were injured in these incidents. Although the Cuban population of Canada is small, attacks happened here with some frequency because of the relative absence of Cuban targets in the United States. In fact, many of the attacks appear to have been made by American residents; this may explain the popularity of Cuban targets in Montreal since US anti-Castro groups were based mainly in New York and Florida. The cessation of activities in 1980 is probably explained by two factors: American police made major inroads into the US groups in the early 1980s, and the Cuban community was becoming more established in that country. (Emigré terrorism tends to occur in recent exile communities, or among immigrants newly arrived in long-established émigré societies.)

Three of the incidents relating to conflict in Yugoslavia took place in 1965 and 1967; directed against Yugoslav missions, they caused little damage and no injury. The assassination of a doctor of Yugoslavian origin in Vancouver in 1977 also seems to have had its roots in the communal tensions of Yugoslavia that were perpetuated by the Serbian and

Croatian communities in Canada. When Serbs and Croats were not attacking each other in their adopted countries, they were hitting targets associated with the Yugoslavian government. Dramatic as many of the attacks of Yugoslavian provenance were between 1966 and the late 1970s, since then they have largely ceased in Canada, as elsewhere, although the conflict that erupted in Yugoslavia in 1991 has resulted in some minor incidents here.

Other external disputes that were catalysts for violence in Canada in the 1970s and 1980s were the Arab-Israeli conflict (which produced a flurry of letter bombs in 1972–73, some with Canadian destinations) and the hardships allegedly experienced by Soviet Jews.

In 1982 a second, deadlier wave of Emigré incidents began with five attacks by two Armenian groups: the Armenian Secret Army for the Liberation of Armenia (ASALA) and the Justice Commandos of the Armenian Genocide (JCAG). These groups had begun operations worldwide in 1975 with frequent sanguinary attacks on Turkish diplomats. The Israeli invasion of Lebanon (1982) disrupted the Beirut-based ASALA, which was further hurt by police arrests in the US as well as a feud within the group itself. Thus the 1982 attacks in Canada came at the apogee of Armenian terrorism; by 1985, when Armenians took over the Turkish embassy in Ottawa, the movement had passed its peak.

A brief flurry of incidents of international terrorism by Sikh groups—dedicated to the establishment of an independent Khalistan—followed the Indian army's attack on Amritsar's Golden Temple in 1984. A Canadian Sikh was convicted in the 1985 Narita bombing, and in 1986 four Canadian Sikhs attempted to kill a Punjab cabinet minister who was visiting Vancouver Island. Two Canadian Sikhs were convicted of conspiring to place a bomb aboard an Air India flight departing from New York in May 1986 (they were released in 1992 after their appeal hearing had been unduly delayed). Finally, in 1988 a young Sikh immigrant shot and wounded the Sikh editor of an Indo-Canadian newspaper in Surrey, BC who had criticized the advocates of violence.

The most recent incident of Emigré terrorism recorded in NSCC 1992 was the 1989 hijacking to Parliament Hill of a Montreal bus bound for New York; the hijacker was a Lebanese-Canadian distraught at the carnage then being wrought in Beirut. Finally, there were two anti-Communist incidents—one an assassination, the other an assault—associated with Romania in 1986; at least one may have been connected with a revival of the Iron Guard, a fascist organization active in Romania before and during the Second World War.

Left-Wing

Emigré politics aside, the other main source of international terrorism in Canada has been Left-Wing opposition to events such as the Vietnam

War and to American policy in Central America. The pipe-bomb wave of 1968 came in protest against the Vietnam war, as did the January 1965 destruction of two US Air Force jets undergoing repairs in Edmonton (one of the earliest anti-Vietnam terrorist incidents anywhere).

Nationalist/Separatist
Seduced by the example of Brazil, where political kidnapping proved highly lucrative at the end of the 1960s, the FLQ made a bid to internationalize their campaign with two diplomatic kidnapping attempts in 1970. One, an attempt on the Israeli consul in Montreal, was thwarted by chance, but the other—the seizure of James Cross, the British commercial attaché in Montreal—led to the 'October Crisis'. The group had earlier protested the Vietnam War with a bomb attack on the United States Consulate-General in Montreal, and had established tenuous links with external groups.

TACTICS
As Table 10.6 demonstrates, bombing has been the main tactic of international terrorism in Canada. Explosive and incendiary bombs (82.3% of incidents) were only slightly less common on the international scene than the domestic one. Yet of the seven attacks since 1983, only one has used bombing (firebombs were used in the 1986 incident). With its symbolic potential, bombing has been the only tactic used by Left-Wing groups, which tend to have a predilection for propagandistic actions. Two of the bombs were incendiaries. Of the remaining 21 devices, 17 were small pipe bombs, inventively rigged but of limited force; the 11 that detonated did little damage. In another incident, attributed to the American 'Weather Underground', a warning enabled police to locate a relatively small device placed near National Defence Headquarters in Ottawa in 1975. In two incidents, however, large quantities of explosives were employed. In the Edmonton attack, 12 sticks of dynamite were used on the three planes that were destroyed or damaged; a fourth jet was also rigged, and an additional 180 to 200 sticks were found in an abandoned car near the airport. Some 500 pounds of dynamite were thought to have been used in the Litton bombing in 1982. As might be expected, the FLQ's single attempt at using a bomb against an international target (the bombing of the US consulate in Montreal in May 1965) used enough dynamite (12 sticks) to cause considerable damage.

Two tactics occur almost solely in the international variety of Canadian terrorism: assassination and hostage-taking in its various forms. There were 10 international incidents in these two categories, representing 16.3% of the total, compared to one domestic incident (0.3%). The deadliness required of an assassination attempt, and the organization normally demanded of a hostage-taking, underscore the difference in lethality between international and domestic terrorism (international incidents are almost twice as likely to inflict casualties). By contrast, arson is notably absent from the inventory of international terrorism in Canada.

It was previously observed that the early Emigré attacks were less lethal than those that followed, and this is reflected in changed tactical choices. Prior to 1977 the only resort to methods other than bombing were the two kidnapping attempts by the FLQ in 1970. From 1977 bombs increasingly became the exception, and assassination and hostage-taking represented a far higher proportion of all incidents than they had before.

TARGETS

With Emigré and Left-Wing groups accounting for fully 95.2% of international incidents, it was rather predictable that the primary targets of this dimension of terrorism should have been American policy in Vietnam and in Central America, and a variety of homeland conflicts.

The planes damaged and destroyed in the 1965 attack at Edmonton were of a type used in the Vietnam War. Three years later, at the height of the war, and on the eve of the American presidential election, terrorists aimed two series of multiple pipe-bomb attacks at Canadian corporations accused of complicity in the war; the bombs were placed outside the homes of executives of aircraft manufacturers Hawker Siddeley, De Havilland, and United Aircraft. The 1982 Litton attack similarly targeted American foreign and defence policy through a Canada-based plant that manufactured parts for the guidance systems of cruise missiles.

Emigré groups also occasionally hit companies seen to be associated with the regimes opposed by the attackers. In some cases these were foreign-owned targets, such as Aeroflot's Montreal office, which was slightly damaged when a Molotov cocktail was thrown at the entrance in 1971. Occasionally, Canadian companies have attracted exile ire, among them businesses involved in trade with Cuba. In 1967 an auction house in Montreal was bombed, injuring an employee, and five years later a forwarding company was targeted.

The study of modern terrorism shows that some groups become locked into a targeting cycle designed more to sustain the groups themselves—primarily by trying to free captured members—than to promote their causes. This happened to the ASALA, which reacted to the arrests of Armenian terrorists in 1980–81 in Switzerland by unleashing two waves of bomb attacks on Swiss targets; one such incident involved the Swiss Air office in Montreal in 1982. In 1982 ASALA bombed an Air Canada freight terminal in Los Angeles in a bid to pressure Canada into releasing four Armenians arrested on extortion charges.

As might be expected, foreign diplomats and missions, along with visiting dignitaries, are high on the Emigré hit list. In all, such targets have been struck by émigrés 24 times (two-thirds of all attacks by this group type). While many of the attacks on diplomatic targets have involved bombs and Molotov cocktails, the Emigré category has been far more prepared than any other to target individuals, most of them diplomats or persons associated with a detested foreign government. Perhaps as a result of the intensity of expatriate politics, the media are also at some risk. Emigrés were implicated in all three incidents involving media targets.

RECENT INCIDENTS IN CANADA

In the two years since the end of the period covered by the NSCC chronology there have been several incidents showing characteristics of terrorism. From a lengthy list of as yet unvalidated events,[11] rather more than a dozen, mostly quite minor, appear to have been terrorist in nature.

The charged political atmosphere in Quebec has continued to generate extremist violence, with the bombing of a *Globe and Mail* vending box in Quebec City in March 1990, an arson attack on the Montreal headquarters of the Société Saint-Jean Baptiste in May 1990 (the tenth anniversary of the 1980 referendum), and a nail bomb attack on a Châteauguay crowd celebrating Canada Day in 1991 (at least seven people were injured). Two bombings bearing the hallmarks of the SOF (a rail line and a gas transmission line near Grand Forks, BC were the targets) occurred within five minutes of each other in April 1990. In August 1990, during the stand-off between Mohawks and troops and police at Oka, Quebec, an Indian blockade of a rail line in BC, intended as a gesture of support, was followed by an arson attack on a rail bridge. A logging bridge near Pemberton, BC, was severely damaged, first by a bomb, and a few days later by arson, in April 1991; it had been the focus of protest by native and environmental groups. There have also been several incidents of tree-spiking in BC (April and May 1990, April 1991), presumably by environmental activists. In December 1991 animal-rights activists were suspected of responsibility in an incendiary attack on trucks belonging to an Edmonton fish market. Abortion clinics have also been subject to violent attack. One in Vancouver was ransacked in February 1990, causing serious damage, and another in Edmonton was the target of an arson attempt in July 1991. In May 1992 a fire destroyed Dr Henry Morgentaler's Toronto abortion clinic; police stated that the fire had been deliberately set.

In the international arena the Gulf War generated much less terrorism than was feared. Two bombs were planted in a shopping centre in Erie County, Ontario, in protest against Canada's participation in the war; they were not detonated. In September 1991 someone threw a Molotov cocktail at the wall of the Iranian embassy, causing minor damage. On 5 April 1992 some 40 individuals, mostly members of the Mujahedin-e-Khalq (MEK, an Iranian opposition group), attacked and ransacked the same embassy to protest an Iranian air raid on the MEK base in Iraq. The Ottawa attack was one of 11 world-wide directed against Iranian missions. The fighting in the former Yugoslavia has not resulted in a spate of terrorism in Canada, as some feared it would. However, the Yugoslavian consulate in Toronto was the target of an abortive Molotov cocktail attack in November 1991, shots were fired at a Serbian church in Vancouver in January 1992, and three Molotov cocktails were thrown at a Croatian church in the same city in March 1992.

ATTACKS ON CANADIAN TARGETS OUTSIDE CANADA

Attacks on Canadian targets in other countries are infrequent, and usually have occurred in countries, such as Lebanon, experiencing a high degree of political violence. Furthermore, Canadian victimization tends to be chance rather than deliberate: Canadians and Canadian property are rarely attacked on the grounds of being Canadian. Data on incidents affecting Canadians, or Canadian interests, outside the country are scarce. However, a chronology of external incidents between 1968 and 1992 indicates that in 8 of 27 cases Canada was indeed the probable focus of attack; in another 14 incidents Canadians and Canadian property were attacked on the grounds less of nationality than of activity or purpose; and in the remaining 5 cases they appear to have been the victims of chance (Kellett, 1988: Annex A, revised 1993). Examples of deliberate attack on this country include the bombing of Canadian facilities in the United States by anti-Castro Cubans during the late 1960s, the 1982 Los Angeles bombing, and a bomb attack on the Canadian embassy in Peru in 1991.

Several factors may account for Canada's limited external victimization. Canada's status as a middle power, its lack of a history of 'imperialism', its relatively low economic profile in areas of conflict, and the availability of more desirable (mainly American) targets have all been advanced as explanations for a low incidence of anti-Canadian terrorism abroad (Kellett, 1988: 158).

COMPARATIVE TERRORIST TRENDS

In February 1992 *The Globe and Mail* reported world-wide terrorism data from an American risk-assessment company under the headline 'Terrorist threat growing' and the sub-heading 'Just when you thought you were

safe' (*Globe and Mail,* 11 Feb. 1992: C1, C8). This claim of escalation contrasts with the data presented so far in this chapter, which suggest a dramatic overall decline in the incidence of terrorism in Canada over the
past three decades. However, NSCC data show that international terrorism
has not shown the same decennial decline in Canada that domestic terrorism has, and is thus not so obviously out of step with the trends
evinced by global statistics. Furthermore, among most Western countries
domestic terrorism appears to have declined from its peaks of the 1970s.

Whether Canadian and global trends converge or diverge, it is
nonetheless instructive to examine terrorism trends elsewhere in order
to learn more about the Canadian experience (Ross and Gurr, 1989).
However, cross-national comparison is not as easy as might be
expected. Global databases, such as those of the State Department and
the RAND Corporation, generally ignore domestic terrorism, concentrating on the international dimension.[12] Because they derive their data
largely from newspapers, they also tend to be skewed towards incidents
affecting the country of origin of a particular database.[13] Many incidents noted in a national database, such as the NSCC's, are overlooked
in a global one. Nonetheless, it may be assumed that national databases
have a certain internal consistency, and also that some broad trends are
discernible in global data. With these caveats, then, national and international statistics, amplified by evidence of a more qualitative nature,
will be used in this section to contrast Canada's experience with that of
other countries.

UNITED STATES

The Kelly Committee felt that Canada's relative freedom from terrorism
has been due in part to geography: 'Canada is far away from the major
terrorist "hot spots" of Western Europe, the Middle East and South and
Central America' (Kelly, 1987: 14). If this explanation is valid, then the
United States should also to some extent be protected by its location in
the Western hemisphere. In fact this has been the case. While the
United States has usually been the principal victim of international terrorism (Kellett, 1988: 83), within its own borders it has been relatively
immune, a blessing that also extends to domestic terrorism. A 1988
RAND study found that '[r]elatively few terrorist incidents occur in the
United States each year' (Hoffman, 1988: 1).

The similarity of American and Canadian experience extends
beyond the actual incidence of terrorism in both countries. It has been
remarked that ideology is not the driving force of North American
society (Mitchell, 1982: 18), and this is reflected in the relatively low
occurrence of both left- and right-wing terrorism in the United States
and Canada. Again as in Canada, left-wing groups in the US have
tended to resort to largely symbolic bombings and to have had

difficulty prolonging their existence. The issues they have protested are also similar to the issues targeted by left-wing extremists in this country. Conversely, ethnic and émigré terrorism constitute a high proportion of all attacks: 'approximately two-thirds of all terrorism in the United States is carried out by ethnic-separatist or émigré terrorists' (Hoffman, 1986: 4).

The biggest difference between Canada and the United States lies in the realm of external victimization. As noted, citizens and property of the US are the primary targets of international terrorism (occasionally being supplanted by those of Israel).

EUROPE

A considerable amount of data relating to domestic terrorism exists for many European countries, allowing an interesting comparison of European and North American experience. Europe has experienced high levels of both domestic and international terrorism, of two main varieties: nationalist and ideological. The former variety is epitomized by secessionist groups such as the Provisional Irish Republican Army (PIRA) and the Basque Euzkadi ta Askatasuna (ETA). Among the ideological groups that may be included are the German Red Army Faction (RAF), the Red Brigades (BR) of Italy, and Action directe of France.

Left-wing groups are less millenarian now than they were twenty years ago. Thus they tend to concentrate on less ambitious goals with a reduced international, and increased domestic, focus (Cordes, 1987: 167), exploiting such issues as the fears felt in the former East Germany at the economic cost of reunification. This change reflects in part a much depleted capability—most groups are now reduced to hard cores of twenty to thirty, and their recent activities have been a pale shadow of those in the dozen years after 1968.

Left-wing tactical and targeting patterns were typified by the BR. An analysis of their operations found that 87% were directed against corporations, and that their tactical repertoire hinged on symbolic bombings; they did not resort to hijackings or barricade-hostage incidents, although kidnapping was part of their tactical armoury. Like the BR, the RAF targeted the 'establishment' and resorted to bombs and assassination. In their use of bomb attacks on businesses, and their occasional resort to surrogate attacks (actions conducted on behalf of a quite different group, or in response to issues remote from their usual concerns or from local problems),[14] left-wing groups in Europe have differed little from their Canadian counterparts; on the other hand, their organizational capability and longevity far exceeded those of groups in North America.

During the early 1980s right-wing terrorism was causing alarm in Europe, although few groups achieved the prominence of the Armed Revolutionary Nuclei (the Italian group implicated in the 1980 Bologna bombing). In Italy and Germany rightist groups followed a strategy of destabilization that produced surprising alliances with left-wing groups. After about 1982 right-wing terrorism abated, although racist and skin-head extremism flourished at the end of the 1980s (European Parliament, 1990). Various émigré groups have operated in Europe, most notably Croatian, Armenian, and South Moluccan ones.

Since the late nineteenth century, nationalism has been a major source of terrorism. In a study of left-wing and nationalist groups in Europe, Hewitt (1984) found that where the former targeted the establishment, and were not notably sanguinary in their attacks, nationalist terrorists were more lethal and struck mainly security-force targets. Hewitt also observed that nationalist terrorists were more parochial, and less likely to attack foreign targets, than were their leftist counterparts (Hewitt, 1984: 26, 28–33). Nationalist groups have tended as well to be larger and more long-lived. While both group types resort mainly to bombs, nationalist terrorists are not only less interested in symbolism but less averse to shedding blood, and thus they are more prepared to use car-bombs (e.g., PIRA, ETA). In its scope, its longevity, its parochialism, and its (relative) willingness to inflict casualties, nationalist terrorism in Canada shares some of the primary characteristics of the European variant.

GLOBAL PATTERNS

The US State Department's annual reports allow some comparison to be made between global patterns of international terrorism and trends and patterns in international terrorism occurring in Canada, most notably in the areas of tactics and targeting. Such comparisons must be made with caution, however, given not only the differing coding procedures of the two data sets, but also regular changes in coding and reporting in the State Department's reports.[15]

State Department data show that the global incidence of international terrorism rose over 70% from 1983 to 1988 (from 500 to 856 incidents), but has declined since, falling to 361 incidents in 1992 (there was a minor upsurge during the 1991 Gulf War).[16] Nonetheless, several incidents in early 1993 (including the bombing of the World Trade Centre) led the Department to warn of 'ominous signs that the problem will escalate' (United States Department of State, 1992: iii).

As for the location of incidents of international terrorism, the State Department data show that the Middle East was the primary venue between 1983 and 1989, particularly when 'spill-over' terrorism (incidents related to the Middle East conflict but occurring in other regions) is considered: from 1984 to 1989 over 40% of all incidents bore the hallmarks of that conflict. After the Middle East, Western Europe and Latin America have been the regions most afflicted, and in the early 1990s

Latin America took over top ranking from the Middle East. North America's share of global incidents between 1983 and 1992 was less than 1%.

Data on casualties show that in no year has the death toll of international terrorism exceeded 1,000—the average for the 1980s was 500 dead and nearly 1,200 wounded—and the number of fatalities has declined precipitously in the early 1990s (to 93 in 1992). This toll contrasts with the losses exacted in more conventional wars: it was estimated that 443,500 people died in 14 wars in 1991 (compared with 291,000 and 16 respectively in 1990)[17] (*Ottawa Citizen*, 28 Dec. 1991: B8).

As in Canada, bombing constitutes the principal tactic of global international terrorism: from 1983 to 1992 it accounted for 58% of all incidents. The next most frequent tactic of international terrorism has been armed attack (including assassination attempts); over the eight-year period it comprised 17% of incidents. Third in overall popularity in recent years has been arson, comprising 19% of attacks prior to 1990. If firebombings (which formed a separate category beginning in 1990) are included, incendiary attacks declined to 14% in 1990–93. Kidnappings accounted for 7% of attacks, most of them occurring in Latin America and the Middle East.

In their targeting data, recent State Department reports distinguish between 'facilities' and 'victims'. Where facilities were the target, the 'Other' category (non-official, non-business targets) was consistently the one most attacked in the years 1987–90, with attacks on business facilities coming a consistent second in frequency. These positions were reversed in 1991 and 1992. Military facilities were almost invariably the least liable to attack. As for victims, the 'Other' category (missionaries and aid workers, tourists, passers-by, and so on) far outstripped the rest, which all varied from second to fifth ranks in frequency of attack.

These statistics indicate that terrorists elsewhere share the preference of Canadian groups for 'soft' targets, and switch their aim when a particular type of target (notably embassies) receives improved protection. They also explain, in the overall switch from official and business targets to more random ones, why public alarm has risen out of proportion to the damage inflicted by international terrorism.

The State Department reports allege that state sponsorship was responsible for 15% of incidents between 1985 and 1990. If so, the limited capabilities and tactical repertoires of Canadian terrorists are hardly surprising, given the marked absence of state sponsorship of terrorism in Canada.

A dozen years ago it was fashionable to predict a trend towards 'technological terrorism'; such predictions have not been borne out. In part, this probably reflects a belief among terrorists that existing tactics and weaponry are adequate to their purposes. However, the capability to acquire and employ high-technology weapons is not beyond many groups. Moreover, authorities on terrorist psychology believe that there are groups, particularly ones subscribing to messianic or apocalyptic visions, that could be attracted to the use of weapons of mass destruction (International Security Studies Program, 1987: 3).

CONCLUSION

Although, over the past thirty years, terrorist incidents have occurred in Canada, on average, approximately every four weeks, they peaked in the early and late 1960s, and in the past decade attacks have been sporadic (if sometimes more dramatic than earlier events). Yet as terrorist attacks in Canada have declined in frequency, elsewhere they have continued to make headlines, and perhaps this has contributed to the public sense of Canadian peaceableness.

While few Canadian incidents have evinced high levels of organizational or technical capability, and many attacks have been crude and ineffective, the past three decades have seen times when terrorist groups posed a substantial security threat. Yet for much of the period public opinion has been able to ignore that threat because the most prolific or dangerous groups have been geographically concentrated (in the Kootenays and in Montreal), or have targeted groups outside the mainstream of society (notably diplomats). Only rarely, therefore, has the central element of terrorism—the instilling of fear and a sense of unpredictability—had any impact on Canadian political life. In these circumstances, a single event—typically a longer-lived incident, such as a hostage-taking—can have a far greater impact than a string of bombings.[18]

There are revealing similarities and differences between terrorism in Canada and terrorism elsewhere. One distinguishing feature is the high proportion of attacks here carried out by the idiosyncratic SOF. The low ideological but high nationalist and émigré content of the balance of Canadian terrorism gives it an affinity to the American brand but renders it quite distinct from the experience of most other Western states. Tactically, Canadian terrorism has been even more conservative than its counterparts elsewhere, relying heavily on methods that generally do not require great technical or logistical capability (a quarter of all attacks have involved the simple tactics of incendiarism, firebombing and arson), and rarely resorting to 'technological terrorism' or tactics (such as barricade hostage-taking) that demand organizational sophistication.

The unique motives (and therefore targets) of the SOF, along with the strong leftward tilt of the nationalist FLQ, have rendered targeting patterns in Canada somewhat dissimilar to those prevailing elsewhere. However, nationalists in Canada, as in other countries, have far preferred domestic to international terrorism, and left-wing and émigré groups have conformed to broader norms in their selection of business and diplomatic targets.

This chapter contributes to the study of one type of political violence in Canada. The evidence presented here shows that while Canada has been far less 'peaceable', where terrorism is concerned, than Canadians generally recognize, it has been relatively fortunate when contrasted with other countries. The comparable American experience (within the US) suggests that geography has played an important role in insulating Canada from international terrorism, and in isolating domestic terrorism from foreign sponsorship and nurture (the European experience). However, the longevity—if no longer the scale—of certain strains of terrorism in this country, and the potential for new types of international terrorism, caution against complacency, just as the modest level of attack warns against excessive reaction to individual incidents.

NOTES

The views expressed are those of the author and are not necessarily those of the Department of National Defence or of the Ministry of the Solicitor General of Canada.

[1] Nuclear war was the most frequently cited problem, and accounted for 13% of those sampled.

[2] The British Prevention of Terrorism (Temporary Provisions) Act was introduced one week after two bloody bombings in Birmingham in 1974. Five days after the kidnap of Aldo Moro in 1978, the Italian Parliament passed Law 191 which made terrorist and subversive aims an aggravating factor in kidnap cases. In the same year, German authorities reacted to the kidnap of Dr Schleyer by granting police additional powers in dealing with certain specified terrorist crimes. Finally, Law 86–1020 was passed in France in September 1986 during a wave of terrorist bombings in Paris (Clutterbuck 1990: 27, 58, 64–5, 92).

[3] A fuller description of the methodology briefly outlined here may be found in NSCC 1992.

[4] Capitalized group references will refer to data from NSCC 1992. The traditional appellations—FLQ, SOF, and so on—will be used in the non-empirical parts of the narrative.

[5] The Air India crash, in which 329 persons died, has often been imputed to terrorism. The RCMP's investigation of the incident continues, and thus the government has not pronounced on whether or not the plane's loss was attributable to terrorist attack. In either case, the event's occurrence outside Canada would exclude it from the NSCC database. Hence, the 329 deaths are not included here among the casualties of terrorism in Canada, although the State Department does incorporate them in its world-wide totals for 1985.

6 In NSCC 1992 their deaths are reported in the separate support activities chronology, and thus are not included in the casualty statistics cited earlier.

7 Morf described five 'waves' up to March 1969, and Laurendeau identified five 'phases' and 11 'networks', some successive, some concurrent, between 1963 and 1970 (Morf 1970; Laurendeau 1974: 58–9, Appendix 2).

8 Migration, even to the Soviet Union (which resorted to conscription, a practice anathema to Doukhobors), was a cherished goal among Doukhobor zealots.

9 The figures for 1968 are somewhat skewed by the occurrence of two multiple-site attacks: 13 pipe bombs exploded in Toronto in just over one hour, and six weeks later four pipe bombs were placed in similar circumstances in Montreal.

10 In fact, both occurred on Vancouver Island.

11 Data collection continues, with over 120 events recorded for 1990–2, but most have not yet been validated or coded because in late 1992 the database was transferred to the Canadian Security Intelligence Service (CSIS); CSIS intends to produce an annual or biennial update for public use.

12 An exception is the Pinkerton Risk Assessment Services database.

13 The State Department reports admit that attacks involving American interests are over-represented in them.

14 In 1982 European leftist groups attacked Israeli offices and businesses over a six-month period in order to demonstrate 'revolutionary solidarity' with the Palestine Liberation Organization, then under pressure as a result of Israel's invasion of Lebanon. Almost all Left-Wing attacks in Canada have wholly or largely protested issues external to this country.

15 Most notably in 1983, when several categories used hitherto, including assassination, were dropped.

16 Unless otherwise indicated, all the statistics cited in this section are derived from the annual State Department reports.

17 The casualty estimate for 1991 includes what has since been recognized as an inflated estimate for the Gulf War.

18 As a resident of Montreal in 1969–70, it comes as a shock to the author now to discover that some four dozen bombings, publicly reported, occurred during that period before the October Crisis transformed the FLQ from (for the author) a crepuscular nuisance into a seemingly pervasive threat, with credence being given to the wildest rumours.

References

Barrett, S.R. (1987). *Is God a Racist? The Right Wing in Canada.* Toronto: University of Toronto Press.

Charters, D.A. (1986a). 'The October Crisis: Implications for Canada's Internal Security', pp. 55–72 in MacDonald (1986).

————— (1986b). 'Canadian security intelligence problems in historical perspective'. Paper delivered to the Conference on Intelligence and Policy, Washington, DC.

Clutterbuck, R. (1990). *Terrorism, Drugs and Crime in Europe after 1992.* London: Routledge.

Cordes, B. (1987). 'When terrorists do the talking: Reflections on terrorist literature', *Journal of Strategic Studies* 10, 4 (December): 150–71.

Crelinsten, R.D. (1987). 'The internal dynamics of the FLQ during the October Crisis of 1970', *Journal of Strategic Studies* 10, 4 (December): 59–89.

European Parliament (1990). 'Report drawn up on behalf of the Committee of Inquiry into Racism and Xenophobia on the findings of the Committee of Inquiry'. Series A, Document A3–195/90, 23 July.

Fournier, L. (1984). *F.L.Q. The Anatomy of an Underground Movement.* Toronto: NC Press Ltd.

————— (1988). 'FLQ: Histoire d'un mouvement clandestin'. Paper delivered to the XIVth International Military History Colloquium, Montreal. In *Conflicts of High and Low Intensity Since the Second World War.* Ottawa: International Commission of Military History.

Financial Post (1962). 'Your score card of Kootenay havoc', 31 March.

Hewitt, C. (1984). *The Effectiveness of Anti-Terrorist Policies.* Lanham: University Press of America, Inc.

Hoffman, B. (1986). 'Terrorism in the United States during 1985'. Paper delivered at Research on Terrorism: An International Academic Conference, Aberdeen.

————— (1988). *Recent Trends and Future Prospects of Terrorism in the United States.* RAND Report R–3618. Santa Monica: The Rand Corporation.

International Security Studies Program (1987). 'The psychology of terrorism', *Security Digest,* May.

Kellett, N.A. (1981). *International Terrorism: A Retrospective and Prospective Examination.* ORAE Report No. R78. Ottawa: Operational Research and Analysis Establishment.

————— (1988). *Contemporary International Terrorism and its Impact on Canada.* ORAE Report No. R100. Ottawa: Operational Research and Analysis Establishment.

Kellett, N.A., B. Beanlands, J. Deacon, H. Jeffrey, and C. Lapalme (1992). *Terrorism in Canada 1960–1989.* Report No. 1990–16. Ottawa. Solicitor General Canada.

Kelly, Hon. W.M. (1987). *Terrorism.* Report of the Senate Special Committee on Terrorism and the Public Safety. Ottawa: Minister of Supply and Services Canada.

———— (1989). *Terrorism*. Report of the Second Senate Special Committee on Terrorism and the Public Safety. Ottawa: Minister of Supply and Services Canada.

Laurendeau, M. (1974). *Les Québécois violents*, rev. ed. Montreal: Les Editions du Boréal Express.

MacDonald, B., ed. (1986). *Terror*. Toronto: Canadian Institute of Strategic Studies.

Mitchell, T.H. (1982). 'Politically-Motivated Terrorism in North America: The Threat and the Response'. Paper delivered to the Canadian Political Science Association, Ottawa.

Morf, G. (1970). *Terror in Québec: Case Studies of the FLQ*. Toronto: Clarke, Irwin & Company Limited.

NSCC 1992. See Kellett et al. (1992).

Ross, J.I. (1988). 'Attributes of domestic political terrorism in Canada, 1960–1985', *Terrorism* 11: 213–33.

————, and T.R. Gurr (1989). 'Why terrorism subsides: A comparative study of Canada and the United States', *Comparative Politics* 21, 4 (July): 405–26.

Schmid, A.P., and A.J. Jongman (1988). *Political Terrorism: A New Guide to Actors, Authors, Concepts, Data Bases, Theories and Literature*. Amsterdam: SWIDOC.

Stone, N. (1988). Personal communication, 3 August.

Torrance, J.M. (1986). *Public Violence in Canada, 1867–1982*. Kingston and Montreal: McGill-Queen's University Press.

United States Department of State (1992). *Patterns of Global Terrorism, 1983–92*. Washington, DC: United States Department of State.

Woodcock, G., and I. Avakumovic (1968). *The Doukhobors*. Toronto: Oxford University Press.

Chapter Eleven

THE RESPONSES OF DEMOCRATIC GOVERNMENTS TO VIOLENCE

JUDY TORRANCE

Democratic governments base their claim to rule on the consent of the governed. They come to power as a result of elections that retain some credibility as mechanisms to express the will of the majority. Once installed, they observe, at least most of the time, the constitution and its conventions that limit their powers and prescribe how these powers may be exercised. Such governments are also not totally shrouded in secrecy; they feel obliged to render an account of their actions, and their characteristic means of formulating and carrying out policy are persuasion and bargaining. In contrast, authoritarian regimes largely ignore the population and rely extensively on the threat of heavy-handed coercion to achieve their aims.

Cross-national surveys of political violence indicate that democracies have higher levels of violence that is not regime-shattering than do authoritarian regimes (Gurr, 1989: 112). In the latter, groups that would challenge either the regime as a whole or a particular government policy find it extremely difficult to organize and remain in existence without being discovered by the omnipresent security forces; they lack the means to communicate their views to a wider audience; they cannot move around the country without attracting suspicion; nor can they easily lay hands on the arms and other resources they need to carry on a violent struggle.

Thus the relationship between violent challenger and government is considerably more complex in democratic regimes. Within them, challenges are both more readily mounted and less easily dealt with by the government. Indeed, one might wonder why democracies are not constantly in a state of crisis, or overwhelmed by various groups of citizens taking up arms on behalf of a particular cause. As we shall see, however, democratic governments do have a number of factors capable of working in their favour. The greatest danger they face, it will be argued, comes from within—the tendency for democracies to transform themselves into authoritarian regimes when confronted by violent challenges.[1]

FORCING THE GOVERNMENT TO PAY ATTENTION

Violent dissident groups have only infrequently been dealt with at the cabinet level in Canada. This does not mean that political violence is a rare phenomenon in the country. Jackson, Kelly, and Mitchell (1975) found 129 incidents of collective violence in Ontario between 1965 and 1975; Frank and Kelly (1979) list 281 incidents of collective violence in Ontario and Quebec between 1963 and 1975; Ross (1988) gives a national total of 415 domestic terrorism events between 1960 and 1985 and (1992) 159 incidents of right-wing violence between 1960 and 1990. However, nearly all these incidents were handled as a matter of routine police work and had no impact on the political level. Since violence is generally employed by challengers as a means of compelling the government to pay attention to their grievances, one might ask why their actions so rarely command the attention of government ministers.

Some violence in society may receive no public attention at all. For example, police often ignore the violence committed within marginalized communities or against lower-status individuals. When this happens, the victims of violent assaults are without legal recourse. Either there is no effective police force within the community, or the victims do not approach the police because of their ignorance, fear of reprisal, or suspicion of the authorities. As the status of the community or victims improves, however, demands for better protection are presented to the government. Thus in recent years spousal assault has become a political issue, at least partly because of the increasing political clout of women's groups. The issue has been debated in Parliament, and police have been instructed to intervene more actively and lay charges.

A spectacular crime that elicits a shocked response from the country can also introduce demands into the political system. One example would be the serial killing in the late 1980s of elderly victims in the Miramichi region of New Brunswick (Maclean and Veniol, 1990). Such crimes typically create widespread fear in the general population, and the media give expression to the public revulsion that they arouse. Demands may then be made not simply that the police arrest the culprit, but that laws and policies be changed to deter others who might engage in similar actions in the future.

Neither spousal assault nor spectacular crime, however, is in itself an example of political violence. While such violence may have political consequences, there is usually no suggestion that the person committing the violence is seeking to influence the political system or to transmit a political message. The incident can thus be defined by the government as a criminal event rather than a political one, requiring limited changes at the bureaucratic level, perhaps, or in the Criminal

Code, but not in more problematic areas involving, for example, the reallocation of social resources, the persuasion of other élites to alter their positions, or the depletion of the government's stock of good will among the electorate.

One subcategory of spectacular crime deserves further mention: mass murder. Such an event can rivet the attention of the country. To the media it is one of the major news stories of the day. As with other spectacular crimes, while there may well be public demands for changes such as tighter gun-control legislation in its aftermath, the incident itself is not readily granted political significance: the murderer is not recognized by the government as a political actor, but rather as a single 'insane' individual representing no one but himself (Leyton, 1986: 15). In fact, however, mass murder is different in that the assailant often has an identifiable political motive.[2] Thus, to take some Canadian cases as examples, in 1966 Paul Joseph Chartier brought a bomb into the House of Commons intending to demand that the House, particularly fractious at that time, put aside its partisan grandstanding and deal with the issues affecting ordinary working people; Corporal Denis Lortie in 1984 left a garbled tape at a radio station saying he was acting against the Parti Québécois government before shooting his way into the National Assembly in Quebec City; and in 1990 Marc Lépine reacted against the changing status of women in Canadian society by shooting down women engineering students at the University of Montreal. Yet even when the message the murderer is attempting to deliver has some discernible political content, we can be quite sure that it is not going to be recognized as such. The government, media, and general population will tend to ignore it, turning instead to explanations focusing on the assailant's mental instabilities, personal inadequacies, or past family life.[3]

Generally, then, the violence of the 'insane' represents no problem for a government. It is a matter for the police to handle. All single assailants, with no ties to an organized movement, are easy to place in this category. Other types of violence with ostensible political motives are similarly easy to keep off-stage politically. In the Ottawa area, attacks on embassies and individual diplomats have occurred several times in recent years. The assailants claim to be responding to injustices perpetrated in their homelands (against Armenians by Turkey, for instance)—that is, to issues unlikely to be found on the agenda of any Canadian government. Hijacking a Greyhound bus and instructing the driver to park it on the Parliamentary lawn in order to protest the situation in Lebanon is an act of such outright political irrelevance as to appear ludicrous, although at the time it was no laughing matter either to the hapless travellers or the 'disturbed' individual involved.

If the violent are to be taken seriously by the government, they must also not be vulnerable to labelling as drunken or overly youthful. Both conditions imply irresponsibility and the lack of a well-thought-out program. The Halifax V-E day riot of 1945 was a spectacular drunken rampage, but there was no suggestion that a political issue was at stake. And the various student-led incidents common in the 1960s (although the student leaders themselves may have earnestly thought they were waging a political campaign against imperialism, capitalism, or racism) were largely dismissed by government and media alike as irrelevant, newsworthy as nuisances but not representing a significant force in the country.

Also firmly relegated to the non-politically-significant category are riots where looting has been a dominant feature. Riots of this type may have originated in an orderly demonstration (for example, the 1992 rioting in Toronto in the wake of a demonstration against the verdict in the Rodney King beating trial in Los Angeles), or they may have suddenly coalesced in response to a particular local grievance (for example, the 1955 Forum riot in Montreal, which erupted after the suspension of the hockey player Maurice Richard). The effect of subsequent looting is to mute the voice of the original protest. The journalistic and governmental concern, if any, tends to focus on the acts of the rioters—what was done, not what was said. The looters themselves are generally dismissed as common thieves.

Another form of group violence that is common but infrequently requires special governmental attention is the kind that occurs during strikes. Such conflict is normally seen as affecting only the employers and employees involved, and picket-line scuffles as no more than might be expected in the situation. Nevertheless, there have been strikes in which the federal or provincial governments have become heavily involved: for example, the Winnipeg general strike of 1919, the General Motors Oshawa strike in 1933, and the Asbestos strike of 1949. Typically, in such cases, employers with established access to the government were pitted against new forms of unionism whose demands and apparent organizational successes posed—in government eyes—a novel threat to the economic stability of the country or province. (See Tunnell, this volume.)

Generally speaking, once a specific type of challenger violence has become routine, it loses its power to shock. The police learn how to cope; laws are adapted to deal with it; and the media lose interest. Such violence may still attract government attention, but with each repetition the amount decreases and the issue devolves to ever lower levels in the bureaucratic hierarchy. Since violent incidents are often influenced by 'contagion', with one challenging group copying the activities of another at home or abroad, their potential impact on the government's agenda tends to diminish over time.

This type of habituation, however, applies only to relatively low-threat types of challenger violence. Standing in contrast are the forms of violence that contest the government's claim to a monopoly of legitimate force in a given area of the country. Civil wars and rebellions dominate a government's agenda, with everything else subordinated to the task of regaining control.

At a lower level of urgency are minor outbreaks of terrorism that do not directly interfere with the government's capacity to govern and during which most people are able to go about their affairs as usual. Nevertheless, such terrorism does impugn the government's claim to provide security for the lives and property of its citizens, and thus it represents a constant thorn in the government's side. The danger for a government is that it will appear incompetent, or be tempted into over-reacting in an arbitrary fashion that alienates popular support. Given the relatively low costs of mounting small-scale terrorist attacks in comparison with other forms of oppositional behaviour, both legitimate and illegitimate, and the care that terrorists may take to hide their traces, such incidents remain among the more difficult forms of violence for governments to deal with.

Recently a number of terrorist incidents have been carried out by single-issue groups. Examples include tree-spiking and other forms of 'ecotage', attacks on institutions accused of treating animals cruelly or against individuals wearing furs, and explosions at abortion clinics. The political monomania of the single-issue groups, their inability to compromise their idealism in the development of a policy acceptable to the nation as a whole, creates an unresolvable policy problem for a democratic government. Given such groups' inevitable failure to secure policy decisions entirely to their liking, it is perhaps not surprising that some of their members should resort to what is euphemistically called 'direct action'. Such behaviour, however, especially given a previous history of failing to influence the government's agenda, is unlikely to be politically effective. Indeed, if the aim is to convince the general public of the justice of their cause, it is more likely to be counterproductive (Ross and Gurr, 1989: 409). Nevertheless, for a government concerned to provide for the security of the population and, perhaps more important, to uphold the traditions of political discourse, these incidents represent a troubling trend.

Another form of challenger violence also requires considerable skill for a government to handle. This is the kind of incident that Turner (1969: 815–31) describes as matching our 'folk concept' of rebellion. While this idea is somewhat nebulous and varies from society to society, it is based on the centuries-old natural 'right' of the oppressed to rebel against an unjust government and on our memories of historical 'heroes' like Robin Hood, or of events like the Fall of the Bastille or the Boston Tea Party. Even though this folk concept is nebulous, and

Canada has few if any such heroes or events of its own to draw upon, I believe it is well enough established that a group conforming to the model will find powerful wellsprings of public support to sustain it in its confrontation with the government.

Turner suggests that to meet the model a group must be labouring under widely recognized grievances that are both serious and long-standing. The movement's spokespersons should be dignified representatives of their community; any violence used should be restrained; and the violent actors should not be open to charges of irresponsibility. The group must have previously tried non-violent means of redress but failed to attract sufficient government attention to resolve the problem. The degree of popular sympathy for the Mohawks involved in the Oka crisis of 1990 suggests that this was one incident that did approach the folk concept of rebellion.

To sum up, a violent event will tend to intrude on the government's agenda if it is the work of an organized group, especially one rising in power; if the violent actor(s) cannot be readily dismissed as insane, criminal, irresponsible, or foreign; if the violence shocks public sensibilities and has not become routinized; if it approximates our folk concept of rebellion; and if it challenges the government's monopoly of legitimate force. Still, it is important to note that these factors vary over time and space. Historically, governments have ignored much more violence than is the case today. One society, even one region of a country, will differ from the next. In countries like Canada, with relatively high standards of public order and a political system unhabituated to violent challengers, it may be easier than elsewhere for such groups to gain the attention of the government.

VIOLENCE AS A POLICY ISSUE

Once a government feels compelled to take action against a challenging group, it can face a number of problems in formulating its policy. These difficulties resemble those associated with other policy areas, but are typically present in a more intense or extreme form. Indeed, Dror (1983: 70) suggests that a government's ability to respond to a terrorist challenge can be taken as a test case of its general ability to govern.

In the first place, governments frequently have very little warning or time for advance planning before an incident occurs. In theory, internal security forces should be able to forewarn of some impending conflicts, so that potential incidents can be nipped in the bud. But even in the most repressive regimes they are not always successful (cf. the 1944 plot to kill Hitler; the conspirators failed but were not discovered until after their bomb had gone off). In democracies, as the record shows, intelligence about potential violent challengers is far from complete (Wilkinson, 1986: 119).

Development of a response is also impeded by the very nature of a violent incident. Collecting reliable information may be all but impossible when rumours abound and lines of communication are severed. Violent challenges are also particularly unstable phenomena and flexibility is required to adapt to frequent, abrupt shifts in the situation. As well the incidents that governments are called upon to deal with are likely to be unprecedented, or to be of a kind that has overwhelmed previous planning exercises (Bell, 1978: 197; Dror, 1983: 84–5). Bourne (1978: 309) notes, for example, that the Canadian government had little contingency planning in place for peacetime emergencies at the time of the October Crisis in 1970.

Another uncertainty is that, at the time, the government has no clear way of knowing when an incident has ended. There is always the possibility that the challengers will regroup and launch a fresh attack, that they will mobilize an ever-widening circle of opposition, or that other groups with similar causes will be inspired to take up arms. It has been characteristic of Canadian governments to respond to major violent challenges by introducing repressive measures for some time after the movements in question have been crushed. Thus, in relation to the October Crisis, Whitaker (1989: 207) points out: 'the historical irony is that the violent separatist movement died with the overwhelming state reaction of the War Measures Act; the next half-decade saw excessive, intrusive (and illegal) counter-subversion activities launched against a movement' that was evolving into a respectable legal political party.

Violent challenges usually constitute an emergency for the government, requiring immediate and extraordinary action. Dror (1983: 87–8) urges 'the need to preserve a "cool" attitude of clinical concern in the face of overwhelming pressure and the heartbreaking impact of tragic choices . . . [and for] protection against emotional overloads, panic effects, and the impact of strain and stress.' His counsel points to the psychological forces that can handicap a government seeking a balanced response to a crisis. Balance may be all the more difficult to achieve because the government itself may well feel on the defensive for its failure to anticipate the trouble and defuse the situation before it reached a crisis point.

The ready development of a government response is further hampered in that the violent challenges requiring government intervention are typically unprecedented and cannot necessarily be handled by the existing decision-making framework. Rather, a new team must be cobbled together—one that can rapidly reach unwieldy proportions, given the numerous agencies that may be drawn into devising or implementing the government's strategy.[4] At the very least, several ministers will want a seat at the table: those responsible for the particular policy areas involved, for the coercive arm, for the region of the country affected, and for departments, like Finance, that may be affected by the decision. Provincial and municipal officials will also have to be brought into the discussions, and individuals not normally included in government decision-making may need to be co-opted so that the government can take advantage of their special knowledge or influence. The ability of such a diverse group to work effectively together cannot be assumed.[5] With no previous history of making trade-offs and accommodating each other's interests, there is the very real possibility of deadlock resulting from the different goals and priorities of the participants.

Many problems confronting governments today—problems like the economy, the environment, and ethnic conflicts—are horrendously complex and, in all likelihood, intractable, at least in the short term. Some may represent structural contradictions beyond the capacity of the political system to resolve with the result that some interests in society will be permanently dissatisfied (Wardlaw, 1986: 203). If such groups turn to violence, nothing much can be done to deal with the root causes of their discontent. As well, other typical features of violent incidents may tie the hands of authorities as they seek a resolution to the crisis. The government may face not one but two challengers to its authority, each bitterly at odds with the other: for example, the provisional IRA versus Protestant extremists in Northern Ireland. A negotiated settlement may also be impossible when the dissident group is divided internally and the violence is undertaken by one faction seeking greater influence within it (cf. the divisions within the Mohawk community during the Oka crisis: Hornung, 1991).

While governments frequently find it difficult to develop a policy that will resolve a violent challenge to their authority, failure to do so can affect the future of the regime itself and the political culture of the nation. Regimes do fall as a result of violence directed against them. Since the Second World War, we have seen ex-dependencies such as Israel, Algeria, Kenya, and Vietnam achieve independence in part through guerrilla warfare and terrorism. In addition, governments have been ousted in innumerable military coups and as a result of civil wars in places like Cuba, Sudan, and Afghanistan. While democratic regimes may be less vulnerable to overthrow, the recent histories of Greece, Chile, and Uruguay indicate they are not totally immune; moreover, they are certainly vulnerable to self-transformation into authoritarian regimes.

Even if the consequences of government decision-making are less than regime-shattering, they can still have profound effects on the political culture of the nation—in particular, on the standards that define the proper means for resolving political disputes. No government can be expected simply to concede to demands violently presented to it. It must not only uphold the standards of political civility and political discourse that enable a democratic nation to function, but maintain its monopoly of legitimate force if violence is not to become endemic in the political process.

In short, the government that is confronted by a violent challenger faces an arduous and potentially disastrous time. Nevertheless, it has three major factors that work initially in its favour. First, it is considerably more powerful than most dissident groups. Its coercive ability is such that virtually no government today can be overthrown by rebel violence without units of the police and armed forces first defecting to the rebel side. As well, it has resources at its disposal—favourable policies, money, prestige, jobs—that it can use to shore up wavering support and that far exceed anything the challengers can offer. It can also rely on the habit of obedience, the result of socialization patterns that instil, however imperfectly, the notion that the lawful edicts of a democratically elected government ought to be obeyed.

Second, the violent challengers, no doubt to their surprise, are probably going to be profoundly unpopular, especially in countries where violent turmoil is uncommon. People do not like having their daily routines disrupted or being held in a state of anxiety and fear. Since the widely recognized effect of an attack on a solidary unit is to increase the cohesion of that unit (Coser, 1956: 87–95), the government may well find itself blessed with a not inconsiderable surge of popular support. Third parties as well will be angry at being elbowed off the government's agenda by the upstart challengers. They and the bureaucracy are far more likely to identify with the government than with those who violently assail it (Wardlaw, 1989: 7–8).

Finally, the government enjoys a key advantage in its privileged capacity to define an incident: that is, to place it in a particular context and to explain its meaning. During a crisis the population will be searching for meaning and eager to believe that the authorities know what they are doing. As Edelman (1971: 79) has explained, 'where people are baffled by complex and threatening events they cannot control they need to believe that the highest official of the state is both benevolent and able to cope.'

This process could be seen at work in the May 1992 riot that followed a peaceful demonstration in Toronto to protest the acquittal of Los Angeles police officers in the beating of Rodney King. In their interpretation of the event, various government leaders clearly distinguished between the demonstration and the riot; only the first was accepted as legitimate protest. In a front-page story, Ontario Premier Bob Rae was quoted as saying: 'Everyone has a right to demonstrate and express their opinions. But nobody has a right to throw bricks through store windows and just basically carry out acts of vandalism' (*Globe and Mail*, 6 May

1992). Evidently no political connotations were to be attached to the rioters' actions; they were not to be seen as fighting racism in the police force. They were quite simply 'vandals'. Well-buried in the inside pages of the 8 May edition of the same paper was a different interpretation: according to this report, 'social activists warned that, despite what politicians and police have been saying, racism was the cause of the rampage . . . [not] "young people having kicks".' But the government-endorsed view of irresponsible youths and greedy looters as the source of the violence was by this point too well entrenched for any counter-interpretation to receive widespread coverage or endorsement in the media.

The government interpretation may, of course, be challenged by established interest groups and opposition politicians trying to adopt and adapt the incident to their own ends. Breton (1972: 50) has noted that the more ambiguous a phenomenon, the greater the opportunity it offers for other groups to structure it to their own advantage. Those not directly involved in the conflict will seek to define it so as to buttress their own positions and demonstrate the justice, urgency, or cogency of their own particular cause, while opposition leaders will use it as evidence to condemn past government policies. The Lépine incident, for example, was promptly interpreted and utilized both by women's groups and by the gun-control lobby to harness the widespread moral outrage and shock to their own ends.

However, third-party manoeuvring rarely damages the government's fundamental interpretation of the event. And it is with this interpretation that the government can strike a crippling blow at its opponents' legitimacy and chances of mobilizing support. If the challengers can be identified as mentally unstable, foreigners, irresponsible, and unrepresentative of the community on whose behalf they purport to act, or if the means they employ can be characterized successfully as criminal, reckless, or vicious, then the government is well on the way to prevailing. The issue has been converted from a political demand to one of law and order. The next step is to send in the police or army.

THE DRIFT TOWARDS VIOLENT AUTHORITARIANISM

It may be taken as axiomatic that a democratic government desires to put an end to violent challenges to its authority and regain control over its agenda as rapidly and as cheaply as possible. Coercion has been identified by Oberschall (1973: 263) as 'the cheapest and most immediately available means of control to the authorities'. Governments generally try to meet violence with violence—or, as they would say, to restore order. While doing so, they tend to make stirring pronouncements to the effect that the government is sworn to uphold the democratic values of the nation; violence (that is, challenger violence) cannot be allowed to disrupt the rule of law and the parliamentary system; and the government is duty-bound to stand firm lest it encourage other groups to take the law into their own hands.

Once the decision to resolve the incident by violence is taken, there is often very little more to be said. Because the government's coercive ability and the resources available to it far exceed those of most challengers, the culprits are usually rounded up in short order, and the government carries on with its previous business. There is, however, no inevitability about this tidy sequence of events. One alternative scenario in particular has occurred often enough to be troubling: a drift towards violent authoritarianism whereby a democratic regime comes to an end not by being overthrown but by gradually transforming itself into a repressive dictatorship.

The slide from democracy to violent authoritarianism is a gradual affair, not easily recognizable as such while it is occurring. It can take a number of forms. In Canada there have been three occasions in this century when the government of the day has clearly started down the path towards repression: around the end of the First World War, at the start of the Depression, and in the latter 1960s and early 1970s. These governments were under domestic attack and deemed it prudent to increase their police and military forces and to enlarge the powers accorded them. Internal security forces were also ordered to broaden and intensify their surveillance; they, and their political masters, then started to take seriously the rumours and wild talk that can always be found in union halls, coffee shops, or campuses. Ever more alarmed, the governments gave further resources to their coercive arm and demanded results of it. Police and soldiers intervened more actively, even pre-emptively, against challengers. Internal security forces started to ignore the legal limitations on their powers; they took shortcuts, infiltrated the challenging groups, and acted as agents provocateurs. As the challengers resisted this onslaught, open violence between citizens and government forces occurred still more frequently.

In each case the possibility of a non-violent resolution of the crisis faded as both sides rejected compromise and the moderates were forced off-stage. Independent critics of the government, whether in the press, the universities, or elsewhere, were silenced (or silenced themselves) in the name of presenting a solid front in the emergency. As these people lost their public voice, a source of ideas for resolving the crisis was also lost. Intermediaries—those who can interpret one side to another and through whom communications normally flow—were now regarded with suspicion by both sides. With the breakdown in dialogue, the possibility of recognizing the validity of each other's viewpoint declined. To the government, the dissidents had become faceless, evil non-citizens or traitors, amenable only to coercion. As well, with more and more resources pouring into the coercive arm, there was less and less available to the government to use creatively to solve the crisis by non-forcible methods. The possibility of widespread reforms to address the grievances of the challenger was probably the first alternative to go. The costs and political risks were considered too high and the outcome too unpredictable. Less expensive 'carrots' came to be seen as incapable of remedying the situation. In this way, the habit of conciliation—traditional among democratic governments—died. The government now found itself boxed into a policy of repression.[6]

For other countries, a number of factors have been identified that aid this transition into violent authoritarianism. Perhaps most important is the nature of the violence facing the regime. Clearly the process is unlikely to be initiated unless the government perceives the challenger as posing a serious threat.[7] Objectively there are certain forms of violence that a government should treat as 'serious'. These would include the violence of a revolutionary group seeking fundamental social and political changes. Also serious would be the group capable of mobilizing a large segment (and particularly an ethnically distinct segment [Wilkinson, 1986: 84–6]) of the population because it is voicing widespread aspirations and has the political skill to build a sustained movement for change. Another serious situation would be one in which a pent-up demand for reform explodes independently in a number of different social segments (Oberschall, 1973: 49). If in any of these cases the challengers, because of either their ideology or their social background, are prevented from operating within the established political channels and thus opt to advance their cause through violence, the seriousness of the threat should be immediately apparent. This will be even more true if the dissident group decides on terrorist tactics, precisely because such a form of violence is so difficult for a government to handle.

A second factor prompting the transition to violent authoritarianism is governmental preoccupation with achieving some great national end. A prime example occurs in countries under attack from foreign foes (cf. the crackdown on union demands and strikes during the First World War in Canada).[8] Less dramatically, a government may become convinced that the country's destiny depends on the accomplishment of some difficult policy feat. The creation of the apartheid system in South Africa (Denemark and Lehman, 1984) and the imposition in Argentina of the anti-inflationary policies demanded by the International Monetary Fund (Pion-Berlin, 1984) are well-known examples. Governmental preoccupations of this nature typically breed impatience with opposition. A government has no time for democratic niceties when it deems the whole future of the country to be at stake.

Third, the ideologies circulating among a society's ruling élites have also been associated with the transition to violent authoritarianism. Lopez (1984: 65–6) suggests that one or more of four ideologies (authoritarianism, militarism, national-security consciousness, and patriarchy) must dominate the thinking of government leaders if state terror is to become established. He argues such an ideology is a *sine qua non*:

> [it] stimulates, rationalizes, and blesses as patriotic political behavior government actions that deny others their basic human dignity and their universal political rights. It reifies the state, making it the highest institutional value to which the ruling élite must maintain their highest commitment.

However, it is unclear whether these ideologies are necessary conditions to the development of violent repression or merely facilitating factors (Franks, 1989: 9); nor is it clear whether, since they were mainly identified in studies focusing on Latin America, they are entirely relevant to countries possessing a different cultural heritage. In Canada, the moral justification that governments have needed to proceed down the path of repression appears to have been linked to their conviction that it was their duty at all costs to preserve order (Torrance, 1977: 478–9). This idea, in turn, may have originated in the identification of this country as the 'peaceable kingdom' and in what McNaught (1975: 138) has identified as 'the basically British belief that both liberty and justice are impossible without order [which] lies at the heart of the Canadian political tradition'.

A fourth factor has to do with the power of example. If the present government has replaced a dictatorial regime, the historical justifications and institutions of violent authoritarianism will already be present for the new government to avail itself of (cf. the transition from the tsarist Okhrana to the OGPU of the new Soviet regime). Alternatively, a government may observe other governments lurching into repression in countries that provide significant reference points by reason of cultural, economic, geographic, or other ties. 'Contagion' is apparently an accelerating factor in the spread of governmental violence just as it is in the spread of certain crimes and protest violence. As examples Gurr (1984: 57) cites the diffusion of secret police agencies in Eastern Europe patterned on the Stalinist model and 'the spreading use among conservative Latin American regimes of enforcement terror by special military units or by vigilante groups operating with the tacit approval of authorities'.

A fifth factor is the pressure of third parties on the government to take ever more stringent actions against the challenger. Third parties, comfortably established in the existing structures of power, may perceive the challenging group as a particular threat to the status quo that serves them well. The government faces not only the threat of such groups transferring their support to a political party, or faction within the governing party, more amenable to their demands, but the far more dangerous possibility of their turning to private acts of terrorism, revenge, or vigilantism. In the latter case, the government will rapidly find itself battling on two fronts in an effort to maintain its monopoly of legitimate violence.

A final factor, relating to the nature of violent challenges as a policy issue, was introduced in the previous section. A government frequently cannot tell at what point it has 'won' the campaign against a challenger. The tendency will thus be to pile on repressive measures long after the challengers have wound down their activities. The governmental urge—even in the face of evidence that the challenger has been defeated—to go one step further, to err on the safe side or deter future challengers, will work against any attempt to rein in the drift to violent authoritarianism. The ability of the government to assess the situation realistically is compromised by the collapse of communications channels between challenger and government, and the silencing of outside sources of opinion. The result may be a distorted governmental perception of the challenger as being far more sinister, organized, and powerful than it actually is.

In some cases the target of increasing governmental violence may not be the population at large but only a section of it, perhaps one concentrated in a particular region of the country (for example, the Kurds in Iraq). This section of the population may also differ from the remainder in ethnicity or religion. A democratic government should face considerably less opposition in responding violently to this segment, and may develop what has been called a 'zone of terror' in relation to it (Gurr, 1984: 53). The rest of the population, left largely undisturbed by emergency measures directed towards a socially distinct segment, may be uninterested in or regard as justified the measures the government is taking. Northern Ireland springs to mind as a prime example of a 'zone of terror'; in Canada one could perhaps include the East Kootenays of British Columbia in the 1950s, where repressive measures were adopted against the Sons of Freedom Doukhobors, and Montreal for a short time in 1970 in the wake of the FLQ kidnappings.

Even when violent repression is not localized, it may be difficult at the time for those subject to it to recognize such repression for what it is. 'State terror' and 'violent authoritarianism' are labels with negative connotations that are more easily applied by those outside the system or distanced from it by time than by those caught up in it. Part of the problem is that there are so many synonyms for violence, some of which have positive connotations and suggest that the government's action is legitimate and justified. Such words also tend to sanitize the gory reality by masking the death, destruction, pain, and horror involved. When a government tells its citizens that it is restoring order, upholding the law, maintaining the peace, or employing force, the populace may well applaud. Differences in behaviour and styles between the forces of the government and those of the challenger may also contribute to the popular perception that the government's resort to violence is legitimate (Wardlaw, 1989: 6–7).

Another obfuscating factor is the tendency, particularly in the initial stages, for governments to clothe their actions in familiar legal trappings. Unlike the United States, Commonwealth countries have a legal legacy of Prevention of Terrorism Acts and special powers under statutes such as the Defence of the Realm Act and the War Measures Act. (Canada updated its legislation in 1988, repealing the War Measures Act and replacing it with the Emergencies Act.) In reading Denmark and Lehman's (1984) account of the emergence of South African state terrorism, the similarities to the Canadian experience are unmistakable. For example, the wording of the South African statutory definition of communism as 'any doctrine that aims at bringing about any political, industrial, social, or economic change by the promotion, threat, or conduct of acts of disturbance or disorder' (Suppression of Communism Act, 1950) is reminiscent of section 98 of the Canadian Criminal Code during the interwar period, which defined an 'unlawful association' as one with the purpose of bringing about 'any governmental industrial or economic change within Canada' by the use, threat, or promotion of violence.

The legislation conferring special powers on the government often includes 'Temporary Measures' as part of its title: for example, the Public Order Temporary Measures Act, the legislation that took effect in December 1970 in place of the War Measures Act. In introducing such legislation, the government typically explains that it needs these unfortunately broad powers only for a short time in order to deal with the particular challenger; once order is restored, the legislation will be allowed to lapse. Thus the usual opposition to restrictions on civil liberties is blunted. Such restrictions, along with the government's employment of violent means, are not generally viewed as the first steps along the path to violent authoritarianism, but rather as temporary aberrations from democratic norms, justifiable in the face of an emergency.

A government may also be able to distance itself from its own agents and thereby deflect awareness of the slide into authoritarianism. It may claim to be unaware of the actions taken by the lower echelons of the bureaucracy: this is the principle of deniability. Or it may simply wash its hands of all responsibility. Death squads, for instance, have more than once been dismissed as private individuals taking the law into their own hands in outrage against the deeds of the challengers.

In addition, it must be recognized that governments may well have strong popular support for their actions not only initially but even as the drift into violent authoritarianism accelerates. As noted earlier, violent challengers disrupt the routines of daily life; they create fears, anxiety, and uncertainty. These are unpleasant psychological states, which people will tend to evade by closing ranks against the disruptive force and believing that the government is beneficial, knows what it is doing, and is in control. In such conditions, governments may hold elections during the emergency and handily win them. While the electoral rules may have been tampered with, and the government may trumpet propaganda emphasizing the threat to the nation, the ability to gain re-election in the midst of crisis (though not necessarily after it has ended)[9] must be attributed in part to the population's desire for security and 'normality'.

In short, the danger in the drift to violent authoritarianism is precisely that it is a drift—an insidiously incremental process. Unlike a sudden change of regime, such as the military coup in Chile in 1973, a drift provides no clear point at which democracy can be said to have died. Rather, the government moves further and further into a policy of repression that attracts little public opposition until finally the regime can no longer be characterized, by outside observers at least, as a democracy. At the time, no one in the government or outside it can tell how long the 'temporary' measures will remain in force or what additional restrictions or coercion will follow. With the wisdom of hindsight, of course, it is apparent that most democracies have been able to overwhelm violent challenges in relatively short order, and thereafter to reverse the drift and return the country if not entirely to the openness obtaining prior to the challenge at least to a lower level of repression. Yet because there can be no certainty that this reversal will take place, and because the drift is so difficult to arrest once under way, a democratic government would be wise to turn to other measures beyond coercion to resolve its difficulties.

RESTRAINTS ON GOVERNMENTAL COERCION

There are, in fact, a number of very practical considerations arguing against the use of coercion, at least in more than minimal amounts. Coercion may be the cheapest means of control, but it is not without costs. Sending the army into the field and asking the police to work long hours of overtime is expensive, and the money will have to be borrowed or found by drawing on existing programs. To be sure, this is more likely to be an annoyance than a restraining factor even for today's permanently cash-strapped governments, if they judge the incident serious enough. Yet the bill in long-term campaigns can be a steep one indeed;

for instance, Wilkinson (1986: 91) gives a figure of nine billion pounds sterling as the total cost to the United Kingdom government of containing the violence in Northern Ireland since 1969.

Financial costs come into play more clearly when a government accelerates the drift towards violent authoritarianism and increases ongoing levels of coercive capacity. Adding more personnel and equipment can quickly distort budgetary allocations and thereby alienate support for the government among third parties. The economy may slow down as public investment dries up or is slowly withdrawn, and private investment is frightened away. The labour force may be depleted by casualties, conscription, and emigration. Balance-of-payments problems can also emerge. As a result, the government's ability to deliver housing, education, and other social programs expected by the population at large may be severely curtailed. Unless the government is blinkered by ideological preoccupations or dedicated to pursuing some great national goal, it will have difficulty justifying even to itself the resulting deformation of the country's economy. The governments of Argentina and South Africa, for example, ran into economic difficulties when they attempted to expand their coercive abilities beyond their countries' ability to pay (Pion-Berlin, 1984: 108–9, 118–19; Denemark and Lehman, 1984: 152, 162).

Another possible restraining factor has to do with the type of challenger involved. The government may well consider it prudent to treat gently a group with powerful allies or one whose future co-operation it wishes to secure. As well, the challenger's tactics may be such that the government cannot strike effectively against it. Mobile groups that hide their identity can rarely be brought to battle by the armed forces. Rather, routine police and intelligence services are called for, unless of course the violence has reached the stage of overwhelming the police, and the army must be called in.

Heavy-handed repression is also just as likely to unite the challenger group as it is to destroy it. Its cohesion, determination, and sense of grievance may rise in the wake of government attacks on its members. Martyrs are a valuable resource to a challenger group (cf. the efforts of the IRA to prolong the hunger strikes of its members). Challengers often seek to provoke the government into clumsy over-reactions that will alienate its popular support. This danger is sufficiently well understood that a number of commentators have encouraged governments to deliberately under-react in such circumstances (Bell, 1978: 278–9; Wardlaw, 1989: 159–60).

In other cases the coercive arm may be incapable of acting. (For some Canadian examples, see Torrance, 1986: 207.) Historically, some incidents have occurred in places that were simply too remote for the army or police to reach; Fort Garry, for instance, was inaccessible to

Canadian military forces throughout the winter of 1869–70, during the first Riel rebellion. During wartime or economic depression, the government may not have enough men in uniform to deploy effectively against a challenger. There may be doubts as to the loyalty of the troops generally or in relation to the particular challenger at hand. The possibility of mutiny and *coup d'état* may also serve as a constraint. Less dramatically, any government will have to consider the professional opinion and morale of the armed forces before committing them to a conflict from which no winners may emerge.

Another factor is the possibility that insurgents will, sooner or later, defeat the armed forces. To re-emphasize an earlier point, there is nothing certain about the outcome of violent conflicts. While, generally, government forces are overwhelmingly superior to those of any challenger and can be expected to succeed, there are no guarantees. Violent challengers can and do overthrow regimes; Afghanistan represents a recent example. And once government forces are committed—once this card has been played—there can be no return to the *status quo ante* (Gurr, 1988: 52).

Such considerations should prompt any prudent government to explore its non-violent options. Moreover, another range of factors, having to do with the government's legitimacy and public opinion, similarly suggests the wisdom of restraint. Democratic governments claim to rule on the basis of the uncoerced consent of the governed. They could face some political embarrassment, therefore, during an election or in the House of Commons, if domestic civil liberties' watchdogs or bodies like Amnesty International have pointed an accusatory finger at their practices.

In addition, of course, democratic governments operate under a host of legal and constitutional restraints on their actions. These restraints govern such matters as what a police officer may or may not do during a riot, the circumstances under which the army may act in aid of the civil power, the legal safeguards surrounding the rights of an accused, the administrative procedures that must be followed in deportation proceedings, and which level of government has responsibility for the enforcement of a particular piece of legislation. All such bureaucratic protocols, legalities, and constitutional provisions hamper the government's freedom of action. It must not be forgotten, for example, that the 'administration of justice', which includes the maintenance of public order, is a provincial responsibility under the Canada Act. For the federal government to become involved in an incident of violence where an area of federal responsibility is not directly affected, it must normally await an invitation. The most formal invitation is the written request from the provincial Attorney-General to the Chief of the Defense Staff, which is required for the deployment of troops in aid of the civil power.

Another potential brake on government action is the bureaucracy—the people who actually have to carry out government orders. Many civil servants have spent their lives operating within prescribed limits and are professionally socialized to respect them. Since overstepping their legal powers may render them personally liable to criminal proceedings or internal disciplinary action, their tendency is towards caution. As one veteran militia officer counselled in 1900, the wise officer 'will do as little as possible, and will do nothing without a positive order from a justice of the peace' (Morton, 1970: 419).

Of course governments can and do amend legislation to enhance their already considerable powers *vis-à-vis* challenging groups. They do bully bureaucrats into doing their bidding, or create new agencies less tied to traditional procedures. Some police or security agents will always be found willing to bend the rules in an effort to advance their careers. The government may in fact already have available élite forces able and willing to carry out various forms of skulduggery at its behest. And the record shows that constitutional demarcations have been ignored in the heat of the moment.

The point is, however, that these actions create political risks. They provide other political élites, the courts, commissions of inquiry, and investigative journalists with damaging material that can place the government on the defensive. While they are unlikely to be questioned in the immediate crisis (supplementary legislation, for example, typically clears Parliament within a day, with few dissenting votes) and indeed may well be widely supported if effective over the short term in putting an end to the incident (Bell, 1978: 151–2), such actions nevertheless often return to haunt a government at a later date. In Canada, the newspapers are still reporting 'scandals' surrounding the FLQ crisis twenty years after the event: who was a paid informant of the RCMP, what exactly the Prime Minister personally authorized, or was informed of and so on.

Finally, a government might question the effectiveness of repression in suppressing dissent. It is impossible to generalize in this regard, as much depends on the nature of the particular challenging group, the time-frame considered, and the ruthlessness of the government's response. Obviously, though, there are limits to what coercion can achieve. As the sole form of response, it is unlikely to keep a group conforming to Turner's folk concept of rebellion off the government agenda for long. It can perhaps give the government some breathing room in which to try and resolve the issues in play. But if these issues are not or cannot be settled in the political arena, they will in all likelihood be settled in the streets—under the watchful eye of the television cameras.

THE ROLE OF THE MEDIA

The freedom of the press is generally considered to be a cornerstone of democratic society. It is the press that is supposed to provide the information the general population needs to determine the electoral fate of the government and to influence the development of its policies. Indications are widespread that governments do fear the power of an independent press to shape public opinion. Many democratic governments make considerable efforts to co-opt the media, with information officers (a.k.a. spin doctors) attempting to ensure that the most favourable interpretations are placed on governmental actions. Authoritarian governments impose censorship, intimidate journalists, or simply shut down opposition papers. Broadcasting facilities are typically among the first targets of coup leaders (Luttwak, 1979: 118–19).

Democratic theory also presupposes a citizen body attentive to all governmental activity and capable of omnivorously absorbing all the information that comes its way. In practice, however, most people are uninterested in trade deficits, budgetary estimates, or diplomatic initiatives. Even on issues that are widely followed, the evidence is that most of us readily absorb only news and opinions that confirm our preexisting beliefs, dismissing the rest as biased. And given the commercial pressures that fuel the inanities of the tabloids and the infotainment of the tube, the amount of useful information being transmitted is open to question.

With respect to violent incidents, there are similarly conflicting opinions as to the role and importance of the press. Some sweeping claims have been made for the power of the media. To take one example, the television camera has been called 'the most powerful weapon available in these modern forms of conflict [mass picketing and terrorism]—a weapon lying in the streets available for either side to pick up and use' (Clutterbuck, 1981: xv). But a more nuanced conclusion emerges when we look more closely at the effects the media can have on an incident and the ways in which a government can influence an ostensibly independent press. In the course of such examination, several of the main themes of this chapter re-emerge.

One thing is certain: violence that has any political connotations will be covered by the media. Even fairly routine, low-level clashes ('strikers damage truck entering plant') will usually receive some coverage, as will the responses of the police and the judiciary. Violence has 'news value': that is, it meets the criteria by which the media sort out which events will be reported to the public. Possible news stories are said to be selected according to whether they are extraordinary and breach our normal expectations, involve élite persons or nations, are dramatic in nature, can be personalized, have negative consequences, or can be incorporated within existing newsworthy themes (Hall et al., 1978: 53; see also Ericson, Baranek, and Chan, 1987: 139–78).

Violence usually bears one or more of these characteristics—in particular, the 'negative consequences'. Violence represents an attack on civil society, with its requirements of security of person and property:

> [It] thus constitutes a critical threshold in society; all acts, especially criminal ones, which transgress that boundary, are, by definition, worthy of news attention. It is often complained that in general 'the news' is too full of violence. . . . Those who so complain do not understand what 'the news' is all about. It is impossible to define 'news values' in ways which would not rank 'violence' at or near the summit of news attention. (Hall et al., 1978: 68)

The role the press can play for and against the contending parties is rather more problematic. Some argue that the media and violent challengers are mutually supportive. The challengers stage a drama and thus provide the newspeople with their story. Preferably, the incident lasts long enough for the media to be able to cover it live, and takes place in a city like Munich with good communications facilities and a large press corps previously assembled to cover an event like the Olympics. The incident itself must offer the reality or prospect of violence, and the outcome must be in doubt. Ideally there is some action or movement going on for the television cameras to capture (Bell, 1978: 112). Most of these criteria were satisfied in the Oka confrontation of 1990, in which the challenging Mohawk group successfully gained access to the media and attracted the extended attention of the country.

According to Bell (1978: 113), 'once a terrorist event is launched before the cameras, the drama by definition is a success.' An opposing view is offered by Hocking (1992), who points out that defining terrorist success in terms of media access is relevant only to some terrorist groups. Nevertheless, Bell's thesis has been widely accepted by government counter-terrorist agencies. The result has been a tendency to think that an incident can be handled simply by controlling the press while ignoring the very real grievances that may have motivated the violence. Counter-terrorist agencies have accordingly attempted to restrict media access to an incident and to 'co-ordinate' the information made available to the press—measures that might be justifiable in wartime but not in situations where the democratic state's existence is not in immediate question.

Nevertheless, given that the media use terrorists and their terrorism as much as terrorists use the media (Schmid and de Graaf, 1982), there is always the possibility that the interests of the media and those of the government will conflict. In some countries it has been alleged that the media have disrupted the government's handling of incidents by revealing information helpful to the challengers, and that hostages have died as a result (Wardlaw, 1989: 78–81). In the excitement or competitive pressure to be first with the story or to unearth fresh angles, the press may eavesdrop on official communications channels or forget what should not be released from confidential background briefings. In Canada, although Bourne (1978: 312) has lamented irresponsible press coverage in the past, there now appears to be in place an informal government-press protocol or code of conduct that restrains any media tendency to actively intervene in an event.

Any protocols of this nature are, of course, precarious: sooner or later, one newspaper or television channel will decide to steal a march on its rivals (Crelinsten, 1989: 331–2). They are also unlikely to extend to novel or spectacular events. Finally, another argument made against censorship, even self-imposed, is that it may drive terrorists to new heights of horror in order to capture the attention they seek.[10]

The media may also contribute inadvertently to the triggering or escalation of violent clashes in a variety of ways. The footage they transmit may create sufficient outrage to set off a riot, as in the Rodney King affair. They may pass a message to potential rioters that there is little or no police presence on the scene. The sight of people in the streets may encourage others to join the fray (although the counter-argument here is that people may instead stay home, close to their television sets, in an effort to keep abreast of events).

The actual arrival of the media on the scene of a clash is unmistakable; their cars and vans clearly label them as does the gear they carry around. As the two sides become aware of the presence of reporters, they alter their behaviour. On the one hand, the police try to act with careful restraint in order to avoid any embarrassing shots of 'police brutality'. On the other, some demonstrators, aware of the protection the press offers them, chant more loudly and act with renewed vigour. Individuals become more daring in the hope of attracting footage that will be widely aired. The violence sometimes escalates as a result.

The media, then, do not simply record violent events. However, their reports on violence carry a number of limitations from the challenger's perspective. In the first place, if the violent group are seeking to transmit a message of any complexity beyond 'we exist; we have a cause' they may well be disappointed. The typical media account tends to record the events that have taken place, the fate of any victims, and the reactions of eye-witnesses and various élite groups to the incident. The issues involved are often ignored (Jackson, Kelly, and Mitchell, 1975: 275; Schmid and de Graaf, 1982: 84–5). Because the scattered background or analytical pieces that do appear take time to produce, they do not usually coincide with the main coverage of the event. The net effect is to delegitimate the challengers and to legitimate the actions of the authorities (Crelinsten, 1992: 216).

In some respects this is not surprising. The very nature of some events precludes the transmission of a challenger's message. A bombing in the night by unknown individuals may make a statement about the existence of a challenger group but no more. The FLQ's hostage-taking had the advantage of prolonging the incident, but because the tactic required the perpetrators to hide themselves, they had no authentic voice during the crisis in the way that the Mohawks did at Oka. Significantly, one of the FLQ demands was that its manifesto be published—an indication of their recognition of the need to communicate their ideas and attach their own interpretation to their actions.

Why do the media so consistently serve violent challengers so poorly in this regard? It is not that the media are a monolithic entity or mere voices or tools of democratic élites (Ericson, Baranek, and Chan, 1989: 378). As we have seen, the media can act in ways that embarrass the authorities and disrupt their planning. A more promising approach is to recognize that news stories are socially constructed artifacts. Violent events belong to the category of the unusual, the unpredictable, the conflictual—all traits that render them newsworthy, but at the same time not readily comprehensible. They need to be brought from the realm of random, chaotic acts into the realm of the intelligible. To this end, they must be identified (that is, named, defined, and related to other known events) and assigned to a social context (that is, placed within a familiar frame of reference) (Hall et al., 1978: 54).

Journalists are subject to a professional code requiring them to strive for objectivity and hence to base their reports not simply on their own impressions but on authoritative statements by those deemed to have special knowledge in the area (Ericson, Baranek, and Chan, 1989: 3–5). This factor, coupled with the time constraints that reporters work under, leads to the 'systematically structured *over-accessing* to the media of those in powerful and privileged institutional positions' (Hall et al., 1978: 58).[11] The government thus has the opportunity to stigmatize a group as 'extreme' or 'irrational,' especially if, like the Sons of Freedom Doukhobors, the group is weak, fragmented, and lacking effective spokespersons.

When alternative interpretations are not given much currency, the media can serve to mobilize public opinion in support of the government's position. They take the definitions of those assumed to have access to specialized information and translate this message into language their audience understands. That audience, in turn, sees its own preconceptions reaffirmed and sends messages to elected representatives or writes letters to the editor reflecting its support of the government's position.

The danger for a government in this situation, however, is that the media may become in effect an amplifying chamber. Because of a spectacular event's newsworthiness, the press tends to give it extensive coverage, with headlines that stress the seriousness of the event. Even if the reportage does not directly push the government into action, it will serve to raise public anxiety, which in turn will be expressed in pressures on the government to become more actively involved. The effect, according to Wardlaw (1986: 202), has been 'to elevate terrorism to undeserved prominence on policy agendas and to grossly inflate the importance of terrorist groups'. For example, press emphasis on the plight of victims, such as hostages, can generate demands for their safety that can distort a government's longer-range planning (Crelinsten, 1992: 215).

Certain changes in communications technology have the potential to undermine the government's ability to define an incident. Desktop publishing, electronic networks, fax machines, and photocopiers all enable a challenger and its allies to circulate their interpretation of events even in the face of censorship. The multiplication of television channels increases the possibility of different viewpoints being aired and makes it more difficult for the authorities to obtain agreement on informal codes with respect to press behaviour during incidents. The spreading availability of videocameras in non-media hands raises the chance that some arresting image will emerge that in a single frame can negate the government's interpretation of events—an image so dramatic that the media will feel compelled to air it repeatedly. The work of amateurs is all the more powerful because of its apparent authenticity in comparison to the ritual dramas so often enacted for the benefit of the media's cameras by challengers and governments alike.

The upshot of these technological developments may be that the world we live in will appear increasingly unintelligible. Yet the human need to make sense of the social environment is strong. In the face of complexity and information overload, the tendency is to simplify drastically and to let others take the responsibility for determining what is going on (Allport and Postman, 1965: 33). As a paradoxical result, the government's pre-eminent role in defining an incident may even be strengthened in the future—a trend that in my view would be dangerous. The reliance on government sources, directly by the media and indirectly by the general population, constricts the flow of information *into* the government. If the government is receiving back only echoes of its own interpretation of events, it runs the risk of isolating itself from reality.

CONCLUSION

Over the last twenty years the literature on governments' policy-making in response to violent challenges to their authority has gradually expanded, concentrating first on responses to guerrilla warfare, then on responses to terrorism, and most recently on the concept of state terrorism. From a Canadian perspective, however, these studies too often are of limited relevance. Partly this is due to the low intensity and episodic nature of challenger violence that Canadian governments have been called upon to deal with in this century. For example they have experienced nothing comparable to the civil war faced by the British government in Northern Ireland, or to the urban unrest that has confronted successive American administrations. When dealing with violent dissidents, Canadian governments have reacted promptly with overwhelming violence of their own (Torrance, 1977: 476–7, 488–9). But because the dissident groups have been crushed in the process, there has been no ongoing use of government violence that would justify applying the label of 'state terror' to the federal government.

The concentration on terrorist incidents has also produced, in my view, a misunderstanding of the role of governments in violent events. I would agree with Wardlaw (1986: 202) that terrorism, because of its 'news value', has received far more attention than it deserves both in the academic literature and in the press. For a democratic government, terrorists—with their typical lack of resources and tiny constituency—usually do not represent a political question. Rather they represent a criminal problem, to be dealt with primarily at the bureaucratic level by instituting procedures such as airport security checks, or issuing identity cards to government employees, and not at the policy level involving a reallocation of the country's social, economic, or political resources.

Indeed, I believe that in general the literature on governmental responses to violence in liberal democracies has tended to overlook the distinction between the relatively rare incidents of challenger violence that the government recognizes as political issues and the great majority that are handled at the bureaucratic level. The distinction is a qualitative one and should not be lost. For example, Ross (1992: 84) records 16 incidents of right-wing violence, mostly perpetrated by skinhead groups, in 1989—the year before the Oka Crisis. In terms of government attention, federal-provincial relations, expenditure of coercive and other governmental resources, location in the governmental hierarchy of decision-making, the intervention of third parties and other élites, media attention, and impact on governmental policies, the Oka Crisis is in a different league from the skinhead incidents and should be compared to a similar political event such as the 1970 October Crisis rather than to events that, while having political content, have no immediate political impact.

Differentiating between great political events and the run-of-the-mill incidents handled mainly by the police leads one to ask why the political system accords different treatment to various challenger groups. By objective indicators, two groups might be engaging in similar types of violence (cf. the bombings carried out in the early 1960s by the Sons of Freedom and the forerunners of the FLQ), but the Sons of Freedom never received the political attention that violent Quebec separatists did. Asking why this should be so prompts inquiry along a number of lines, including the resources at the command of the challenger group, the nature of its grievances, the amount and type of media attention it can attract, the government's perception of the challenger, the resources available to the government, how the challenger's program fits with other governmental priorities, and whether it is feasible for the government to define the group as essentially non-political.

Such a detailed inquiry may help governments prepare for future major incidents by reminding them that the violence that will thrust itself upon their agendas will probably not be the kind that has become routine—that variety will be dealt with at lower levels of the political hierarchy. Rather, governments generally have to deal with the unprecedented variety of violence, and they should prepare to be taken by surprise. What 'worked' for them in the past may not do so the next time around. They may be called upon to develop not minor policy changes or procedural amendments, but—under highly difficult circumstances—a new consensus on the distribution of social values. It is their political skill that will be called upon.

How the challenging group will react to their efforts is the great unknown. Such groups, after all, are deliberately eschewing the established modes of political discourse that democratic politicians are accustomed to dealing with. Instead they are appealing to the great tribal emotions of ethnicity, religion, or, more rarely, class (even while their leaders may be assessing the odds with cool rationality), or drawing upon powerful symbols of justice and liberty.

Government coercion may manage to extinguish one outburst, only to have the conflict rekindle elsewhere. Governmental concessions may be scornfully rejected as too little, too late. In the face of a recalcitrant and resourceful challenger, the incident can drag on, and it is in these circumstances that the drift towards violent authoritarianism may gather speed. Added to the difficulties and pressures confronting any government as it formulates its policy, therefore, should be the knowledge that if its initial response is ineffective, its next steps may well lead it down a path of repression that undermines the basis of its legitimacy as a democratic government.

Notes

[1] For the purposes of this chapter, I follow Tilly's (1978: 52) definition of a challenger as a group that seeks to apply pooled resources to influence the government but that, unlike other contenders in the political system, lacks low-cost access to the resources controlled by the government. I identify the key players involved in the government response to the violence of challenging groups as follows:

(1) The government: the central core of decision-makers surrounding the leading elected political figure in the country. In parliamentary democracies, the term is roughly coterminous with 'cabinet'.

(2) Other political élites: the holders of legislative and judicial offices who are provided by the constitution with certain powers that can be used to thwart the government. In federal states, the government members of the component territorial units also fall within this category.

(3) The bureaucracy: the non-elected servants of the government to be found working within the various government departments and including the police, security agencies, and armed forces. The last three are sometimes collectively referred to as the 'coercive arm' of the state.

(4) Third parties: those who are not politicians or government employees, but who, like Tilly's 'contenders', have ready access to the government and whom the government wishes to conciliate. They are 'third' parties in that they are not usually immediately involved in the confrontation between the government and challenger.

(5) The public at large and the mass media, the major informational linkage between the public and the government.

[2] In contrast, serial killers (those who kill usually one victim at a time) typically lack this dimension. Such murderers are usually not seeking to pull off a spectacular incident to draw attention to an issue they espouse (Norris, 1986: 17–21). In yet another category are the mentally unstable individuals who carry out assaults on government figures and other prominent members of society. These assailants may well have no political motive or indeed any identifiable motive apart from the desire to draw attention to themselves. Their actions, however, can have political consequences if government members are killed or incapacitated.

[3] We are perhaps too quick to dismiss these motivations. Such murderers are products of their society; the particular cause they espouse may signal currents of opinion that the political élite and media have failed or refused to recognize (Leyton, 1986: 26–32).

[4] In the United States, efforts 'to ensure effective coordination of policies and plans as well as a rapid and effective government response to the challenge of terror violence' produced a working group of over 30 agencies, subsequently scaled back to a 'small' group 'composed of the State, Defense, Justice, Treasury and Energy departments as well as representatives of the FBI, CIA, FAA, the Joint Chiefs of Staff, and the National Security Council staff' (Quainton, 1983: 53–4).

5 In particular, the division of powers in a federal state can represent a powerful brake on the freedom of action of all levels of government. Some Canadian examples are disputes involving the militia (Morton, 1970: 409, 413); the inability of the federal and Saskatchewan governments to collaborate in halting the On-to-Ottawa trek in 1935 (Liversedge, 1973: 229–30); and the federal government's refusal to provide reinforcements requested by Ontario in the 1937 Oshawa strike (Abella, 1974: 109–12). See also Bourne (1978: 310–12).

6 Cf. Bonante's (1979) concept of 'blocked societies': those whose governments are incapable of introducing change but that are too strong to be overthrown. He notes that while governments can readily increase the size of their coercive arm, it is far from simple to reverse the process. Once fully institutionalized, a coercive apparatus takes on a life of its own.

7 Bell (1978: 268–9) and many subsequent commentators have urged governments to carefully evaluate the seriousness and nature of the challenge facing them, but concede this is difficult in practice. The uncertainties of the situation, coupled with fears for the future or even for their own personal safety, do not aid government members in reaching a balanced assessment, but rather foster a tendency to perceive an incident as more serious than it is. The fears expressed in Montreal, Quebec City, and Ottawa, during the 1970 October Crisis, of an 'apprehended insurrection' provide one example of this tendency.

8 It is not, of course, necessary to have an invading army actually crossing the frontier; it is sufficient for the government to be convinced that an external enemy is waiting to pounce.

9 Note that in elections following major government-challenger conflicts the Canadian electorate has consistently punished the government party. The government losses in each case can be attributed to several factors other than its handling of the incident. However, the pattern does suggest that, once the immediate crisis is over, the population may blame the government for not resolving the conflict before it reached the stage of open violence.

10 Many of the books on terrorism that appeared *circa* 1970–85 contain gloomy speculations about the possible future tactics that terrorist groups might employ—for example, selecting nuclear power stations and water supplies as targets, or using nuclear, biological, and chemical weapons—in order to maintain media attention. However, these forebodings have not been borne out, and the media, whether by giving too much or too little attention, would not appear to have been a factor. Rather the main cause seems to have been the declining willingness of states such as Iran, Libya, and the former Soviet Union to supply and train the groups involved.

11 In times of uncertainty this tendency is probably reinforced by the psychological need—which will be experienced by journalists as much as by everybody else—to believe that established powers are beneficent, know what is going on, and are in control, and to the further need to close ranks in the face of disruptive threats to social stability.

REFERENCES

Abella, I. (1974). 'Oshawa 1937'. Pp. 93–128 in I. Abella, ed., *On Strike: Six Key Labour Struggles in Canada, 1919–1949.* Toronto: James Lewis and Samuel.

Allport, G. and L. Postman (1965). *The Psychology of Rumor.* New York: Russell.

Bell, J.B. (1978). *A Time of Terror: How Democratic Societies Respond to Revolutionary Violence.* New York: Basic Books.

Bonante, L. (1979). 'Some unanticipated consequences of terrorism', *Journal of Peace Research* 16: 197–211.

Bourne, R. (1978). 'Terrorist incident management and jurisdictional issues: A Canadian perspective', *Terrorism: An International Journal* 1: 307–13.

Breton, R. (1972). 'The socio-political dynamics of the October events', *Canadian Review of Sociology and Anthropology* 9: 33–56.

Clutterbuck, R. (1981). *The Media and Political Violence.* London: Macmillan.

Coser, L.A. (1956). *The Functions of Social Conflict.* New York: Free Press.

Crelinsten, R.D. (1989). 'Terrorism and the media: Problems, solutions and counterproblems'. *Political Communication and Persuasion* 6: 311–39.

——— (1992). 'Victims' perspectives'. Pp. 208–38 in D. Paletz and A. Schmid, eds, *Terrorism and the Media.* Newbury Park: Sage Publications.

Denemark, R.A. and H.P. Lehman (1984) 'South African state terror: The costs of continuing repressions'. Pp. 143–65 in M. Stohl and G. Lopez, eds, *The State as Terrorist: The Dynamics of Governmental Violence and Repression.* New York: Greenwood Press.

Dror, Y. (1983). 'Terrorism as a challenge to the democratic capacity to govern'. Pp. 65–90 in M. Crenshaw, ed., *Terrorism, Legitimacy, and Power: The Consequences of Political Terrorism.* Middleton, CT: Wesleyan University Press.

Edelman, M. (1971). *Politics as Symbolic Action: Mass Arousal and Quiescence.* Chicago: Markham.

Ericson, R., P. Baranek, and J. Chan (1987). *Visualizing Deviance: A Study of News Organizations.* Toronto: University of Toronto Press.

——— (1989). *Negotiating Control: A Study of News Sources.* Toronto: University of Toronto Press.

Frank, J.A., and M. Kelly (1979). ' "Street politics" in Canada: An examination of mediating conditions', *Canadian Journal of Political Science* 23: 593–614.

Franks, C.E.S. (1989). 'Introduction'. Pp. 1–20 in C.E.S. Franks, ed., *Dissent and the State.* Toronto: Oxford University Press.

Gurr, T.R. (1984). 'The political origins of state violence and terror: A theoretical analysis'. Pp. 45–71 in M. Stohl and G. Lopez, eds., *The State as Terrorist: The Dynamics of Governmental Violence and Repression.* New York: Greenwood Press.

——— (1988). 'War, revolution, and the growth of the coercive state', *Comparative Political Studies* 21: 45–65.

——— (1989). 'Protest and rebellion in the 1960s: The United States in world perspective'. Pp. 101–30 in T.R. Gurr, ed., *Violence in America, Vol. 2: Protest, Rebellion, Reform.* Newbury Park: Sage Publications.

Hall, S., et al. (1978). *Policing the Crisis: Mugging, the State, and Law and Order.* New York: Holmes and Meier.

Hocking, J.J. (1992). 'Governments' perspectives'. Pp. 86–104 in D. Paletz and A. Schmid, eds, *Terrorism and the Media.* Newbury Park: Sage Publications.

Hornung, R. (1991) *One Nation under the Gun: Inside the Mohawk Civil War.* Toronto: Stoddart.

Jackson, R.J., M.J. Kelly, and T.H. Mitchell (1975). 'Collective conflict, violence and the media'. Pp. 228–314 in Royal Commission on Violence in the Communications Industry. *Report, Vol. V: Learning from the Media.* Toronto: Queen's Printer for Ontario.

Leyton, E. (1986). *Hunting Humans: The Rise of the Modern Multiple Murderer.* Toronto: McClelland and Stewart.

Liversedge, R. (1973). *Recollections of the On to Ottawa Trek with Documents Related to the Vancouver Strike and the On to Ottawa Trek,* ed. V. Hoar. Toronto: McClelland and Stewart.

Lopez, G.A. (1984). 'A scheme for the analysis of government as terrorist'. Pp. 59–81 in M. Stohl and G. Lopez, eds, *The State as Terrorist: The Dynamics of Governmental Violence and Repression.* New York: Greenwood Press.

Luttwak, E. (1979). *Coups d'Etat: A Practical Handbook.* Cambridge, MA: Harvard University Press.

Maclean, R., and A. Veniol (1990). *Terror: Murder and Panic in New Brunswick.* Toronto: McClelland and Stewart.

McNaught, K. (1975). 'Political trials and the Canadian political tradition'. Pp. 137–61 in M. Friedland, ed., *Courts and Trials.* Toronto: University of Toronto Press.

Morton, D. (1970). 'Aid to the civil power: The Canadian militia in support of social order', *Canadian Historical Review* 51: 407–25.

Norris, J. (1986). *Serial Killers: The Growing Menace.* New York: Doubleday.

Oberschall, A. (1973). *Social Conflict and Social Movements.* Englewood Cliffs, NJ: Prentice-Hall.

Pion-Berlin, D. (1984). 'The political economy of state repression in Argentina'. Pp. 99–122 in M. Stohl and G. Lopez, eds, *The State as Terrorist: The Dynamics of Governmental Violence and Repression.* New York: Greenwood Press.

Quainton, A. (1983). 'Terrorism and political violence: A permanent challenge to governments'. Pp. 52–64 in M. Crenshaw, ed., *Terrorism, Legitimacy, and Power: The Consequences of Political Terrorism.* Middleton, CT: Wesleyan University Press.

Ross, J.I. (1988). 'Attributes of domestic political terrorism in Canada, 1960–1985', *Terrorism* 11: 213–33.

——— (1992). 'Contemporary radical right-wing violence in Canada: A quantitative analysis', *Terrorism and Political Violence* 4: 72–101.

Ross, J.I. and T.R. Gurr (1989). 'Why terrorism subsides: A comparative study of Canada and the United States', *Comparative Politics* 21: 405–26.

Schmid, P., and J. de Graaf (1982). *Violence as Communication: Insurgent Terrorism and the Western News Media.* London and Beverly Hills: Sage Publications.

Tilly, C. (1978). *From Mobilization to Revolution.* Reading, MA: Addison-Wesley.

Torrance, J. (1977). 'The response of Canadian governments to violence', *Canadian Journal of Political Science* 10: 473–96.

——— (1986) *Public Violence in Canada, 1867–1982.* Kingston: McGill-Queen's University Press.

Turner, R.H. (1969). 'The public perception of protest', *American Sociological Review* 34: 815–31.

Wardlaw, G. (1986). 'Terrorism, counter-terrorism, and the democratic society', pp. 189–206 in M. Stohl and G. Lopez, eds, *Government Violence and Repression: An Agenda for Research.* New York: Greenwood Press.

——— (1989). *Political Terrorism: Theory, Tactics, and Counter-Measures,* 2nd ed. New York: Cambridge University Press.

Whitaker, R. (1989). 'Left-wing dissent and the State: Canada in the cold war era'. Pp. 191–210 in C.E.S. Franks, ed., *Dissent and the State.* Toronto: Oxford University Press.

Wilkinson, P. (1986). *Terrorism and the Liberal State,* 2nd ed. New York: New York University Press.

Chapter Twelve

CONCLUSION: SUMMARY AND FUTURE DIRECTIONS

JEFFREY IAN ROSS

What have we learned from the contributors to this volume? The notion that Canada is a peaceable kingdom has been challenged by evidence presented in this book. Canada is not immune from criminal and political violence. Violence in Canadian society is not a contemporary social and policy problem as the media and some politicians would have us believe. To the contrary, the historical roots of this violence can be traced to preconfederation times. Moreover, this violence is not caused or experienced by a narrow subset of the Canadian population; no social group is immune as perpetrators and victims. In short, violence is committed by a variety of actors, against a multitude of citizens, in a number of contexts.

Most of the contributors to *Violence in Canada* briefly reviewed the types, patterns, data adequacy, causes, and effects of a particular subtype of violence in Canada. In an effort to integrate these chapters, the editor reviews the arguments about the subprocesses of violence put forth by these authors.

TYPES OF VIOLENCE

In general, the discussions in this book have focused on overt physical violence rather than on psychological or structural violence. The most common distinction is between violence against persons and against property (especially evident in labour violence and terrorism). Within this distinction, violence can differ based on its purposes, sources, and causes. For example, some contributors (e.g., Tunnell and Welch) used the terms symbolic, expressive, and instrumental to refer to the intent of actors who resort to violence. Others (e.g., Long) differentiate between individual and collective types of violence, to distinguish the number of people who engage in violent acts. With perhaps the exception of some acts of terrorism (e.g., Kellett), most political violence (e.g., labour violence) and some racial violence is collective. On the other hand, most criminal violence is individual. Some authors introduce other distinctions such as public violence (Tunnell) which is violence committed for a public good; public police violence (Ross) which is police violence that is detected by the police hierarchy or nonpolice actors'; or corporate violence (e.g., Knafla), which refers to violence caused by a business in negligence or provision of poor working conditions that lead to physical injuries or death to workers. A logical extension of corporate violence is state-corporate violence (e.g., Tunnell) which consists of violence that is caused by government negligence of corporate practices which lead to physical injury or death to workers and citizens.

Violence can also be based on the type of target and intent. It may be directed outwards against persons and property or inwards, as in the case of suicide. Even with homicides, there are different types of violence including culpable and nonculpable. There are also gradations accounted for in the Criminal Code of Canada; for example, murder is classified into two categories, namely first and second degree.[1]

Although the focus of this volume is on overt physical violence, most of the researchers acknowledged the presence and importance of psychological or structural violence. Subsumed under this classification are such acts as threats, browbeating, or social harms such as restriction of educational and employment opportunities, loss of job security, loss of income, and adultery (e.g., DeKeseredy and Ellis, Kellett, Tunnell). In this type of violence, the perception of the victim, rather than that of the observer, is most important. Most researchers argue, or it can be inferred from their analyses, that psychological or structural violence can be a step in the process that leads to physical violence.

PATTERNS OF VIOLENCE

Rates of violence vary not only with time and space (e.g., across regions, or in rural versus urban locales), but according to the personal characteristics of both victims and perpetrators (age, race, gender, etc.).

For example, Knafla writes that in the late nineteenth and early twentieth centuries, aboriginals, mixed bloods, and orientals became the victims and perpetrators of violence. Between 1870 and 1919, the number of convictions of individuals on a per capita basis for crimes of violence were twice as high in Saskatchewan and Alberta as those found in the rest of Canada combined. Western Canada had more recorded homicides per capita; a higher percentage of persons convicted for capital crimes; and stiffer penalties (i.e., executions) (Knafla, p. 26).

In terms of social groups, Native Canadians have higher offending rates for violent crimes than those of the general population (Long, Gartner). One of the reasons for this pattern is that their political struggles have been more violent over the past three decades, than in previous times. In the main, homicide by and against Native Canadians has increased in the 1960s and 1970s, suicide reached alarming proportions until the 1980s, and although researchers concede that family violence in Native communities is high, data are not sophisticated enough to determine whether it is rising, declining, or stable.

In general, violence by and against labour is increasing. It is primarily property violence and the few cases of violence against a person usually result in minimal injuries. Rarely do deaths occur in the context of labour violence. Moreover, the mining industry seems to be the most violent in labour struggles.

With the exception of homicide, longitudinal research on violence against women in Canada has not been conducted. On the other hand, periodic contemporary research on intimate violence indicates high levels in the general population (DeKeseredy and Ellis). DeKeseredy and Ellis warn that it is wrong to assume that we are experiencing an epidemic of violence against women in Canada; rather, 'violence against women has existed in Western societies for centuries.' They add, the incidence of violence against women is difficult to determine mainly because record-keeping began in earnest only in the early 1980s. Relying on the extant data, they claim that 'today's men are no more violent, and possibly less so, than their ancestors' (p. 115).

According to Cabrera, rates of violence by and against children are also difficult to substantiate. There are, however, a number of case studies suggesting that such violence has dire and long-lasting consequences for both victims and perpetrators. But the perception that our children are out of control is fuelled by exploitative and sensationalized public, media, and governmental reports about this social and policy problem. Similarly, crime by and against the elderly has been exaggerated by media reports. Contrary to popular belief, Canadian Uniform Crime Reports and victimization studies indicate that violence by and against this age group declines with age (Sacco). In other words, the elderly are less likely than younger adults to be perpetrators and victims of violence.

Homicide, the most serious of violent actions, increased after the early 1970s and then plateaued in the 1980s, averaging about 2 per 100,000 population. The Yukon and Northwest Territories have had the lion's share of homicides both in the contemporary period and since the 1920s (Gartner).

Public police violence has remained fairly consistent over the past sixteen years (Ross). This phenomenon as documented in published reports from *The Globe and Mail* is largely concentrated in Ontario, and the majority of real or alleged victims and perpetrators are young males. On the other hand, violence by prisoners against other prisoners has been increasing. Welch, citing a Correction Service of Canada report, notes that 'violence directed toward staff has been decreasing steadily over the last few years; the bad news is that violence directed toward inmates has not' (p. 266).

With regard to terrorism, Kellett identifies two basic types: domestic and international. He further differentiates among several types of perpetrators, including left-wing, right-wing, religious, nationalist/separatist, single issue, and émigré. Despite media hype, oppositional political terrorism reached a few peaks during the 1960s, but subsided during the 1970s. The types of groups engaging in terrorism differed throughout the contemporary period.

DATA ADEQUACY

Unfortunately, most of the authors lament the problem of obtaining adequate data on violence, regardless of the type, perpetrators, victims, and context. Some of the problems include considerable variability, unreliability, and contradictions among data sets. Among causes of poor data are problems of definitions, failure to report acts of violence, different reporting measures, lack of public education, and the cost of collecting the data.

Data can be gathered using victim, offender, community, or event-based measures; each has its advantages and disadvantages. Additionally, there are what can be classified as official statistics, victimization statistics, and statistics based on media reports. Official statistics are available from two sources: public-health organizations and criminal-justice agencies. According to Gartner, '[t]hese institutions differ somewhat in their measurement and reporting procedures and in the purposes for which they gather data on homicides' (p. 188). Victimization studies have periodically been performed in Canada. And media-based statistics include what is generally referred to as events data analysis (e.g., Kellett, Ross). In short, neither official, victimization, nor media events data are adequately reliable sources of statistics. Long and others recognize the limited reliability and generalizability of all statistics.

When the state fails to collect data on violence, Canadian academics have displayed their resourcefulness by constructing their own unique data sets (e.g., DeKeseredy and Ellis, Gartner, Ross). Alternatively, others have been relatively creative with what is available to minimize the problem of data sufficiency. For instance, Knafla used official public records such as judicial or criminal court records and coroner inquest records, and literary evidence, including unofficial records such as correspondence, memoirs, and newspapers. Similarly Tunnell used a sample of post-1960 cases to illustrate typical examples of violent behaviour by labour, capital, and the state. These incidents characterize the types of clashes that took place. Long, on the other hand, used a large number and variety of sources including government reports, consultant reports, etc. Others relied on a variety of sources such as a series of victimization surveys produced by both government and academic researchers (e.g, DeKeseredy and Ellis), a series of academic and governmental reports on the rates of violence by and against children (e.g., Cabrera), victimization studies and the Canadian Uniform Crime Reports (e.g, Sacco); Solicitor General of Canada statistics, in particular Canadian Correctional Services data, reports from government inquiries, and a victimization study conducted in prisons (e.g., Welch), and a data set developed at the National Security Coordination Centre based on other data bases and media reports (e.g., Kellett).

CAUSES OF VIOLENCE

Both the wider academic literature and the contributors to *Violence in Canada* point to five basic causes of violent crime: interpersonal conflict situations (over status, resources, power, control, and reputation), presence of weapons, influence of drugs and/or alcohol, media facilitation, and cultural or subcultural reinforcement.

Each of the different subtypes of violence by and against Canadians has its own particular constellation of causes. Knafla suggests that racist attitudes towards francophones, aboriginals, and Métis who inhabited the Western frontier, revenge, a subculture of violence, and the inability of the Canadian government, through its representative agencies, to adequately police the land are dominant causes in frontier violence. Although Long points to acculturation theory, internal colonialism, and other mitigating factors, he also mentions such subprocesses as marginalization, increased bureaucratization of the government, ideology, and relative deprivation as causes of Native Canadian political and criminal violence. Tunnell argues that because the issues have changed, the causes of labour violence in Canada have shifted over the years from pay, to working conditions, to the right to collectively bargain, to job security. Labour violence is cast in a marxist dynamic where labour, capital, and the state support the interests of capital. Violence is the natural outcome of this relationship. Cabrera briefly touches on the plethora of research on the causes of violence by and against children and cites factors such as socially acceptable punishment patterns, including discipline, and a history of being abused as children, as prominent causes. And Sacco suggests that routine activities and life style theories are the best explanations to explain violence by and against the elderly in Canada.

With regard to violence by police officers, Ross suggest two basic causes: structural and psychological. These two broad categories encompass individual, situational, organizational, community, and legal explanations for violence by police officers. Similarly, Welch suggests that there are three dominant causes of prison violence: the violent inmate, the social climate of violence, and overcrowding. Prison violence, he argues, is a problem of advanced capitalism because the state and capital simultaneously create high expectations, but must control those who engage in crime to achieve the unfulfilled material rewards.

EFFECTS OF VIOLENCE

Most of the contributors also looked at the effects of their selected subtype of violence. These outcomes transcend both government and public responses. In the main, the Canadian government responds to violence either through the various public bureaucracies that it has created (e.g., police, prisons, jails), the legal system (through the creation of new laws), or in a parliamentary fashion with the establishment of Royal Commissions, parliamentary task forces (e.g., MacGuigan), or Senate Committees (e.g., Kelly).

Much of the Canadian criminal justice system's treatment of violence is somewhat contradictory. There is a tendency to respond to violence with violence in particular prisons, which reproduce violence in society, or police whose violence is often the result of criminal violence. Although it may seem utopian to suggest that we should passively respond to violence with something other than violence, conflict resolution or mediation techniques are rarely emphasized or implemented. Alternatively, the Canadian government often encourages repressive tactics by focusing public attention on the threat of violence, thereby convincing the public that an iron fist or repressive policies are required responses (e.g., Welch, Torrance).

This is not to suggest that Canadians are simply docile, immobilized by fear, or totally dependent on governmental action. There are a number of private organizations involved in the prevention or control of violence. In addition to conventional organizations (e.g., Canadian Chiefs of Police Association) lobbying for changes in the Criminal Code, a series of advocacy groups have been formed such as Canadians Against Violence Everywhere Advocating Its Termination.

In other instances, Knafla notes that periodically Canadians, particularly those who lived on the Western frontier, have taken law and order into their own hands and engaged in vigilante justice. In many cases, the severe environmental conditions were used as justifications for public excesses against suspected and actual criminal offenders. Alternatively, violent offenders were tolerated and told to go their separate ways. This points to the trend that community norms often predicate the public and judicial response to violence.

An interesting consequence of violence at the individual and collective levels is Long's contention that both political and criminal violence by and against Native Canadians has resulted in the 'revitalization of native spirituality and the rediscovery of some almost forgotten cultural traditions' including but not limited to the development of community-based health education, justice and economic development programs run by and for native people (p. 63).

The effects of violence by labour include clashes with the militia, police, scabs, and private security guards; police are often placed in between the right of business owners to run his or her business and the rights of striking workers. In many incidents, strikers were fired, arrested, charged with criminal offences, and sometimes convicted. In some cases workers got their demands, in others they did not. Tunnell-concludes that workers' gains have only been achieved through conflict, in particular violent conflict.

Violence against women has stimulated 'state-sponsored reports, the federal government's establishment of the Canadian Panel on Violence Against Women, two federally funded national surveys, . . . the creation of special community organizations . . . , and, many academic journal articles and books' (DeKeseredy and Ellis, p. 97). Media and public attention to this issue have produced what DeKeseredy and Ellis label 'atrocity tales' which dominate television talk shows, newspaper reports, and feature films. Not only has violence against women stimulated academic research and awareness in popular culture, but it has also led to better policing practices, mediation efforts, calls for economic equality, the development of alternative social services, and profeminist programs for violent males (DeKeseredy and Ellis).

The effects of violence against children include violence by these same children; responses include national and international awareness of the vulnerability of children and the need to protect them, but little in terms of policy. Cabrera suggests the changes must be made to the judicial system and the therapeutic community to implement better methods of detection, obtaining children's testimony, and the healing of children who have been subjected to violence. Violence by and against another group that is also vulnerable, namely the elderly, has stimulated an increasing number of newspaper and academic articles, books, grants and awards, governmental inquiries, and elderly advocacy groups. The periodic victimization of the elderly has led to an increase in fear and a popular perception that the elderly are the prime targets of violence.

Ross looked at a variety of effects of public police violence in Canada, including better controls, demands for further education, and the introduction of community policing. In a similar vein, Welch describes a variety of responses to prison violence including civil and prisoner's rights movements, which took place both inside and outside prisons, as well as the introduction of 'super' maximum security facilities, special handling units, and greater reliance on administrative segregation.

Although Kellett does not pay much attention to effects, he suggests that besides fear, some of the responses to terrorism in Canada lie at the governmental level, including the creation of the National Security Coordination Centre, the Joint Task Force Two, the Counter-Terrorism Task Force, the Senate Special Committee on Terrorism and Public Safety, and media attention.

Torrance, who specifically looked at the responses of the government to political violence, suggested that governments will pay more attention to violence 'if it is the work of an organized group, especially one rising in power, if the violent actor(s) cannot be readily dismissed as insane, criminals, irresponsible, or foreign; if the violence shocks public sensibilities and has not become routinized; if it approximates our folk concept of rebellion; and if it challenges the government's monopoly of legitimate force' (p. 318). On the other hand, she argues that 'Once a government feels compelled to take action against a challenging group, it can face a number of problems in formulating its policy' (p. 318). Torrance makes a case for the view that although there are a number of restraints on governmental powers, many democratic states, such as Canada, have a propensity to drift into violent authoritarianism.

SUGGESTIONS FOR FUTURE RESEARCH

Victim-perpetrator-context dynamics are practically unlimited. Among the most notable omissions from this book are discussions of 'Violence in Psychiatric Hospitals', 'Violence By and Against Probation Officers', 'Violence Against Municipal Police', 'Violence in Schools', 'Violence By and Against Racial Groups', 'Violence By and Against the Helping Professions', 'Government Responses to Criminal Violence', 'Suicide', 'Nongovernmental Responses to Political and Criminal Violence', 'Future of Criminal and Political Violence in Canada', and 'Violence By and Against Women in Prisons'. Future research should focus on these topics.

Additionally, not all the contributors to this work were able to look at violence perpetrated both by and against the particular group in question: that is, clearly violence is part of an interaction that, once started, acquires a momentum, and reproduces, such that all sides to a conflict may be using violence. Such multiple interactions need further exploration.

One theme salient in this volume is that researchers, the public, and policy-makers interested in better data must increasingly pressure the government or funding bodies to collect additional types of statistics on criminal and political violence. This effort might include the funding of nontraditional collection methods (i.e., victimization studies, etc.). The general consensus is that research needs to be more collaborative, rigorous and comprehensive in nature (Long).

The authors were instructed to focus on physical violence rather than on psychological and structural violence. Nevertheless, almost all of them acknowledged a strong linkage between psychological and structural processes. To have a comprehensive understanding of violence in general, future research should develop the linkages among the three.

Comparatively, Canada has experienced less violence than the United States but it still ranks high amongst advanced industrialized countries. This book represents the most comprehensive treatment of the various subtypes of violence in Canada. Raising social consciousness to the violence that Canadians experience and engage in has a dual purpose: to challenge the myth of the peaceable kingdom, and to work toward creating a society that is less violent.

NOTES

Special thanks to Natasha J. Cabrera for comments on this chapter.

1 Gartner also notes that Canadian researchers separate criminal homicides into different subtypes: 'differentiating homicides according to the prior relationship between victim and offender, the social roles or demographic characteristics of the victims and offenders, or the features of the precipitating incident' (p. 188).

CONTRIBUTORS

NATASHA J. CABRERA is an educational psychologist and study director for the Roundtable on Head Start Research for the National Research Council in Washington. She received her PhD from the University of Denver and specializes in issues connected to critical thinking, learning, and child development. Her published work includes chapters and articles in academic journals.

WALTER S. DEKESEREDY is an Associate Professor of Sociology at Carleton University. He has published over two dozen articles which have appeared in academic journals such as *Crime, Law and Social Change, Journal of Family Violence, Canadian Journal of Sociology, International Review of Victimology*, and *Sociological Spectrum.* He is the author of *Women Abuse in Dating Relationships: The Role of Male Peer Support* and co-author of *Woman Abuse: Sociological Perspectives* (with Ronald Hinch) and the forthcoming second edition of *The Wrong Stuff: An Introduction to the Sociological Study of Deviance* (with Desmond Ellis). DeKeseredy is Associate Editor of *Justice Quarterly* and in 1993, he received Carleton University's Research Achievement Award.

DESMOND ELLIS is a Professor of Sociology at York University and a member of the LaMarsh Centre for Research on Violence and Conflict Resolution. He has contributed a number of articles on woman abuse among separating couples. Co-author of *The Wrong Stuff,* Ellis is presently completing a project on the impact of lawyers and mediators on post-separation abuse and starting two others (sibling violence, and intimate femicide).

ROSEMARY GARTNER is Professor of Sociology at the University of Toronto, where she is also affiliated with the Centre of Criminology and the Faculty of Law. Her research on homicide and criminal offending has appeared in *American Sociological Review, Law and Society Review, Social Problems, Social Forces, Journal of Criminal Law and Criminology,* and other journals. She is co-author (with Dane Archer) of *Violence and Crime in Cross-National Perspective,* winner of the Distinguished Scholarship Award from the criminology section of the American Sociological Association and the Behavioral Sciences Prize from the American Association for the Advancement of Science. Her current research includes historical and comparative studies of homicide and femicide (the killing of women).

TED ROBERT GURR is Distinguished University Professor of Government and Politics and Distinguished Scholar at the Center for International Development and Conflict Management at the University of Maryland (College Park). His 14 books and monographs include *Why Men Rebel* (recipient of the Woodrow Wilson Foundation Award as the best book in political science of 1970) and *The Politics of Crime and Conflict: A Comparative History of Four Cities.* In 1988–89 he was a Jennings Randolph Peace Fellow of the U.S. Institute of Peace in Washington, DC.

ANTHONY KELLETT is a defence scientist with the Department of National Defence. During his tenure at the DND, he was seconded to the Privy Council Office and to the Police and Security Branch of Solicitor General Canada for terms of one year each. His book *Combat Motivation: The Behavior of Soldiers in Battle* has been reprinted and translated into Portuguese, and he has a dozen chapters and articles published on a variety of subjects. Kellett specializes in terrorism, military motivation, and organizational structure, and has developed a global geopolitical database. In 1982, Kellett was awarded the Public Service of Canada Merit Award for 'an exceptional and distinguished contribution to the effectiveness and efficiency of the Public Service'.

LOUIS KNAFLA is a Professor of History at the University of Calgary. He is the author of several books and articles on the history of crime in Canada and Great Britain. His work includes *Law & Justice in a New Land: Essays in Western Canadian Legal History, Kent at Law 1602*, and he has edited recently with Susan Binnie, *Law, Society and the State: Essays in Modern Legal History*, and with Clive Emsley, *Crime Histories and Histories of Crime: Studies in the Historiography of Crime and Criminal Justice in Modern History*. He is the Editor of the journal *Criminal Justice History*, and is currently President-Elect of the Canadian Law and Society Association.

DAVID A. LONG is an Assistant Professor of Sociology at The King's College in Edmonton. He has authored a number of publications on the movements of Native peoples in Canada, and is co-editor with Olive Dickason of a forthcoming book, *Contemporary Aboriginal Issues in Socio-historical Perspective* with Harcourt, Brace Jovanovich. In 1990–91, Long received the inaugural awarding of the Grant Notly Memorial Postdoctoral Fellowship at the University of Alberta.

JEFFREY IAN ROSS is a Senior Research Associate, Center for Communitarian Policy Studies at George Washington University. He has conducted research, written, and lectured on political and criminal violence and policing for over a decade. His work has appeared in academic journals such as *Canadian Journal of Political Science, Comparative Politics, Conflict Quarterly, Contemporary Sociology, International Journal of Group Tensions, Journal of Peace Research, Justice Quarterly, Local Government Studies, Low Intensity Conflict and Law Enforcement, Peace and Change, Police Studies, Terrorism, Terrorism and Political Violence*, and a variety of chapters in academic books, as well as articles in popular magazines in Canada and the United States. He is the editor of *Controlling State Crime*. In 1986, Ross was the lead expert witness for the Senate of Canada's Special Committee on Terrorism and Public Safety.

VINCENT F. SACCO is a Professor of Sociology at Queen's University, Kingston, Ontario. He has authored numerous articles in the areas of crime prevention, family violence, and fear of crime. With Ezzat Fattah, he is the co-author of *Crime and Victimization of the Elderly*. He has recently completed (with Leslie Kennedy) an introductory criminology textbook entitled The Criminal Event.

JUDY TORRANCE is a federal public servant working in a field unrelated to the content of her chapter. She received her PhD in Political Science from York University in 1975. Her published work on political violence includes a book chapter, an article in the *Canadian Journal of Political Science*, and a full-length study, *Public Violence in Canada*.

KENNETH D. TUNNELL is an Associate Professor at Eastern Kentucky University. He received his PhD in Sociology at the University of Tennessee in 1988. He has published in *Journal of Criminal Justice Education, Justice Quarterly, Qualitative Sociology, Sociological Spectrum,* and *The Journal of Popular Culture.* He is the author of *Choosing Crime: The Criminal Calculus of Property Offenders* and the editor of *Political Crime in Contemporary America: A Critical Approach.* His ongoing research interests include qualitative approaches to understanding crime and criminals, as well as the political economy of crime and social control.

MICHAEL WELCH is an Associate Professor in the Administration of Justice Program at Rutgers University, New Brunswick, New Jersey. He has published articles which have appeared in *Social Justice, American Journal of Criminal Justice, Journal of Crime and Justice, Dialectical Anthropology, Journal of Offender Counseling, Services, and Rehabilitation,* as well as numerous chapters. He is author of *Corrections: A Critical Approach.* His research interests include corrections and social control. Welch has correctional experience at the federal, state, and local levels.

INDEX

Aboriginal people: and correctional system, 255-6; customary law, 14, 29; demographic trends, 50-1; and Hudson's Bay Co., 12, 14, 15; and justice system, 18, 45, 52, 54; organizations, 46, 47; political activism, xiii, 45-7, 48, 63; pre-contact societies, 44; socio-economic conditions, 51-2; and treaty process, 15, 45; and White Paper on Indian Policy (1969), 40, 46; *see also* Aboriginal people, violence by and against

Aboriginal people, violence by and against, ix, 5, 345-6, 348-9; and alcohol, 62-3; and colonialism, 40-1, 42, 47-8, 61, 62, 206; criminal/physical violence, 50-61; data, 42-4; family violence, 43, 55-7, 66; and gender, 62; homicide, x, xi, 52-4, 205, 206; political violence, 40, 41, 42, 45-50, 47, 48-9; and powerlessness, 49-50, 62; responses to, xiii, xv, 42, 45, 63-9; and self-determination, 64-5, 67, 68; and social/cultural change, 61; and state-initiated violence, 42; suicide, 57-61; young offenders, 135, 143; *see also* Frontier violence

'Accidental death', 4, 23-5; *see also* Corporate violence

Acculturation theory, 61

Action directe, 305

Administration of Justice Act (1886), 21

Age: and fear of crime, 166; and homicide offending, 199-200, 206-9; and homicide victimization, 160-1, 199-200, 206-9; and police violence, 233, 234; and victimization, 160-3

Alberta: frontier violence, 21-3, 26-7; homicide rates, 196; suicide rates, 25-6; terrorism, 288

Armed Revolutionary Nuclei, 305-6

Armée de libération du Québec (ALQ), 289, 290

Armée révolutionnaire du Québec (ARQ), 289, 290

Armenian Secret Army for the Liberation of Armenia (ASALA), 299, 301

Assiniboia frontier, 12-13, 18, 21

Atlantic provinces: homicide rates, xii, 195, 196, 197

Authoritarianism, xv, 313; 'drift towards', 320, 322-8

Authority, respect for, ix

Badgley Report (1984), 133

Batoche, battle of, 15

Beechgrove Children's Centre, 140

Begbie, Matthew Baillie, 18

Born with a Tooth, Milton, 48

British Columbia: frontier violence, 18-21, 24, 26-7; homicide, 195, 196-7; suicide, 25; terrorism, 288, 291-2, 296; *see also* Pacific frontier

Canada: as 'peaceable kingdom', viii-x, 3, 11, 28, 50, 93, 115, 250, 284-5, 325

Canada Evidence Act, 127, 142

Canada Jurisdiction Act (1803), 13

Canadian Centre for Justice Statistics, 156

Canadian Manufacturers Association, 90

Canadian Pacific Railway, 18, 21, 25

Canadian Urban Victimization ('seven cities') Survey (CUVS; 1982), 100, 101, 105, 157, 158-9, 160, 161

Cardinal, Harold, 46

Challenger disaster, 92

Challenger violence: 'contagion' effect, 316; definitions, 339n.1; and 'folk concept of rebellion', 317-18, 331; and media, 332-6, 337; political impact, 337-8; public responses, 321; 'routinized', 316-17; *see also* Government responses; Terrorism

Chartier, Paul Joseph, 315

Children, violence against, x, 346; data, 127-9; and gender, 133; incidence, 128-9; offenders, 133; physical, 127, 129, 130-2; police responses, 130, 142, 144-5; reporting of, 128; reproduction of, xiii, 131, 133, 136; responses to, xiv, 139-45; sexual, 128-9, 130, 132-4; treatment programs, 140

Children, violence by, 346, 348, 350; against family members, 134, 135, 136, 174; as consequence of abuse, 127, 136, 138-9; and criminal justice system, 141-5; data, 127; and gender, 134, 138; homicide, 129; incidence, 129; physical, 134-7; public reactions to, 126, 134, 143; regional variations, 143; sexual, 137-9; and television, 137; treatment programs, 141-2

'Claims-making', xiv, 155

Class: and correctional system, 251, 252, 253; see also Inequality

Coke, Sir Edward, 28

Colonialism: and aboriginal violence, 42, 47-8, 206; internal, 41, 47, 61, 62; structural effects, 40

Conflict Tactics Scale (CTS), 99, 101, 103-4, 105, 173

Corporate violence, 23-5, 78, 79; and limited liability, 25; state-, 91-3, 94, 345

Correctional Services of Canada (CSC), 253-4, 264, 275; mission statement, 254

Correctional system: 'cascading', 275; and class, 251, 252, 253; classification system, 275; contemporary, 253-9; and crime/social control, 252, 271-5; history, 251-3; imprisonment rates, 250, 254-5; informal rules of social control, 269-70; institution types, 255; overcrowding, 259-60; Penitentiary Act (1868), 252; placement procedures, 260; protective custody, 276; responsibility for, 253-4; reform efforts, 253; and reproduction of violence, 250, 270, 271, 274-5, 277, 278; social climate, 259; Special Handling Units (SHUs), 275-6; Sub-Committee on the Penitentiary System (MacGuigan

Commission), 261; transfer of prisoners, 276, 277; treatment/rehabilitation model, 253; see also Prisoners; Prisons; Prison violence

Crime: fear of, 154, 166-71, 197, 273, 314; 'street', 115, 153, 154, 162, 230

Cypress Hills 'massacre' (1873), 21

Direct Action (Squamish Five), 292-3, 300, 301

Doukhobors, 291; Sons of Freedom (SOF), 287, 288, 291-2, 293, 294, 295-6, 302, 308, 326, 335, 338

Drugs: and homicide, 210-11, 212; and prison violence, 266, 270, 278; and young offenders, 136

'Ecotage', 317

Elder abuse, 154-5, 156, 177; by caregivers, 157-8, 172, 173, 174; causes, 171-2; and dependency, 172, 173; and gender, 171; spousal, 172, 173; and substance abuse, 172; see also Elderly, violence against

Elderly, violence against, xiii-xiv, 6, 97-8, 36, 348, 350; data, 156-8; and fear of crime, 166-71, 176-7; and lifestyle/routine activities, 161-2, 175; physical effects, 163-5; psychological effects, 165; reporting, 165-6; risk factors, 158-60, 161-3; as social problem, 153-5; victimization rates, 176, 177, 209; see also Elder abuse; Elderly, violence by

Elderly, violence by, 6, 155, 174-6, 177; and gender, 175, 176; and race, 176; and routine activities, 175

Emergency Measures Act, 327

Euzkadi ta Askatasuna (ETA), 305, 306

Family violence, 42, 43, 55-7, 154-5; see also Children; Elder abuse; Women, violence against

Female's Safety survey (1992), 133

Firearms, x; and homicide, 210, 211, 212; police use of, 226, 227

Friction directe, 293

Front de libération du Québec (FLQ), 289-91, 293. 295, 300, 308, 326, 331, 335

Frontier violence, ix, 4, 348; and absence of authority, 14, 15; corporate violence, 23-5; 'frontier' defined, 11; and 'frontier justice', 21; and legal culture, 13-14, 29-30; and racism, 13, 15; reporting, 20, 21, 27; sexual offences, 23; statistics, 26-7; suicide, 25-6; and US 'Code of the West', 29; *see also* Hudson's Bay Company

Gagnon, Charles, 290
Gender: and elder abuse, 171; and elderly victimization, 160; and fear of crime, 166, 168, 170; and homicide offending, 54, 203-4; and homicide victimization, 53, 200-3; and police violence, 233, 234; and prison violence, 250; and suicide, 59; and violence against children, 133; and violence by children, 134
General Social Survey (GSS), 100-1, 105, 157, 158, 160, 168-70, 270
Government responses to political violence, xiii, 7, 45, 316; and ability to define incident, 321-2, 326-7, 336; bureaucratic restraints on, 331; 'contagion' effect, 325; creation of 'zone of terror', 326; and 'deniability', 327; drift towards authoritarianism, 313, 320, 322-8; and élite ideology, 325; and financial costs, 328-9; and 'folk concept of rebellion', 331; legal/constitutional restraints on, 330, 331; and media, 336; and national priorities, 324; and perception of challenger, 324, 326, 329; political risks, 331; and popular support, 328; and public opinion, 330; and special powers (emergency measures), 327, 328; and status of community/victims, 314; and third-party pressure, 325-6
Groupe action directe, 29

'History, Whig', 11
Holmes, Oliver Wendell, 28
Holt-Dubois gang, 22
Homicide, 6, 346; aboriginal people, 42, 52-4; and activity patterns, 200, 203; and age, 160-1, 199-200, 206-9; Canada-US comparisons, 209-12, 213;

of children, 130-1; cultural factors, 196, 206; data, 108-9; 'death by legal intervention', 226-7; definitions, 186-8, 189; elderly offenders, 175; and English common law, 28; and family relationships, 135; and firearms, 210, 211, 212; and gender, 53, 54, 135, 200-4, 206; mass murder, 211, 315; motivation, 186; multiple, 105; murder-suicide, 105; non-criminal, 187-8; in prisons, 250, 265, 266, 267, 270; provincial-regional variations, 195-7, 206, 209; and race, 135, 199-200, 205-6; reporting, 99, 189; social factors, 186, 196; 'stranger', 161, 192-3, 194, 195, 197, 201, 203, 205; and substance abuse, 210-11; trends, 191-5; unsolved, 195, 197; urban/rural variations, 197-9, 209; victimization, x, xi, 160-1; and victim-offender relationships, 192-5201-3, 205, 208-9, 210; young offenders, 129, 135; *see also* Homicide rates; Infanticide
Homicide rates, x, xi; Canada (1921-90), 191, 193; international comparisons, 212; major cities, 199; by province, 196; Toronto, 193-5
Hudson's Bay Company (HBC): charter, 12, 13, 14, 17; conflict with North West Company, 12-13, 15; and customary law, 14; legal authority 12, 13, 14, 17; prosecution of crime, 15-16, 17

Immigration, xii, xv
Imperial chicken processing plant fire (1991), 92
Indian Act, 46, 48
Indian Association of Alberta, 46
Indian Chiefs of Alberta, 46
Inequality, structural, xv, 50, 110-12, 116, 271-4; *see also* Poverty
Infanticide, 130, 187, 189, 192
Inuit: Coronation Gulf, 16; suicide rates, 59-60
Irish Republican Army, *see* Provisional IRA

James, Jesse, 18
Japan, x

Judicature Act (1886), 14
Justice Commandos of the Armenian Genocide (JCAG), 299
Justice system: and aboriginal people, 18, 52-3, 54; and social control, 18, 84, 272, 273, 274, 277

'Kamloops outlaws', 18

Labour violence, xii, 5, 346, 348, 350; in construction industry, 81, 85; and differential power relations, 78-80, 84, 85, 94; and divisions within working class, 80-1, 83-4; early history, 80-4; and economic violence, 81, 84; in mining industry, 81, 89; and police, 79, 82-3, 84, 85, 86, 87, 88, 91; as public/political violence, 78, 82, 93; recent history, 84-91; and state support for capital, 78, 79, 85 (see also State-corporate violence); and union formation, 83; see also Strikes; Unions
Law: aboriginal, 29; common, 14, 17, 18, 25, 28; criminal, 10, 17, 18, 23; customary, 14, 29; municipal, 29, 30; two traditions, 4, 28-9, 30
'Law and order', viii, 253, 272
Lépine, Marc, 315, 322
Litton Industries bombing, see Direct Action
Lorraine, Henri, 93
Lortie, Denis, 315

Macdonald, John A., 14
Mackenzie district, 15-18
Mackenzie River murders, 16
McLean gang, 18
McLoughlin case, 17
Manitoba: frontier violence, 26; homicide rates, 196; see also Assiniboia
Manslaughter, 54, 187, 191; see also Homicide
Marshall, Donald, 52
Media: and aboriginal activism, 48; and escalation of violence, 334; and government, 332, 334, 335-6; and public policy, xiv, 314, 332, 335-6; reporting of police violence, 229; and terrorism, 333-4, 337
Métis, 13, 14, 15; 'mixed bloods', 18

Mexico, 28
Minorities, xi, xv, 22, 345; fear of crime, 166; and justice/law enforcement system, 18-19, 22; see also Aboriginal people; Métis; Race
Monarchy, constitutional, 29
Mujahedin-e-Khalq (MEK), 303
Mulroney, Brian, 90
Multiculturalism, viii, x-xii, xv
Murder, see Homicide

National Crime Victimization Survey (US; NCVS), 160, 163-4
National Indian Brotherhood (NIB), 46
Negligence, corporate, 4; see also Corporate violence
New Brunswick: homicide, 196, 314; terrorism, 288
Newfoundland: homicide, 195, 196
New Right, 271-2
North West Company (NWC), 12, 13, 15
North-West Rebellion (1885), 14-15, 21, 42, 45
Northwest Territories: frontier violence, 21-3, 24-5, 26-7; homicide, 195, 196
Nova Scotia: homicide, 196

October Crisis (1970), 290, 291, 293, 300, 319, 337
Oka Crisis (1990), 42, 47, 48-9, 302, 318, 320, 333, 335, 337-8
Ontario: crime statistics (1891-1911), 26-7; homicide, 196, 197; political violence, 314; terrorism, 288
Ontario Race Relations and Policing task force, 108
On-to-Ottawa trek (1935), 82-3
Osborne, Helen Betty, 52

Pacific frontier, 16-18
Police: and labour violence, 79, 82-3, 84, 85, 86, 87, 88, 91; municipal, 223; responses to violence, 106-8, 130, 142, 144-5, 314; see also Police violence
Police violence, ix, 6, 346, 348, 350; and age, 233, 234; Canada (1977-92), 228-36; citizens' complaints, 226; control mechanisms, 225, 237-41; data, 225-7; definitions, 223; and firearms, 226, 227; and gender, 233, 234; literature

review, 224-5; media reporting of, 229; and race/ethnicity, xi, 252, 253; sanctions, 235, 236; temporal distribution, 230-1; types, 223, 225, 228-9, 232, 233

Political violence, 4, 78; aboriginal, 40, 41, 42, 45-50; incidence, 314; political impact, 314; and regime type, 313; *see also* Challenger violence; Labour violence; Terrorism

Poverty, viii-ix, xi, 136; and fear of crime, 166

Prairie provinces: homicide, 196, 199; *see also* Frontier violence

Prince Edward Island: homicide, 195, 196

Prisoners: alienation/fragmentation, 269-70, 274, 278; 'inmate code', 266, 269; prisoners' rights movement, xii, 262, 278; profiles, 256, 257; social networks, 260; solidarity, 269, 278; *see also* Correctional system; Prison violence

Prisoners' Rights Group (PRG), 262

Prisons, 252-3; Archambault, 263-4; British Columbia penitentiary, 261-2, 276; Kent, 263; Kingston penitentiary, 252, 260-1; Matsqui, 262-3; Millhaven, 261, 275; Oakalla, 261

Prison Victimization Project, 266, 269

Prison violence, ix, xii, 7, 346, 348-9; and class, 274-5; collective, 258, 277-8; contagion effect, 260-1; control strategies, 275-7; data, 264-5; and drugs, 266, 270, 278; expressive, 264; and gender, 250; homicide, 270; instrumental, 264, 270, 277, 278; individual, 257-8, 278; and institutional type, 259; 'major' incidents, 264, 265, 266, 267; 'minor' incidents, 264, 266, 268; motives and goals, 256-9; permitted/encouraged, 275; and prisoner fragmentation, 269-70, 274, 278; reporting of, 264; riots/disturbances, 260-4; sociopolitical causes, xv, 271-5; sources of, 259-60; types of aggression, 257-9; victimization, 250, 266, 270, 274-5; *see also* Correctional system; Prisoners; Prisons

Protest movements, xii

Provisional Irish Republican Army (PIRA), 305, 306, 320, 329

Public Order Temporary Measures Act, 327

Quebec: crime statistics (1891-1911), 26-7; homicide rates, xii, 196-7, 199, 204, 209; political violence, 314; terrorism, 289-91

Race: and correctional system, 257; and homicide, 199-200, 205-6; *see also* Minorities

Racism, 13, 15, 16

Rae, Bob, 321

Red Army Faction (RAF), 305

Red Brigades (BR), 305

Red River 'Rebellion', 14, 21, 42, 45

Rex v. Weir (1910), 23

Riel, Louis, 14-15

Right-wing violence, 314, 337

Royal Commission on Aboriginal Peoples (RCAP), 42-3

Rupert's Land, 12, 14

Saskatchewan: doctors' strike (1962), 89; frontier violence, 21, 26; homicide, 196

Sayer trial, 13-14

Scott, Thomas, 14

Selkirk, Thomas Douglas, Earl of, 12

Seven Oaks incident (1816), 12-13

Simpson, George, 17

Sovereignty, parliamentary, 28, 29

Sproule case, 18, 19

Squamish Five, *see* Direct Action

State-corporate violence, 78, 79, 91-3, 94, 345

Strikes: Asbestos (1949), 316; General Motors (1933), 316; Holmes factory (1937), 83-4; Hormel (1960), 84; International Nickel Co., 86; Lachine (1843), 80-1; *La Presse* (1971), 86; Ontario doctors (1986), 89-90; Pacific Western Airlines (PWA; 1986), 88-9; postal, 86-8; Royal Oak mines, Inc. (1992), 89; Steel Co. of Canada, 86; Val Rita cooperative raid (1963), 85; Winnipeg general (1919), 24-5, 81-2, 316

Suicide, 41, 345; aboriginal people, 57-61; and gender, 59; murder-suicide, 105; western frontier, 25-6

Terrorism, ix-x, xii, xiii, 7, 317, 347; casualties, 288, 289, 295, 301, 307; comparative trends, 303-8; as criminal, not political, problem, 337; data, 285-6; definitions, 286-7, 293; domestic, 287-96, 301, 304, 314; Emigré, 287, 288, 289, 290, 297, 298-9, 301, 302; in Europe, 305-6, 309; external victimization, 303, 304; global patterns, 306-8; incidence/location, 287-9, 306-7; international, 296-302, 304, 306, 309, 315; Left-Wing, 287, 289, 290, 292-3, 297, 299-300, 301; and media, 333-4, 337; Nationalist/Separatist, 287, 288, 289-91, 292, 294, 295, 297, 298, 300; political impact, 308; public perceptions, 284, 285-6, 307, 309; recent incidents, 302-3; Right-Wing, 287, 289, 290, 293; Senate Special Committee on Terrorism and the Public Safety (Kelly Commission), 285; Single-Issue, 287, 290, 293, 297, 317; 'spill-over', 306; 'state terror', 325, 326, 337; support activities, 287; surrogate attacks, 305; symbolic, 295, 300, 304, 305; tactics, 287, 293-5, 297, 298, 300-1, 305, 306, 307, 308; targets, 295-6, 302, 303, 305, 306, 307, 308-9; 'technological', 307-8; in US, 304-5, 309; see also Challenger violence; Government responses; Political violence
Thom, Adam, 13-14, 15, 16
Toronto: 1992 riot, 316, 321-2
Trudeau, Pierre Elliott, 50, 87
Two Axe-Early, Mary, 48

Uniform Crime Reporting System (UCR), 107, 156, 159-60, 163, 188, 190
Unions: Canadian Association of Smelter and Allied Workers (CASAW), 89; Canadian Maritime Union (CMU), 85; Canadian Union of Postal Workers (CUPW), 88; Letter Carriers Union (LCUC), 87; Longshoremen's Union of the St Lawrence, 86; Ontario Medical Association (OMA), 90; Public Service of Canada (PSAC; 1991), 90; Seafarers' International Union (SIU), 85; Teamsters' Union, 85-6; United Steelworkers of America, 88
United States, ix, 1, 11; 'Code of the West', 28, 29; homicide, 209-13; labour violence, 79; minorities, xi; multiculturalism, x; 'No Duty to Retreat' rule, 28; poverty, viii-ix; prisons, 271; terrorism, ix-x, 304-5, 309; violence against children, viii-ix; violence against women, viii-ix, x, 103, 115; 'war on crime', 271

Vallières, Pierre, 290
Vancouver Urban Survey (1984), 170
Violence: causes, 348-9; collective, 314, 344; data, 347-8; definitions, 10, 41; expressive, 78, 256, 258-9, 344; impact on victims, xiii; instrumental, 78, 256-8, 270; interpersonal, viii, ix, x, xi; 'legal' use of, 15; literature review, 1-2; psychological, 3-4, 345; public, 78, 92, 93, 229, 344; public responses to, xiii-xv; 'recreational', 13; sensitization to, xiv; social, viii, ix, xi, xii; social consequences of, viii, xii-xiii; structural, 3-4, 345

War Measures Act, 327
Weather Underground, 300
White Paper on Indian Policy (1969), 40, 42
Women, violence against, ix, x, xiii, 5-6, 346; aboriginal women, 55-7; and age, 104; and class, 110; Canada/US comparisons, 115; Canadian Panel on Violence against Women, 97, 101; in cohabiting relationships, 99-103; cultural/structural causes, 108, 112-14; in dating relationships, 103-5; definitions, 98-9; and economic dependence, 110-11, 112; homicide, 200-3; left-realist responses to, 110-12; and mediation, 108-10; Ottawa Regional Coordinating Committee to End Violence against Women, 97; and patriarchy, 112, 114; police responses to, 106-8, 314; post-separation, 105-6; reporting, 55-6, 99; responses to, xiv-

xv, 106-15, 350; 'risk markers', 101-3, 104; and structural inequality, 110-12, 116; treatment programs for offenders, 113-15; wife-abuse surveys (table), 102; *see also* Family violence

Women's Safety Project, 100, 101
Workplace death, 24-5, 92-3, 189

Young Offenders Act, 126, 127, 141-2, 143
Yukon, 195, 196